Sports Photography: From Snapshots to Great Shots

Bill Frakes

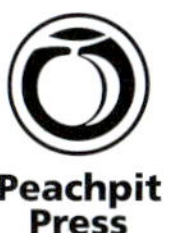

Sports Photography: From Snapshots to Great Shots
Bill Frakes

Peachpit Press
www.peachpit.com

To report errors, please send a note to errata@peachpit.com
Peachpit Press is a division of Pearson Education.

Project Editor: Valerie Witte
Production Editor: Tracey Croom
Development and Copy Editor: Anne Marie Walker
Proofreader: Cari Wilson
Composition: Danielle Foster
Indexer: Valerie Haynes Perry
Cover Image: Bill Frakes
Cover Design: Aren Straiger
Interior Design: Riezebos Holzbaur Design Group
Back Cover Author Photo: Laura Heald

ISBN-13: 978-0-321-88570-8
ISBN–10: 0-321-88570-8

9 8 7 6 5 4 3 2 1

Printed and bound in the United States of America

DEDICATION

To the athletes and coaches, those kids of all ages, who play the games that fuel my images.

ACKNOWLEDGMENTS

While writing this book I felt like a wrestler trying to make weight. Each chapter could have been a book in itself. To fit so many different sports between the covers of a simple how-to guide, I had to shed a lot of excess tonnage.

I am very lucky to work at Straw Hat Visuals with Laura Heald and Sara Tanner. Laura is there every day splitting the load, making me laugh, and stealing my food. Every project comes through the office we share; I simply couldn't do it without her. Sara is the most Southern person I know, and I went to school at Ole Miss, so that's saying something. She's always there providing strong logistical support and sweetness.

During the eight months I was in the writing process, I was traveling constantly— about 200,000 miles—to some of the best sporting events on the planet. This book came together at the Olympics, at the Kentucky Derby, during March Madness, at the BCS national championship game, and at a prom dress rugby game. Those events provided a lot of inspiration and energy. I can't say enough about the people I photograph.

My colleagues at *Sports Illustrated* are incredible. The editors, photographers, and writers are very talented, and I've always been surprised to be in their midst.

I owe a big debt of gratitude to my editor on the book, Anne Marie Walker, who skillfully and graciously kept this project on track. I put her through a lot, and her delicate touch saved a lot of what my writer friends would surely call "bad stuff." Valerie Witte was there for us, too, providing counsel and guidance when we needed it.

For my entire life, I have been surrounded by teachers. My Mom taught me about art, creativity, and just plain hard work. My Dad brought imagination and storytelling to the mix. Now my daughter Havana supplies the fuel. She is constantly in motion, challenging me, pushing the limits of her vision, and making me want to show her the world through my photographs and films.

Contents

Introduction

This book has been in the back of my mind for quite a while.

I shoot pictures every day. I'm a storyteller, and this is the best, surest way for me to communicate. I want to share what I am privileged to see, and reveal it to the biggest crowds I can.

The desire to teach is in my blood, and the desire to share knowledge comes as a direct result of having had terrific mentors help me along the way.

WHY I LOVE COVERING SPORTS

I started shooting sports in my 20s, working as a staff photographer for the *Miami Herald*. The craft was different then: The lenses were slower, the cameras had to be focused manually—which is more difficult—and the frames captured were far fewer. Working with film required more light and gave me less latitude, and it took much longer to process the images. Before I pressed the shutter, I had to be sure the photograph would be sharp and depict an important moment.

In the early 90s, I joined the staff of *Sports Illustrated* as a photographer. Since then I've travelled around the world covering every sport you can imagine.

At some of the world's greatest sporting events, I've had the best seat in the house. But at the heart of my existence is making meaningful photographs no matter where I am. Shooting a little league game is every bit as important to me as shooting the World Series.

Over the past 25 years, I've covered 10 Olympics, 25 Super Bowls, 10 NCAA basketball tournaments, 25 Kentucky Derbies, and all the events in between. Photographing ten-year-old Eli Manning playing catch with his dad in front of their New Orleans home in 1991 was as much fun as picturing him winning his second Super Bowl in 2012.

It's not just about access. Great shots are everywhere; you just have to look for them.

THE GOAL OF THIS BOOK

The ability to make photographs is changing rapidly in the sports photography arena, but the fundamentals are still the same. Newer cameras—because of their larger sensors, faster lenses, and bigger cards—are actually making sports photography more accessible to more people. Finding the action, capturing the personalities of the athletes, and experiencing the ambience of the crowds are the elements that give you the feel of the game. They are the guts of sports photography and they haven't, and won't, change.

This book explains how I do what I do. It includes everything from the gear I use to how to gain access to events. I'll show you how I approach the sports I shoot and discuss how each requires a different mind-set and a different approach. Chapter by chapter I'll lead you through the process of making great sports photographs of athletes at all levels.

WHO THIS BOOK IS FOR

This book is designed for photographers of all levels who want to raise their game. It takes you through the thought processes of telling the story by capturing penultimate action and salient moments away from the motion. Technique is important too; therefore, I'll spend time analyzing not only the tools, but the reasoning behind why I stand where I stand—or crouch, or kneel, or sit.

My objective is to teach you, whether you are a novice, amateur, or skilled photographer, how to put the viewers of your photographs into a front-row seat.

SHOOTING SPORTS

Covering sports well means thinking ahead and understanding the athletes' motivations and reactions. It's all about anticipating, preparing, and moving.

Understanding the game—knowing the personalities and tendencies of the participants—is very helpful. But the most important part of the equation is knowing yourself, being prepared to respond, and staying in the moment.

The crux of my exploration of athletic competition is the intersection of motion and emotion, the sometimes chance. But more often it is the calculated inclusion of art, commerce, and athleticism into sport, which so heavily influences the functioning of society through participation and observation. I want to capture the peak moment, which will hopefully enlighten and engage the viewer in a way that defines the game.

Sports photography needs to be about motion and emotion, style and scene, and place and purpose. At its best, it is the intersection of art and athleticism.

1

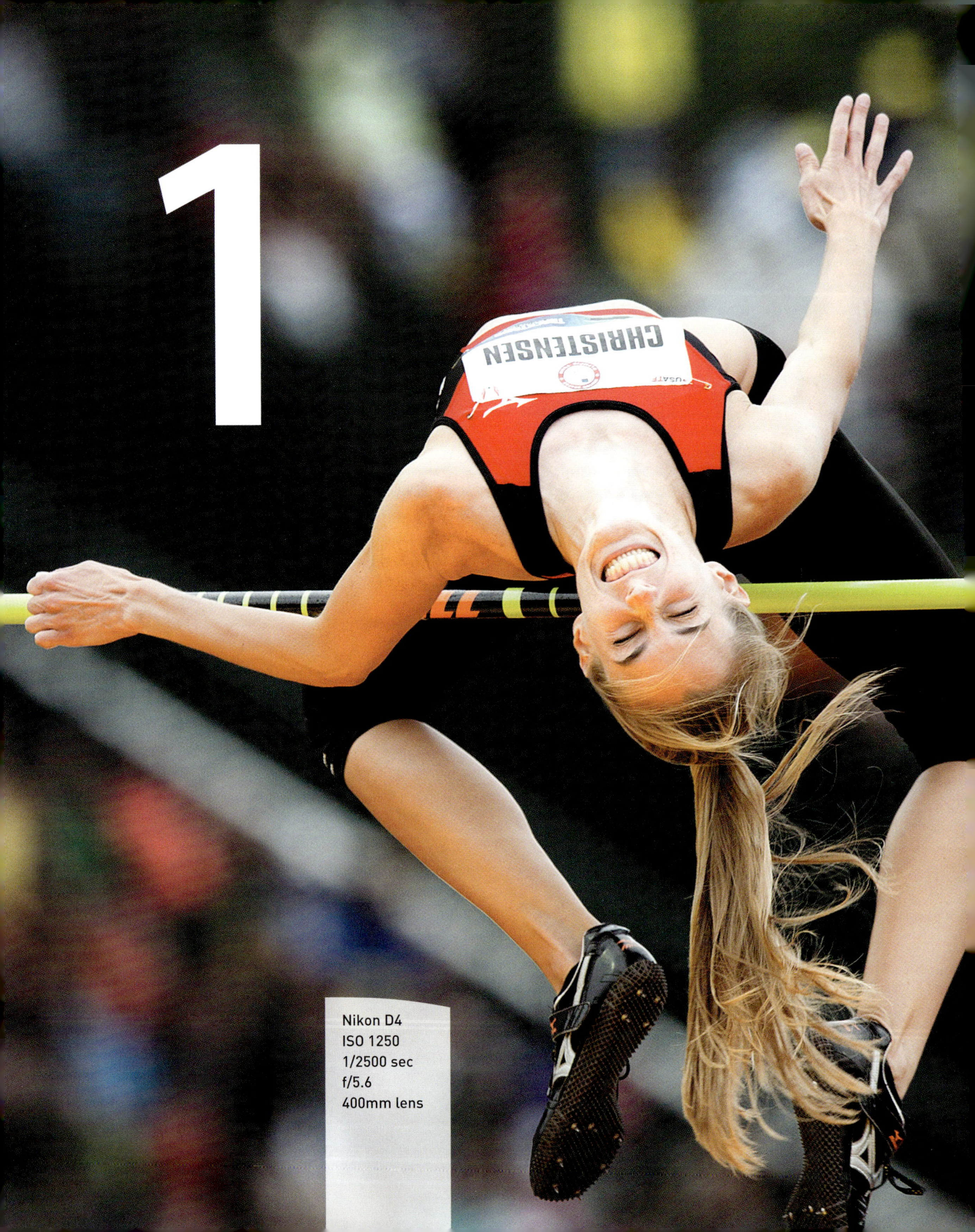

Nikon D4
ISO 1250
1/2500 sec
f/5.6
400mm lens

In the Bag

EQUIPMENT ESSENTIALS FOR PHOTOGRAPHING SPORTS

I use my cameras and lenses like painters use their brushes.

Photography is writing with light. Sometimes you can control it, and sometimes you have to work so that it doesn't control you. Having the right gear for the situation helps, but finding the right situation for the gear you have is just as important.

Rebecca Christensen competes in the women's high jump during the 2012 USATF Olympic Trials. She finished sixth overall and did not qualify for the 2012 Olympic Games in London.

PORING OVER THE PICTURE

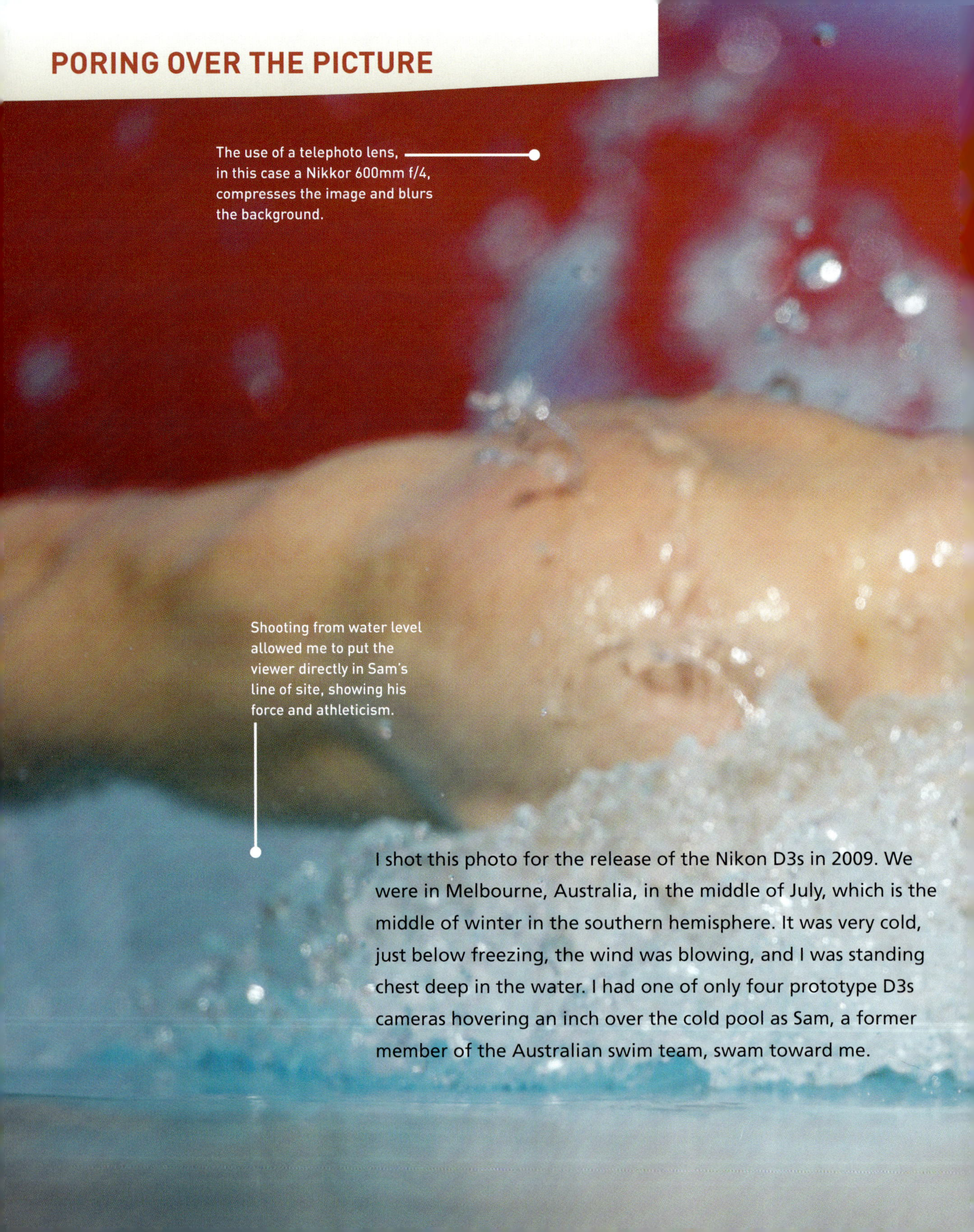

The use of a telephoto lens, in this case a Nikkor 600mm f/4, compresses the image and blurs the background.

Shooting from water level allowed me to put the viewer directly in Sam's line of site, showing his force and athleticism.

I shot this photo for the release of the Nikon D3s in 2009. We were in Melbourne, Australia, in the middle of July, which is the middle of winter in the southern hemisphere. It was very cold, just below freezing, the wind was blowing, and I was standing chest deep in the water. I had one of only four prototype D3s cameras hovering an inch over the cold pool as Sam, a former member of the Australian swim team, swam toward me.

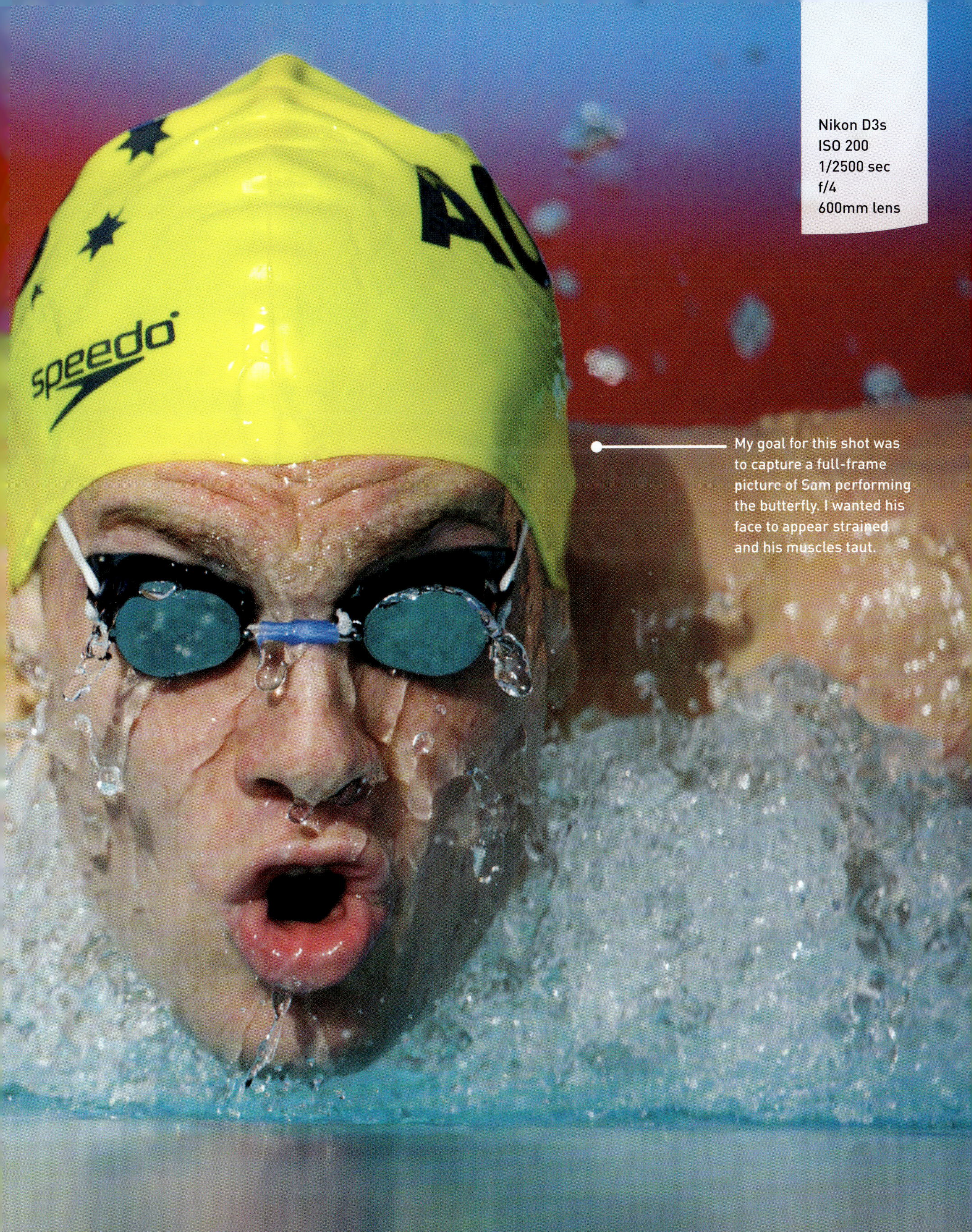

Nikon D3s
ISO 200
1/2500 sec
f/4
600mm lens

My goal for this shot was to capture a full-frame picture of Sam performing the butterfly. I wanted his face to appear strained and his muscles taut.

GEAR ISN'T EVERYTHING

You can produce terrific images with any camera. How you go about doing that is the piece of the puzzle that is controlled by you and your photographic acumen.

At many athletic events, access is tightly controlled. This makes a photographer's job more difficult but far from impossible. A number of factors influence access:

- The safety of the athletes and the spectators.
- The sanctity of the competition—not interfering with the game being played or the people who are watching, and showing common courtesy.
- The ability of the facility to accommodate photographers given how much space there is to work in.
- Who owns the rights to take and use photographs and in what fashion (issues related to rights' holders). This is not a universal concern but is increasingly an issue.

To some extent, access is important because it can dictate what's in your bag. Unlike many other photographic disciplines, sports photographers are constrained to work in fixed positions, which means bringing the right gear in order to work within the limits imposed. Although no special access was needed to shoot **Figure 1.1**, I still had to be aware of my safety and those of the players. Because I could not be on the

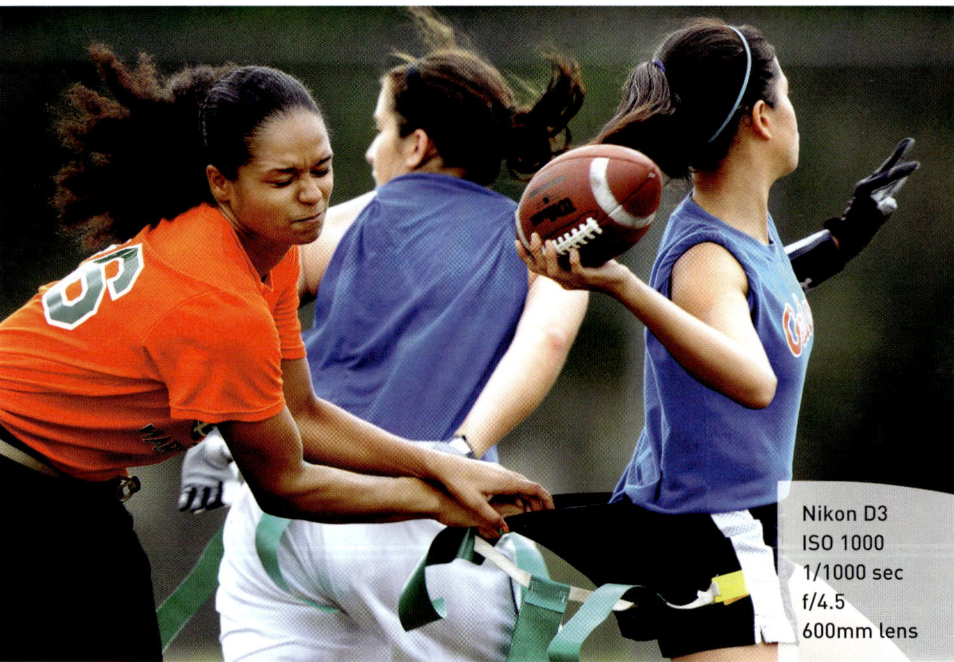

FIGURE 1.1
A women's flag football game in Gainesville, Florida.

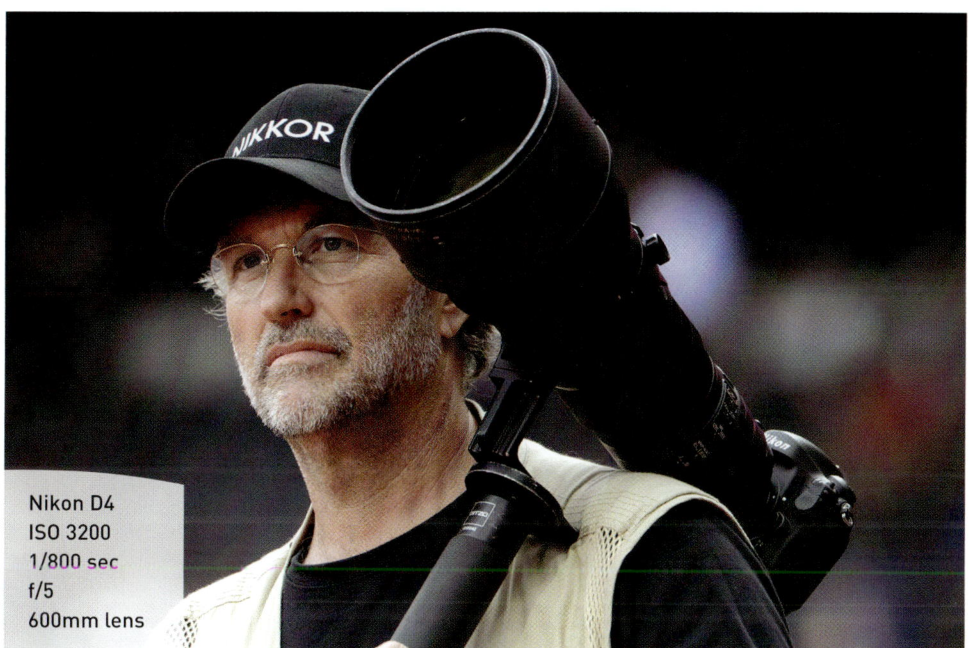

Nikon D4
ISO 3200
1/800 sec
f/5
600mm lens

FIGURE 1.2 This image of me was taken by Laura Heald at the Olympic Stadium in London in August, 2012.

field with them, I had to have the right gear and shoot from a good location. I shot Figure 1.1 with a telephoto lens.

Sports photographers are notorious for being gear crazy. Although having certain pieces of equipment absolutely makes shots easier and better, it is important to remember that you make photographs with your heart, your mind, your eye, and your soul (**Figure 1.2**). The technical means necessary to take your vision and transfer it to a viewing medium where you can share it with your readers should be just an extension of those elements.

To make sports photographs, you need a camera, a lens, and a memory card.

CAMERAS

When you're choosing a DSLR camera body, you have many options. The best cameras can run as much as $6,000. These cameras will have the biggest sensors and thus create the highest-quality images, and will shoot up to 11 frames per second. The more expensive the camera, the more bells and whistles it is likely to have. And although you can use all these features to do different, wonderful things, they are not necessary in every situation.

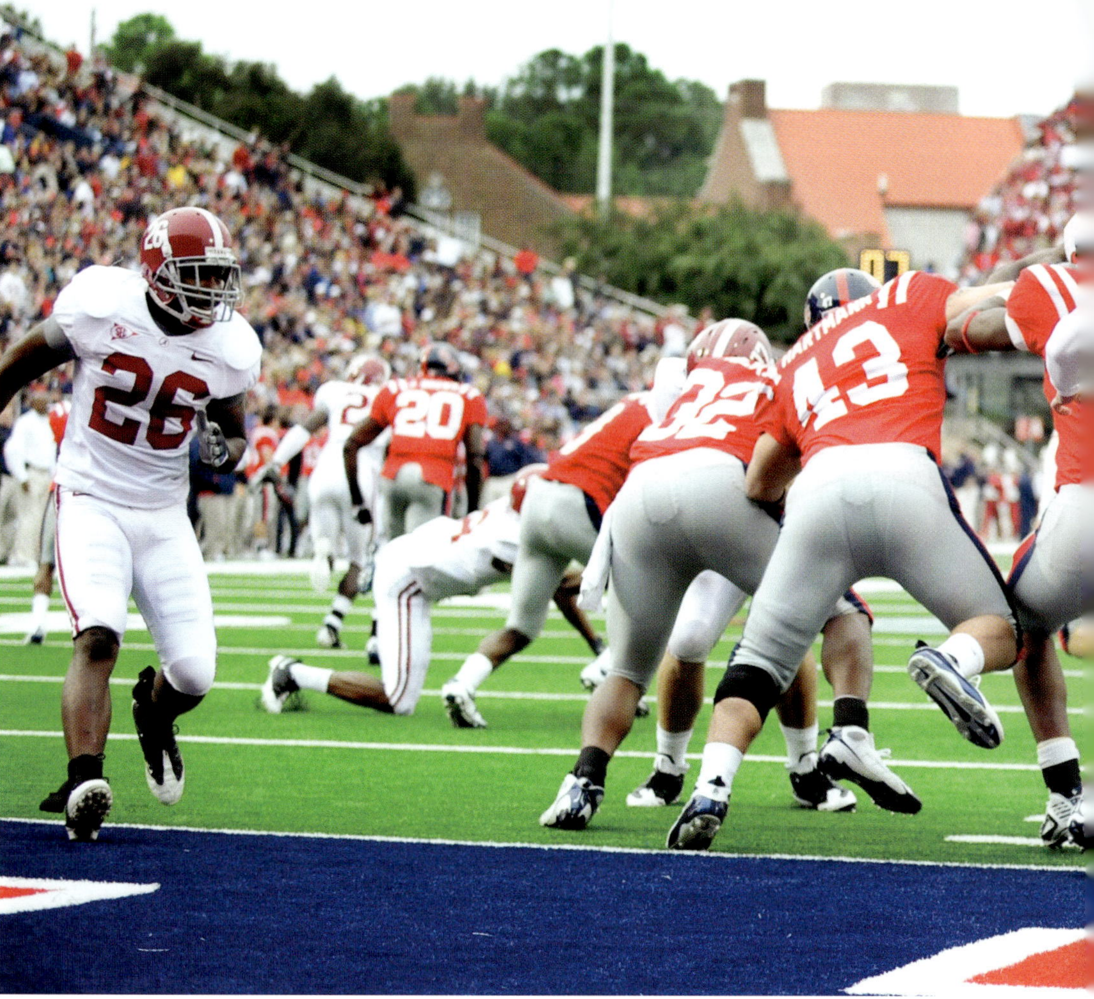

But don't let the high price point of photo equipment scare you. Smaller, less-expensive cameras are also very good. The best camera for its price point is the Nikon D7000, which costs about $1,000. It handles low-light files well, shoots 6 frames per second, and gives you a large file to work with later (i.e., for post processing and printing).

My camera of choice is the Nikon D4. It is the biggest, most robust camera on the market. When I'm shooting for a publication like *Sports Illustrated*, I need to know the camera is going to react when I press the button and react the way I tell it to, so I invest in the best cameras I can find.

But I also use cameras like the Nikon D800, D600, and D7000 when I don't need the speed of the D4. These cameras are smaller, more lightweight, and less expensive, and still produce multipurpose high-quality images that can be used across various platforms.

At football games I like to carry a small camera with a secondary lens on it for the type of photo you see in **Figure 1.3**.

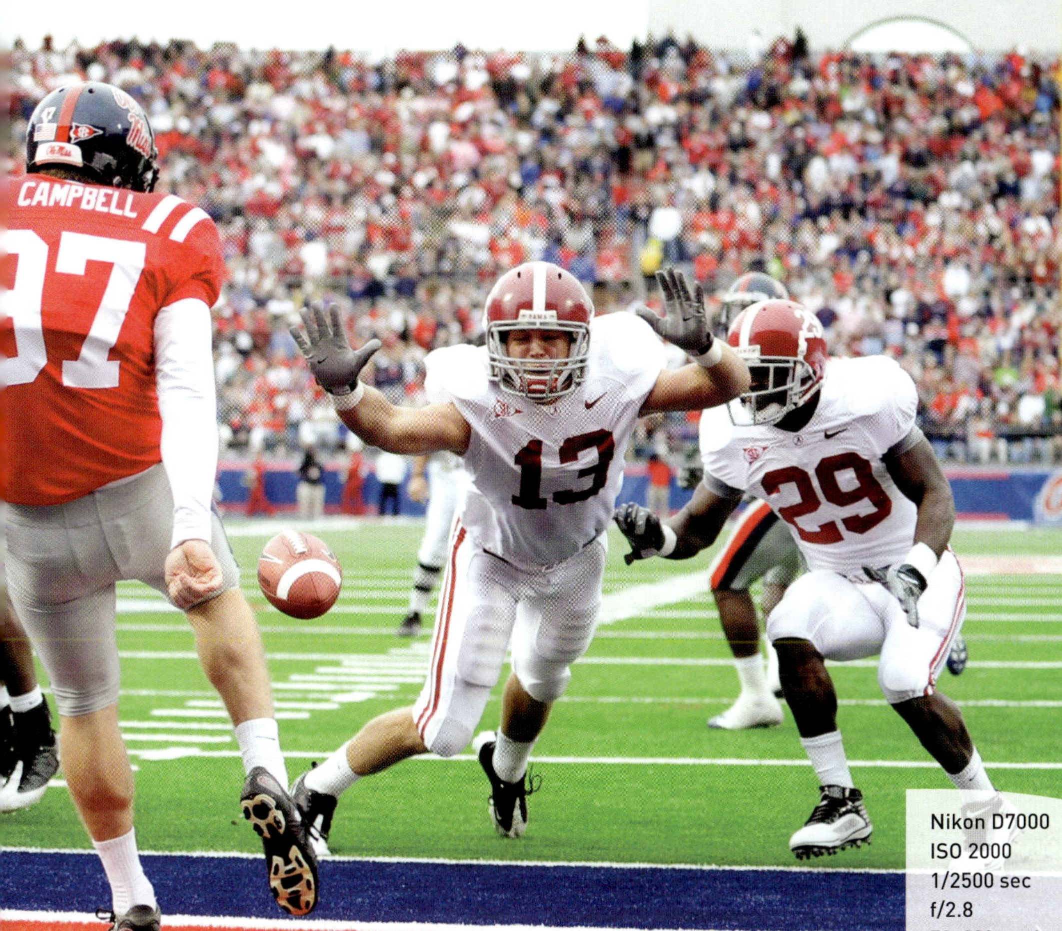

FIGURE 1.3
I knew Alabama would try to block a punt coming out of the end zone, so I was ready for it with my 70–200mm f/2.8 lens (set at 70mm) on my Nikon D7000.

LENSES

The camera is important, but equally critical is your choice in lenses. Part of the reason I shoot with Nikon cameras is that Nikon also makes some of the best optics in the world. Every sports photographer needs certain lenses, namely, a wide-angle and a telephoto lens. And the faster—meaning the lower the aperture setting, allowing more light to reach the sensor—the better. Lenses, like camera bodies, vary greatly in price and use.

Sports photographers live by their telephoto lenses. I'm a fan of prime lenses—fixed focal length—but those lenses tend to be more expensive than others. For a lower price point, the lens I recommend most is the Nikkor 70–300mm f/5.6. It is very sharp and offers a photographer a wide range of focal lengths.

The wide-angle lens is used less often but can still be very important to a sports photographer, especially in the context of a story. For some events, like the discus

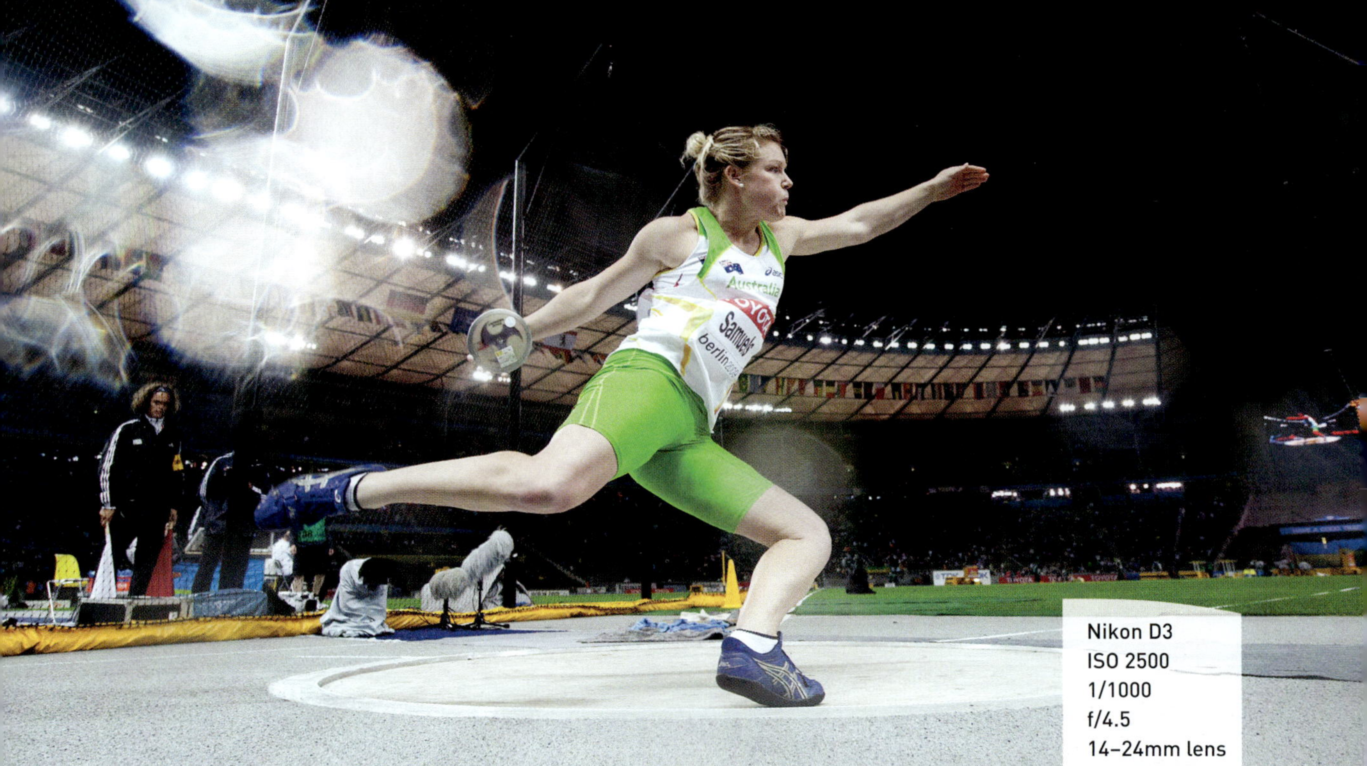

Nikon D3
ISO 2500
1/1000
f/4.5
14–24mm lens

FIGURE 1.4
The wide-angle lens allows viewers to see the stadium and the discus thrower's form, and the flare on the left side of the frame shows you it was wet outside.

throw, I like to use a wide-angle lens to show the environment. In the photo in **Figure 1.4** the net is important, so I used the Nikkor 14–24mm f/2.8 lens. However, you have several options in this range.

The most popular lenses for sports photographers include:

- 14–24 f/2.8
- 16–35 f/2.8
- 24–70 f/2.8
- 70–200 f/2.8
- 300 f/2.8
- 400 f/2.8
- 600 f/4

For the shot in **Figure 1.5**, I chose a telephoto lens so I could concentrate on the faces of the athletes.

MEMORY CARDS

Memory cards are the equivalent of film in the digital age. Different cameras use different kinds of memory cards. Compact flash (CF) and SDHC are the most common types. However, the Nikon D4 is a new camera and with it you use a new kind of memory card, the XQD card. I always buy the biggest and fastest cards I can find—fast being the most important thing for me. When shooting sports, you are recording

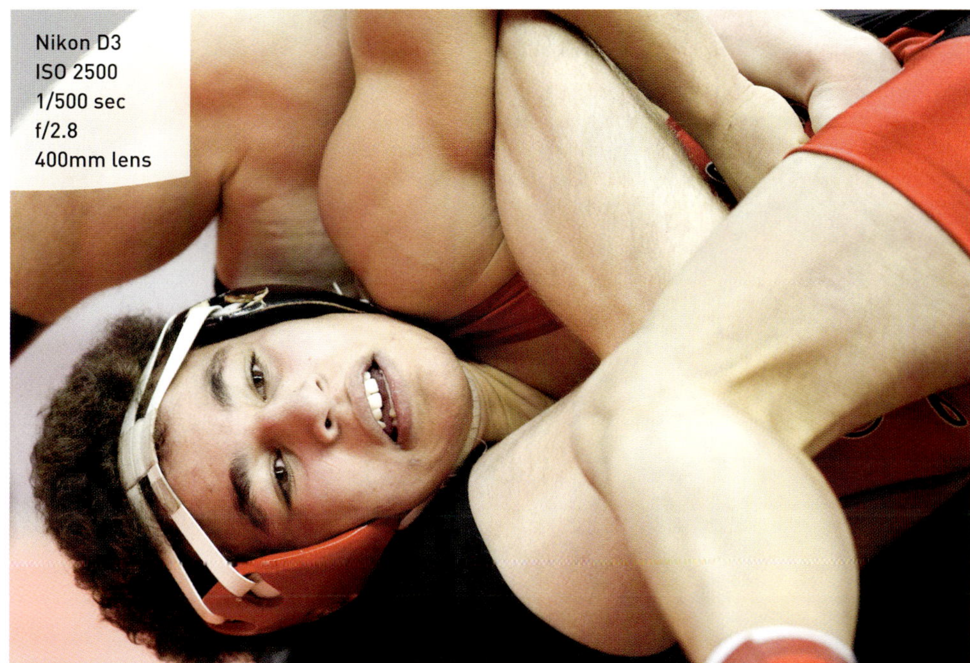

FIGURE 1.5
Nebraska State High School Wrestling Championships.

a lot of information in a short amount of time, and you want a card that can keep up. The faster cards are more expensive but earn their worth in the speed with which they record what you shoot.

SUPPORTS, STROBES, AND CASES

The essential equipment in sports photography, or any type of digital photography, consists of a camera, a lens, and a memory card. But taking care of those cameras and lenses is just as important when you're preparing to cover a game or setting up a portrait shoot. Investing in a few simple items will make the difference in how well your camera equipment serves your creative vision.

SUPPORTS

Many people forget to factor tripods and monopods into their gear. The common misconception is that supports are only necessary when you're shooting at a low shutter speed. That is one reason, but it is not the only reason.

Tripods and monopods are used best as composition aids. I always have at least one monopod and one tripod with me everywhere I go. If I'm using a long lens, like a Nikkor 400mm f/2.8 or 600mm f/4, I'll always have it on some kind of support.

A monopod is a must have for a sports photographer. Tripods are important as well, but most sidelines do not allow tripods for safety reasons. I use tripods mostly for remote cameras or when I'm shooting video.

Monopods and tripods aren't the only support equipment you can use. There is a plethora of grip gear and smaller supports I'll discuss later when I break down how I cover each sport.

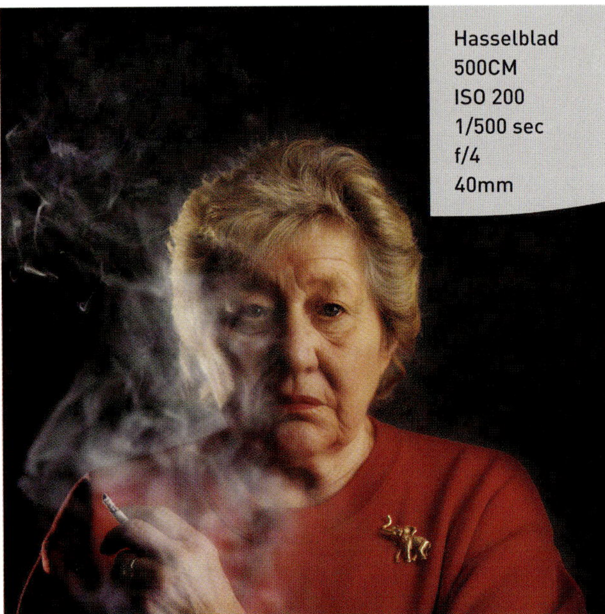

FIGURE 1.6
The controversial owner of the Cincinnati Reds, Marge Schott.

STROBES

Strobes, or electronic flashes, are also an important accessory for a sports photographer. But you can't use strobes for every sport; not every sport requires them, and some do not allow them at all. I mainly use strobes for portraits, basketball, and hockey.

For the most part, I use big, powerful strobes so I have as much control as possible. I mainly use strobes in portrait situations when I direct the athletes and the shoot. Using extra light to knock down a background or accent a feature of their body that is unique, attractive, or an important part of their persona helps take my portraits to the next level. In **Figure 1.6**, a portrait of Marge Schott, I used dramatic lighting, the subject's pose, and the smoke from her seemingly omnipresent cigarette to emphasize her toughness.

CASES

How you pack your gear is ultimately important to achieving good results in your final product. When I show up to an assignment, I need to be confident that my equipment will work as soon as I arrive. The best way to ensure that happens is to pack it properly.

The camera gear can only produce the results you allow it to produce, and upkeep is critical. Clean the lenses with soft cloths designed for that purpose. Have the sensors cleaned and the camera functions checked to be sure the autofocus is working properly, the sync speeds are correct, and the sensor is spotless.

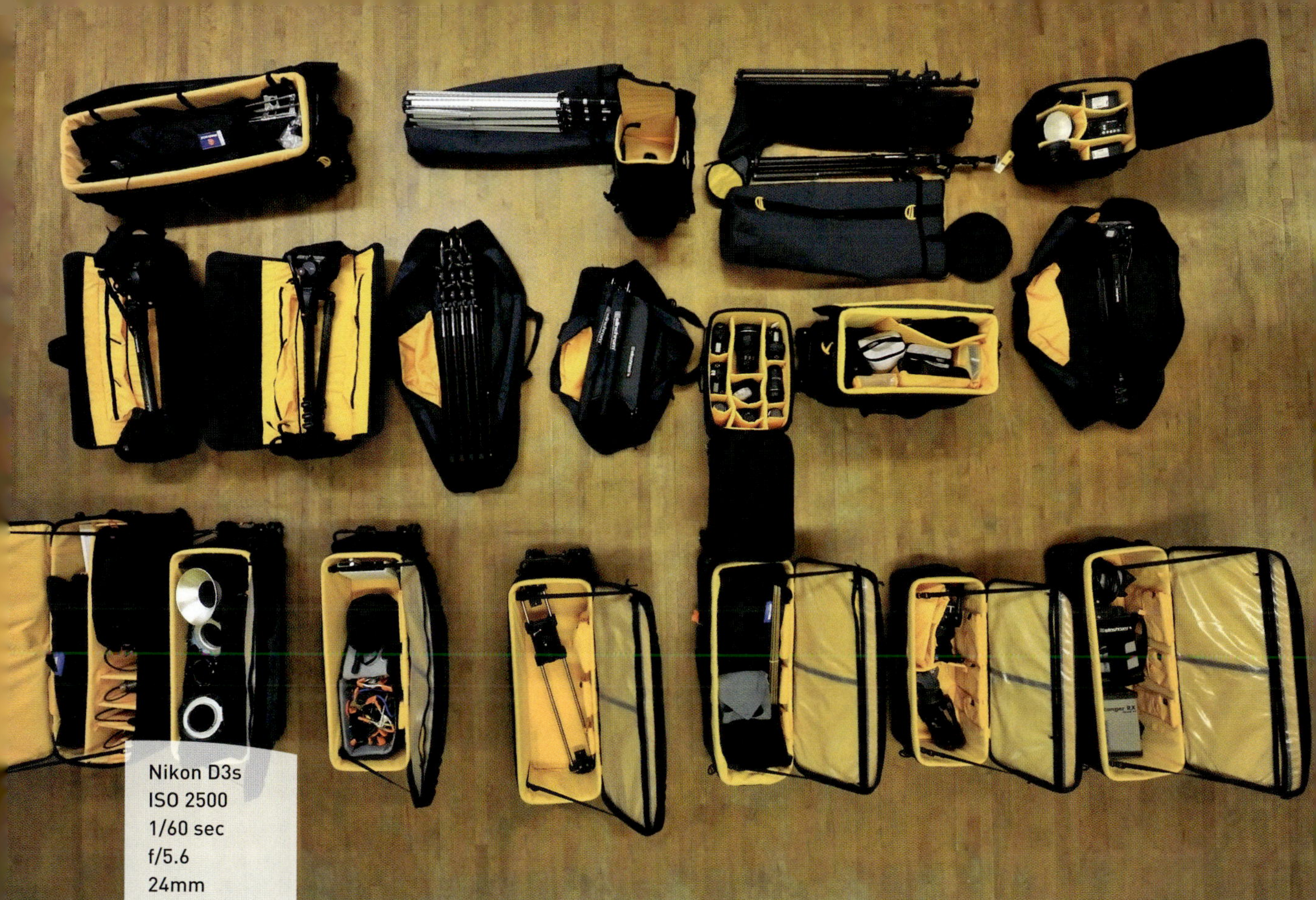

Nikon D3s
ISO 2500
1/60 sec
f/5.6
24mm

FIGURE 1.7
These are some of the loaded cases I travel with.

Make sure to pack your gear securely for travel. To do this, I pack all my equipment—cameras, lenses, and supports—in Kata bags (**Figure 1.7**). The Kata Flyby 76 is my camera bag of choice because I tend to travel with a lot of equipment, and this bag allows me to bring it all and carry it safely. The Flyby 74 is a smaller option I frequently use as well.

To transport support equipment, like tripods and monopods, I use the Kata LW-99. It is lightweight but rugged and robust at the same time.

Having some sort of transporter to carry extra lenses, cards, and batteries while you're on the field of play is also very important. Once you are on a sideline or a court it is not easy to leave, so you want to make sure you have everything you might need.

Some photographers like photo vests, but I prefer small waist bags. I find the more pockets I have the easier it is to lose something. The waist pack allows me to keep accessories in one, easily accessible spot.

INSIDE MY BAG

When I go to a game or a portrait shoot, I pack seriously, and by most standards heavily, because my images will frequently be viewed by millions. But even if they weren't, I would still want to have options when I'm shooting.

For most games, this is my minimum must-bring list:

- Four Nikon DSLR camera bodies (currently that includes three D4s and one D800)
- 14–24mm f/2.8 lens
- 24–120mm f/4 lens
- 200mm f/2 lens
- 400mm f/2.8 lens
- 600mm f/4.0 lens
- One Nikon SB 910 strobe
- Four PocketWizards (remote flash and camera triggers) with appropriate connectors
- Gitzo tripod with Manfrotto 409 head
- Gitzo monopod
- Sekonic Spot/Flash meter
- Sekonic Color temperature meter
- Lasolite tri grip
- Manfrotto Super Clamps and ballheads
- Manfrotto Poncho
- Lightware rain covers
- Gaffer tape
- SD, CF, and XQD cards
- Card readers
- Computers

I pack all this gear in Kata rolling cases and backpacks. Along with securely packing your gear, protecting your equipment from rain and other elements must be a priority as well. I realize that my camera options are more vast than most photographers'. Since I work for Sports Illustrated, I have to pack for every possibility.

If you only have one DSLR body, though, and want to be able to cover a sporting event, I would recommend bringing a zoom lens with that camera. My personal favorite zoom lens is the Nikkor 28-300 f/3.5-5.6. This lens is extremely sharp for the focal lengths it covers. The only downside is that it is a relatively slow lens, meaning the aperture values (f/5.6 at 300mm) force greater depth of field and do not allow you to use high shutter speeds in low light.

Another good zoom lens is the 70-200mm f/2.8. The fixed f/2.8 aperture throughout the focal reach makes this lens very fast. However, 200mm is not very long, so if you choose this option I recommend buying a teleconverter 1.4x. A teleconverter 1.4 magnifies your focal length 1.4 times. So if you have a 70-200mm, a teleconverter 1.4x gives you a 98-280mm. Keep in mind that using a teleconverter changes your exposure and relative sharpness; the more you add on to your lens, the more light you lose.

Chapter 1 Assignments

Having the right gear is important, but practice makes perfect. Here are some assignments to help you hone your skills.

Stopping Action with Different Shutter Speeds

Select a subject that is moving in a fairly consistent manner. Position yourself so that you have to make photographs of the subject as it approaches you, passes you, and goes away from you. Try a wide range of shutter speeds from fast to slow. Then analyze how the different shutter speeds allow you to capture the action differently from extreme stop action to blurs. Also, pay attention to where the subject is relative to your position and how that affects how the different shutter speeds emphasize the motion.

Comparing Aperture and Focus

Choose a still subject—an apple or a chair, for example. Turn your camera to manual mode and shoot one frame at aperture f/2.8 (or the widest aperture your lens will allow) and one at f/16 (or the smallest aperture your lens will allow). Look at the difference between the two photos in terms of what is or is not in focus. Try various apertures from several different positions and make note of how position and aperture affect the final product.

Using the Light

For this assignment find a window and a model. The model can be a friend, a spouse, a son, or a daughter. Place the model in front of the window and have the model turn his or her face in various directions. Pay attention to how the light hits your model from different angles. Use your feet as well; don't just stay in one place. Try different exposures. This will help you understand how light affects a photo and how exposure uses light.

Share your results with the book's Flickr group!
Join the group here: flickr.com/groups/sportsphotographyfromsnapshotstogreatshots.

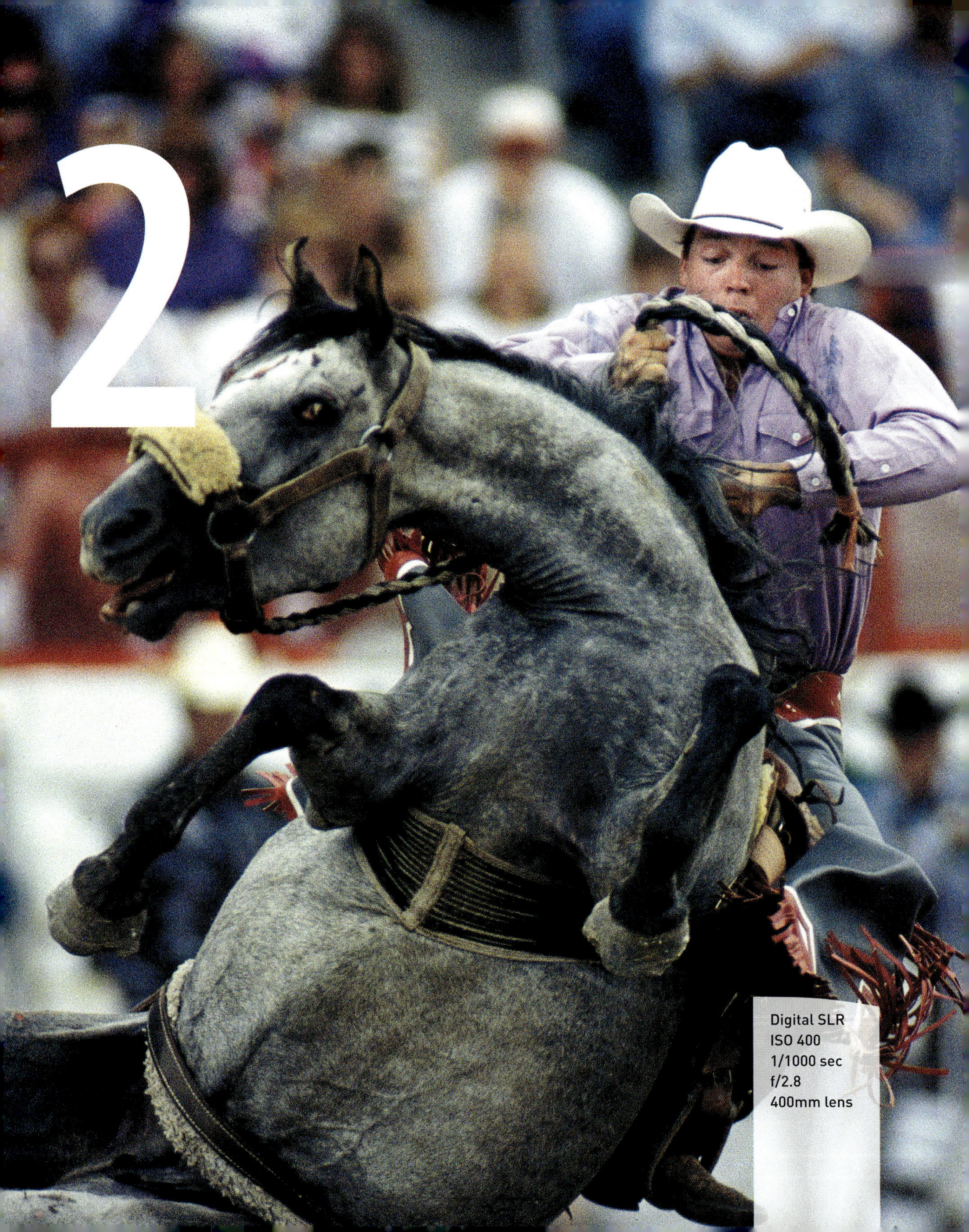

2

Digital SLR
ISO 400
1/1000 sec
f/2.8
400mm lens

Getting Started

THE FUNDAMENTALS OF SPORTS PHOTOGRAPHY

It's passion for images that pushes me to excel and makes me work harder, longer, and more creatively. I use technology not just to make my life easier, but to make my images better and to do something that I couldn't do before.

A rodeo cowboy struggles to stay on his bronc during Cheyenne Frontier Days.

PORING OVER THE PICTURE

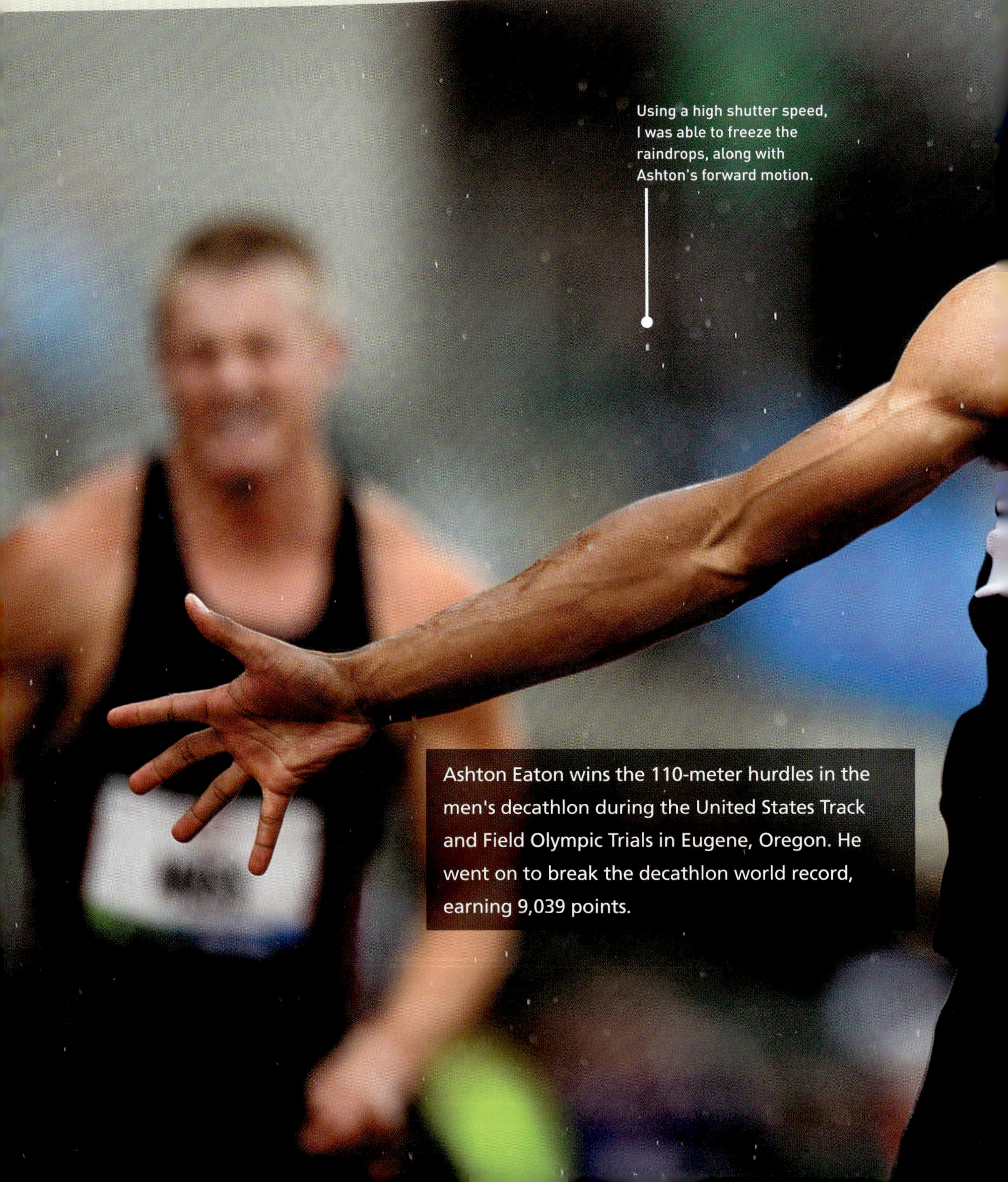

Using a high shutter speed, I was able to freeze the raindrops, along with Ashton's forward motion.

Ashton Eaton wins the 110-meter hurdles in the men's decathlon during the United States Track and Field Olympic Trials in Eugene, Oregon. He went on to break the decathlon world record, earning 9,039 points.

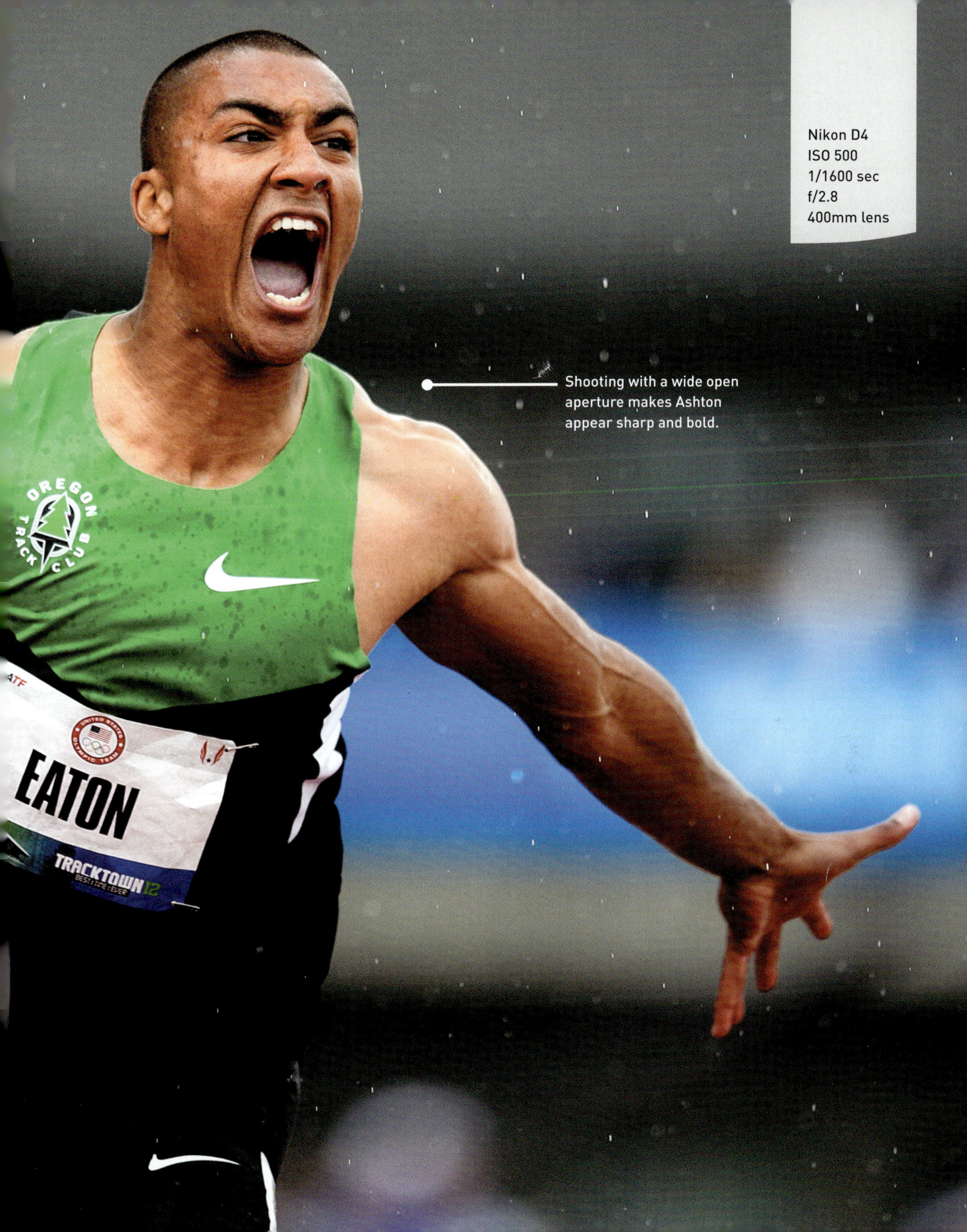

Nikon D4
ISO 500
1/1600 sec
f/2.8
400mm lens

Shooting with a wide open aperture makes Ashton appear sharp and bold.

GETTING STARTED

To be successful on any level, it's important to identify what you are trying to say with your images and how to physically make that happen. Therefore, you need to understand light and composition, your image content, how to access the subject matter you want to photograph, and technical considerations relating to running cameras, lenses, lights, supports, and post-processing devices.

You'll learn about all of these aspects of sports photography throughout this chapter and the book. Although the learning curve initially sounds intimidating, the skills you need to achieve your goals are approachable and can easily be learned.

Simple as it sounds, practice and hard work are the key ingredients to success as a sports photographer. So much of what is necessary to make great sports images is having the knowledge to anticipate the action. Thereafter, timing and reflexes take over. Practice, quite literally, makes perfect.

Learning to see is a combination of inherent talent, personal discipline, and passion for the subject. Learning to run the camera is similar to how athletes learn the games bit by bit, beginning as children and mastering the mechanics and the strategies as they grow.

The technical parts of the process are not as difficult as they initially might seem. Running the camera is basically simple math. Each camera has advantages and liabilities. You need to learn and understand how to use them to your advantage. There is no secret formula for making great images, but there are a lot of guidelines and techniques that can help.

The toughest skill to learn is how to critique your own work accurately. If you are too easy on yourself, you won't grow. If you are too hard on yourself, you can stifle your own growth.

Learning to see is the first step and involves a few essential components: recognizing what is important to include and what is necessary to exclude in terms of subject matter, deciding what looks attractive, and combining these elements to tell the story in the best way.

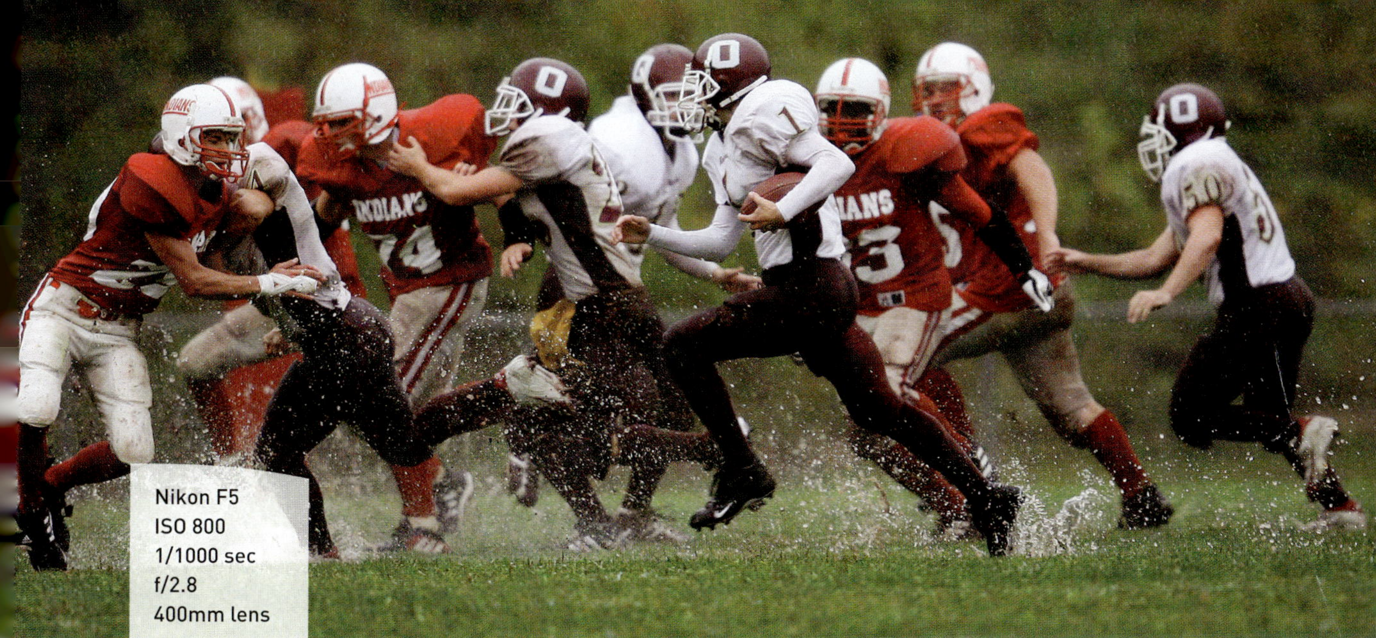

FIGURE 2.1
High school football in the rain. Using a high shutter speed and a telephoto lens, I was able to freeze the action and the water.

CAMERA BASICS

Understanding the camera is important but only to the extent you need to be able to communicate your ideas about the image. The primary elements to think about are shutter speed, aperture, white balance, and depth of field.

SHUTTER SPEED

Shutter speed is the key to controlling motion. It's simple: The higher the shutter speed, the greater the ability of the camera to stop motion. Experimentation is the best way to really understand how shutter speed works. You first have to consider how you want the final image to appear. Do you want to freeze the action? Blur it? Do a combination of blur and frozen motion using a panning technique? Or, do you want to combine the blur and frozen motion using a panning technique and then add a flash to stop the action at the right moment, making the subject stand out even more?

These are all ways of rendering action images. But you first need to decide how you want to render the action and then use the appropriate technique.

USING A FAST SHUTTER SPEED

You can freeze the action by using a fast enough shutter speed to literally stop the action perfectly (**Figure 2.1**).

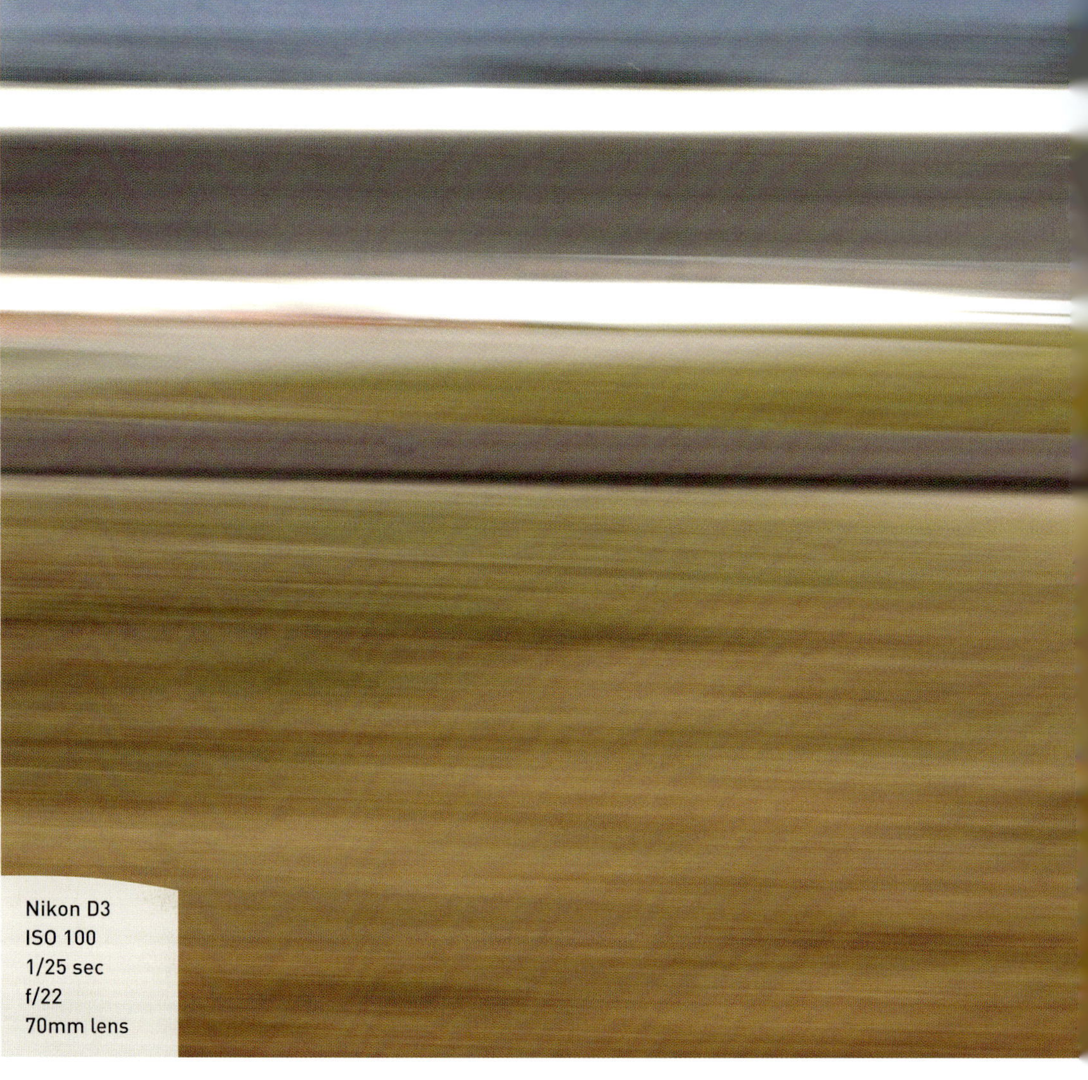
Nikon D3
ISO 100
1/25 sec
f/22
70mm lens

A faster shutter speed is necessary to stop action moving parallel to the camera. The closer the subject is to the lens as it moves parallel to the front of the lens, the faster the shutter speed will need to be to freeze the action.

Movement captured, especially with a long lens, as it moves directly toward the camera can be frozen with a significantly slower shutter speed.

BLURRING THE ACTION

Blurring the action is the easiest motion to achieve in an image and the toughest to make look good. Blurring involves using a slow enough shutter speed that the motion of the subject is rendered as a blur. The camera can be stationary or in motion during the exposure. If the camera is in motion, the speed at which the camera is moving has to be different than the speed at which the subject is moving.

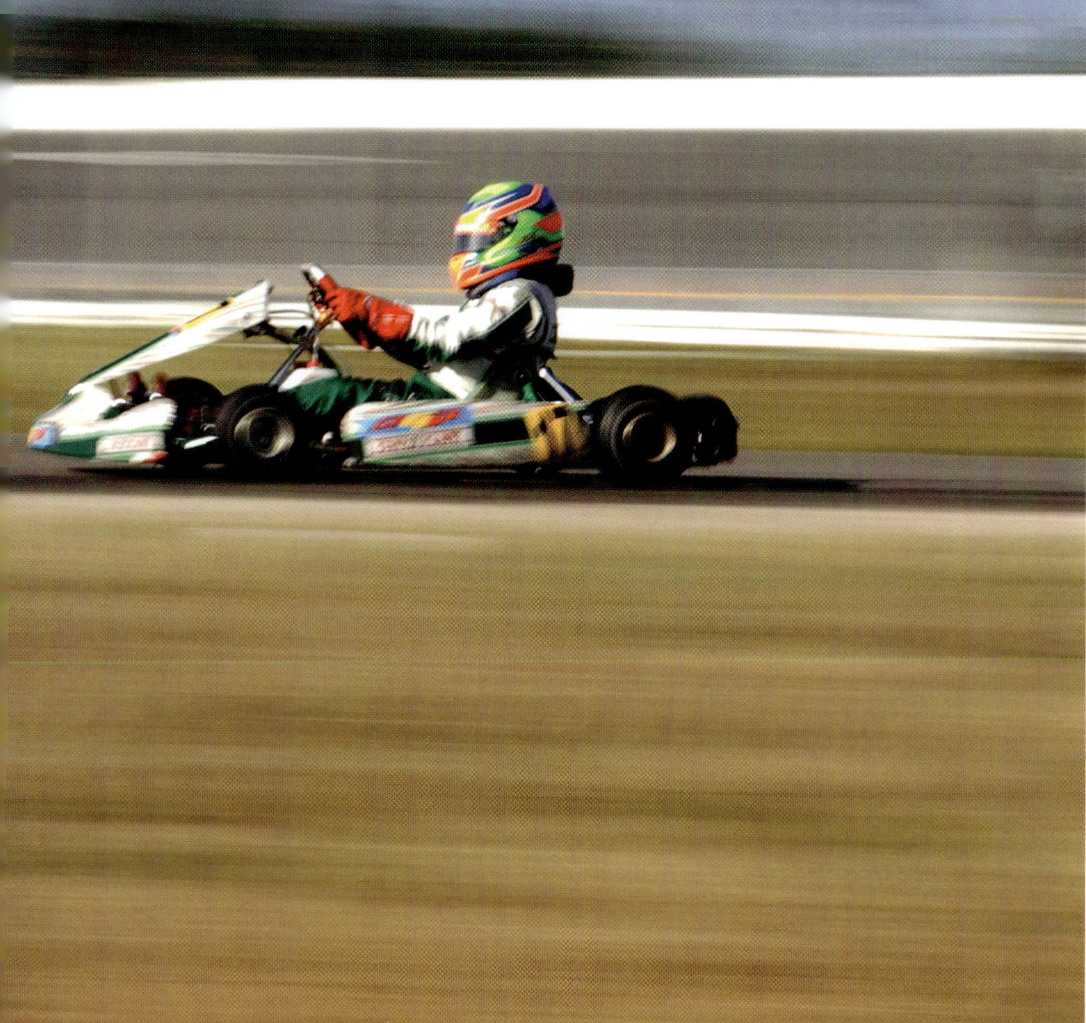

FIGURE 2.2
Go-kart racing at the Daytona International Speedway.

PANNING THE ACTION

Panning is a technique that involves moving the camera in parallel to the action being photographed. It is achieved by keeping the subject in the same position of the frame for the duration of the exposure. The duration of the exposure must be long enough to allow the background to blur due to the movement of the camera. Simply put, it is necessary to focus the camera on the action you want to freeze using a slow enough shutter speed and then moving the camera in an even motion, keeping the camera level at the same speed as the moving subject you want to freeze. Again, this is easier than it sounds and is a very basic and necessary skill you need to master (**Figure 2.2**).

By setting the camera to rear curtain sync, you can do a pan and fire the flash while panning. This will illuminate the subject and help freeze the motion.

Each sport has different, important considerations relative to how to capture the various forms of action, and these will be discussed in later chapters.

NOTE

Rear curtain sync is a setting on the camera whereby the camera fires the flash just before the shutter shuts. This causes anything in motion to appear to be a streak until the light from the flash illuminates it, rendering it sharp, provided that the lens is focused properly. It's a technique used to demonstrate speed in still images.

APERTURE

Used in combination with shutter speed, the aperture controls how much light reaches the film/imaging plane. The aperture is normally called an F stop. The greater the F stop, the more light it will allow to reach the film or image sensor, which allows a faster shutter speed or a lower ISO to be used.

NOTE

The imaging plane is the exact place the image is captured, whether it is film or a sensor.

Aperture is also an important part of focus considerations. How much of the image do you want in focus? The larger the opening of the aperture (lower numbers enlarge the opening), the less that will be in focus—every time with every lens. With longer lenses you can see the change in depth of field faster, but the same rules apply for wide-angle lenses as well.

WHITE BALANCE

Digital cameras make setting the white balance easy. Auto white balance is so good that the camera will get you close to the ideal setting almost every time. As long as you shoot RAW you will be able to make perfect final corrections during postproduction.

I always want very tight control over the technical part of the photographic process. I want every camera set to very tight technical tolerances. This is particularly important when I'm using multiple cameras (remotes) to capture images simultaneously. It helps with quality control, and that not only makes the images better but allows me to work much faster on deadline because I spend very little time in postproduction.

TIP

I use a Sekonic color temperature meter to determine the Kelvin number and then dial in the precise color temperature I want in every situation.

DEPTH OF FIELD

Entire books have been written about depth of field. What you need to know is that it greatly affects the look of a photograph.

Depth of field is the amount of the image that is in sharp focus, from the nearest to the farthest element in the image. Three factors control this critical part of composition:

- **Aperture.** The wider the aperture, the smaller the amount of the image that will be in focus.
- **Distance from the lens to the subject.** The closer to the lens the subject is, the smaller the amount of the image that will be in focus.
- **Lens length.** The longer the lens is, the smaller the amount of the image that will be in focus.

The combination of these three elements controls the amount of the image that will be in focus.

CAMERA SUPPORTS

Auxiliary equipment can also be helpful in making photographs in an efficient, comfortable, and accurate manner. Tripod use is extremely important and is always undervalued. People tend to use tripods only in slow shutter speed situations. However, they are important not only for stability but for consistency of composition. I also use them for remote cameras.

Monopods are a must when you're shooting sports. For many major sports, access is tightly regulated, and for security reasons, tripods are not allowed. I always have either a Nikkor 400mm f/2.8 or 600mm f/4 over my shoulder with a Gitzo Series 5 6X monopod with G-lock. It is big and strong but lightweight at the same time. It gives me better control over composition and stability, which is important when I'm using telephoto lenses. Having a long lens helps me get close to the action without physically putting myself in the middle of the action.

TIP

Many photographers make the mistake of trying to find the lightest tripod possible. Although that makes the tripod easier to carry, it makes it less stable with longer lenses or in windy conditions. Sand bags can be added to the tripod to help provide additional weight.

SPORTS PHOTOGRAPHY AS A TEACHING TOOL

Many collegiate and professional sports teams hire photographers and videographers to provide images to athletes and coaches to use for critical analysis of the athletes' performance. Prior to the shoot, the photographer needs to talk with the coaches and athletes to determine what kind of angles and sequences need to be shot so that afterwards the participants can analyze the images and help improve their performance by using the information in the photographs to alter their body movements.

SPORTS PHOTOGRAPHY FOR ADVERTISING AND PROMOTIONAL PURPOSES

Sports photographs made for advertising and promotional purposes are normally done as controlled shoots where the athletes perform for the camera and the photographs produced are used to sell or endorse products.

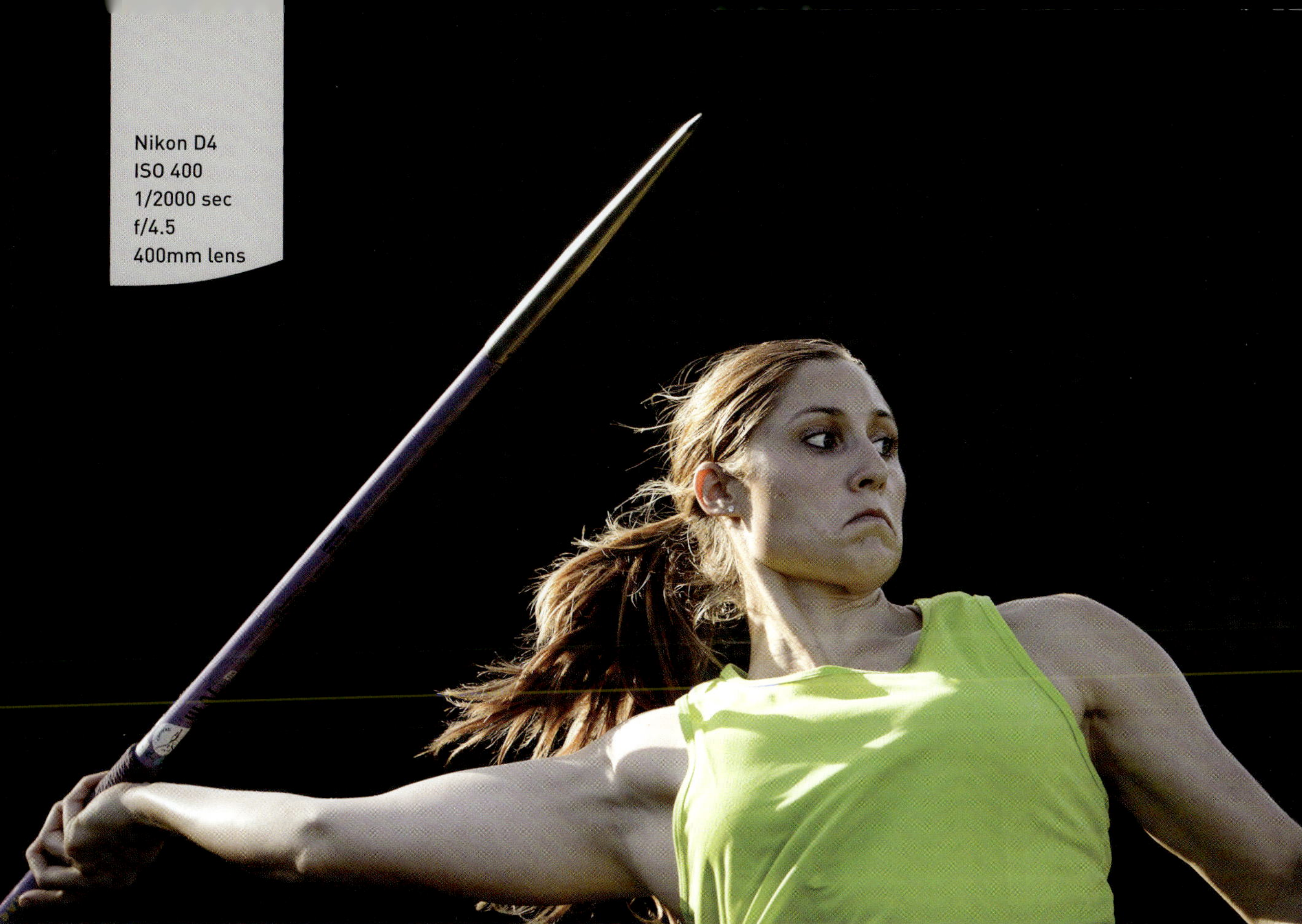

FIGURE 2.3
Kara Patterson models for an endorsement of the Nikon D4.

For the release of the Nikon D4, I photographed Kara Patterson, the USATF National Champion in women's javelin at the time, to demonstrate various camera functions (**Figure 2.3**). For the shoot, Kara acted as a model. She stood where I asked her to stand and threw where I asked her to throw. This situation is similar to a portrait because I had control over access and timing.

SPORTS PHOTOGRAPHY AS JOURNALISM

Providing images to publications for editorial use is often done in combination with a written story. In these situations, most publications want the photographs and words to work together to support each other. At a minimum, a caption is normally attached to the photograph to provide additional information. One of *Life* magazine's great picture editors, Wilson Hicks, was quoted as saying, "No photograph should need a caption, but every photograph must have one."

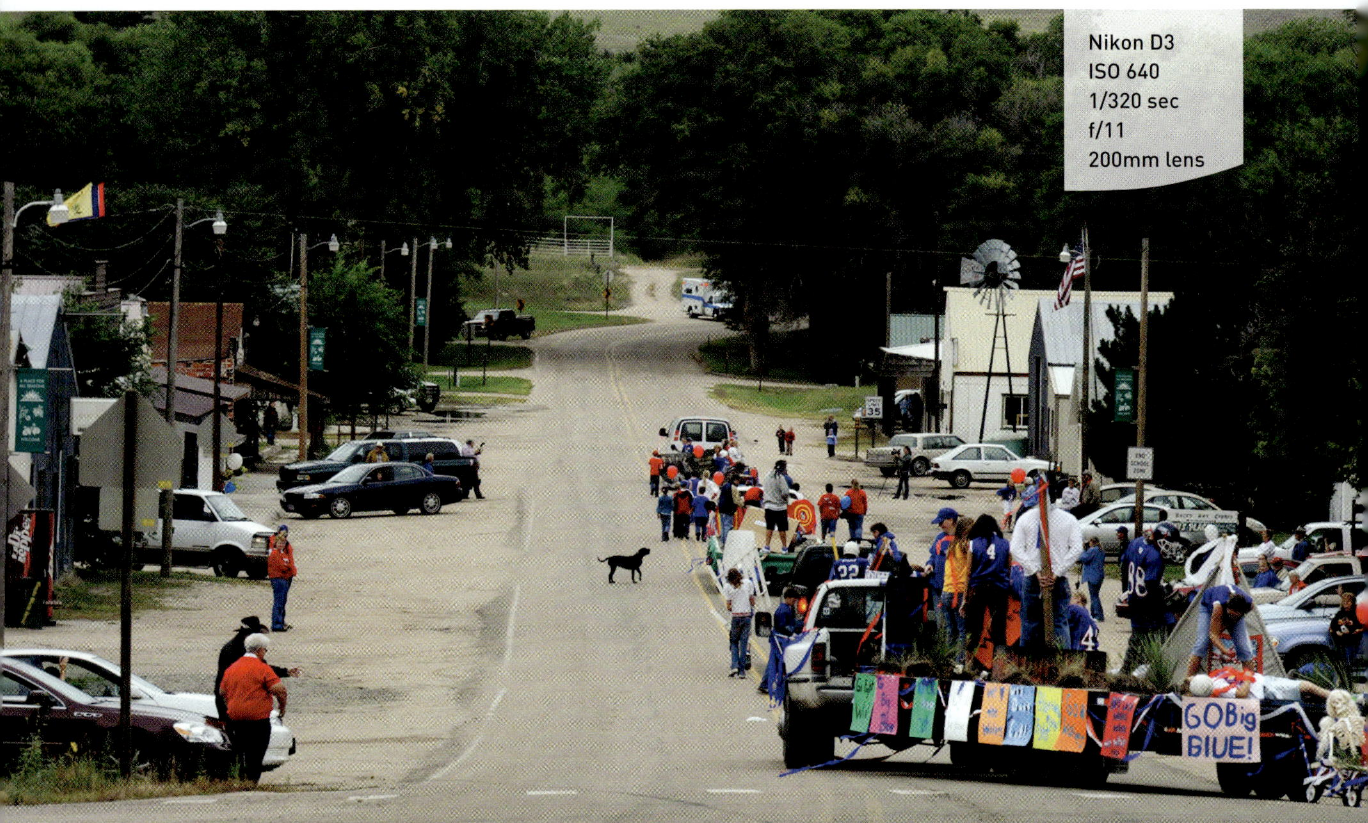

FIGURE 2.4
The Arthur High School Homecoming Parade.

FINDING THE STORY

Finding the story can mean a literal story consisting of a combination of words and pictures or a single storytelling image.

Sports photography isn't just about big events. But when I am covering big events, often my goal is to tell a specific story about a team or athlete. Many of my favorite images do not include major athletes and were not taken at major events. Finding lower-profile stories generally allows for greater access to subjects, and better access usually allows for better photos.

One of my favorite sports stories, shot at Arthur High School in Arthur, Nebraska, is about a six-man football team—the Arthur Wolves (**Figure 2.4**). It wasn't fancy. It was just a simple story about the love of football and community.

Arthur is deep in the sand hills of western Nebraska. The population of the town is 145 people, and the high school consisted of 28 students that year. Every boy but one was on the football team, and the quarterback also played in the band. I was in town for homecoming week and the story ran in *SI for Kids* (**Figure 2.5** and **Figure 2.6**).

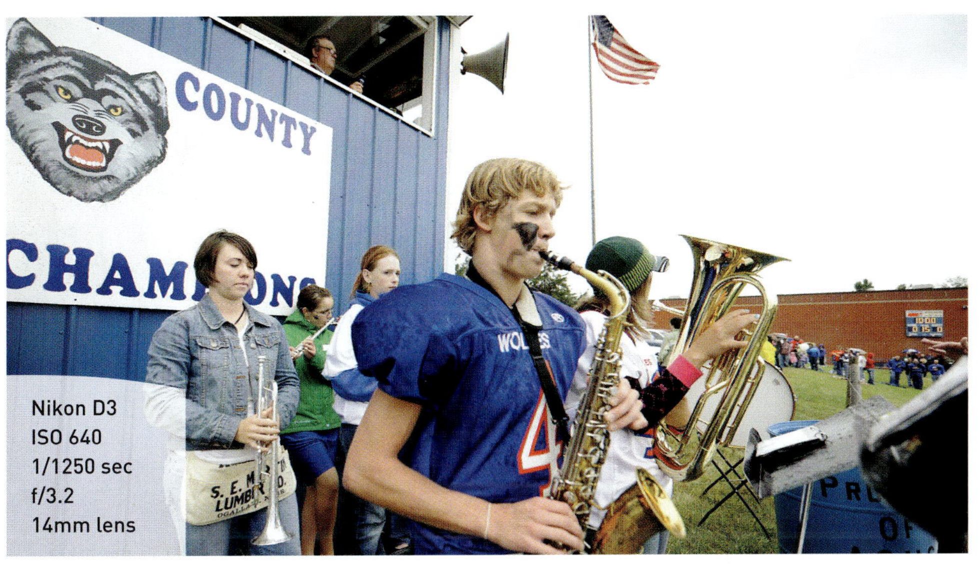

Nikon D3
ISO 640
1/1250 sec
f/3.2
14mm lens

FIGURE 2.5
The quarterback plays his part of the *Star Spangled Banner* before the game.

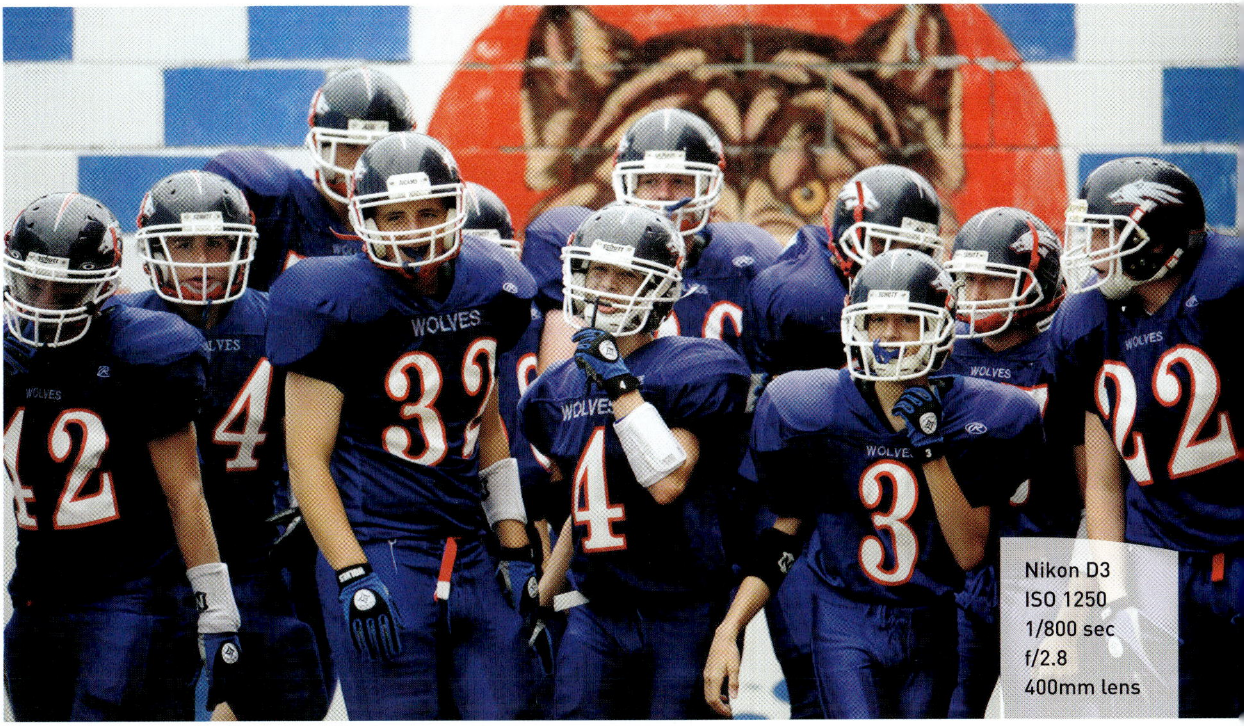

Nikon D3
ISO 1250
1/800 sec
f/2.8
400mm lens

FIGURE 2.6
The team makes its way onto the field to start the game.

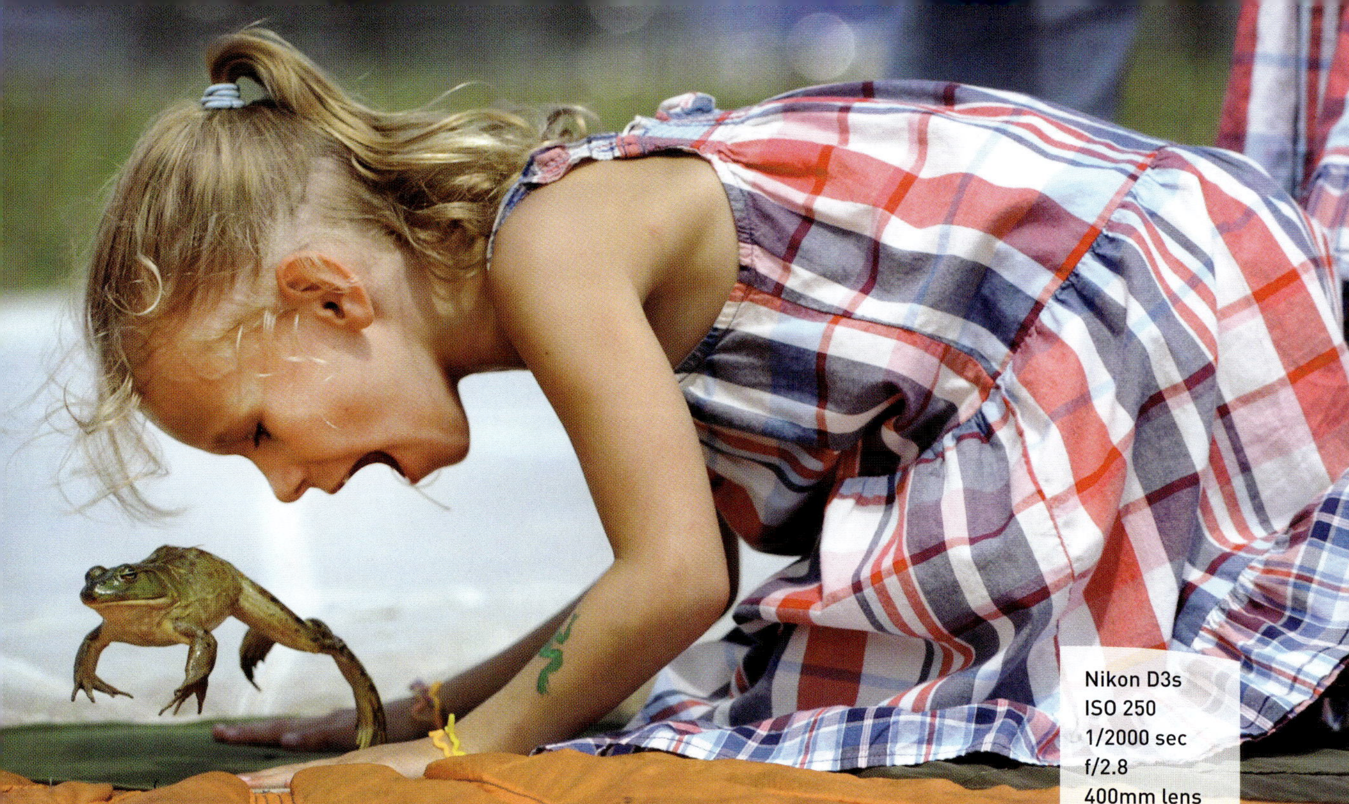

FIGURE 2.7
A little girl screams at a frog to encourage it to jump during the competition.

Stories similar to the one I shot in Arthur are everywhere. People do seek me out if they have a story they think *Sports Illustrated* should feature, but most often I find stories on my own. Community calendars are extremely helpful in this regard. In fact, I covered a frog jumping festival in Ohio after picking up a community calendar in the Cincinnati airport (**Figure 2.7**).

Internet search engines are also a good place to look for local events. In the summer of 2010, I wanted to find something fun to run on SI.com and in the digital edition of *Sports Illustrated* before football season started. I was fortunate to find a watermelon festival in Georgia, just a couple hours from my home in Jacksonville (**Figure 2.8**). SI.com and digital publishing in general have provided me with many more opportunities to show my work.

Often, great stories are right in your backyard. Five years ago I met a 12-year-old local skater named Cason Kirk. We did a story on skateboarding at the famous Kona Skate Park in Jacksonville, Florida. Since then, I've had the joy of watching Cason grow into one of the world's best young skaters (**Figure 2.9**).

Events and stories like these are fun to shoot and generally allow a lot of access, which brings us to the next important subject.

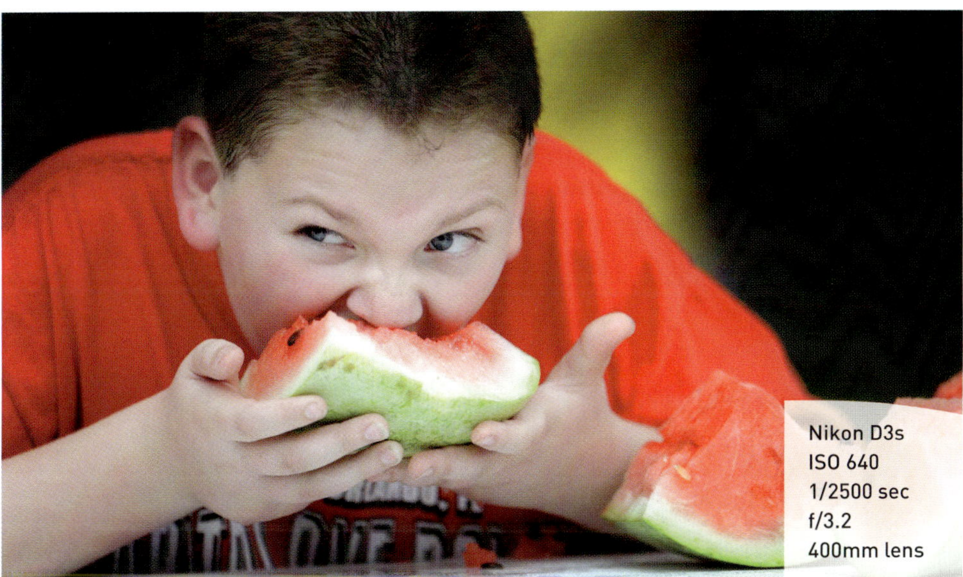

Nikon D3s
ISO 640
1/2500 sec
f/3.2
400mm lens

FIGURE 2.8
A boy eats a slice of watermelon during the watermelon eating contest.

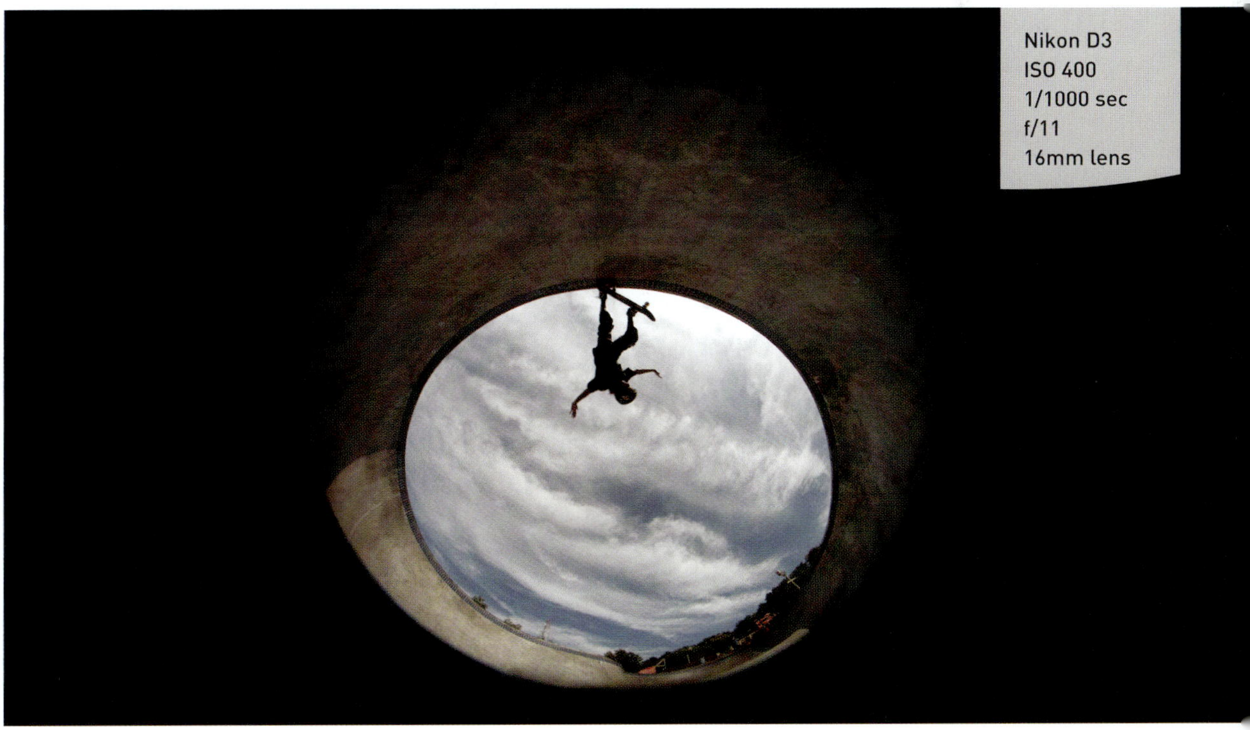

Nikon D3
ISO 400
1/1000 sec
f/11
16mm lens

FIGURE 2.9
Cason Kirk skates above me at Kona Skate Park.

GAINING ACCESS

For journalism, and also strictly as a fan, access is the hardest part of covering sports. Certain events are simply off limits if you are not a member of the credentialed media. Access is determined by two main factors: the safety of the athletes and spectators, and the rules of various athletic departments/federations and television broadcast.

Every situation will be slightly different, and it is very important to ask the right questions. If you don't, you won't be prepared and you'll make costly mistakes, which will put you and those around you at risk. Here are a few questions I ask in every situation:

- What can and can't I do?
- Where can I physically be?
- What can I use the images for?

ACTION AND FEATURE PORTRAITS

Not all sports photography is pure action. Much of my time is spent planning and executing high-quality portraits.

Features, the action away from the action, is another very important element of sports photography. These images define the culture of the sport.

Whether a portrait is environmental, showing the person you are photographing in a setting that helps define who they are, is action based, or is against a backdrop, proper lighting is critical when you're shooting a portrait.

LIGHTING

Light shapes a photograph. In a controlled portrait situation you can use light however you see fit; you are less at the mercy of natural elements than you are when you're shooting an event. Sometimes you introduce light through strobes or continuous light sources; sometimes mother nature offers a far superior option.

HIGHLIGHTING POWER AND GRACE

Candace Parker is one of the best athletes I've ever photographed. When she was the star of the Tennessee women's basketball team, I photographed her for a cover story in *Time* magazine (**Figure 2.10**).

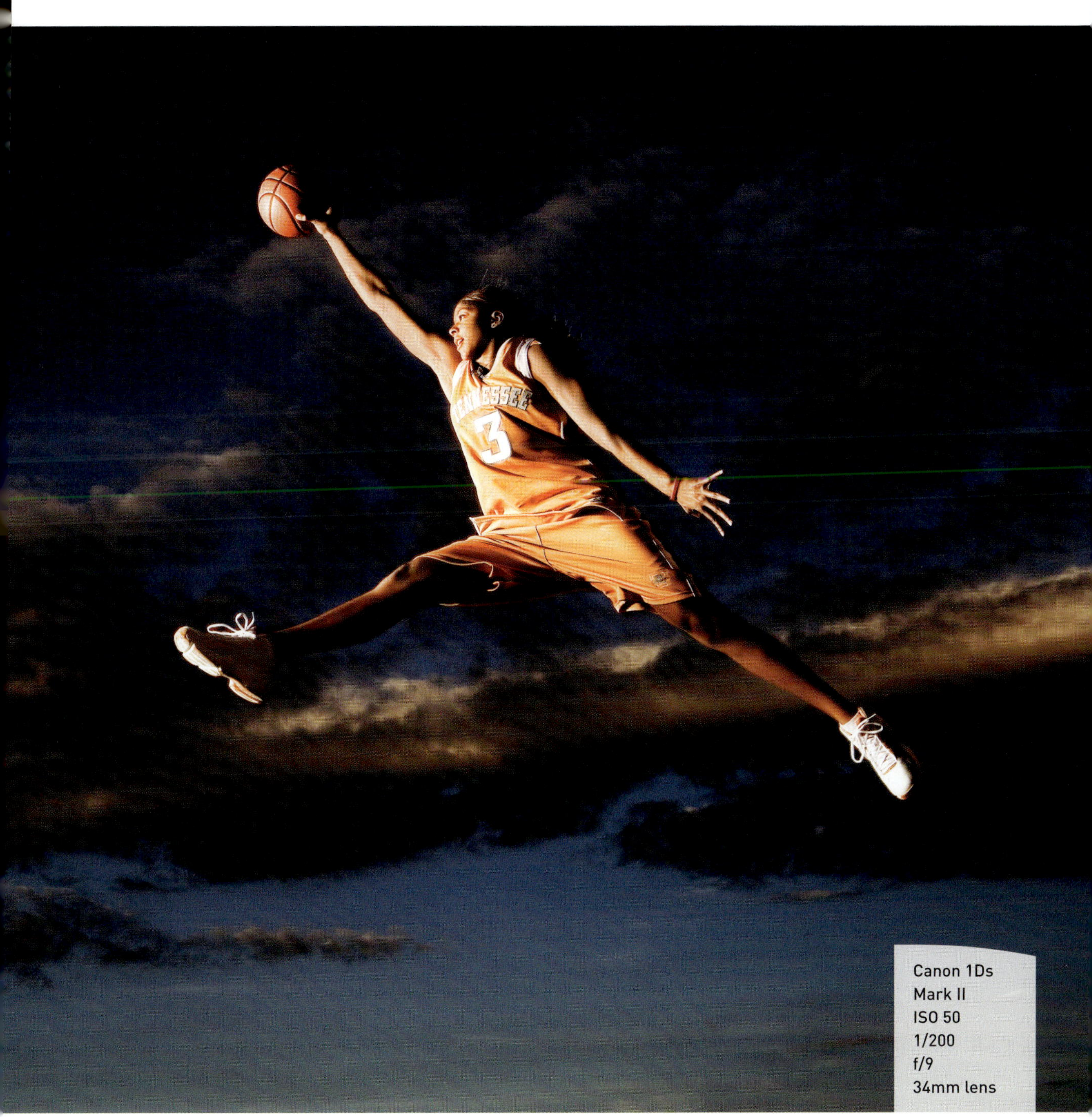

Canon 1Ds
Mark II
ISO 50
1/200
f/9
34mm lens

FIGURE 2.10
Candace Parker jumps across a Tennessee sky for a portrait.

Candace is strong and powerful but also graceful and elegant at the same time. To show this, I wanted the light to accentuate her beauty and her body to emphasize her strength. I lit this portrait with two Elinchrome 2400 watt/second strobe heads and softened that light with two large Elinchrome octabox light diffusers. I stacked the lights—one at 10 feet above the ground and one at 18 feet—using huge Avenger light stands.

Candace was jumping on a trampoline and palming the ball effortlessly. I waited for sunset so that the orange and blue sky would complement her uniform colors and make a lovely image. By pumping in a lot of light, I was able to make the sky go a little darker and make her stand out.

TIP

Adding extra light to your principal subject allows you to expose your subject normally, and if you keep the extra light from spilling onto anything in the background, it allows you to let the background go darker, which adds drama to the image.

ANTICIPATING THE HIT

Jevon Kearse's nickname is "The Freak." He was a dominant defensive figure throughout his career in the NFL. When I was assigned to shoot him for the cover of *Sports Illustrated*, I wanted to show viewers what a quarterback sees when Jevon is coming at him (**Figure 2.11**).

To do this, I put gymnastic pads on the floor, stretched out flat on my back, and let Jevon jump over me. To keep it simple and to make sure Jevon was the only focus of the photo, I shot him against a pure white backdrop in a sound stage.

Because he needed to be moving very fast in close proximity to me, I decided to shoot him with a wide-angle lens. That meant I needed to be able to shoot at a fast shutter speed, even with strobe, in order to freeze the action.

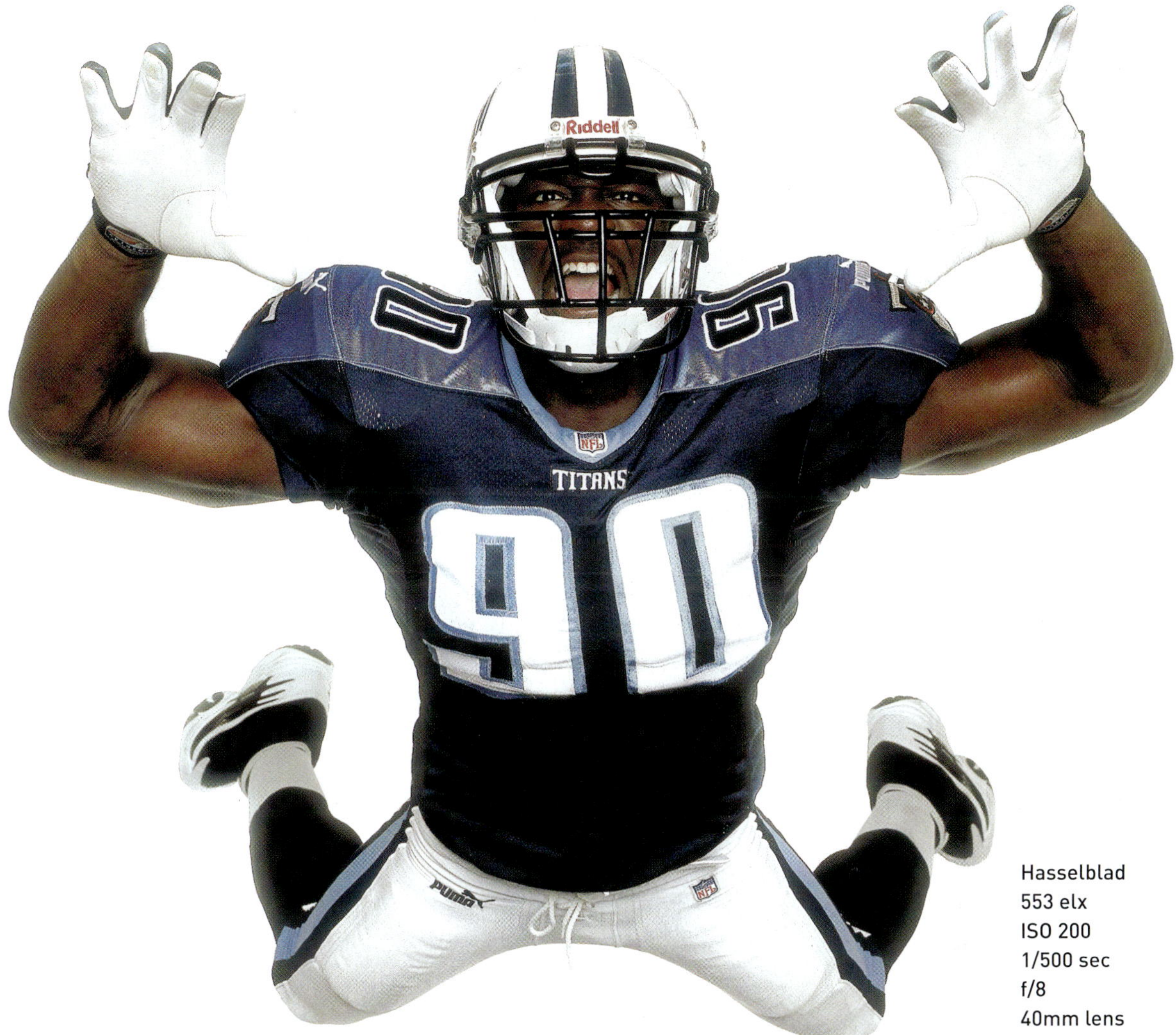

Hasselblad
553 elx
ISO 200
1/500 sec
f/8
40mm lens

FIGURE 2.11
Jevon Kearse in tackle mode. I used 6 Speedotron black line strobes with quad heads to shorten the flash duration.

FIGURE 2.12
A happy-go-lucky Rebecca Twig.

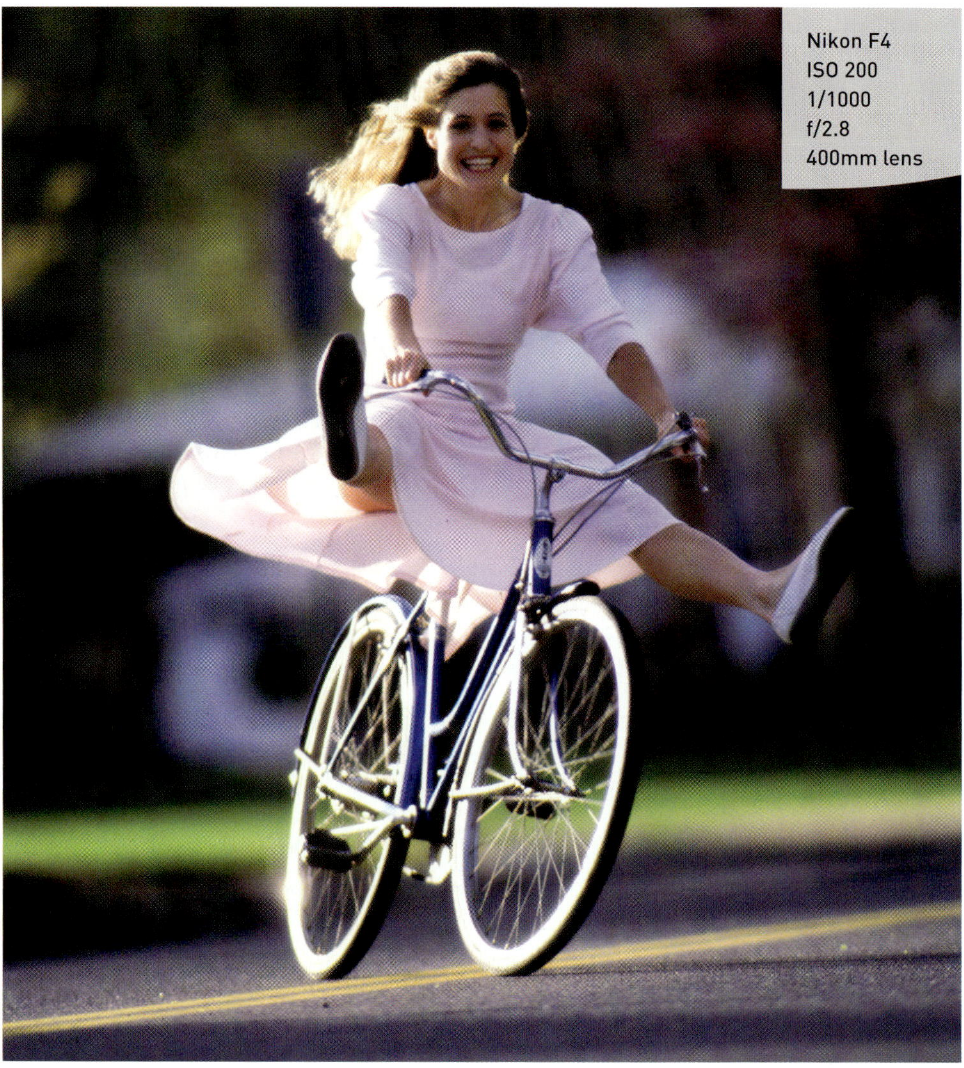

Nikon F4
ISO 200
1/1000
f/2.8
400mm lens

SHOWCASING THE OTHER SIDE

For an Olympic preview story, I traveled to Colorado Springs to photograph Rebecca Twigg, a six time world track cycling champion and Olympic medalist. She is an incredibly fit, strong, and tough athlete. So tough in fact that she won a world championship with a broken collarbone. For this feature, I chose to photograph her in a pink dress on a low-tech, old-school bicycle to emphasis her upbeat personality and happy demeanor (**Figure 2.12**).

Chapter 2 Assignments

The following assignments will help you gain technical control of your camera.

White Balance and Mixed Light

Find a game being played under artificial light. Set your white balance on automatic, and then try each of the other white balance settings. Compare the results. Look especially at how the different white balance settings affect skin tones.

Distance and Depth of Field

Take a portrait of someone who will cooperate with you and let you take your time making photographs. You will need that person to stay relatively still so you can make accurate comparisons. Take one portrait two feet away from your subject and one from ten feet away. Make sure your camera settings are the same for both portraits. Look at the difference your proximity to the subject makes on depth of field. Using a person as the subject has the added bonus of seeing what effect depth of field has on people; it's important to not distort or overly compress a person's features.

Repeat the exercise on an inanimate object. This time take five pictures from two feet away using different aperture settings, from the widest to the narrowest aperture your lens allows. Then do the same thing from ten feet away. Compare the differences.

Being able to know how to use depth of field to predict what will be in focus in your compositions is a major part of being able to control your photographic vision.

Practice Panning

Stand safely on the side of a road where traffic is constantly flowing. Practice panning at different speeds as the cars pass by you. Pay attention to the different effects you get by changing the speed at which you pan the camera. Making smooth pans is a combination of keeping the camera/lens moving at a constant speed and level. If you have a tripod with a head that allows panning, try doing the pan on the tripod, and then try panning using a handheld method. Compare the differences.

Share your results with the book's Flickr group!
Join the group here: flickr.com/groups/sportsphotographyfromsnapshotstogreatshots.

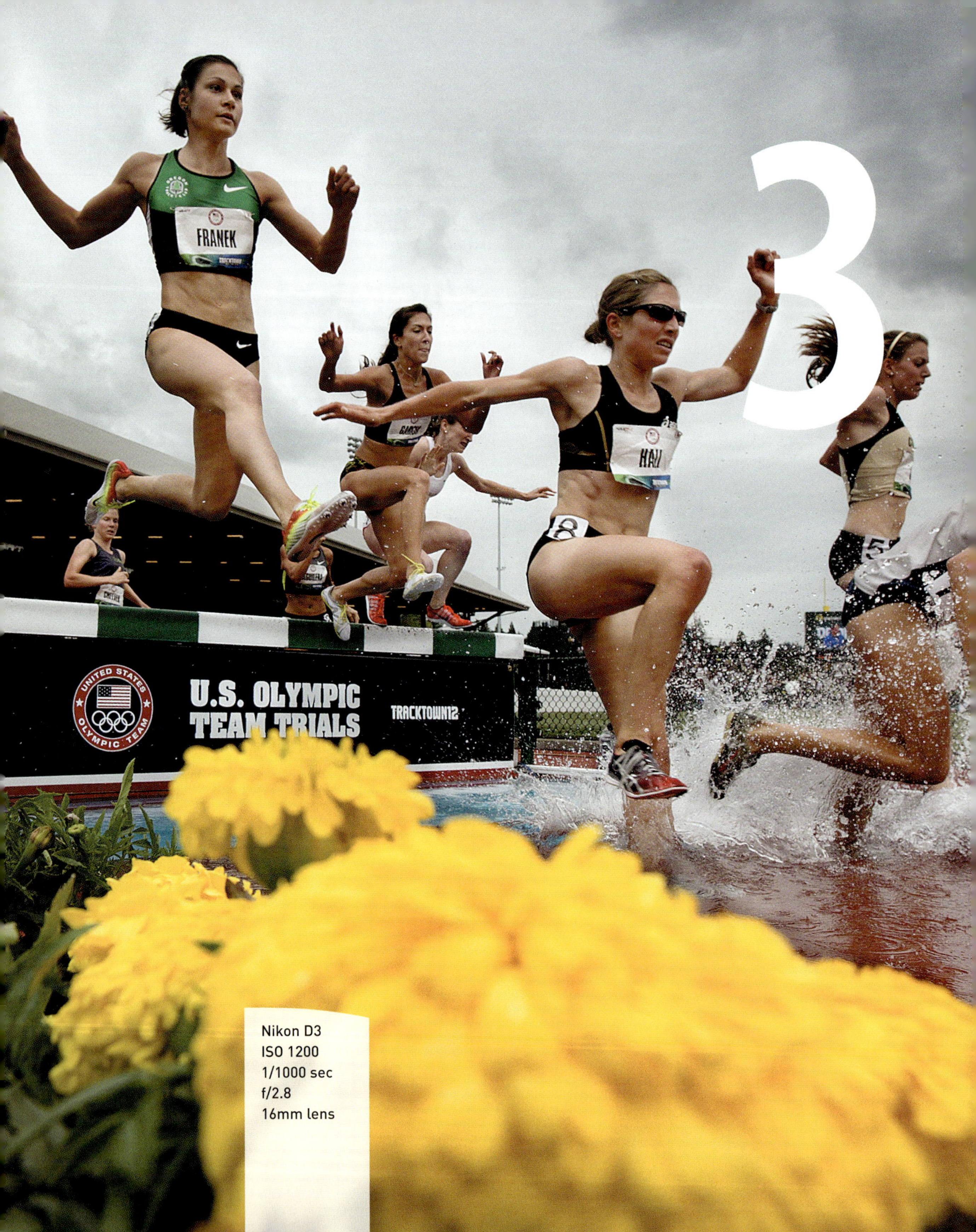

3

Nikon D3
ISO 1200
1/1000 sec
f/2.8
16mm lens

The Right Perspective

SHOOTING WITH SHORT AND LONG LENSES

The camera is only part of the equipment you need to make a photo. Although having a good camera will help with the final quality of your pictures, the lens you use, and how you use it, is also critical. Professional photographers discuss cameras and lenses as individual elements.

I always advise beginning photographers to invest their money in good lenses. Camera bodies change constantly, but a good lens can perform perfectly for many years. I buy new cameras every couple of years but still use lenses that I bought when I started my career 30 years ago.

This chapter walks you through the different kinds of lenses and explains when to use them and why.

The final of the women's 3000m steeplechase at the USATF Olympic Trials in 2012 in Eugene, Oregon.

PORING OVER THE PICTURE

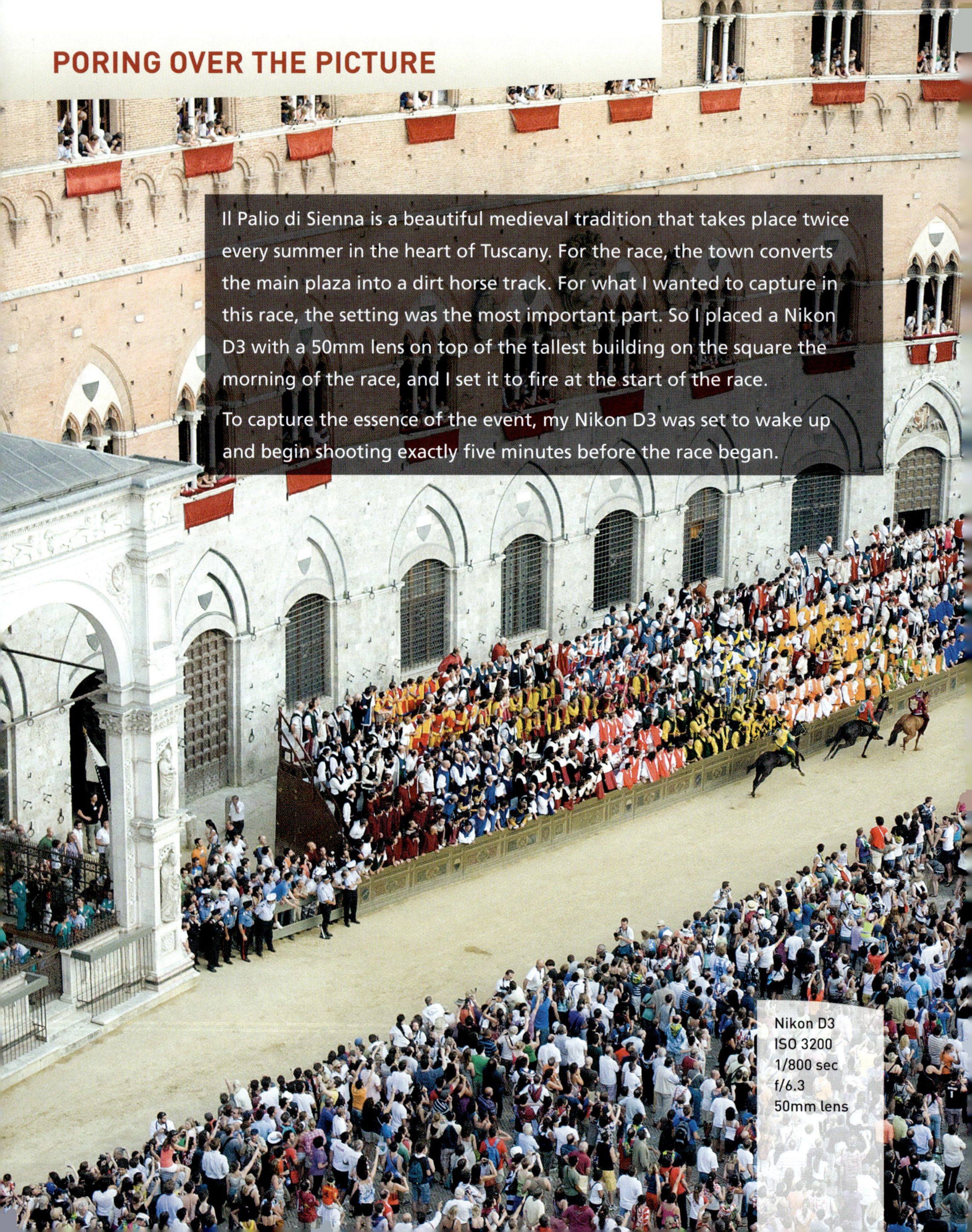

Il Palio di Sienna is a beautiful medieval tradition that takes place twice every summer in the heart of Tuscany. For the race, the town converts the main plaza into a dirt horse track. For what I wanted to capture in this race, the setting was the most important part. So I placed a Nikon D3 with a 50mm lens on top of the tallest building on the square the morning of the race, and I set it to fire at the start of the race.

To capture the essence of the event, my Nikon D3 was set to wake up and begin shooting exactly five minutes before the race began.

Nikon D3
ISO 3200
1/800 sec
f/6.3
50mm lens

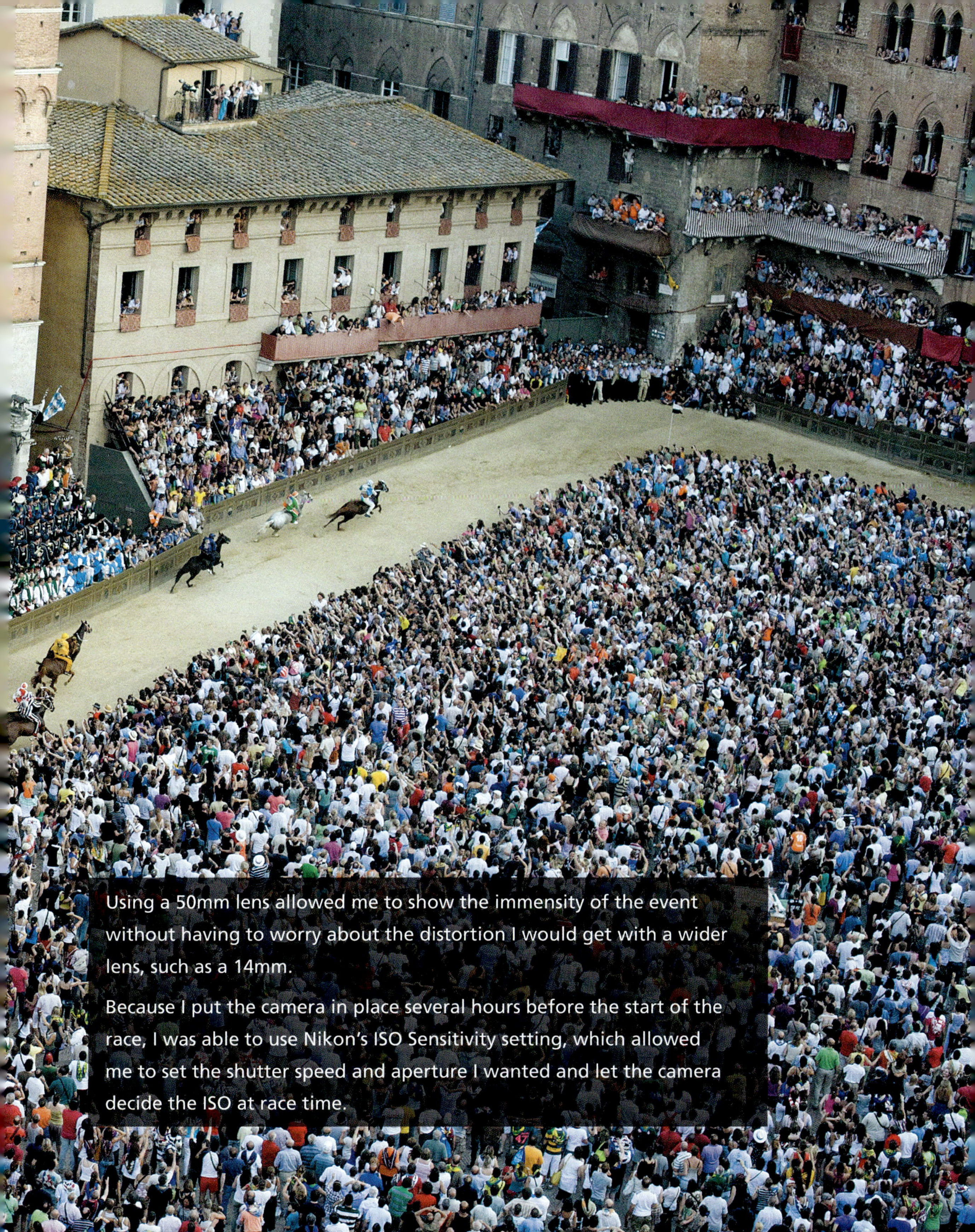

Using a 50mm lens allowed me to show the immensity of the event without having to worry about the distortion I would get with a wider lens, such as a 14mm.

Because I put the camera in place several hours before the start of the race, I was able to use Nikon's ISO Sensitivity setting, which allowed me to set the shutter speed and aperture I wanted and let the camera decide the ISO at race time.

SHORT LENSES: FROM SUPER WIDE TO NORMAL

A short lens is any lens ranging from 6mm to 70mm. Common lenses in this range are 14mm, 24mm, 14–24mm, 16–35mm, 35mm, 24–70mm, and 50mm, although there are other, less common options as well.

INTIMACY

Wide-angle lenses allow a point of view that draws the viewer right into the heart of the situation. With a wide-angle lens attached, you can position the camera very close to the subject matter and still produce sweeping views of the field of play (**Figure 3.1**).

> **TIP**
>
> When you're using a wide-angle lens, be sure to keep it level to reduce distortion. If you tilt a wide-angle lens, buildings will warp toward the center and faces will look like almonds. To change perspective, use your feet and knees; move closer or farther away, or kneel or bend down to get a different perspective.

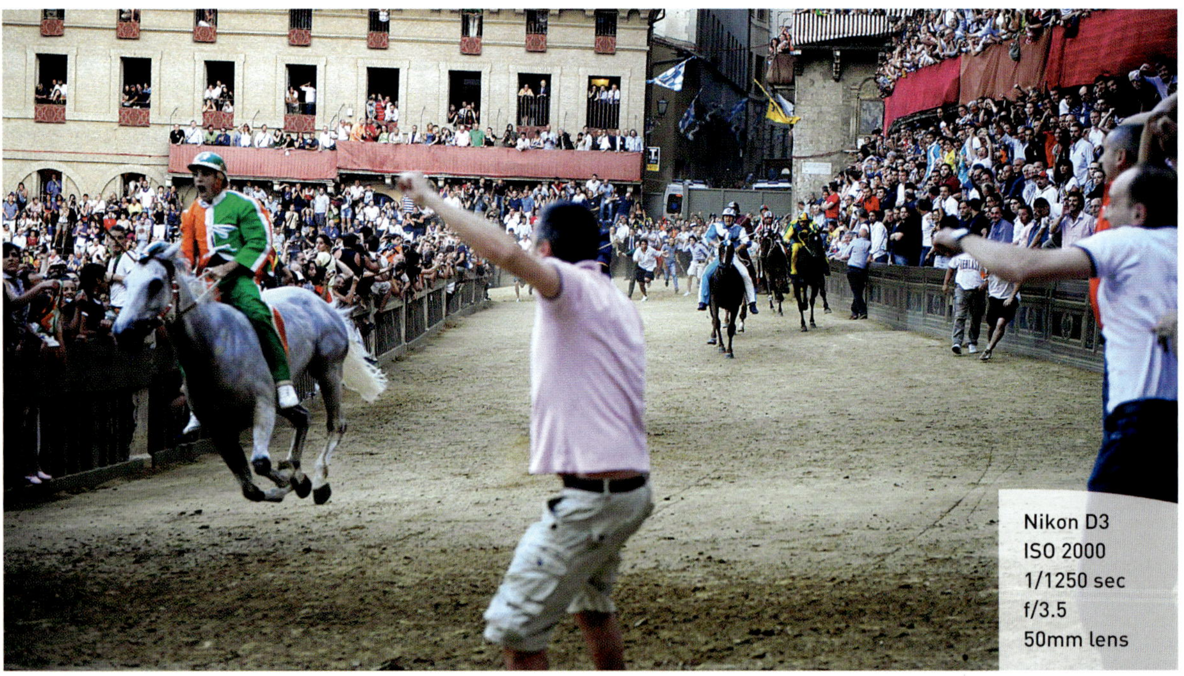

Nikon D3
ISO 2000
1/1250 sec
f/3.5
50mm lens

FIGURE 3.1 Fans celebrate as the winning horse crosses the finish line at Il Palio di Sienna.

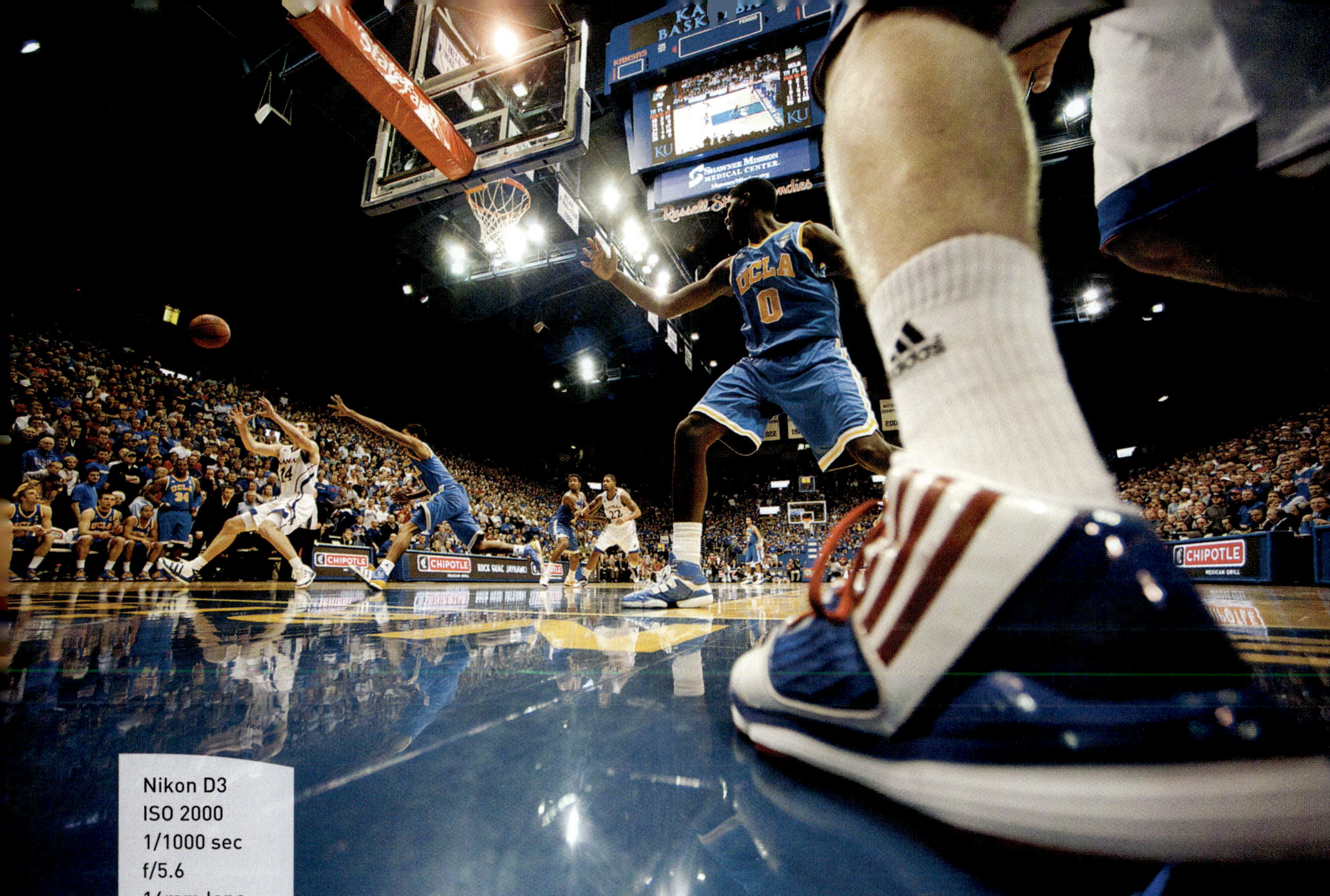

Nikon D3
ISO 2000
1/1000 sec
f/5.6
14mm lens

FIGURE 3.2 Kansas University plays the University of California, Los Angeles.

PROXIMITY

Wide-angle lenses allow you to work in much closer physical proximity to the subject matter, particularly people. The lenses are smaller, easier to handle, require less stabilization or support, and are much more portable than long lenses. That means that you can get closer to the subject physically (**Figure 3.2**).

TIP

Subjects moving across the focal plane close to the lens will require a faster shutter to stop the action.

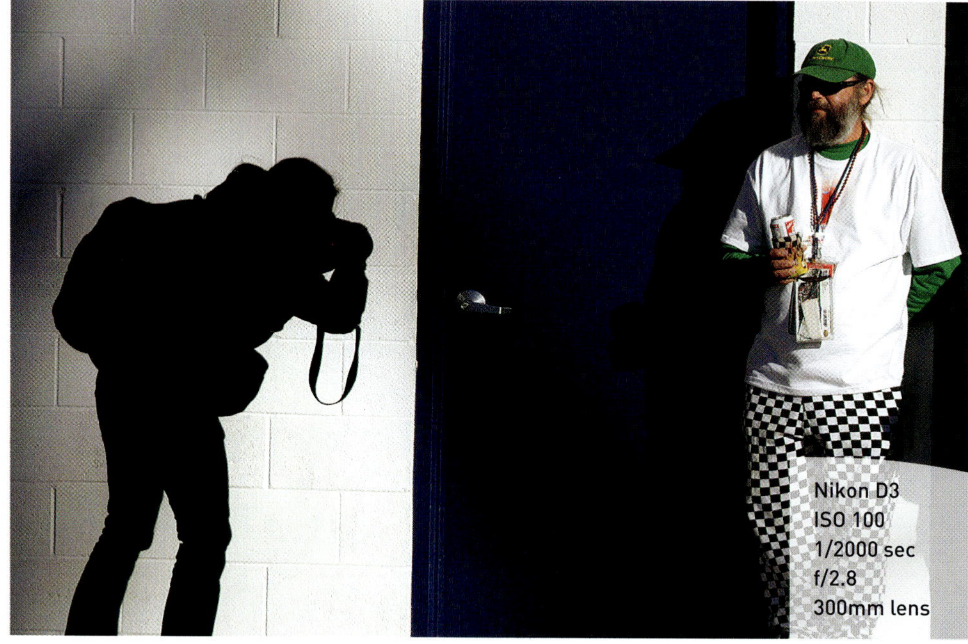

FIGURE 3.3
Using a wide-angle lens, photographer Laura Heald gets close to a subject during a NASCAR race in Las Vegas, Nevada.

Physical closeness also allows you to have increased communication visually, both literally and figuratively, with the subject. You can communicate with your eyes, with words, and with gestures in a way that you can't when the subjects are not right in front of you (**Figure 3.3**).

ANGLE

Wide-angle lenses help you provide a different perspective of a subject than is possible with long lenses. They are best used to provide context by placing the main subject of the photograph in the overall scene (**Figure 3.4**).

> **TIP**
>
> Focus is critical. It's harder to tell what's in sharp focus with a wide-angle lens than it is with a long lens. For this reason, many good shots are lost due to a lack of precision.

Use wide-angle lenses to do *overall* images, which show as much of the environment or scene as possible. A scenic or panoramic image can set the stage for a picture story or simply show readers something added, like a sunset (**Figure 3.5**).

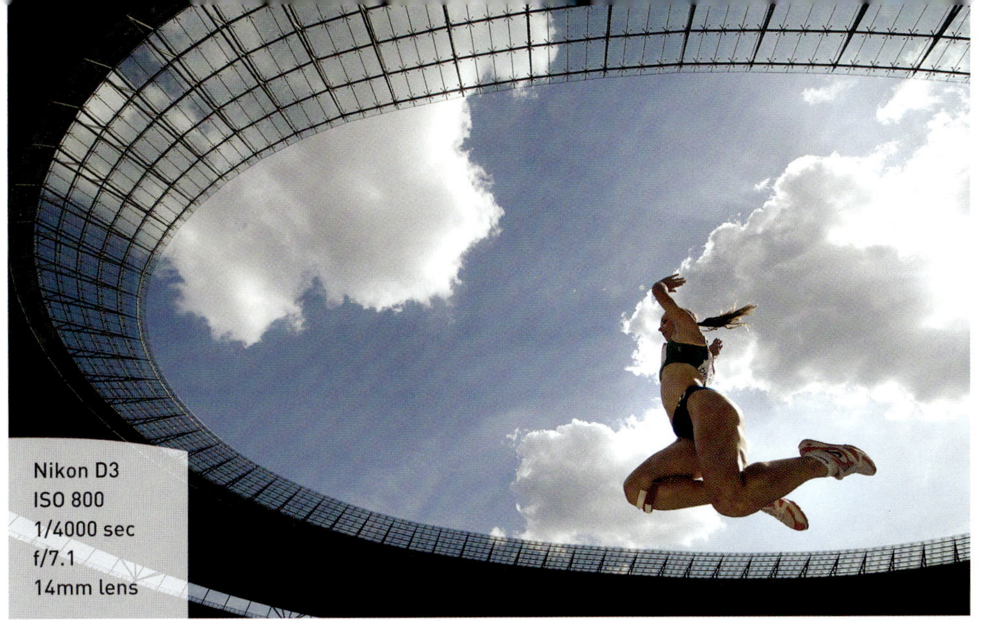

FIGURE 3.4
A long jumper competes in the 2010 IAAF World Athletics Championships in Berlin, Germany.

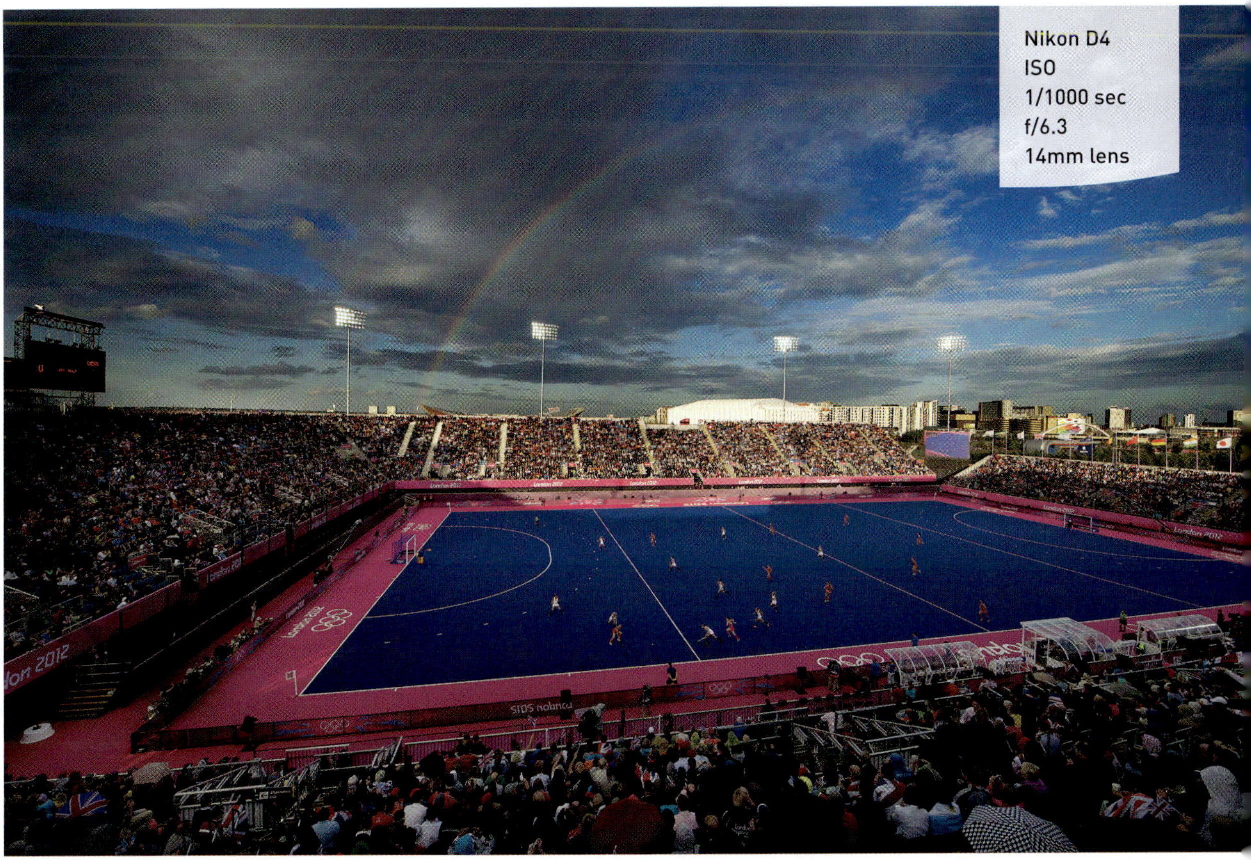

Nikon D4
ISO
1/1000 sec
f/6.3
14mm lens

FIGURE 3.5
A rainbow forms over the field hockey arena at the 2012 Olympic Games in London, England.

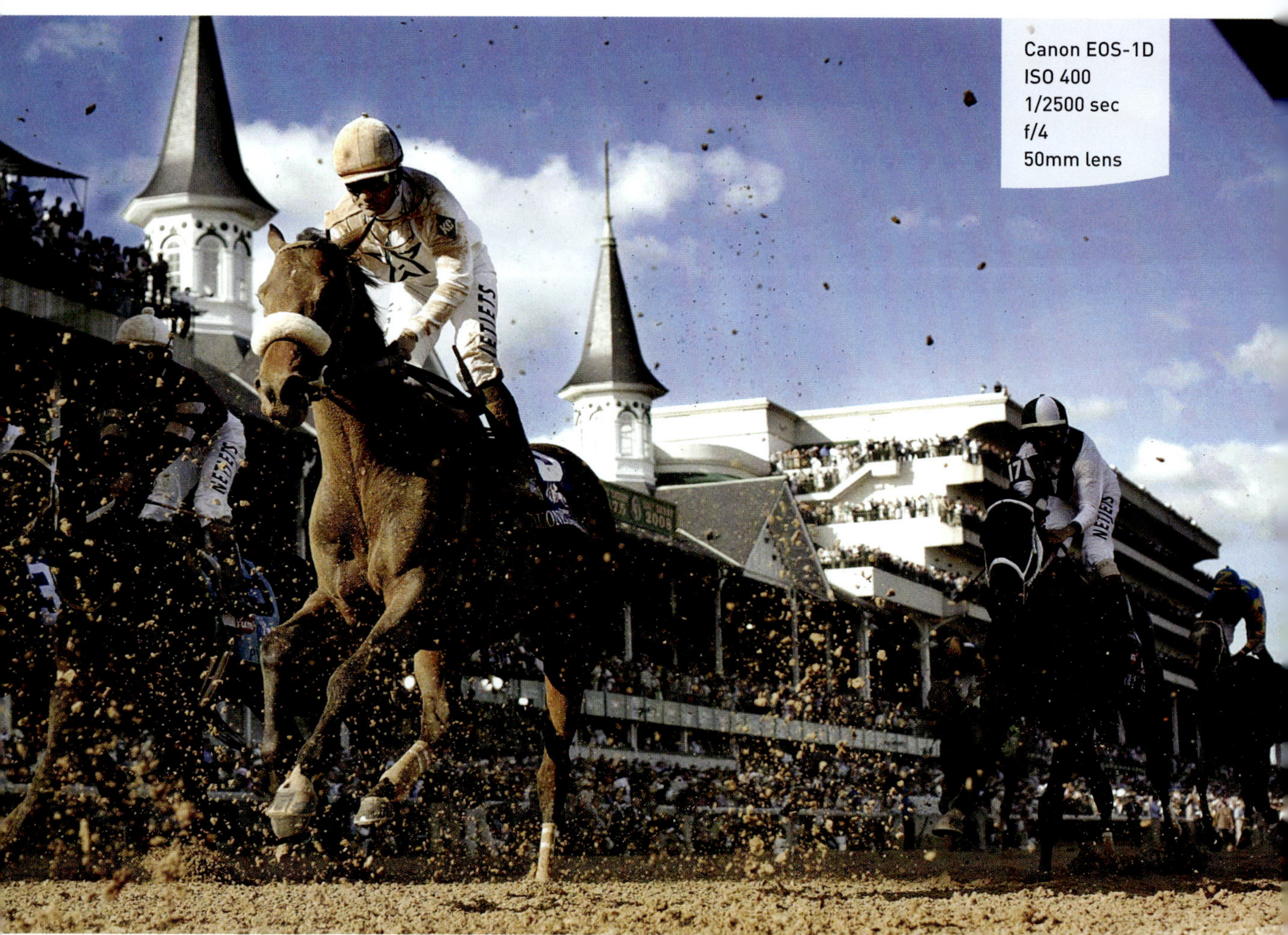

Canon EOS-1D
ISO 400
1/2500 sec
f/4
50mm lens

FIGURE 3.6
The Kentucky Derby.

When used wide open, the f-stop set to maximum aperture, and the front of the lens close to the subject matter, a wide-angle lens can provide a close-up view that will look much different than those produced by long lenses. Long lenses compress the background, whereas wide-angle lenses expand them, creating a very different look (**Figure 3.6**).

> **TIP**
>
> Be careful not to interfere with the action. Remember that you are there to record the game, not inadvertently become part of it.

LONG LENSES

Long lenses are any lenses above 70mm. The most common lenses in this range are 70–200mm, 70–300mm, 200mm, 300mm, 400mm, 500mm, and 600mm. My personal favorite is the Nikkor 600mm f/4, because it works for my photographic style, which is bold, simple, and clean. This particular focal length affords me the opportunities to position myself in places that I prefer to work, because it is a long focal length, is fast, and is incredibly sharp when used properly. Many other more affordable and less-intrusive options are also available.

INTIMACY

Long lenses allow you to reach out into the game and isolate segments of the action, making it easier to focus the viewers' attention on a smaller part of the overall scene. You first have to decide how you want to render the action and then use one of the techniques discussed in Chapter 2, "Getting Started: The Fundamentals of Sports Photography" (**Figure 3.7**).

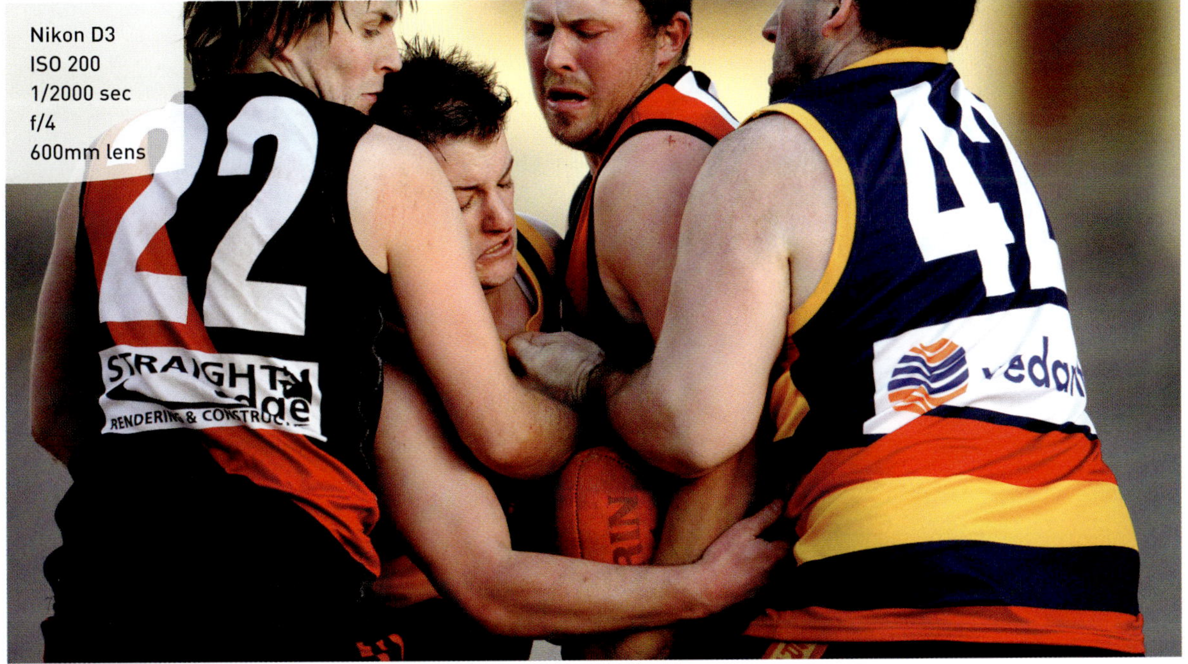

FIGURE 3.7
Aussie Rules football in Queenstown, Tasmania. Shooting with a long lens placed me in the center of the action while I sat in the safety of the sidelines.

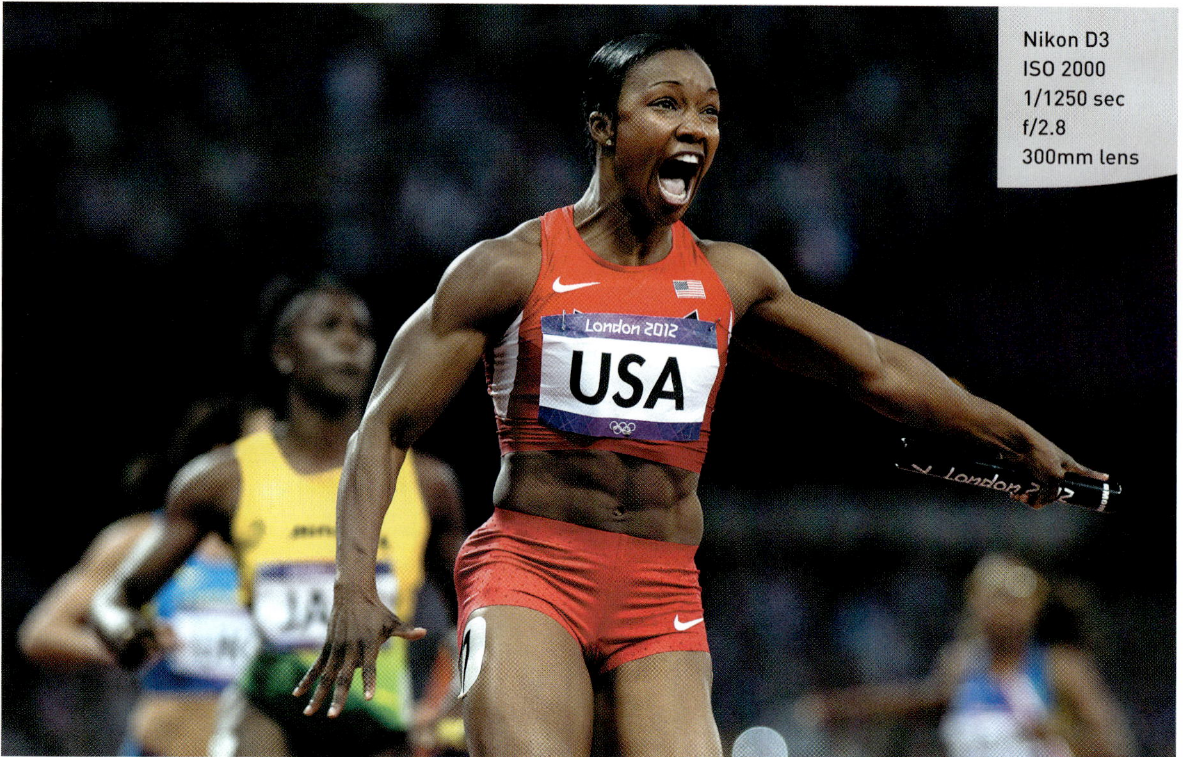

FIGURE 3.8
Carmelita Jeter celebrates as she crosses the finish line in the women's 4x100 meter relays during the 2012 Olympic Games in London. Jeter, along with Allyson Felix, Tianna Madison, and Bianca Knight, won the relay and shattered the existing world record.

PROXIMITY

Long lenses give you the ability to remain relatively distant from the action while still placing the viewer smack in the middle of what's happening on the field of play. Long lenses are often heavy and can be harder to balance than shorter lenses. You can use tripods or monopods to support the cameras with long lenses attached and keep them stable (refer to Chapter 2).

Athletes move quickly. Using long lenses allows you to track the action without having to move with the subject to track him or her. With long lenses, you can stay in one place and let the action come to you. For example, I can't run alongside Usain Bolt, but with a long lens I can position myself to allow him to run to me. This keeps everyone safe and ensures that I don't interfere with the action (**Figure 3.8**).

ANGLE

Because you are isolating segments of the action by using a long lens and the decreased depth of field that goes along with using it, you can gain greater control of the angle of your shots. Showing only pieces of the playing surface affords you much more opportunity to configure your shots tightly without needing to worry about the horizon or nonessential subject matter. It also gives you the chance to make images from many different, slightly askew positions (**Figure 3.9**).

You can use a long lens and carefully monitor the depth of field. Increase the depth of field as necessary to keep enough elements in focus to allow you to shoot overalls of the action, resulting in isolation while offering context.

TIP

Use increased depth of field with long lenses to increase the amount of the image that will be sharp while still benefiting from the compression that goes along with using a long lens.

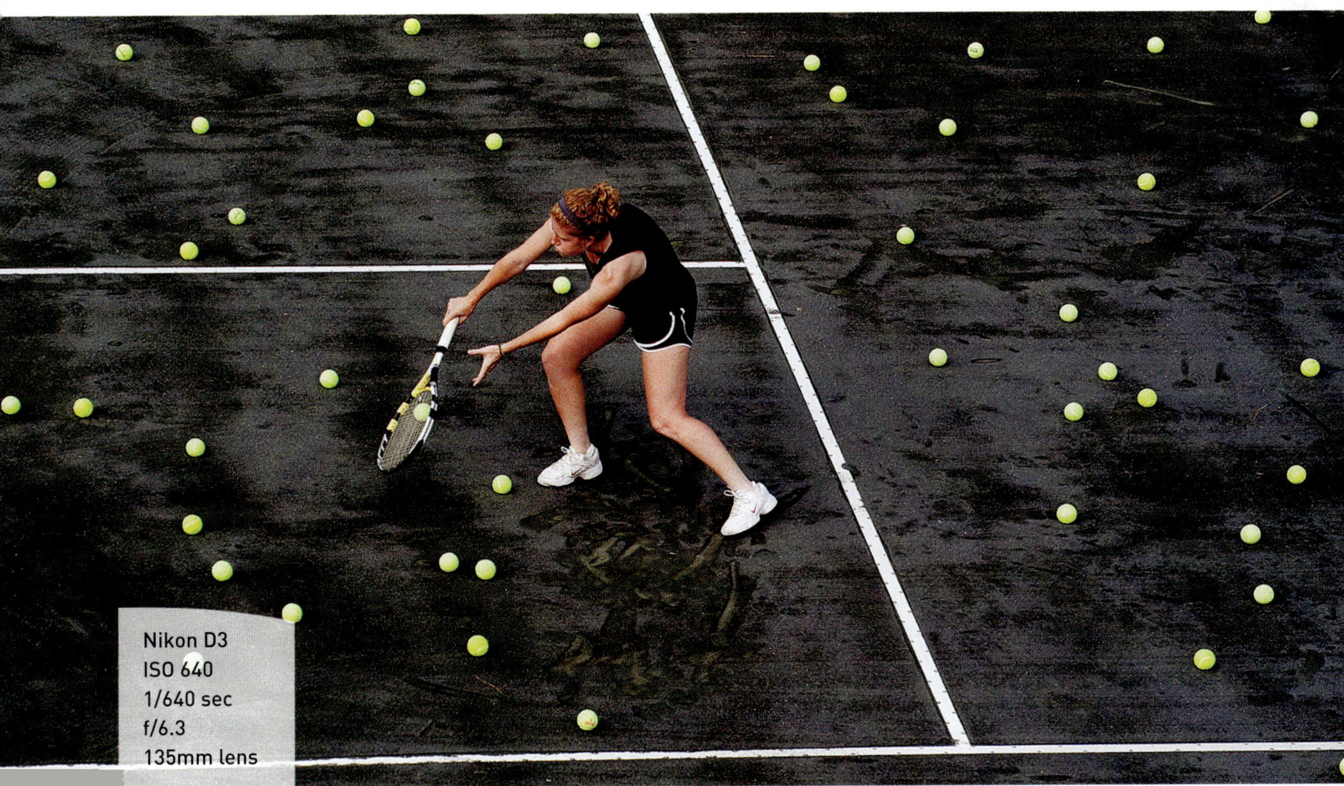

Nikon D3
ISO 640
1/640 sec
f/6.3
135mm lens

FIGURE 3.9
A tennis player practices her volleys.

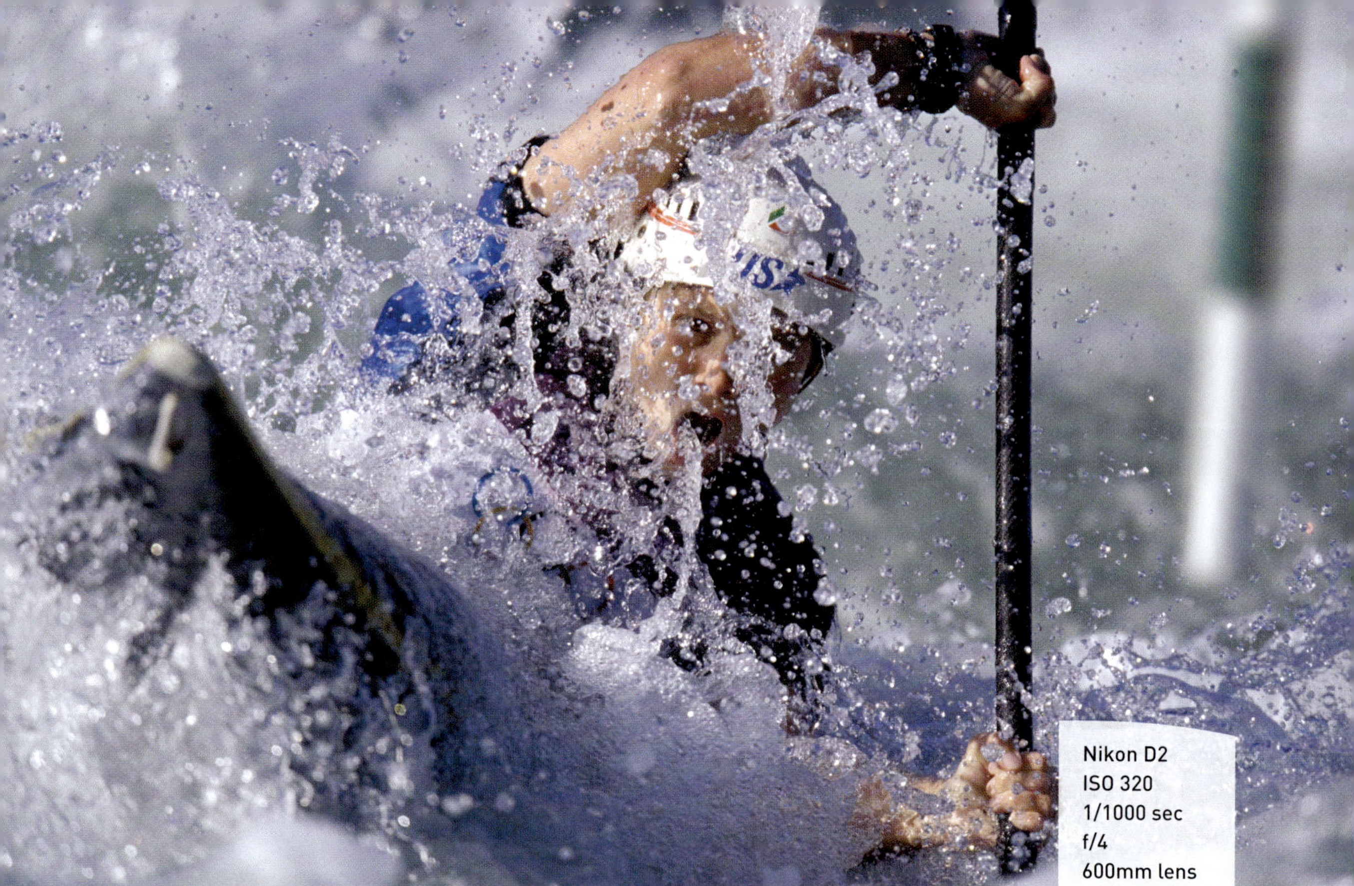

FIGURE 3.10
A kayaker at the Olympic games in Athens, Greece.

One of the main benefits of using longer lenses is cleaner, simpler backgrounds, which make the action you want to emphasize pop. The image in **Figure 3.10** was taken during the Olympic kayaking competition in Greece. I waited for the kayaker to be positioned where I wanted him, used a long lens wide open to isolate him from the background and foreground clutter, calculated the exposure, and used a shutter speed that would freeze the splashing water.

TIP

Use long lenses to eliminate messy, cluttered backgrounds, drawing the viewer's interest directly to the subject you want to showcase.

Chapter 3 Assignments

There is no better way to understand the differences in focal length than to see them for yourself. Just like practicing a perfect curve ball or spiral, you also need to hone your photo skills. The following exercises will get you out in the action and allow you to contrast and compare situations.

Try each exercise using a wide-angle lens and then a long lens. Compare the advantages and disadvantages of each lens.

Shooting Action with a Wide-angle Lens

Find a basketball game in progress, perhaps at a local playground or gym. Sitting a safe distance behind the hoop along the baseline, photograph players driving to the basket using a wide-angle lens. Use shallow depth of field and as fast a shutter speed as possible. Then use medium depth (f/16 or f/22) and a fast shutter speed. A slow shutter speed will probably not yield an image you can use, but to see the difference, try using a slow shutter speed at medium depth of field as well.

When you review the images, pay close attention to distortion, the ability of the shutter to stop the action, and clutter—in the action and in the background.

Shooting Action with a Long Lens

When the players are on the other end of the court, use a long lens to try to isolate action. Do the same thing as they race down the court toward you. For this exercise, use shallow depth of field and a fast shutter speed. Then try using greater depth of field and a fast shutter speed. Compare the results.

Creating Short and Long Lens Portraits

At the conclusion of the game, make portraits with the short and long lenses, respectively. Pay attention to how you are able to place the players in context differently with each lens.

Share your results with the book's Flickr group!
Join the group here: flickr.com/groups/sportsphotographyfromsnapshotstogreatshots.

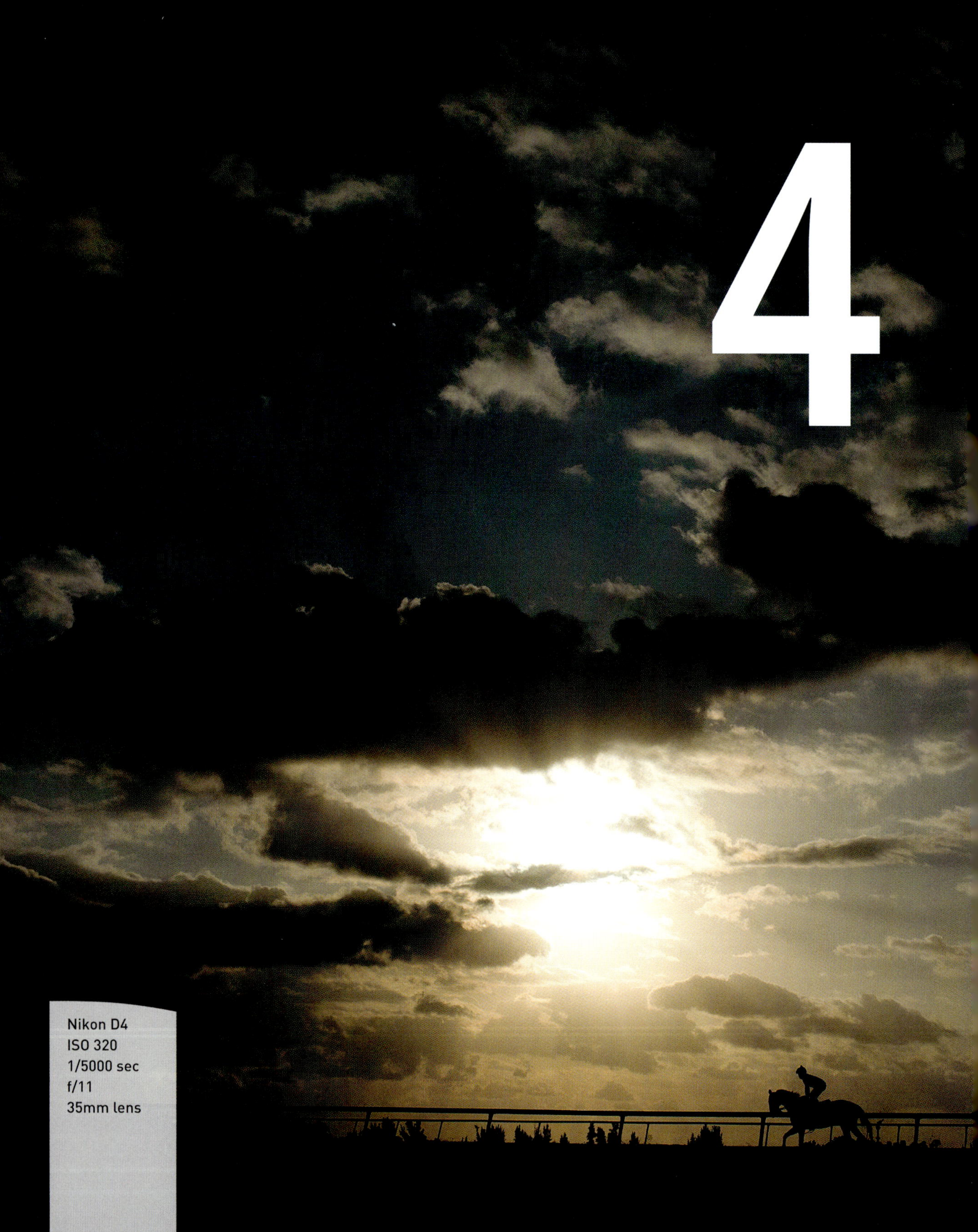

4

Nikon D4
ISO 320
1/5000 sec
f/11
35mm lens

Finding the Light

USING THE RIGHT LIGHT

Light is the single most important component in a photograph. The amount and texture of light can drastically change the content of the picture in good ways and bad. A large quantity of light does not mean you have good quality light.

This chapter walks you through the many types of light available—ambient light, both daylight and artificial—and how to use them to your advantage.

Future winner of the Belmont Stakes, Union Rags breezes in the early morning sun in Florida in May 2012.

PORING OVER THE PICTURE

At the Australian Open, I decided to climb to the roof to shoot Venus Williams from an elevated position to capture a different kind of image. The angle combined with the strong directional light allowed me to make a very graphic action photograph that was powerful, yet simple. From the ground, the light would be entirely different, cutting her body in half, and the shadow would be barely visible.

The shadow is a key element in the composition, suggesting motion and depth. She is running out of the dark into the light with the light coming from above and behind her. I exposed for her and let everything else fall into place.

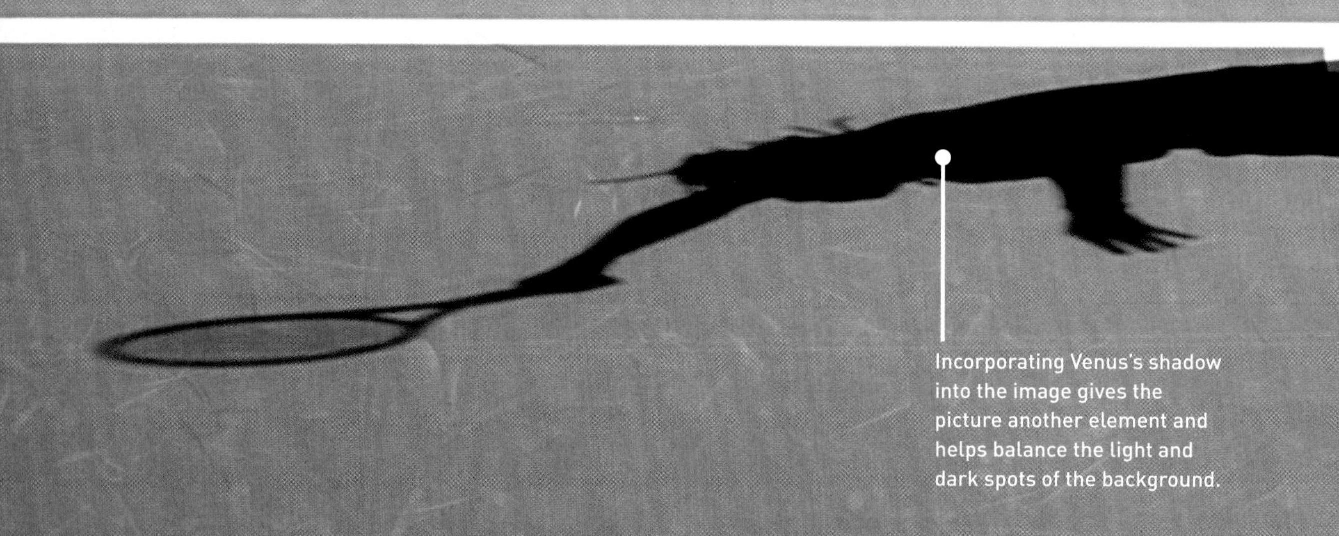

Incorporating Venus's shadow into the image gives the picture another element and helps balance the light and dark spots of the background.

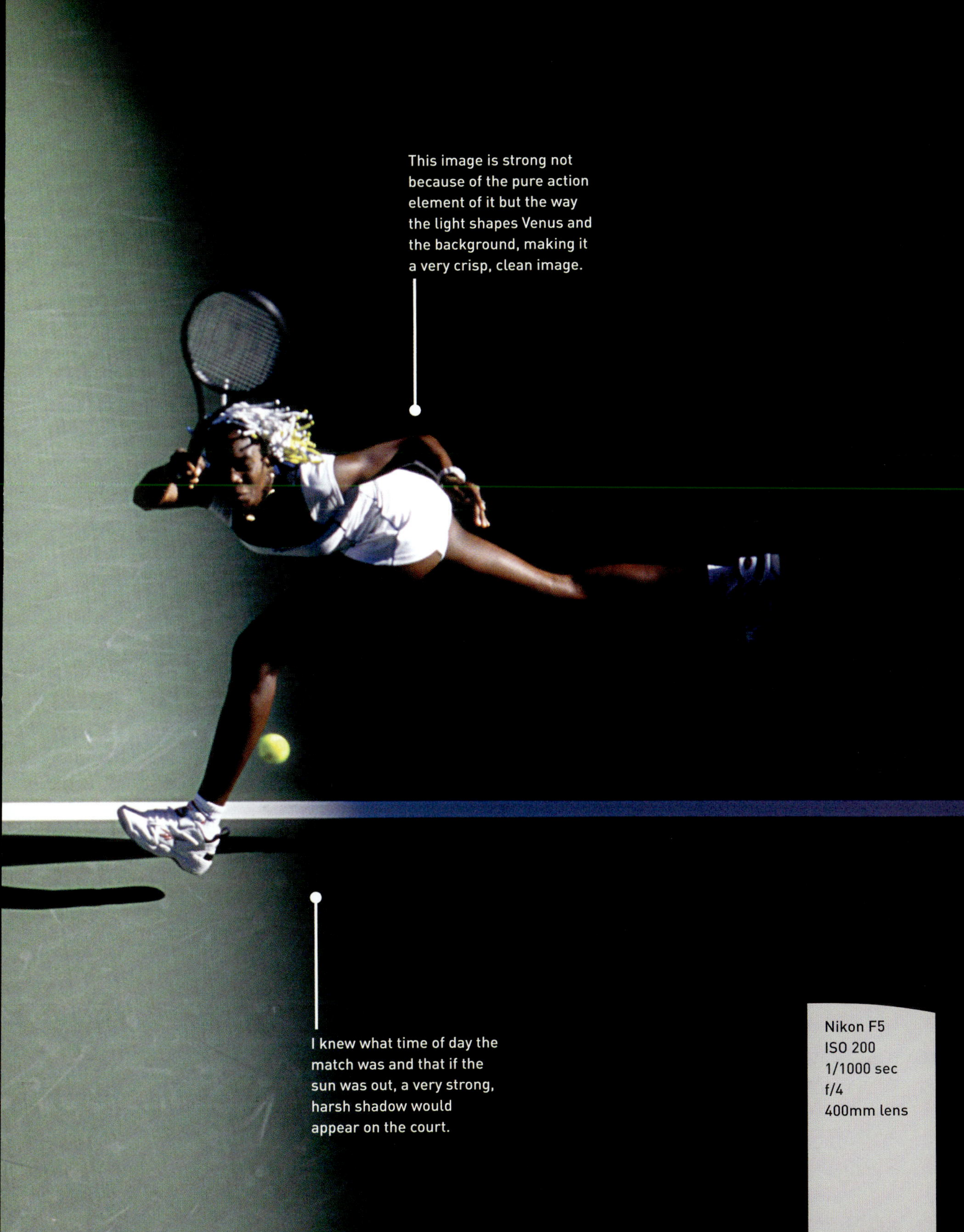
This image is strong not because of the pure action element of it but the way the light shapes Venus and the background, making it a very crisp, clean image.
I knew what time of day the match was and that if the sun was out, a very strong, harsh shadow would appear on the court.
Nikon F5
ISO 200
1/1000 sec
f/4
400mm lens

AMBIENT LIGHT

Ambient light can be sunlight, or it can be artificial light that is provided at a stadium or arena. It is simply light you can't control that but you have to learn to use.

TIP

Quality, not quantity, is the most important consideration when working with light. When evaluating light, be sure to prioritize direction, color, and texture over the amount if you want your images to be beautiful.

DAYLIGHT

You must learn to use the light that is present at game time. It is what it is. The key consideration to remember is that there is no one correct exposure. You have to look at the situation, decide what part of the subject matter is most important to you, and then expose to amplify that part of the image. You can also help yourself massively by paying attention to where the light is coming from and positioning yourself to take advantage of it.

Often, the light is constantly changing. Therefore, you should monitor the exposure settings each time before you shoot and make sure that you have the camera set to do what you want it to do. You should drive the equipment instead of letting the equipment drive you.

THE GOLDEN HOUR

Ideally, the best time to make dramatically lit images is the hour before sunset. This lighting is often referred to as "liquid light." Its qualities are rich, full, golden, and very directional. It's perfect for making front and backlit images, and it normally changes quickly (**Figure 4.1**).

TIP

When you're shooting backlit, be sure to calculate the exposure of the subject's face first. Otherwise, you'll end up with a significantly underexposed image.

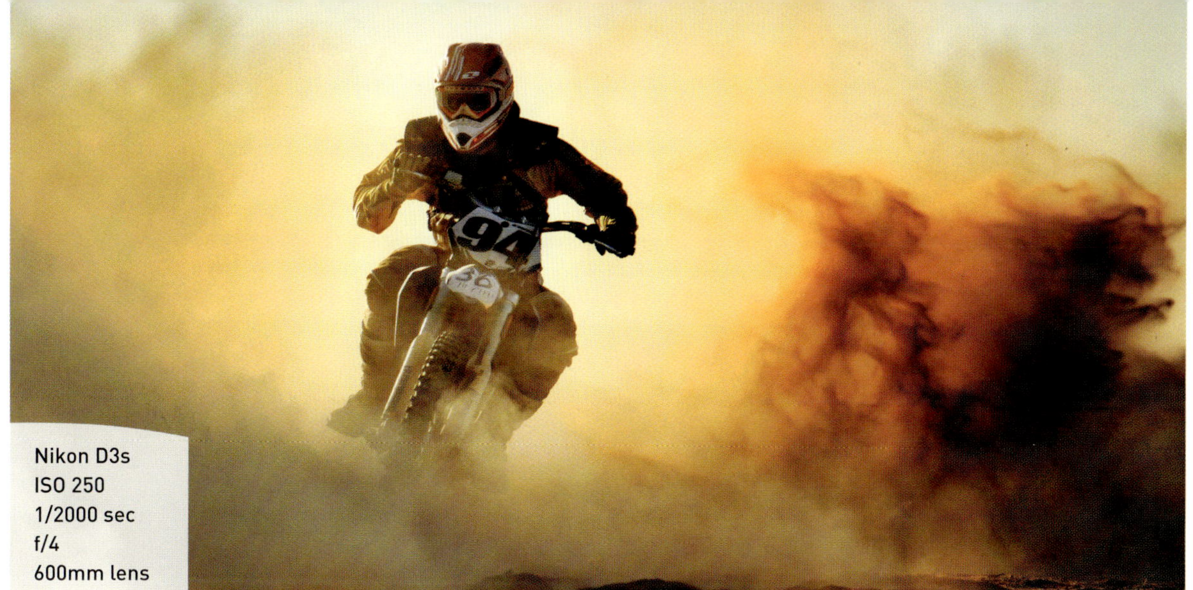

Nikon D3s
ISO 250
1/2000 sec
f/4
600mm lens

FIGURE 4.1
This motorcycle race was shot in the Australian Outback at sunset. I sat facing west so the backlight would amplify the dust being kicked up by the motorcycles.

MIDDAY HARSHNESS

Working from an elevated position or getting very low is often the best way to deal with ugly light. Sports equipment the athletes wear—uniforms, hats, or helmets—is particularly difficult to expose for during the middle of the day (**Figure 4.2**).

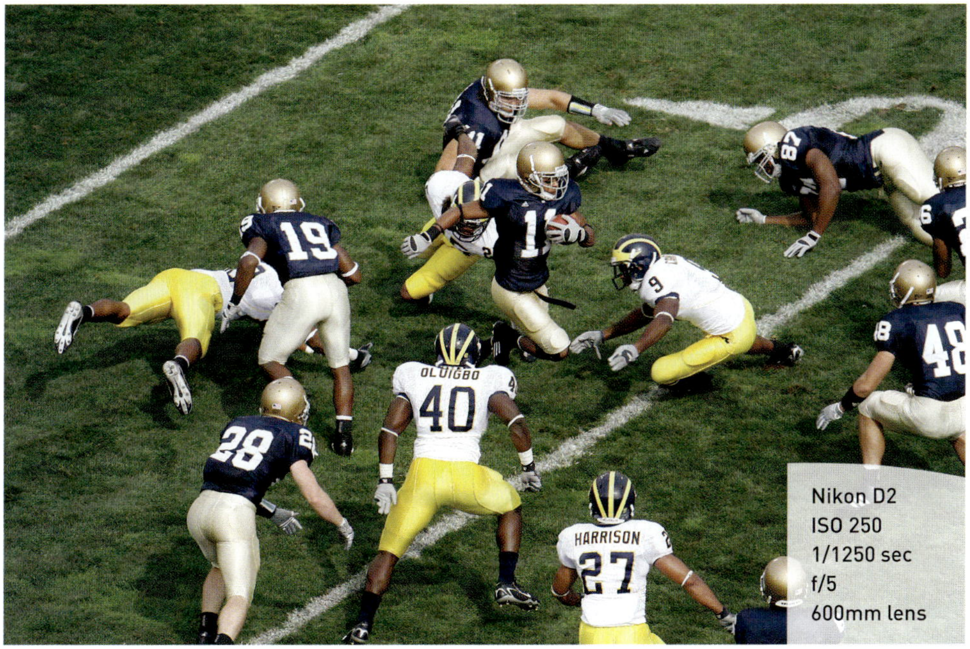

Nikon D2
ISO 250
1/1250 sec
f/5
600mm lens

FIGURE 4.2
Notre Dame vs. Michigan was a noon game in Ann Arbor, Michigan. Football is very difficult to shoot in midday light, so I decided to shoot from an elevated position and take advantage of shadows and patterns.

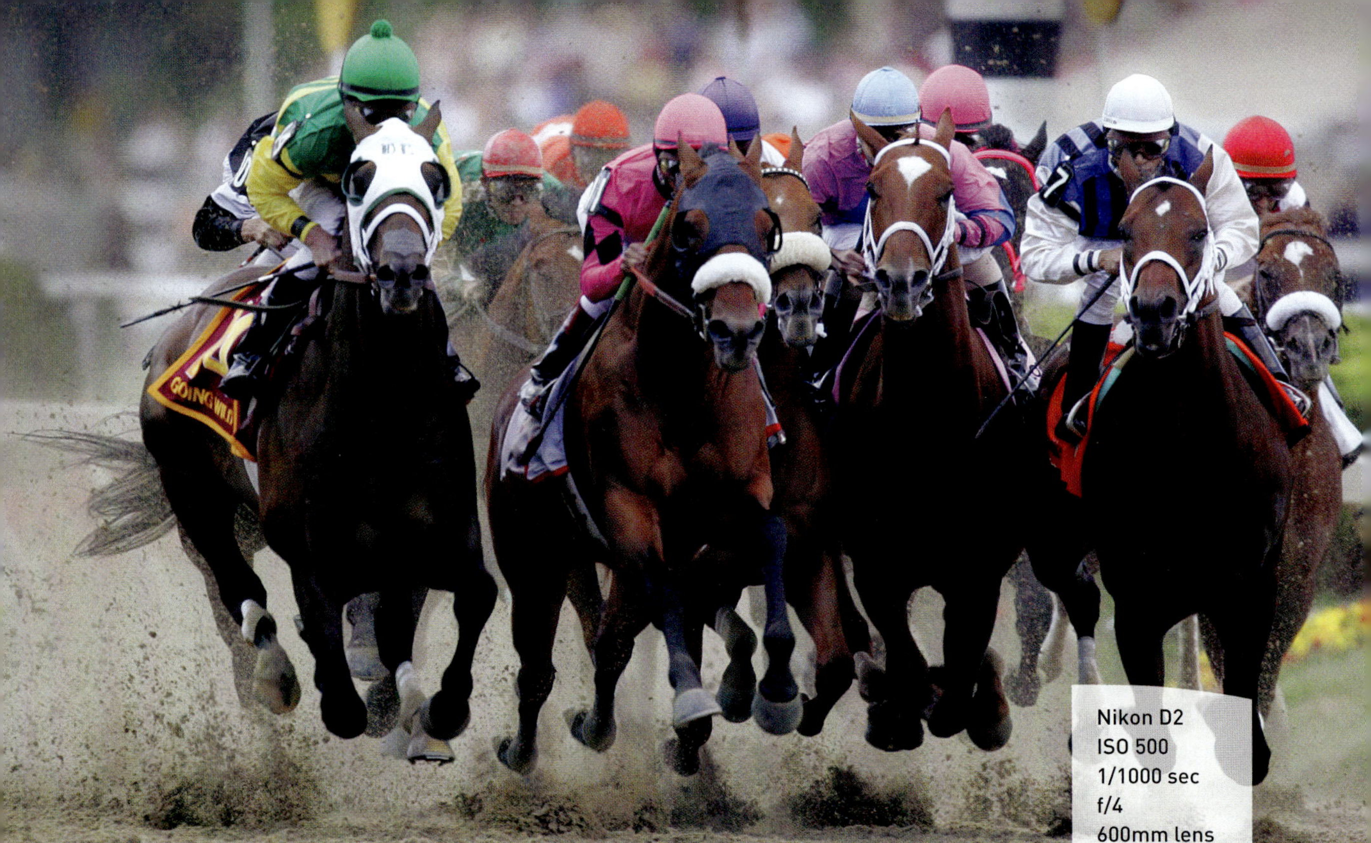

FIGURE 4.3 Overcast weather casts a nice, even light across the whole field, making the image easier to read.

OVERCAST DECEPTION

There is a common misconception that you need bright sunlight to make photographs. The truth is actually quite the opposite. Flat, soft light has the potential to be simply lovely and is by far the easiest light to work with. Overcast light is wonderful when you're shooting action sports. The tonal range is condensed, and you can expose in a way to capture highlights and shadows well. This is especially important for sports where faces are obscured by helmets, and where hats can cause dark shadows on foreheads and eyes.

I love shooting horse racing in overcast weather (**Figure 4.3**). When the sun is shining, it is very difficult to expose for the skin tone of the riders, which can mix with the generally dark coats of the horses and the light tan mud.

> **TIP**
>
> In overcast situations, you have to be sure that the camera's color balance is correct and isn't recording too much blue. The clouds filter the light, and the result is often a blue cast if the camera's color temperature is not set to cloudy.

ARTIFICIAL LIGHT

Artificial light is usually the ugliest light possible and is frequently the light you will have to deal with. When you're working under these lights, you will have limited options. To stop action, you'll need to use the fastest lens you have and work with the highest ISO settings your camera will produce acceptable images with.

Color temperature will be important. Auto normally works fine, but if you can identify the color temperature of the light, set your camera accordingly.

Pay attention to the direction of the lights, and make sure that you note any places on the playing surface where it is brighter or darker. The light might appear to be roughly consistent, but patches of dark and light can make a big exposure difference, as can the angle the light is coming from. For example, the exposure from an elevated position and the exposure at the field of play will be very different. In basketball, the higher you go the brighter it will be, because basketball courts reflect light.

Basketball is one of the many sports that takes place indoors (**Figure 4.4**). The good thing about shooting inside is that the light never changes. The bad news is that you have no control over what that light is.

FIGURE 4.4 Kobe Bryant wipes his face during a game in 2005. To make this image, I got as low to the floor as I could and shot up to reduce the effect of the ambient light by putting him against the black ceiling.

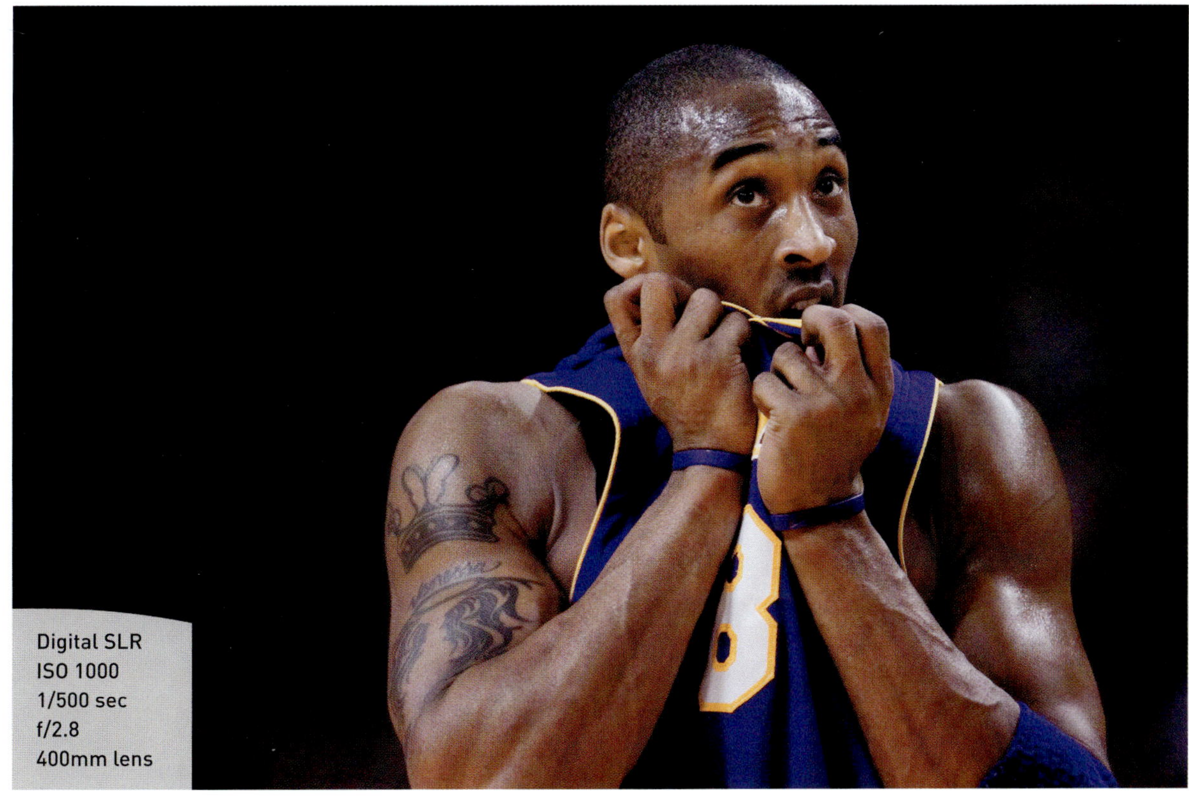

Digital SLR
ISO 1000
1/500 sec
f/2.8
400mm lens

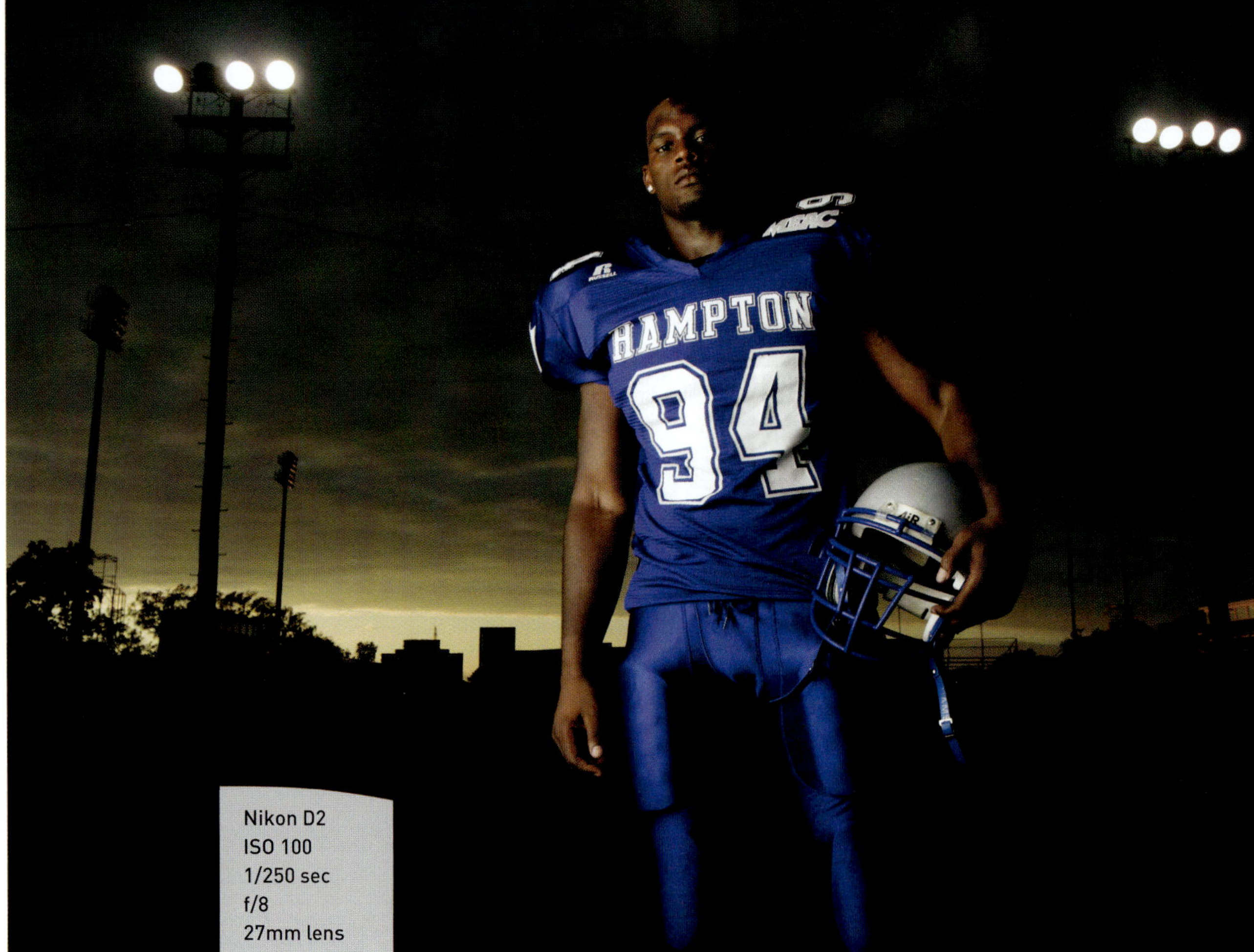

Nikon D2
ISO 100
1/250 sec
f/8
27mm lens

FIGURE 4.5
Placing the sunset in the background gives viewers more information and adds an interesting element to the photo.

STROBES

Strobes provide that necessary flash of light when you need it most. One of my favorite ways to use strobes is in combination with natural—or ambient—light. Without a strobe, the subject in **Figure 4.5** would have been in silhouette. But by introducing light, I was able to draw him out of the background while still including it.

TIP

When you're shooting backlit, you can fashion a longer lens hood from cardboard, attaching it to your normal lens hood with gaffer tape or strong rubber bands. This will help eliminate lens flare.

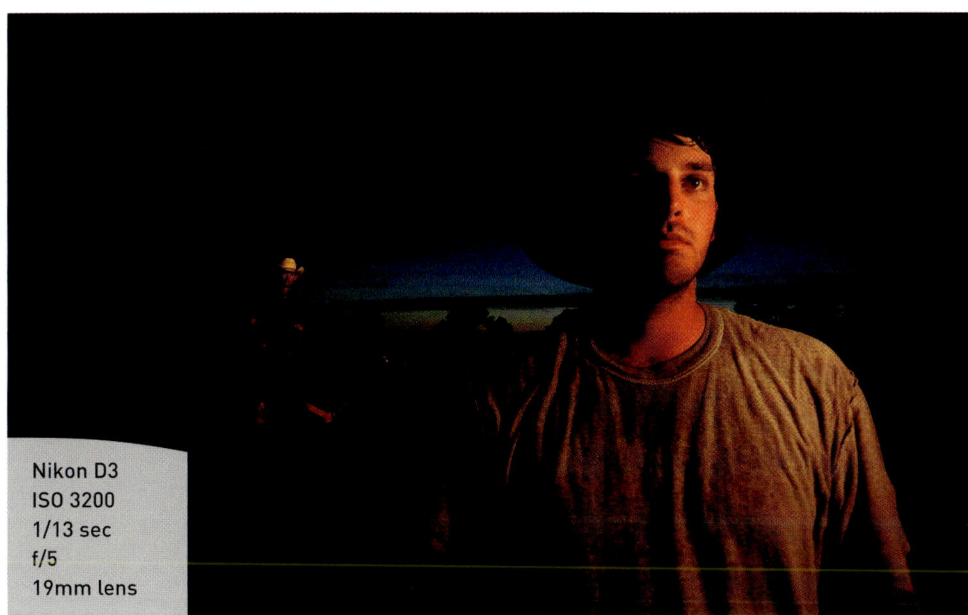

FIGURE 4.6
Using the Nikon SB-900 and a slow shutter speed, I was able to illuminate both cowboys and maintain the dusk light in the background.

ON-CAMERA FLASH

On-camera flashes are small, less powerful lights that normally fit in the hot shoe of your camera. They are lightweight and usually work automatically with the camera, allowing the sensors in the camera and the flash to communicate with each other and provide an acceptable amount of light for normal situations.

These flashes put out a small amount of light, which means they cannot sufficiently illuminate a very large area. They have a short flash duration, which means the burst of light is short and therefore has greater stopping power (**Figure 4.6**).

BIG STROBES

Big strobes provide significantly more light. They are large, require more power, and normally have slow flash durations. They are not automatic, so they do not communicate with cameras directly.

The advantage of using a big strobe is the size of the area that it can light. Use big powerful strobes that you can place a good distance from the playing surface at angles that will not disturb the competition, or use the artificial light that is in place. Small strobes are not powerful enough to get the job done and will likely not be allowed for security reasons.

TIP

If you can't get access to big strobes, you'll have to use the ambient light that already exists. It's your only other option.

STROBES FOR PORTRAITS

The size of a strobe unit doesn't matter nearly as much for portraits. The key to good portraiture is controlling the light by shaping it, modifying it, and making it provide the tone and style you want.

I made the portrait of Danny Woodhead in **Figure 4.7** after he broke the NCAA all-time rushing record at Chadron State University in Chadron, Nebraska. For the portrait, I wanted to show the small environment he was in, even though he was one of the best college football players ever.

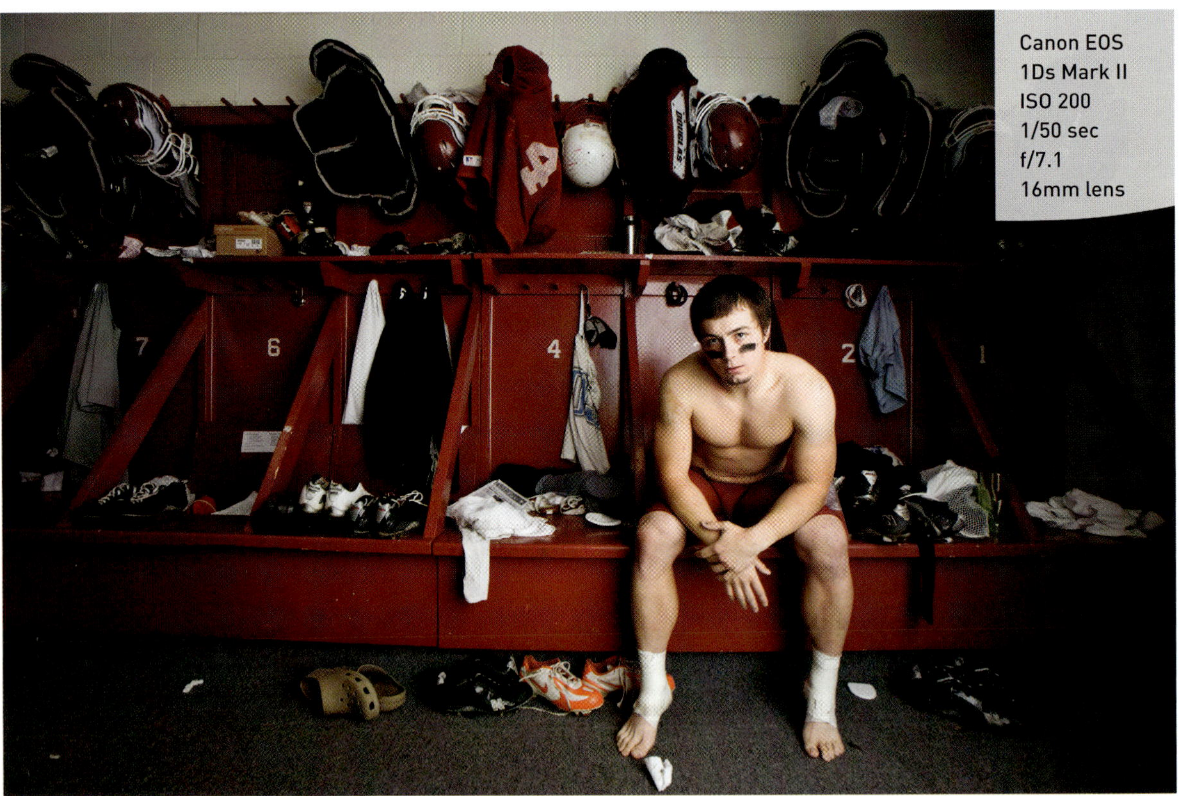

Canon EOS 1Ds Mark II
ISO 200
1/50 sec
f/7.1
16mm lens

FIGURE 4.7
I used a large strobe—an Elinchrome 1200 watt/second strobe with a Chimera octabox—to illuminate the whole locker room around Danny.

Chapter 4 Assignments

Noticing a change in light is a learned skill. Over the course of my career, I have come to think in terms of exposure—quality first and then quantity. When I walk outside and see gorgeous light, I want to find something to photograph; it's always my initial reaction and it's a labor of love. Usually, the light becomes such an important part of the content that I can photograph almost anything and be happy.

When I have to make a photo because the assignment or situation calls for that, I take a different approach. I analyze the situation and decide how to use the light to enhance the content I have to use.

The following exercises will help you think in terms of exposure, making the transition from observer to photographer more seamless. Remember that there is no right or wrong exposure, just the exposure you want to make.

Shooting at Different Times of Day

Find an object—a silver garbage can or mailbox, for example. Put it in a location where it won't be disturbed or be in anyone's way. Photograph it using the same lens from the same angle at noon, at 3:00 p.m., and 30 minutes before sunset. Compare the shadows, the tones, and the textures created by the light. Notice how the light changes the mood of the photograph.

Shooting at Different Angles

Go to a high school football or baseball field. Shoot a person standing 15 yards from the sideline. Then climb to the top of the stands and shoot the same person from as high an angle as you can. Compare the shadows, the tones, and the textures created by the light. Decide how you can use the angle to your benefit to take advantage of different lighting conditions.

Changing Your Perspective

Find a football game. Shoot half of the game from the end zones and half of the game from the sidelines. Notice how changing your position on the field gives you not only an altered perspective, but also significantly different opportunities to make photographs. Take note of what you capture where and when.

Share your results with the book's Flickr group!
Join the group here: flickr.com/groups/sportsphotographyfromsnapshotstogreatshots.

5

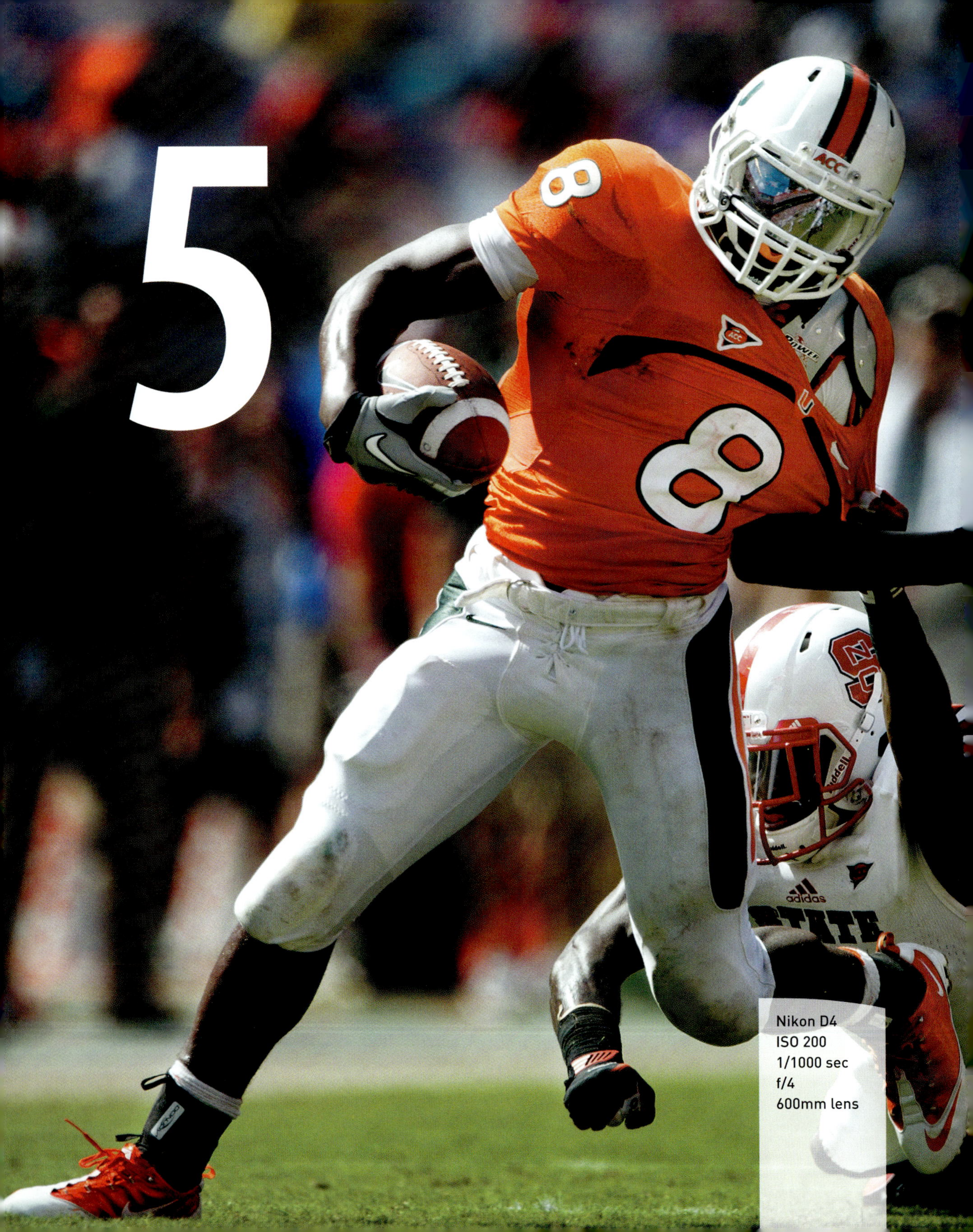

Nikon D4
ISO 200
1/1000 sec
f/4
600mm lens

Shooting Football

BIG HITS, BIG REACTIONS

Football is the most popular American sport and the one I get asked about shooting most often. Of the sports I'll explain in this book, football is the easiest to cover because it is predictable and there's lots of action. It may also be the most difficult to cover because the game happens on a fairly large surface, the athletes' faces are often obscured, you're usually subject to the elements, and the ball takes funny bounces.

University of Miami running back Duke Johnson is dragged down by a North Carolina State defender.

PORING OVER THE PICTURE

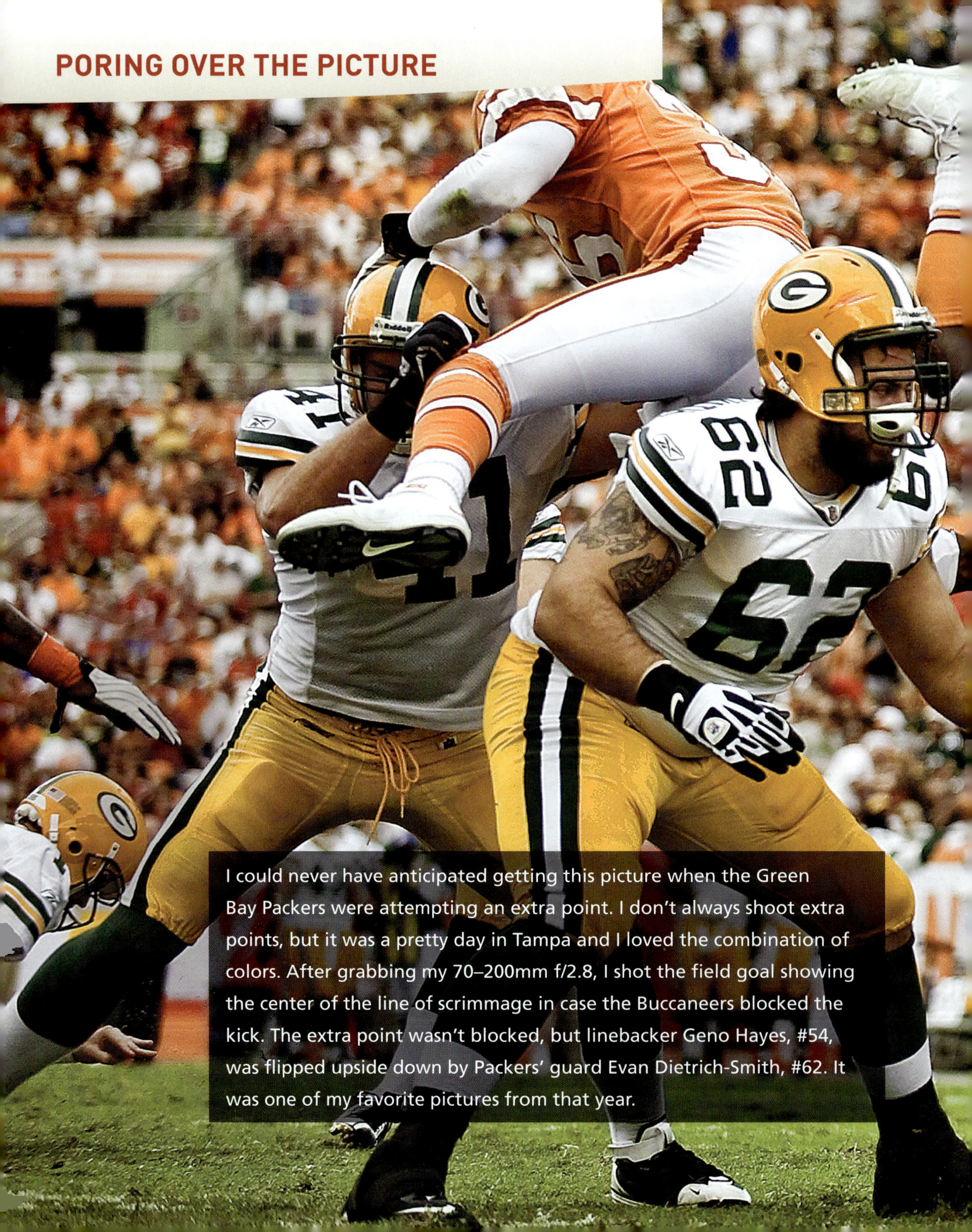

I could never have anticipated getting this picture when the Green Bay Packers were attempting an extra point. I don't always shoot extra points, but it was a pretty day in Tampa and I loved the combination of colors. After grabbing my 70–200mm f/2.8, I shot the field goal showing the center of the line of scrimmage in case the Buccaneers blocked the kick. The extra point wasn't blocked, but linebacker Geno Hayes, #54, was flipped upside down by Packers' guard Evan Dietrich-Smith, #62. It was one of my favorite pictures from that year.

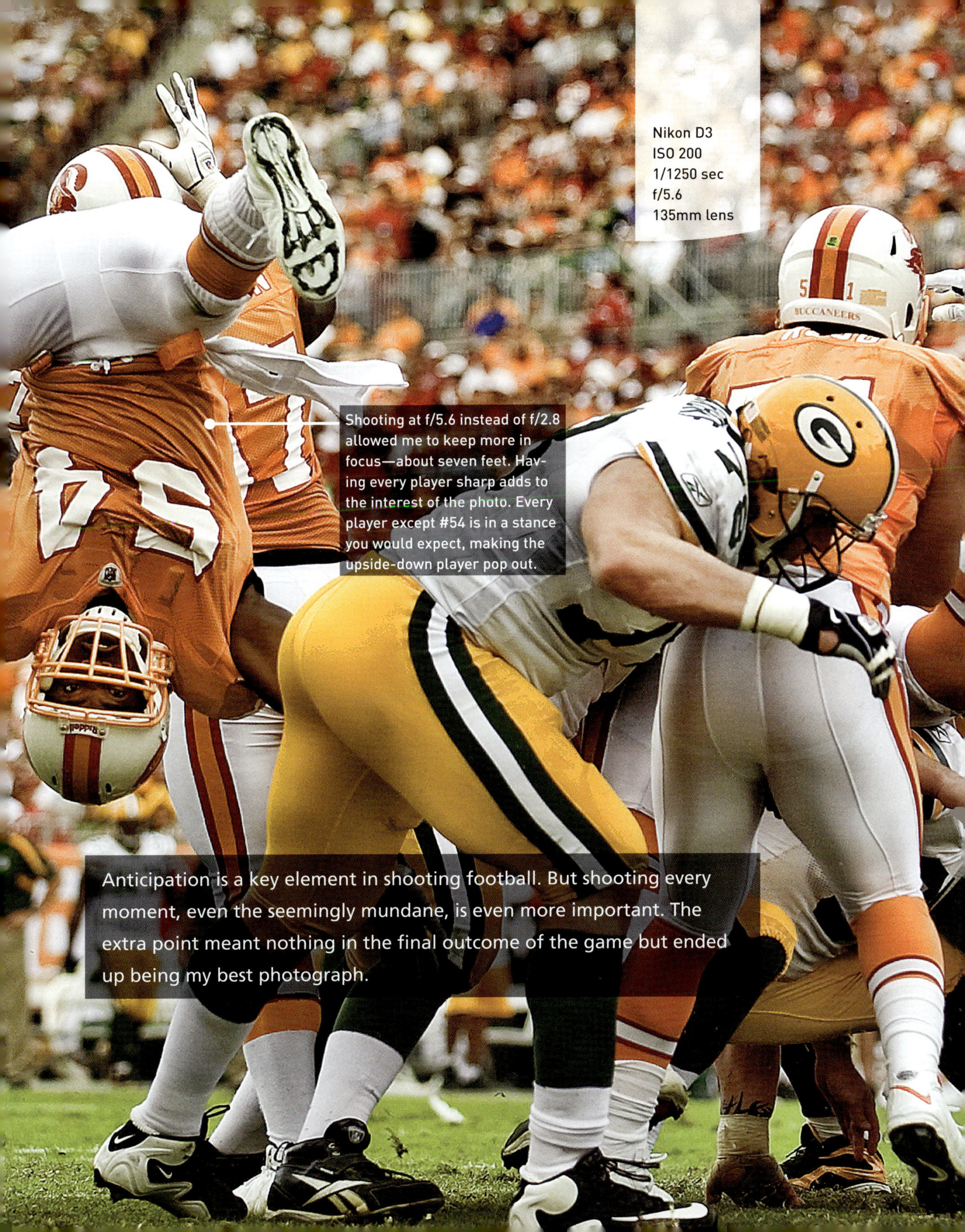

Nikon D3
ISO 200
1/1250 sec
f/5.6
135mm lens

Shooting at f/5.6 instead of f/2.8 allowed me to keep more in focus—about seven feet. Having every player sharp adds to the interest of the photo. Every player except #54 is in a stance you would expect, making the upside-down player pop out.

Anticipation is a key element in shooting football. But shooting every moment, even the seemingly mundane, is even more important. The extra point meant nothing in the final outcome of the game but ended up being my best photograph.

FOOTBALL: HOW TO GET THE BEST SHOTS

There are many breaks in the action during football games. This gives you a chance to anticipate what will happen and prepare for it.

WHERE TO POSITION YOURSELF

Pro and college football is played in large stadiums, and the field of play area is relatively large. Each stadium has its own credentialing rules, but there are four general areas to shoot from: end zones, sidelines, stands, and catwalks. Catwalks are only found in indoor stadiums and are normally very difficult to access.

High school games are usually played in smaller stadiums and are normally easy to gain access to.

Credentialing and space issues aside, the process of covering the games is basically the same. With each step up the food chain, the athletes get faster and stronger, access gets tougher, and the harder it gets to make emotional images.

I've covered more than 25 Super Bowls, at least that many big bowl games, and thousands of regular season NFL and NCAA games. But my favorite memories are from small-town high school games (**Figure 5.1**).

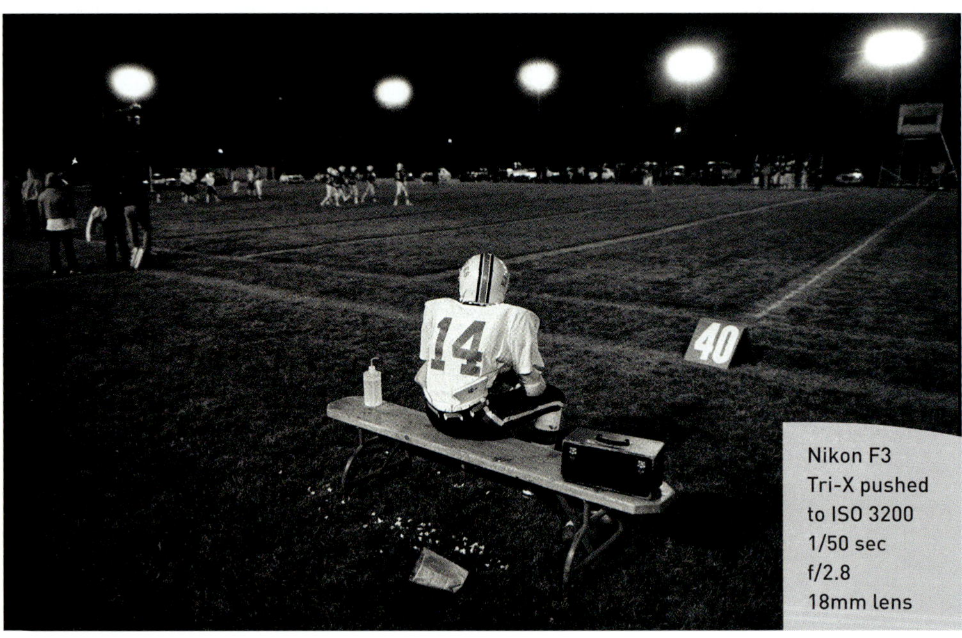

Nikon F3
Tri-X pushed to ISO 3200
1/50 sec
f/2.8
18mm lens

FIGURE 5.1 This photo was taken at a high school football game in Lyman, Nebraska. This was taken before the digital age took over photography, and was shot on Kodak Tri-X film, pushed three stops. Quiet moments like these are some of my favorite sports photos.

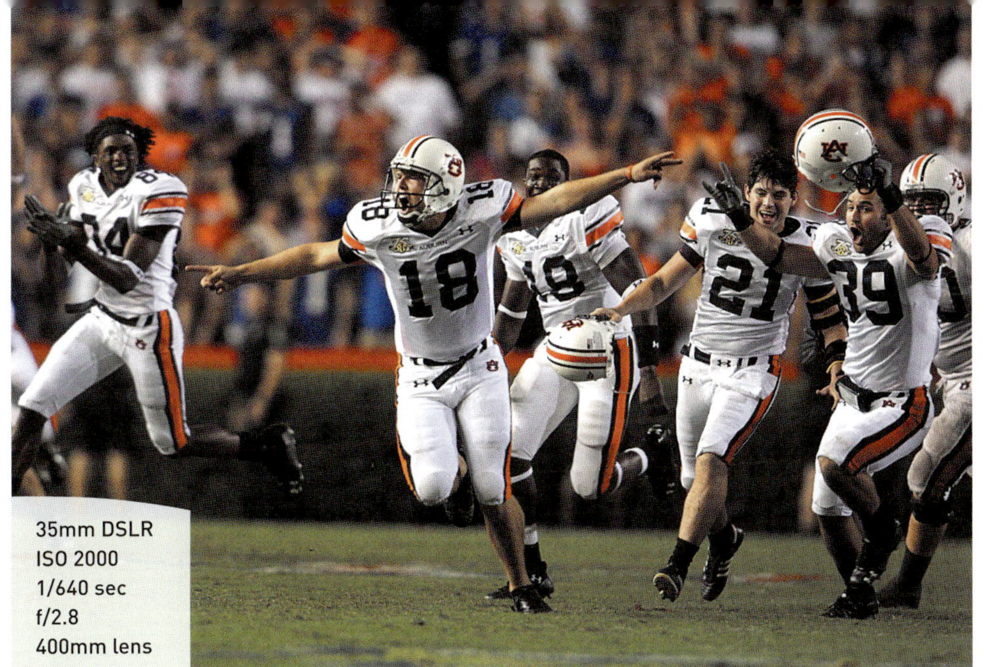

FIGURE 5.2
In this picture, Auburn kicked a field goal to beat the Florida Gators at Florida Field in the last second of the game.

SHOOTING FROM THE END ZONES

If I'm covering a game from field level, I generally shoot from the end zones. This gives me a head-on view of the action. If a running back or receiver breaks free, I'm in the best position to capture the moment. At the other end zone, if I get behind an offense, I am in prime position to capture a sack or fumble.

If a team is attempting a game-winning kick, I like to go to the opposite end zone to show the whole scene and capture the reaction of the players (**Figure 5.2** and **Figure 5.3**). Whether the field goal is made, blocked, or missed, there is always a big reaction from the fans and players that a tight shot of just the kicker won't show. I'll use the longest lens I have when play is at the end of the field opposite me and use progressively shorter lenses as the action gets closer to me. I always have a camera with a normal (35mm to 50mm) lens hanging around my neck. It is typically referred to as a "chest camera."

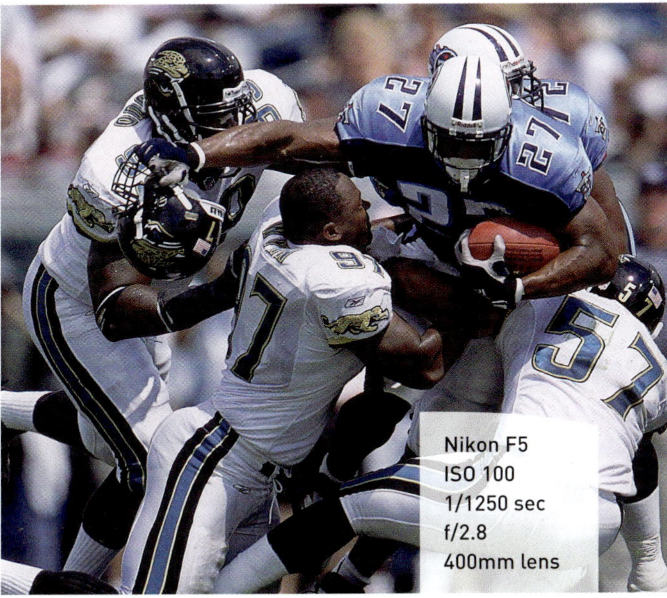

FIGURE 5.3
The end zone is a great location to capture images like these. I love how it appears that the running back is coming directly toward me. The fact that he removed a Jaguar helmet in the process just adds to the interest of the photo.

TIP

Prefocus the chest camera on a spot directly in front of you and use gaffer tape to secure the focus position. Be sure to set the camera on manual focus when you do this.

TIP

The first frame you take with the chest camera will usually be the best one, so be sure you have the f-stop set so that you have at least five feet of depth of field. A scale on your lens should provide you with that information.

SHOOTING FROM THE SIDELINES

Shooting on the sidelines offers a slightly different perspective from shooting in an end zone. Instead of capturing action that is moving away from you (north and south or end zone to end zone, as football players like to say), the sidelines give you side-to-side action. If there is a screen pass to a sideline, a sack just behind the line of scrimmage, or a sweep, the sideline is a prime place to be (**Figure 5.4**).

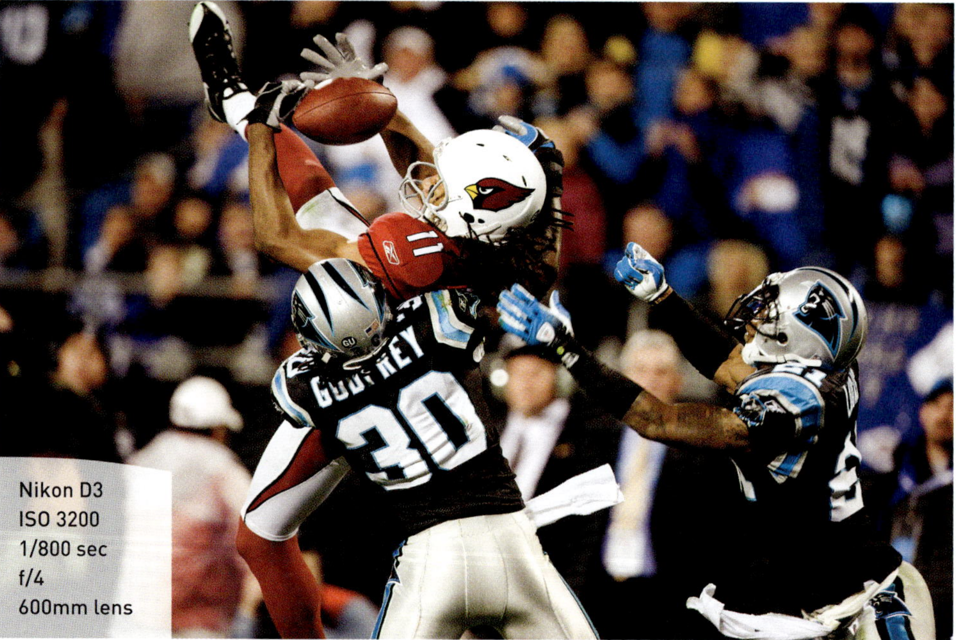

Nikon D3
ISO 3200
1/800 sec
f/4
600mm lens

FIGURE 5.4
Sidelines are a great place to capture receivers in midair, like this Larry Fitzgerald catch.

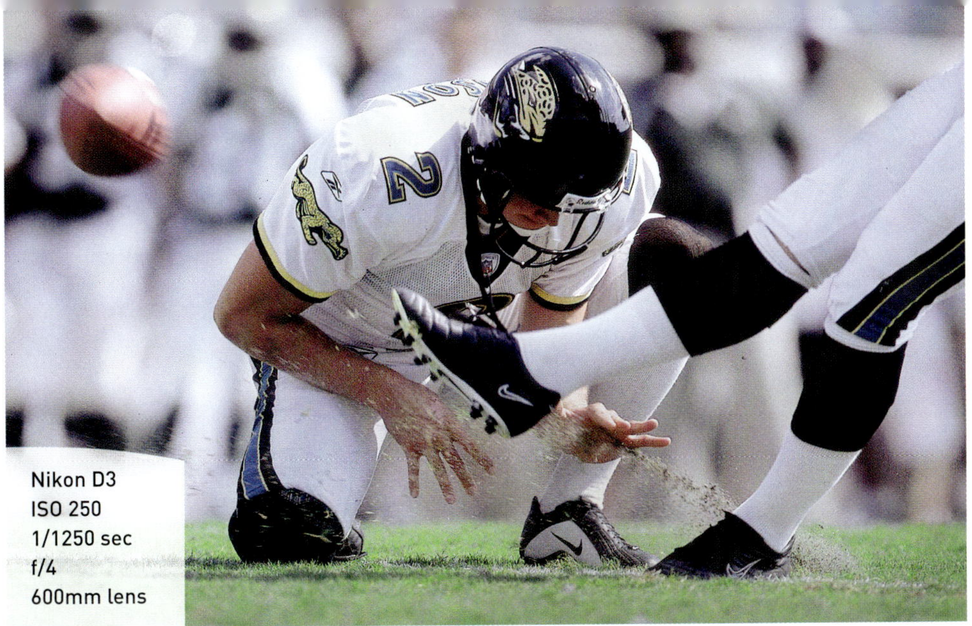

FIGURE 5.5
This shot is not a high-action photo in the traditional sense. However, it does show a lot of motion.

By positioning myself on the sidelines directly next to the spot of the kick, I was able to capture an aspect of the game that is frequently overlooked (**Figure 5.5**).

Sidelines offer great views of quarterbacks throwing and getting hit (**Figure 5.6**).

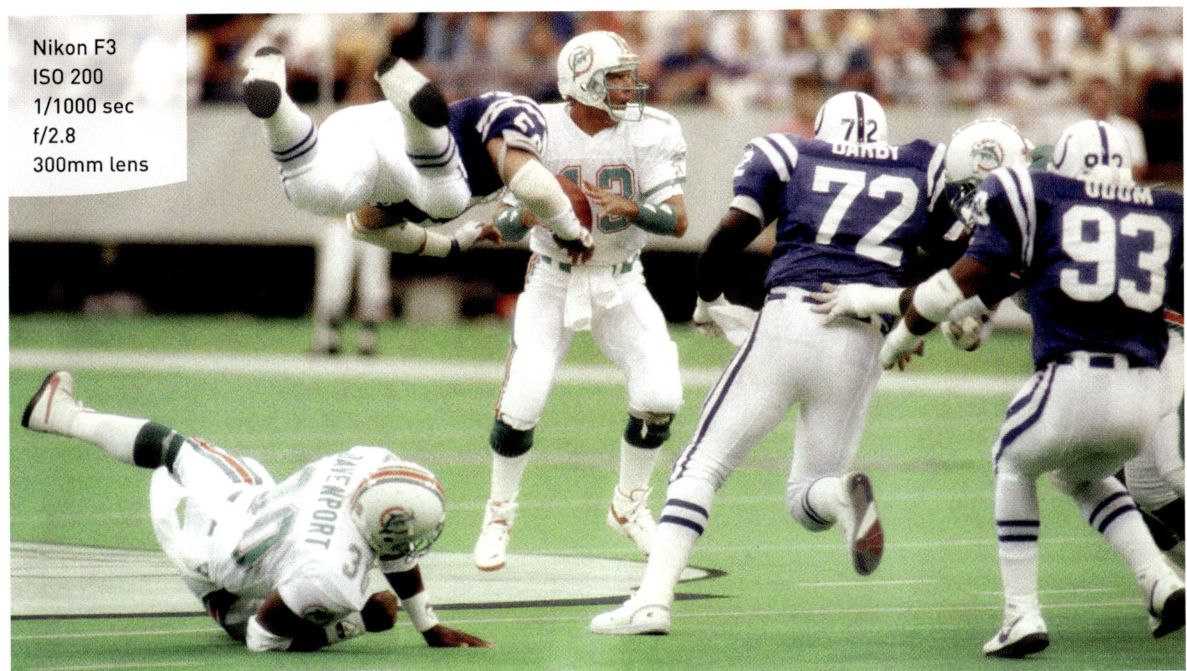

FIGURE 5.6
In this photo, Dan Marino is about to get crunched by Barry Krause of the Indianapolis Colts. If I was shooting from the end zone, I would be blocked from taking this shot by the linemen.

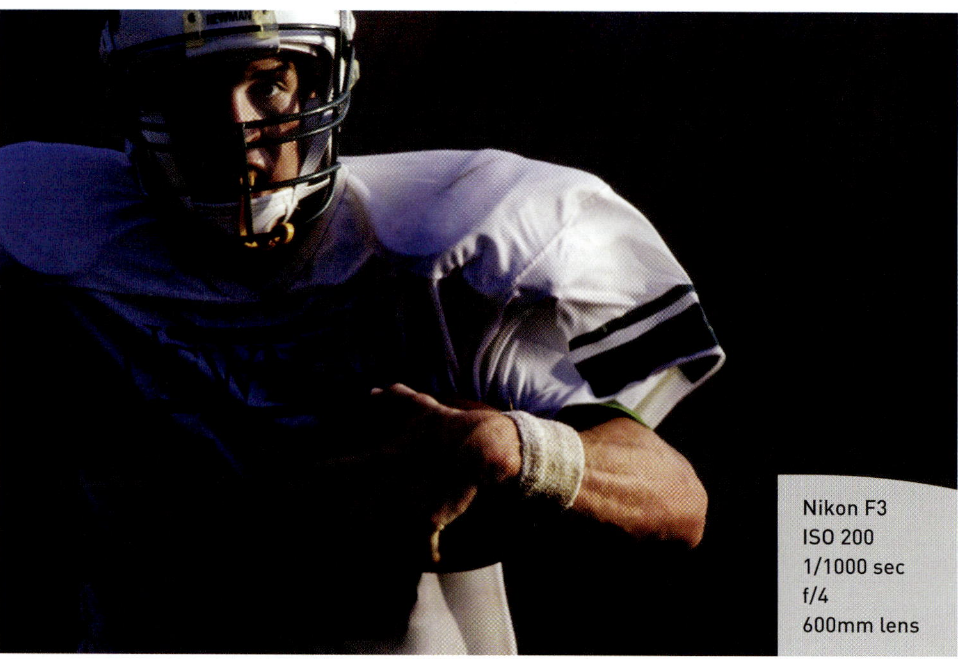

FIGURE 5.7
Peyton Manning in high school.

Nikon F3
ISO 200
1/1000 sec
f/4
600mm lens

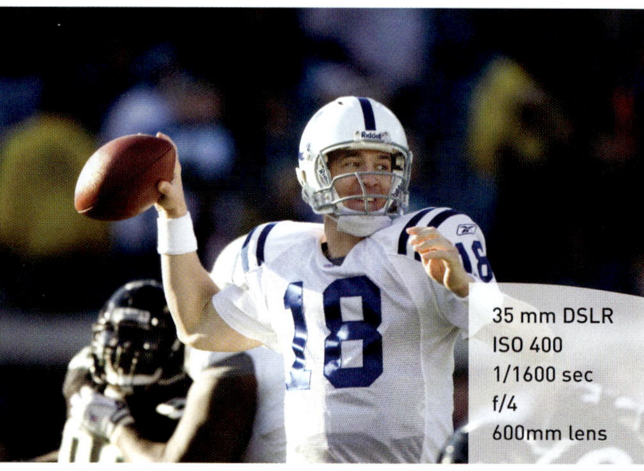

FIGURE 5.8
Peyton Manning and the Colts play against the Jacksonville Jaguars.

35 mm DSLR
ISO 400
1/1600 sec
f/4
600mm lens

I've been photographing Peyton Manning since he was a high school athlete (**Figure 5.7**). Peyton is credited with having the fastest and most analytical mind among NFL players. My favorite images of Peyton all involve his intensity (**Figure 5.8**). The only thing you can be sure of is when he is on the field, it's going to be exciting.

I generally pick my field level spot based on the specific assignment I am covering. If I'm at a game to shoot a running back, for example, I'll position myself in the end zone. If I'm covering an outside linebacker or offensive tackle, I'll be on the sidelines. If you can't see the player because he is obscured by other players, you can't do your job, so you have to have a clean line of sight.

TIP

When the play starts, don't be concerned if an official is obscuring your view. He will move as the action does.

SHOOTING FROM THE GRANDSTANDS OR BLEACHERS

Shooting from the stands gives you an elevated look at the field and allows you to make beautiful graphic photos. From the stands, the most important details are shape and light. I love to go into the stands to make overalls of the stadiums with wide-angles lenses—as discussed in Chapter 3.

The photo in **Figure 5.9** was made as the Southern Methodist University (SMU) Mustangs took the field for their homecoming game in 2001. SMU was a football powerhouse until the school was given the "death penalty" in 1987 for paying players. The program has never fully recovered, and the dark, foreboding skies and empty grandstands in the figure help tell that story.

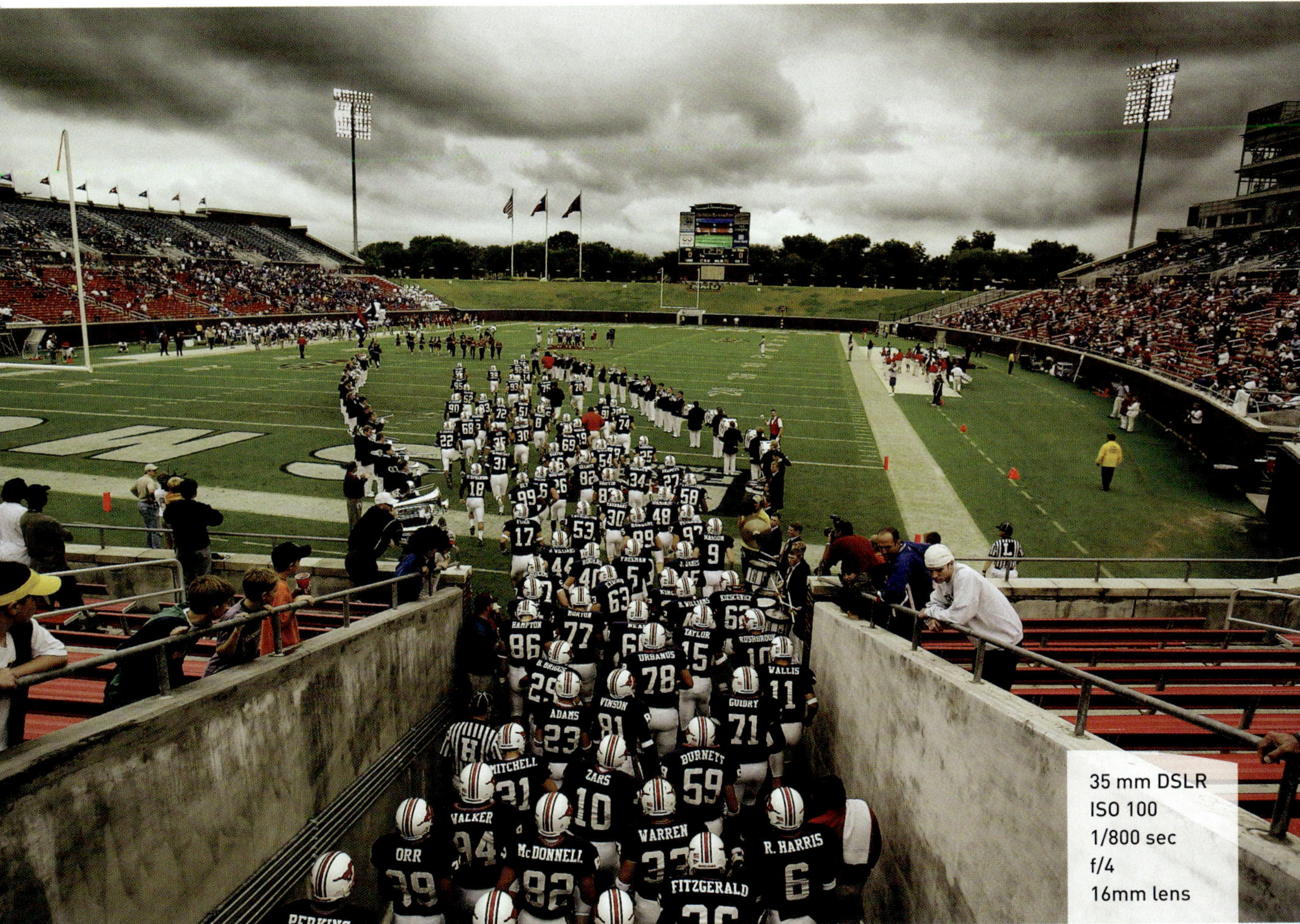

35 mm DSLR
ISO 100
1/800 sec
f/4
16mm lens

FIGURE 5.9
The use of a high angle and a wide-angle lens made this picture possible.

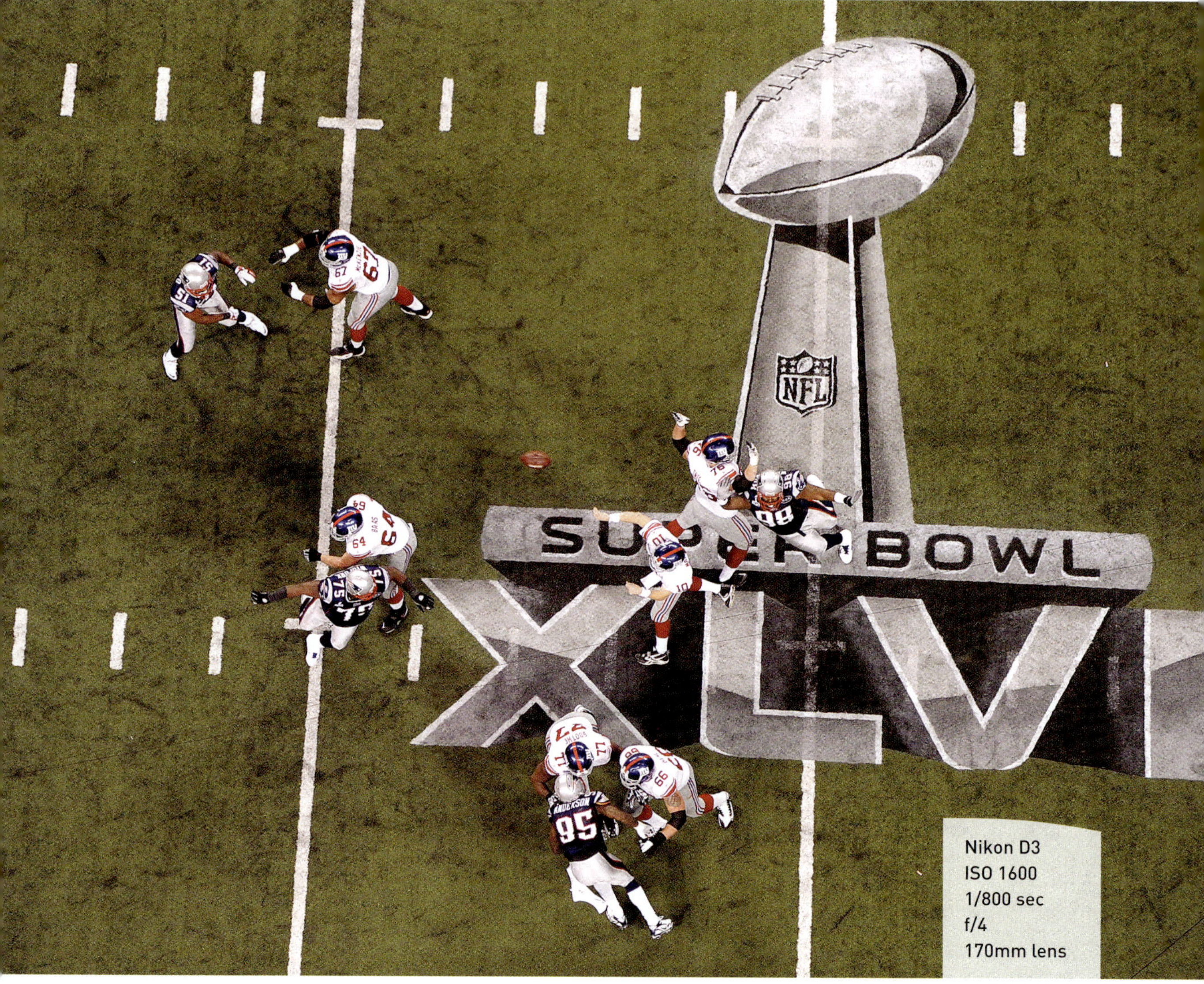

FIGURE 5.10
Because of the dome, I was able to place remote cameras in the catwalks and make a nice, graphic picture of Eli Manning throwing a pass.

SHOOTING FROM CATWALKS

Obviously, not all football stadiums have catwalks. Catwalks are only found in domes. For Super Bowl XLVI, which was played at Lucas Oil Stadium in Indianapolis, I put remote cameras in the catwalks over the 50-yard line and the Super Bowl logo so that I could fire them when the teams passed over those sections of the field (**Figure 5.10**).

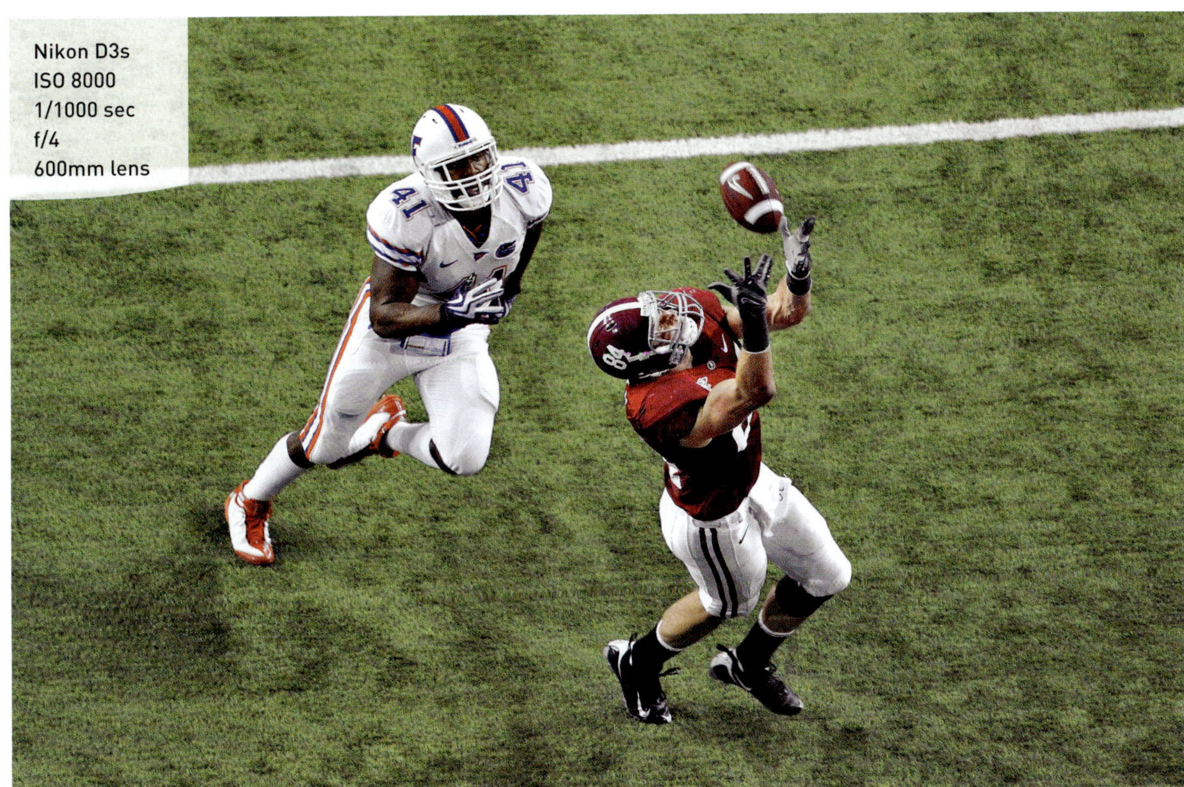

FIGURE 5.11
Being almost directly overhead, I was able to capture the players' faces as the play happened. *Sports Illustrated* used this photo as the cover the week after the game.

In **Figure 5.11**, Alabama tight end Colin Peek catches a touchdown pass against the Florida Gators in the 2010 SEC Championship Game in the Georgia Dome. The Georgia Dome has three levels of catwalks. For this picture, I positioned myself on the first level because Alabama was driving and I knew that Alabama quarterback Greg McElroy would soon try a down field pass.

SETTINGS AND LIGHTING

Camera settings for football vary greatly depending on when and where the game is played. Carefully consider how much you want to be in focus in each frame. After you calculate the depth of field, make sure you have a fast enough shutter speed, and then use the ISO settings on your camera to make it work.

A one o'clock game in Miami will have drastically different settings from an eight o'clock game in Green Bay. As discussed in Chapter 4, keep in mind that light is extremely important and managing it has to be one of your principal concerns.

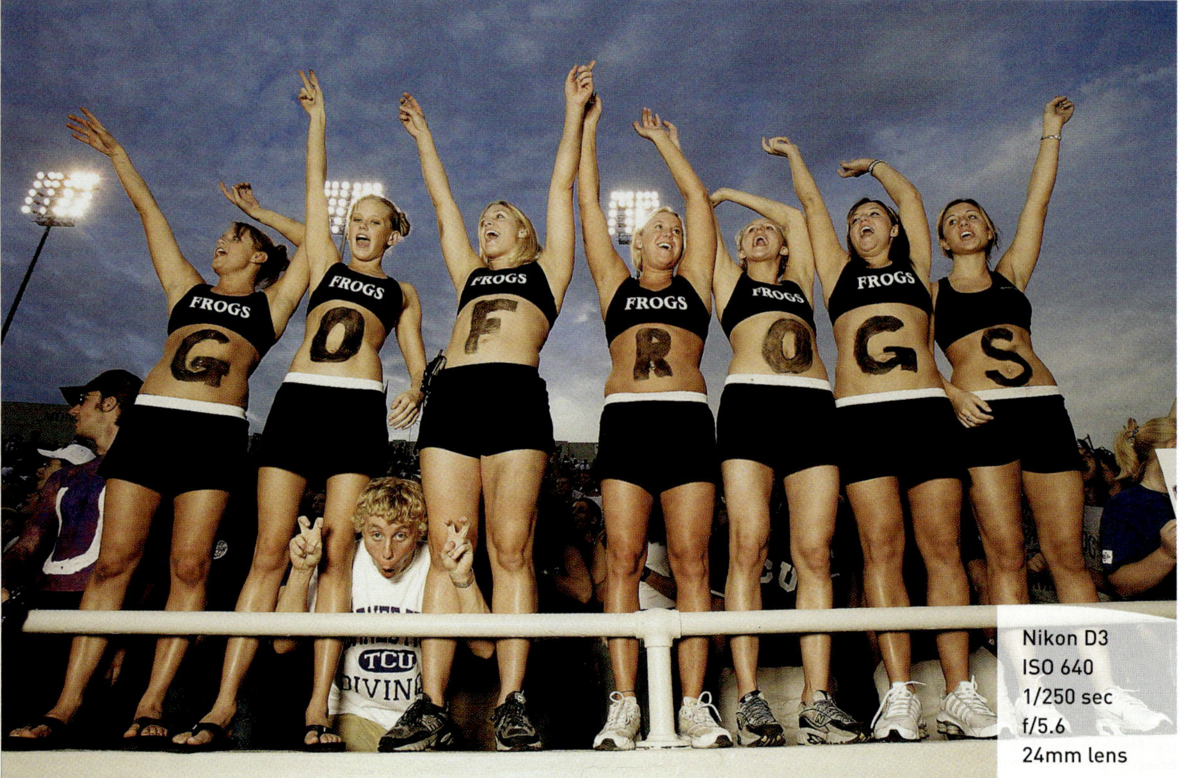

Nikon D3
ISO 640
1/250 sec
f/5.6
24mm lens

FIGURE 5.12
Big hits and touchdowns aren't the only great pictures you can make at a football game. Always be on the lookout for wacky fans, like this image taken at TCU.

I never shoot football with a shutter speed less than 1/1000 of a second if I can possibly help it. Freezing action is extremely important in football, and it is a rare occasion that I would employ a pan or blur. Pans and blurs work best in sports where you can predict the action, such as track and field or horse racing. You can predict those sports because they run, for the most part, in straight lines and do not vary their paths.

Football isn't all about peak action, either. There are opportunities to make truly stunning photos of candid portraits of the participants when the light is right. Don't forget the fans either (**Figure 5.12**)!

TIP

When the action on the field stops, turn your attention to the bench and look for emotion from the participants there.

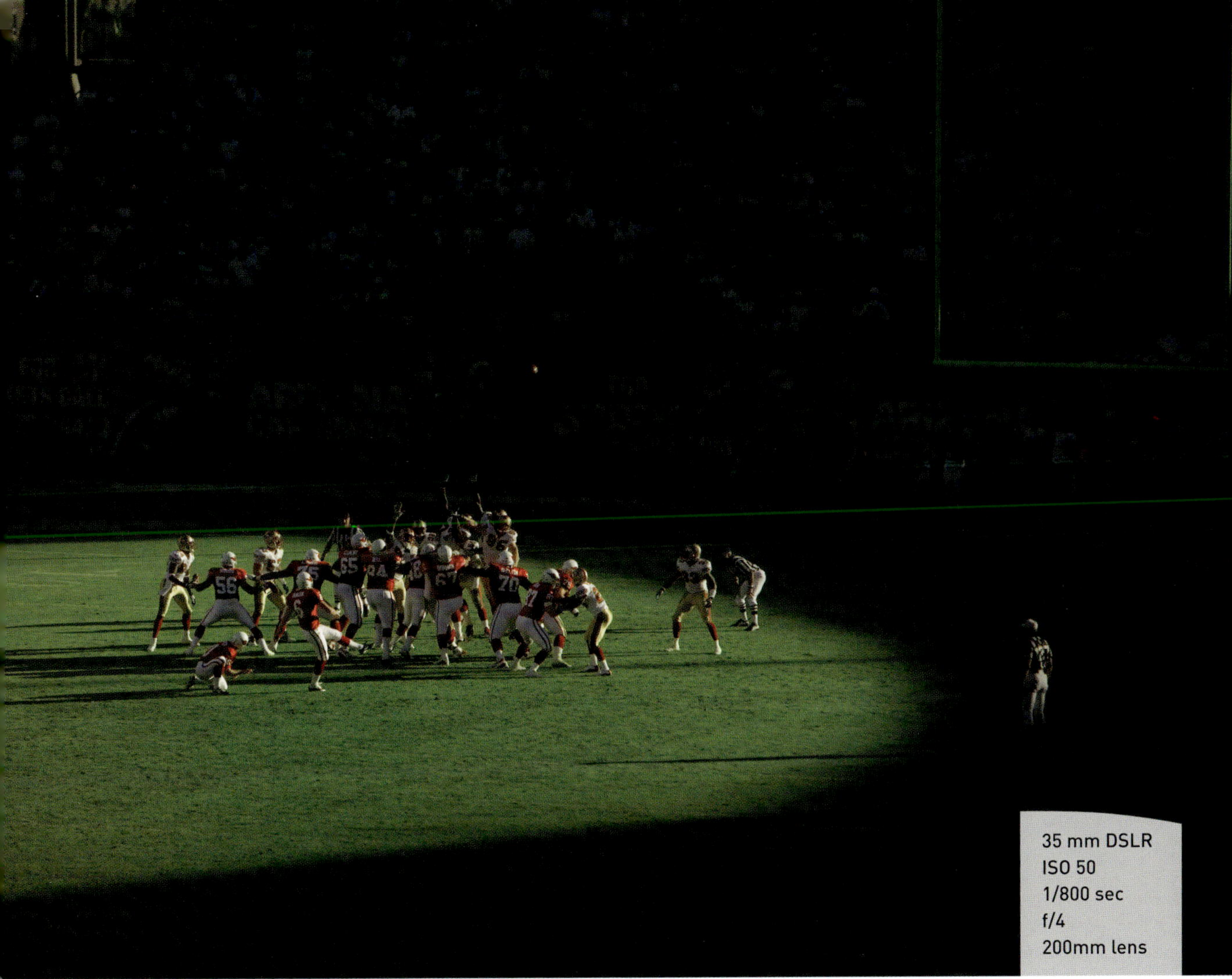

FIGURE 5.13

Because I had my camera set to manual, I was able to stop down, underexpose, and make a different and beautiful image.

Figure 5.13 shows the Cardinals kicking a field goal to beat the 49ers in overtime. The moment was important, but the way the light shaped the field and captured the action within it gave it a powerful dynamic tension. I exposed for the bright sunlight, which let the shadows go very dark. This is an example of where the camera would have picked a different, flatter exposure to try to bring the shadows into the light.

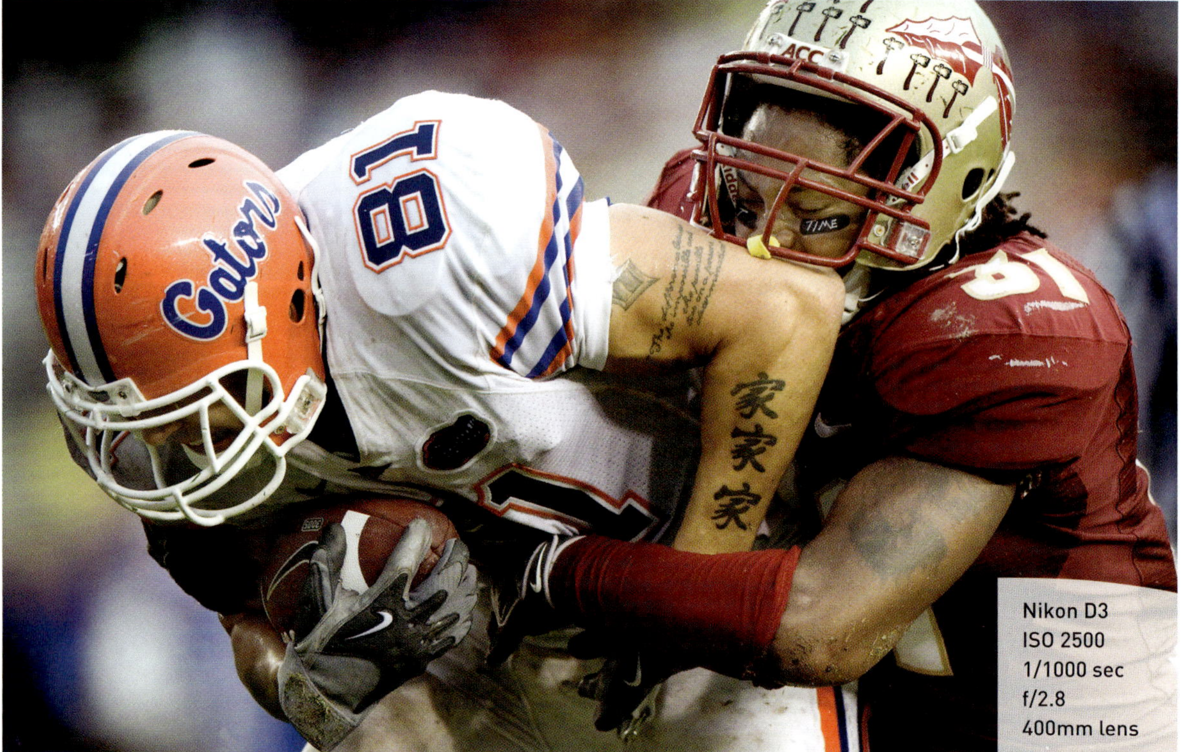

Nikon D3
ISO 2500
1/1000 sec
f/2.8
400mm lens

FIGURE 5.14
Although this is an action shot, the graphics of the image are what make it great.

Figure 5.14 shows an action shot, but it isn't really about the action. What makes this image work are the tattoos on #81 Aaron Hernandez's arm compared to the tomahawks on the defender's helmet, the angle at which Hernandez's elbow is positioned, and the look on the defender's face.

COVERING THE ACTION

Capturing key moments in football is all about anticipation. The more you know about the sport and each team playing, the better your pictures will be.

> **TIP**
>
> If a team runs a play successfully, the team will nearly always try the same play again in similar situations. Being aware of the team's tendencies will help you anticipate the action.

Having control over your camera is also hugely important when you're covering football. You need to be one with your equipment. The camera has to be an extension of your mind, or you won't be able to react quickly enough.

The game, for the most part, is played outside, which makes for changing conditions. Bright sunshine that changes to cloud cover can make for up to six or seven stops' difference in exposure. Correcting for that quickly can be the difference between a great image and an unusable one.

> **TIP**
>
> Check the light immediately before the play begins. Think about not only the basic ambient exposure, but also about the exposure inside the helmets, which will often be darker than that on the jersey, especially white jerseys.

COVERING THE MOMENTS AFTER THE GAME

What happens after the game can be as important as what happened during the game. The players, fans, and coaches will react. They always do. That can be the defining picture of the game just as easily as an action image (**Figure 5.15**).

Figure 5.16 on the next page shows the University of Florida quarterback Tim Tebow high-fiving fans after his last game in The Swamp. The outcome of the game didn't matter, but this moment did.

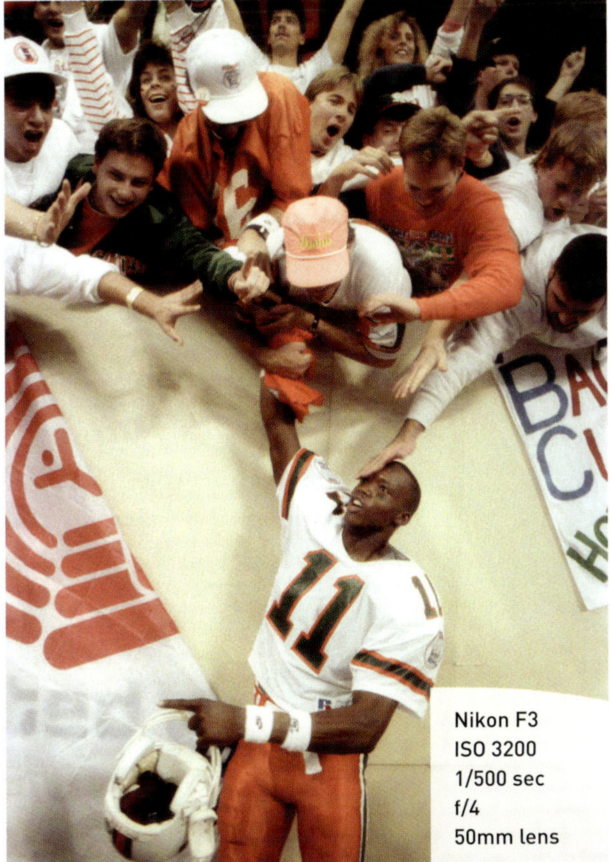

FIGURE 5.15
This image was taken during the post game celebration after a National Championship.

FIGURE 5.16
This photograph speaks to Tebow's personality and how widely popular he was at the University of Florida.

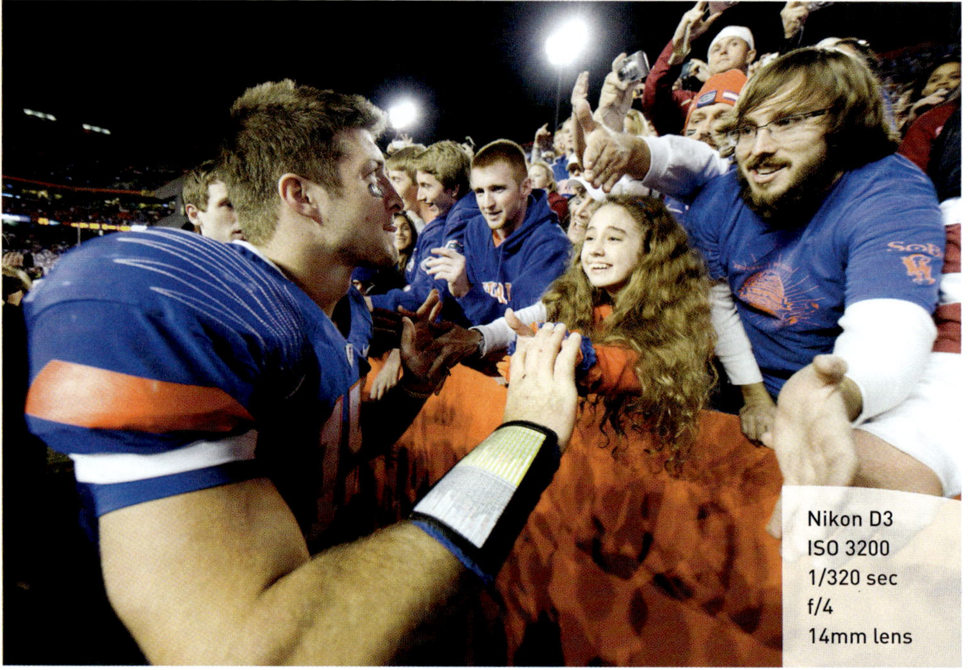

Nikon D3
ISO 3200
1/320 sec
f/4
14mm lens

SUGGESTIONS FOR SHOOTING FOOTBALL

Be patient when you're shooting. Pay careful attention to the action away from the ball. Many great photographs happen after the play is whistled dead (**Figure 5.17**).

Never give up on the action. Running backs can bust through a pack of defenders, players can celebrate a big play, or things that seem ordinary can end up resulting in surprising photos.

Figure out what the offensive and defensive tendencies are for each team. Anticipate what they will do instead of just trying to react quickly after the play starts. Football is a game of carefully calculated and choreographed movements. Luck favors the prepared.

Remember that the teams won't stop a football game for inclement weather, so come prepared for the elements. Dress accordingly, and protect your cameras from the cold and wet. Many companies make gear to protect your cameras and lenses; be sure to check them out.

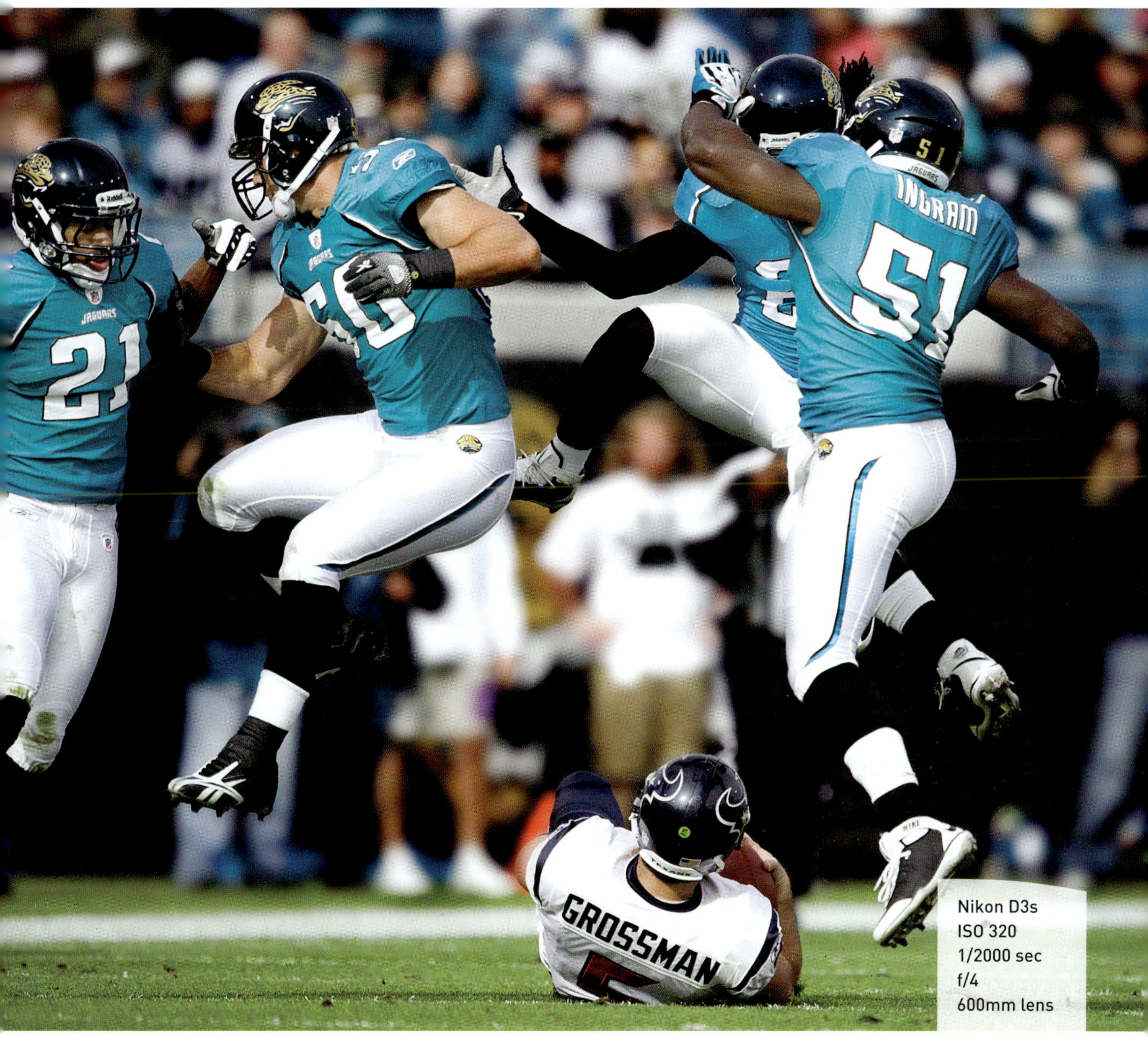

Nikon D3s
ISO 320
1/2000 sec
f/4
600mm lens

FIGURE 5.17
The Jacksonville Jaguars celebrate after sacking Texans quarterback Rex Grossman. If I had stopped shooting when Grossman went down, I would have missed this moment.

Until the teams head to the huddle, keep your eyes on the field. You not only want to be sure you don't miss any images, you also have to protect yourself. If you are watching only the ball, you may miss a player coming at you full speed, and trust me, they are bigger, stronger, and faster than you. Add to that the fact that they are wearing pads and like to hit, and you can be sure that almost no collision will come out in your favor.

One funny exception to this, however, occurred while I was covering a University of Miami vs. Notre Dame game in South Bend. The teams didn't like each other, and there was a lot of pushing, shoving, and yelling going on as they took the field. I was where I was supposed to be, covering the conflict. One of the Notre Dame defensive backs was looking back shouting at the Miami players, and ran right into me. I saw him coming and tried to move, but there was nowhere for me to go. My back was literally against the wall. He hit me, but I got my hands up in time to steer him away. He went to the ground. To his great chagrin, the other players saw what happened and he got a serious ribbing as they laughed and yelled, "You just got knocked down by a photographer." It was funny. And in all fairness, at 6'5" and 220 pounds, I was bigger than he was.

But it almost never turns out that way. Every year several photographers and TV camera operators get badly injured because they aren't paying attention. Don't let that be you.

Chapter 5 Assignments

The following exercises will help you learn how to gauge where to position yourself in relation to the action on the field. They will also help you learn how quickly you can focus and anticipate action.

Shooting from Different Field Positions

Call your local Pop Warner or high school football team and ask permission to shoot a few games. Take a variety of lenses with you, from wide-angle to telephoto lenses. Try to shoot from every position—end zone, sidelines, and grandstands—using a variety of focal lengths. Make sure your camera is in manual mode so you can control what you capture.

Shooting with Two Cameras

Find two athletes who will run toward you at full speed as you follow focus on them with the longest lens you have. When they get close, switch to your "chest" camera and make images as they continue toward you. As the athletes get closer, you'll have to change to a shorter lens to keep the athletes in the frame. Practice until you can judge accurately how to set your chest camera and until you learn how to change cameras while the athletes are running at full speed right toward you.

Practice Manual Focus

Have an athlete run toward you carrying a football and then have the athlete drop the football on the ground. Try to keep the athlete and the football in the frame. To do this, you will most likely have to manually focus the lens. If you try to follow the ball with autofocus, you'll have trouble keeping your composition intact. Do this exercise using manual focus, and then repeat it using autofocus. Compare your ability to compose tight images with each method.

Share your results with the book's Flickr group!
Join the group here: flickr.com/groups/sportsphotographyfromsnapshotstogreatshots.

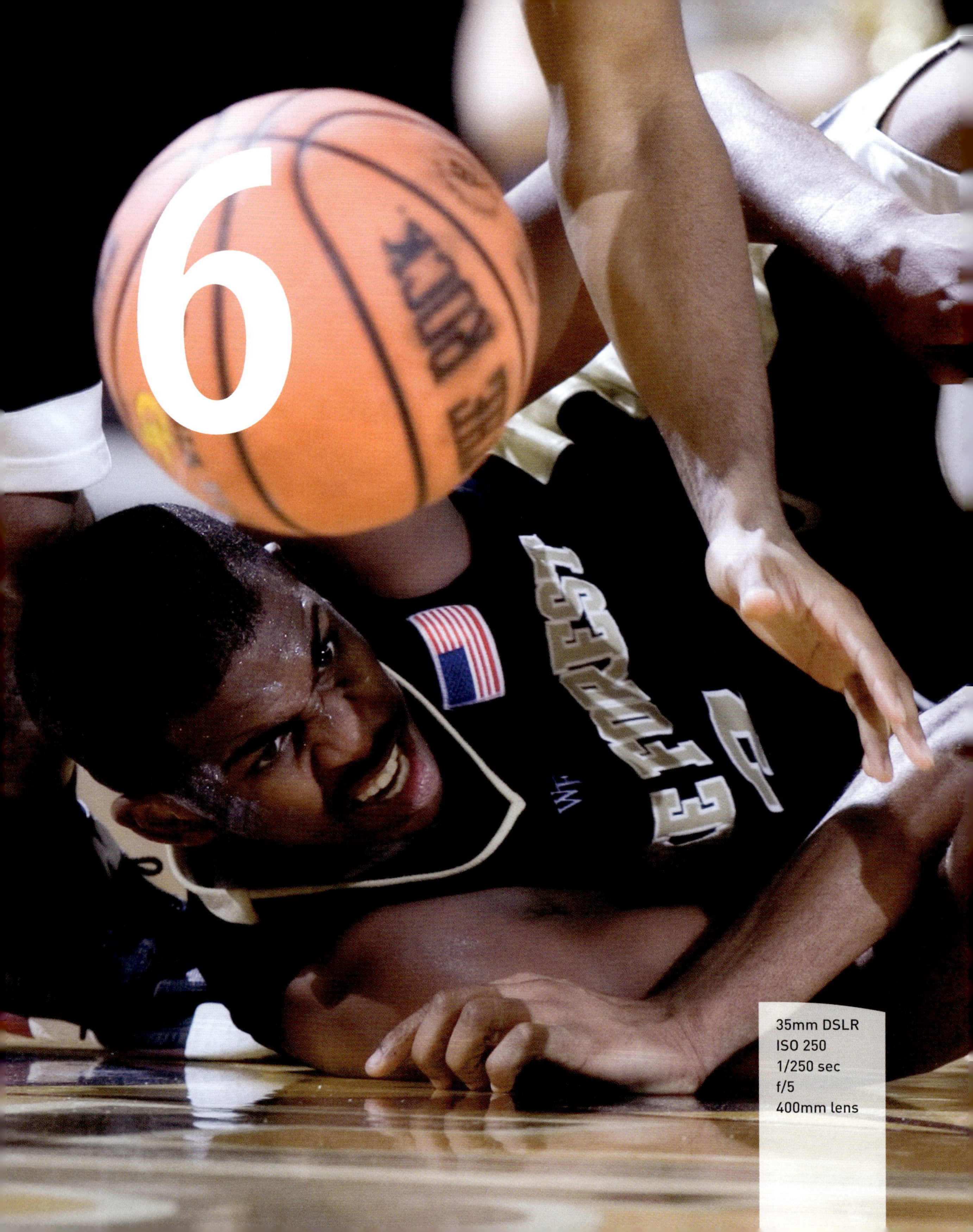

6

35mm DSLR
ISO 250
1/250 sec
f/5
400mm lens

Shooting Basketball

COVERING THE ACTION FROM ALL ANGLES

Basketball is full of action, and that makes for a lot of great opportunities for fantastic shots. It's a very fast, physical sport. But the downside of shooting basketball is that you have limited space courtside to take advantage of those chances.

This chapter reveals different ways to cover the game and what to consider when you're trying to make an image.

Timing is everything. For this game, I was shooting on strobe, meaning I could take only one picture every three seconds. This moment happened in a fraction of a second. I was able to make this image because I was ready and able to anticipate the action.

PORING OVER THE PICTURE

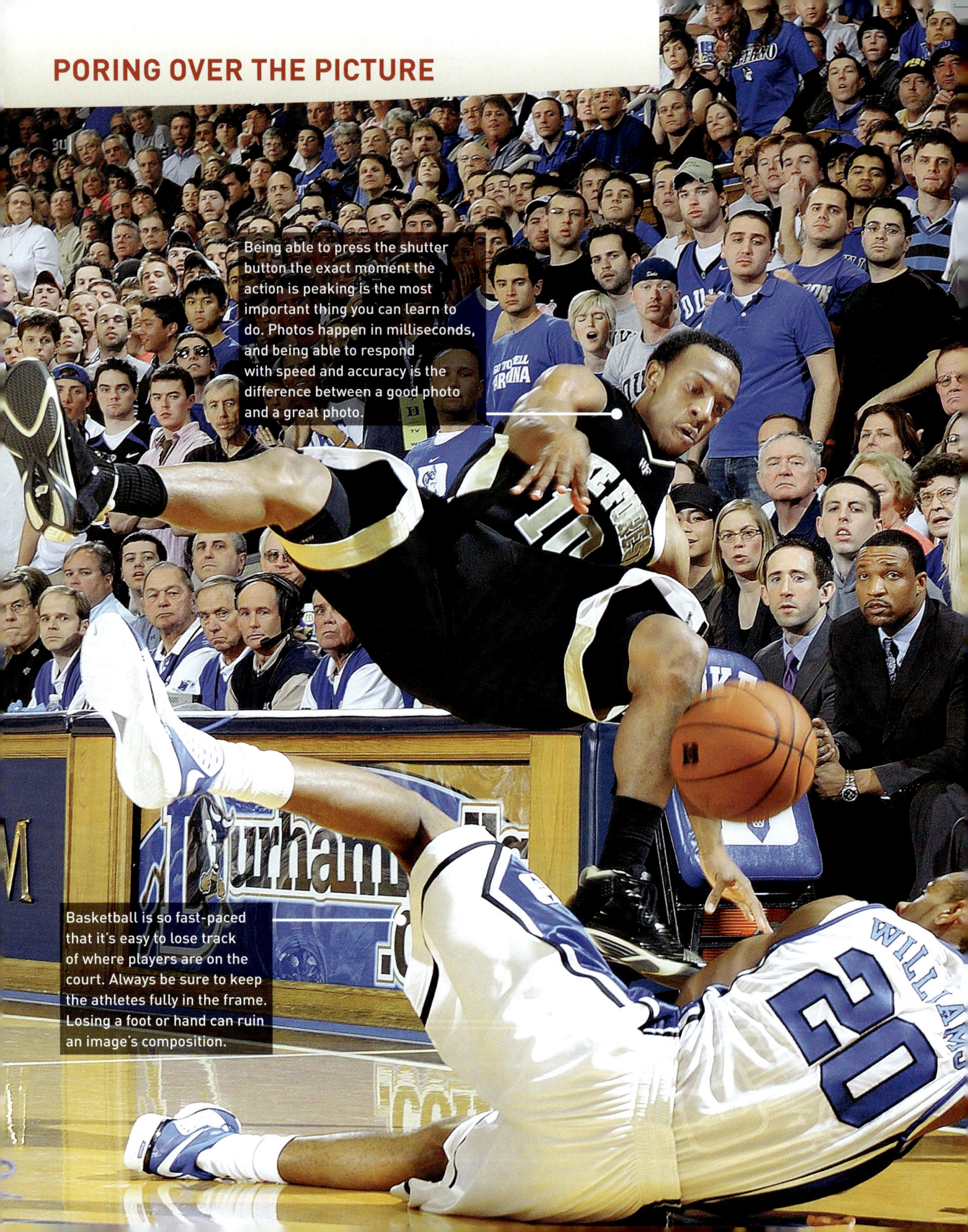

Being able to press the shutter button the exact moment the action is peaking is the most important thing you can learn to do. Photos happen in milliseconds, and being able to respond with speed and accuracy is the difference between a good photo and a great photo.

Basketball is so fast-paced that it's easy to lose track of where players are on the court. Always be sure to keep the athletes fully in the frame. Losing a foot or hand can ruin an image's composition.

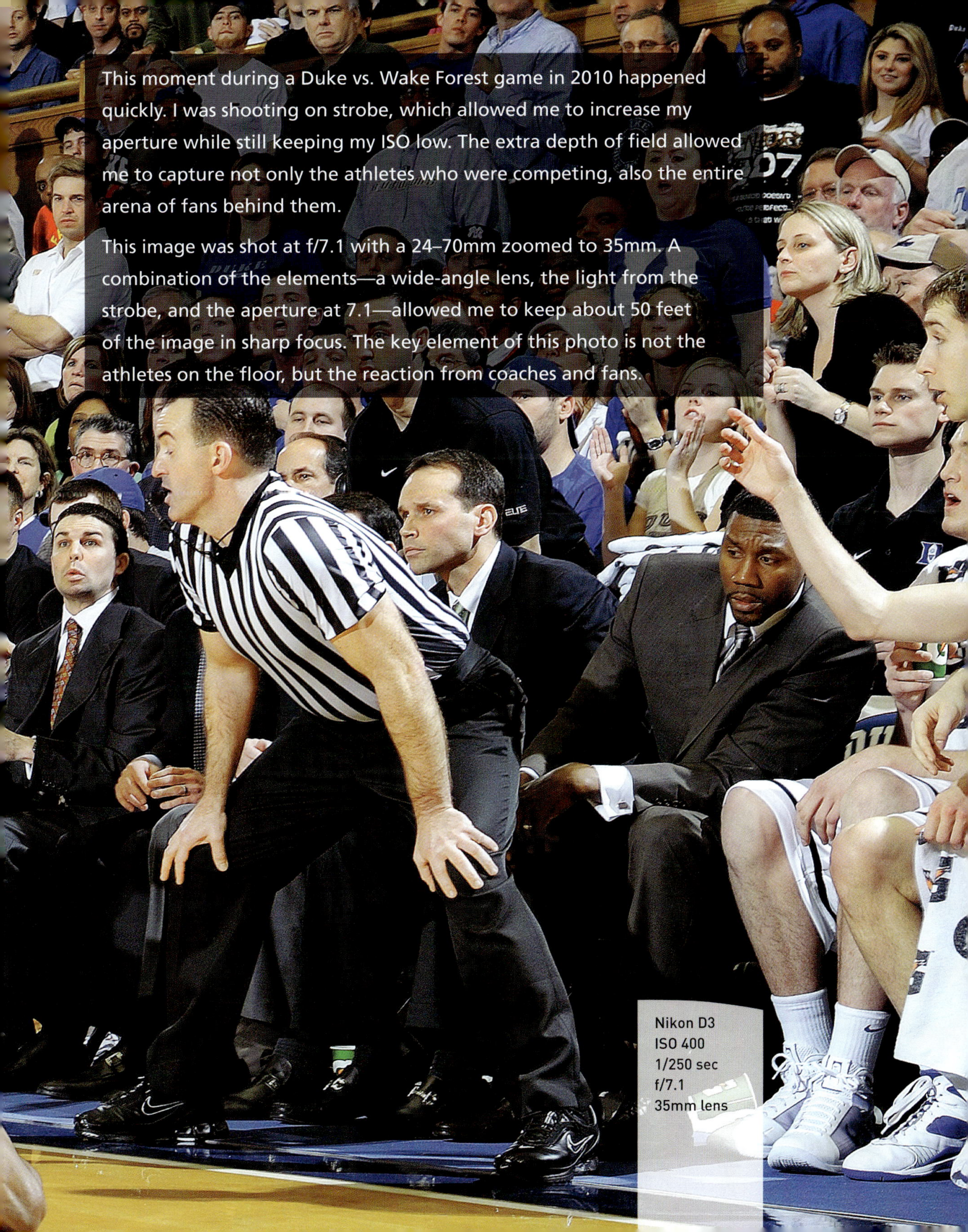

This moment during a Duke vs. Wake Forest game in 2010 happened quickly. I was shooting on strobe, which allowed me to increase my aperture while still keeping my ISO low. The extra depth of field allowed me to capture not only the athletes who were competing, also the entire arena of fans behind them.

This image was shot at f/7.1 with a 24–70mm zoomed to 35mm. A combination of the elements—a wide-angle lens, the light from the strobe, and the aperture at 7.1—allowed me to keep about 50 feet of the image in sharp focus. The key element of this photo is not the athletes on the floor, but the reaction from coaches and fans.

Nikon D3
ISO 400
1/250 sec
f/7.1
35mm lens

BASKETBALL: HOW TO GET THE BEST SHOTS

Of all the sports, basketball has the least amount of room to work. Most of the time it is necessary to be seated, and that makes it difficult to move quickly. In small gyms you may be able to stand against a wall, but that is the exception, not the rule.

Lighting is also a challenge when you're shooting basketball games.

LIGHTING

You need to consider two kinds of basketball: indoor and outdoor. Indoor games can be difficult to cover because of limited space and poor lighting conditions.

Those of you shooting indoor basketball at high schools or little league games will also be challenged by bad light. Even with the improved sensors available in contemporary cameras, the light is frequently uneven, poorly focused, and has an ugly color temperature.

You can solve some of the lighting issues by using small strobes. However, before you do, you need to check with the officials in charge. Many places don't allow you to use a flash on your camera because it is distracting to the players, and because it can become a safety issue for the athletes. Always keep in mind that the game is about the athletes, not about you.

If using a small strobe on your camera is not an option, you'll have to use the highest ISO setting you are comfortable with. This is a quality issue and one only you can determine.

You'll need to use the fastest, wide aperture optics you can afford to allow the most light possible to reach the camera's sensor. After you set the camera for the highest ISO and the lens to the widest aperture possible, you can set the shutter speed. Hopefully, the shutter speed can be 1/500 or faster so you have a chance to stop the action.

Outdoor basketball allows you even better opportunities to create great images. Some of the best basketball being played in the world happens during unregulated playground play. Just because a game isn't professional doesn't mean it's not a good game. When it happens during the day, the light can be wonderful; you just need to take advantage of it using the techniques discussed in Chapter 4 (**Figure 6.1**).

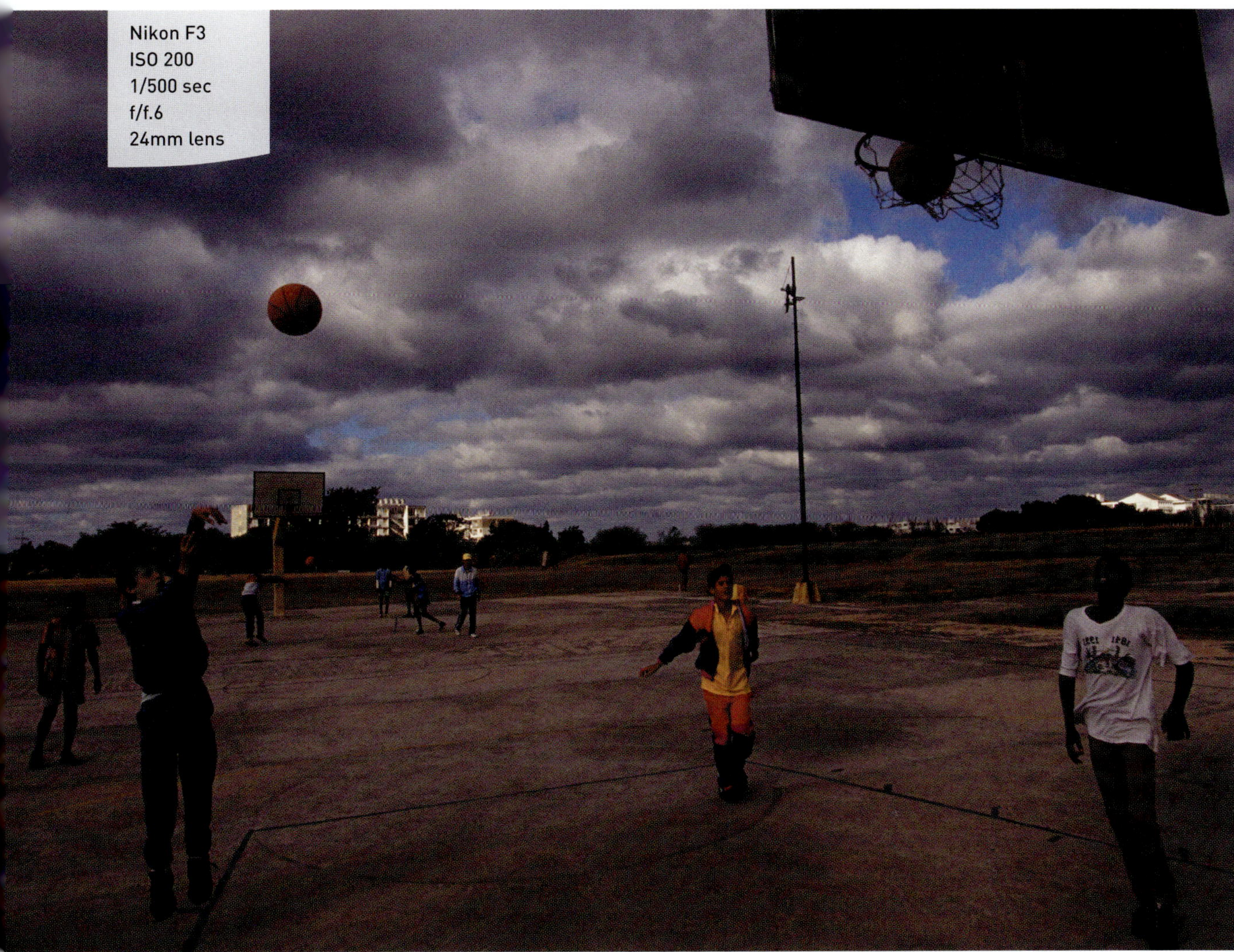

FIGURE 6.1
A group of kids play a pick-up game in Havana, Cuba.

TIP

In most arenas, the light on the athletes' faces will be much better when they are looking up because all of the light is coming from above.

COVERING THE ACTION

Making good action shots during basketball games—as in every sport—is all about anticipation.

The field of play in basketball is the smallest of all the major team sports, and the game moves at an extremely fast pace. Therefore, knowing the tendencies of certain players is important. For example, LeBron James is big and powerful, and he dominates with his size and strength. So when he gets the ball, I'm ready for a dunk, power layup, or just a big hit on another player (**Figure 6.2**).

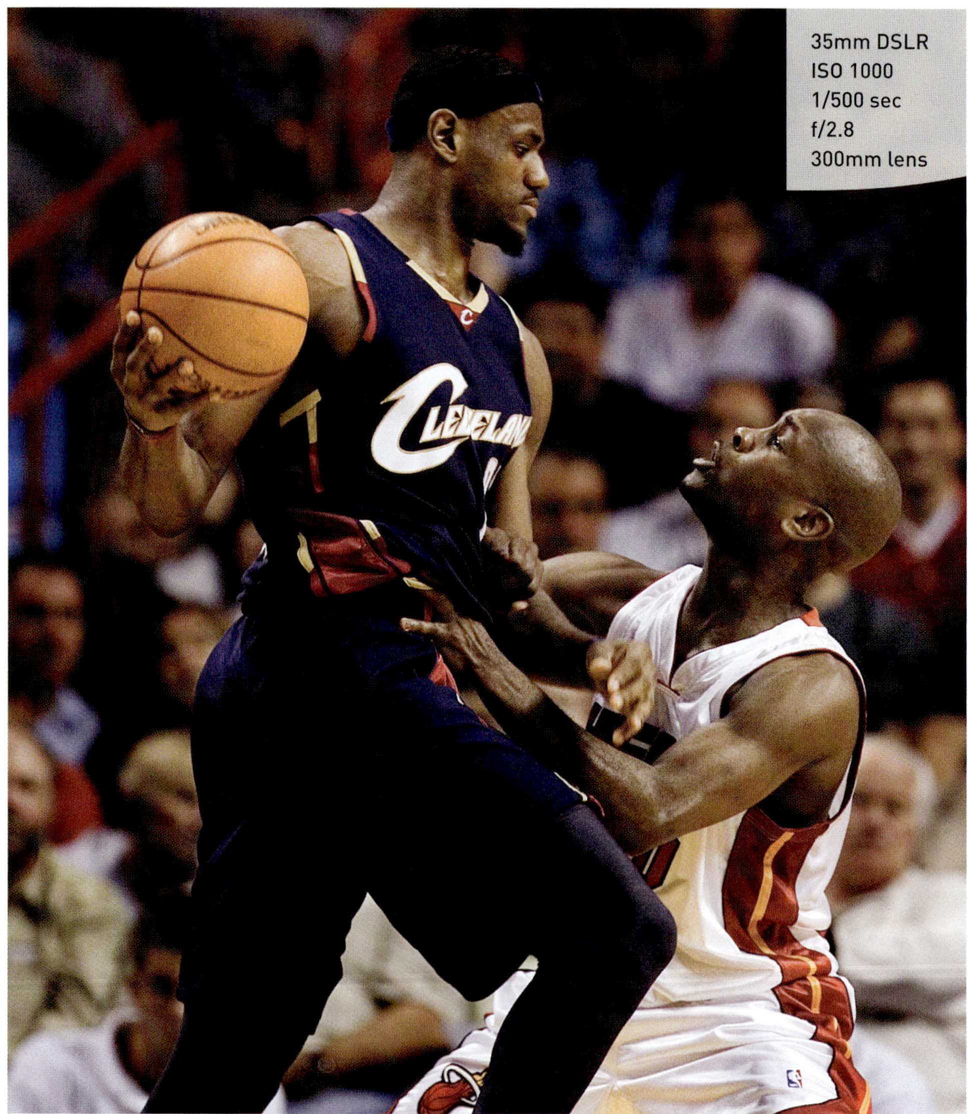

FIGURE 6.2
Understanding how certain athletes play the game always helps me figure out how to approach a game. LeBron James is one of the most dominant players in the sport, and this photo shows that.

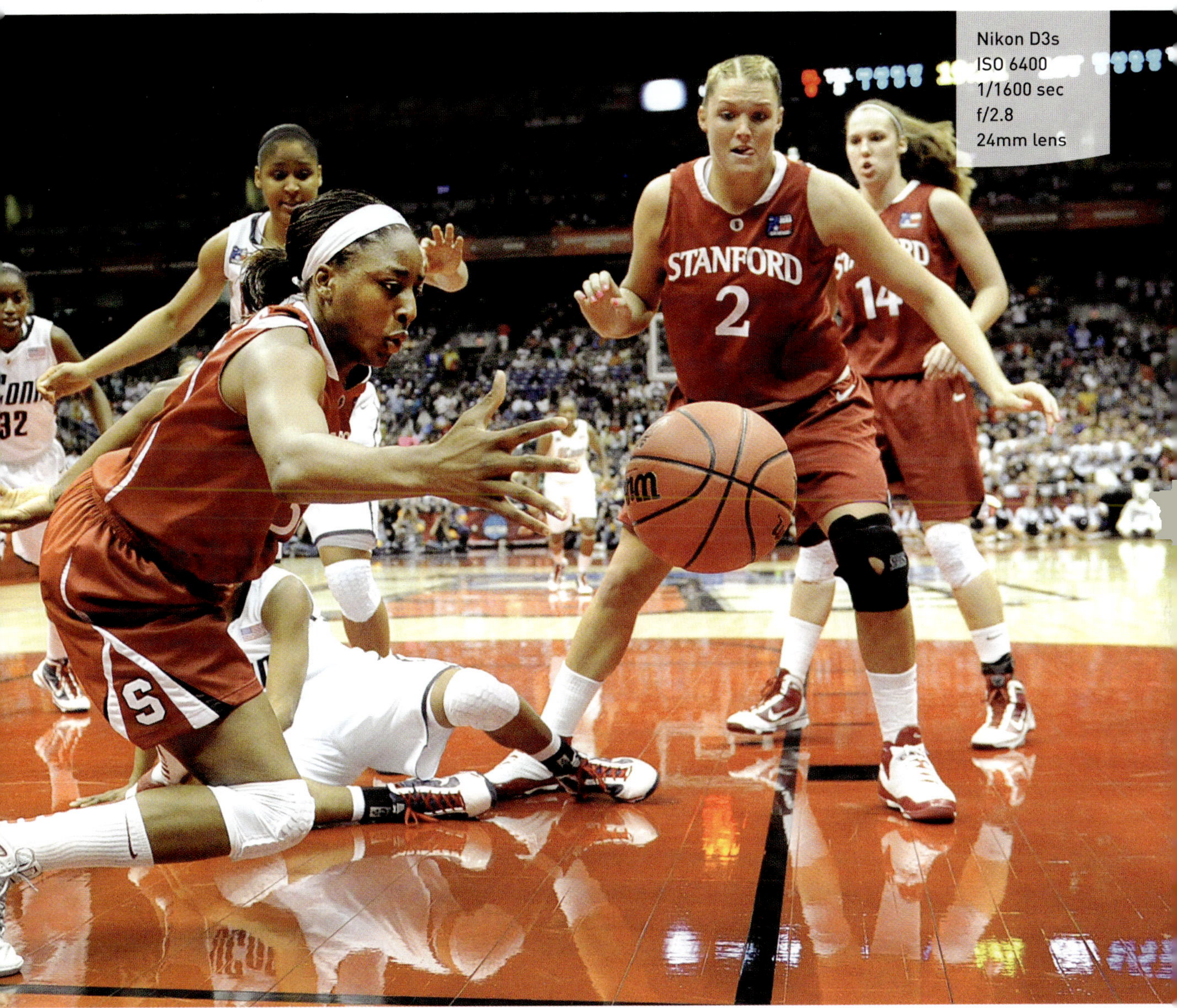

FIGURE 6.3
Stanford vs. UConn in the 2010 Women's NCAA Championship Game in San Antonio, Texas. For tough, physical games like this one, I always focus on the game near the hoop. The women are physical, but most of the action stays low.

Women's basketball is a very different game from the men's game. It's the same sport with slightly different mechanics. It too is fast and physical, but for the most part it is much closer to the ground. To cover women's basketball well, you have to be aware of how the game is played and what key players on each team excel at (**Figure 6.3**).

FIGURE 6.4
In this picture, all the action is centered around the player on the ground, and the action is relatively stationary, giving photographers a chance to focus and make a nice picture.

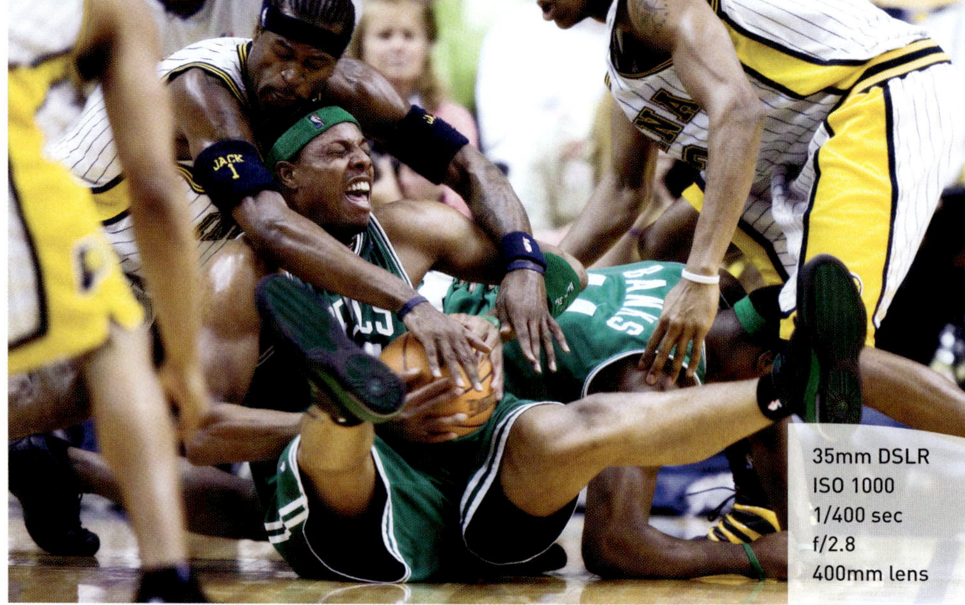

35mm DSLR
ISO 1000
1/400 sec
f/2.8
400mm lens

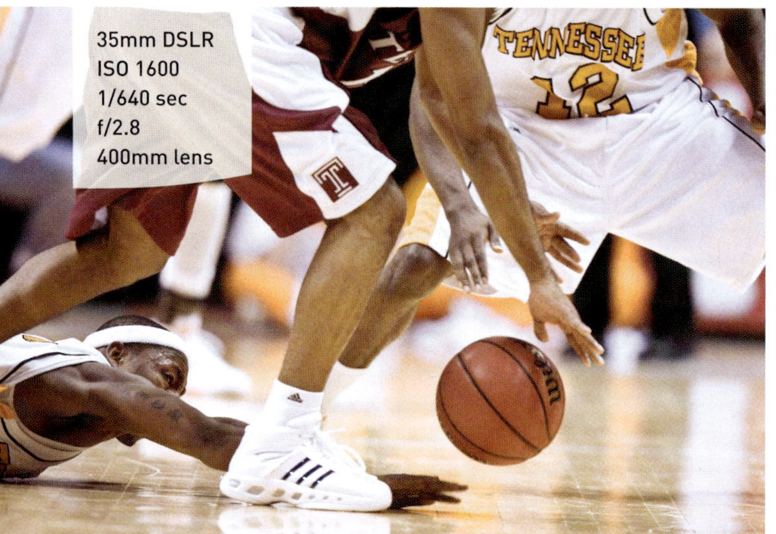

35mm DSLR
ISO 1600
1/640 sec
f/2.8
400mm lens

FIGURE 6.5
Sometimes a dive to the floor happens quickly, so you always have to be alert and ready to focus and fire quickly.

Some of my favorite shots in both men's and women's basketball come when the game gets scrappy. By that I mean the ball gets loose, the players dive for it (which never happens in baseball), and their faces strain as they fight for the ball. No matter how close the game is or how much the outcome matters, the best players will always fight for possession, which makes for great photos (**Figure 6.4** and **Figure 6.5**).

More than with any other sport, you have to think and move quickly to get great shots of basketball. The confined space and speed of the game keeps even the best photographers on their toes.

TIP

Place the camera on the floor/ground pointed at the basket. Be sure to have the floor and the ceiling in the frame. With the camera at that angle, the players will appear to be jumping even higher.

TIP

Eventually the action will involve the basket. By concentrating your focus on the hoop, you'll make good pictures at every game. The images may not be of every player or every play, but it is the highest percentage shot in all of sports photography.

COVERING THE MOMENTS AFTER THE GAME

The end of a game yields a winner and a loser. If the game is close or if it is during a tournament, the reactions of fans and players to the outcome can be very important from a journalistic standpoint. I always make it a point to position myself or a remote camera in a place that can best capture the post-game celebrations. This location will change from game to game because of the physical limitations imposed by the conditions of the competition and the facility. But there will be some place that will not be blocked, where you can place the camera's focus on the winners or the losers (**Figure 6.6**).

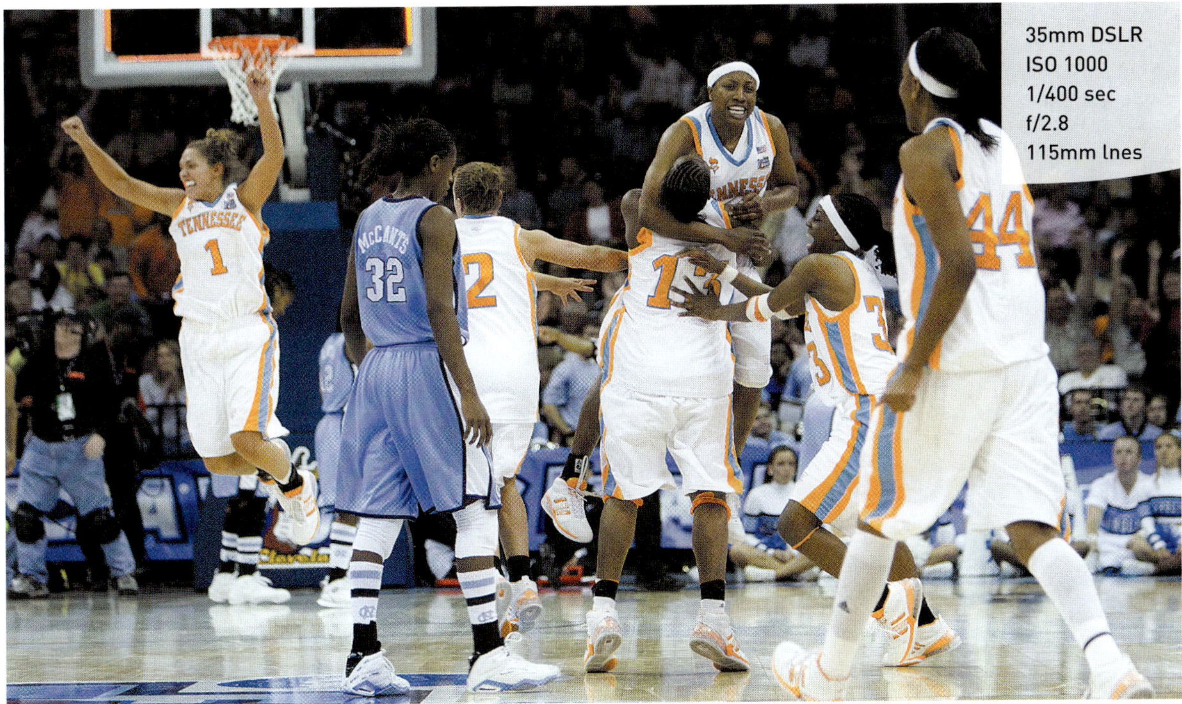

FIGURE 6.6
The Tennessee women's basketball team celebrates winning a national championship.

TIP

You can easily refer to the game clock to help you get ready for the post-game reaction. The players will be on the bench until the final seconds, and then the winners will jump up and race onto the court. The losing team will stay on the bench. The emotions are amplified during big games.

HOW I COVER BASKETBALL

As a *Sports Illustrated* staff photographer, I am given access and opportunities that most photographers are not. Still, I believe it's instructional to give you a look behind the curtain at how my basketball images are made.

When I cover a major game, I am given one spot on the floor by the basket, and that is where I have to stay for the game. Being in one spot gives me one look at the game. Because I never know when and where the best moments will occur, I employ the use of remote cameras to fully cover games.

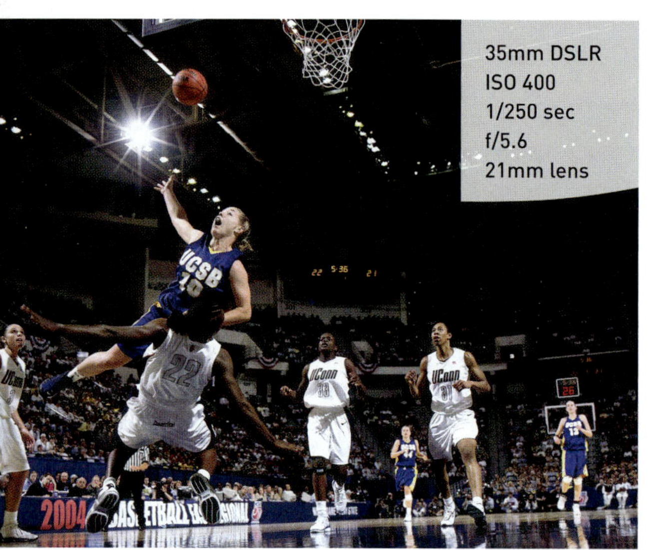

FIGURE 6.7
The floor remote provides a different point of view. This angle shows the crowd, other players, the score, and the time left in the game. Including internal identifiers like these in a shot can be extremely important.

REMOTE CAMERAS

For an NBA or NCAA game, I generally arrive at the arena five or six hours before tip-off. Because I can't physically move during the action, I position cameras in places where I know the action will happen to get great shots.

In basketball, one fact is guaranteed: All action, at some point, will move to the hoop. With that in mind, I place my remote cameras in locations where they can capture the best action in and around the basket. There are several remote positions that I try to employ in every game.

One of my favorite remote placements is a wide-angle lens on the floor looking up from the baseline at the basket. This camera has a low ratio of success, but when it works, it offers a very different look at the game (**Figure 6.7**).

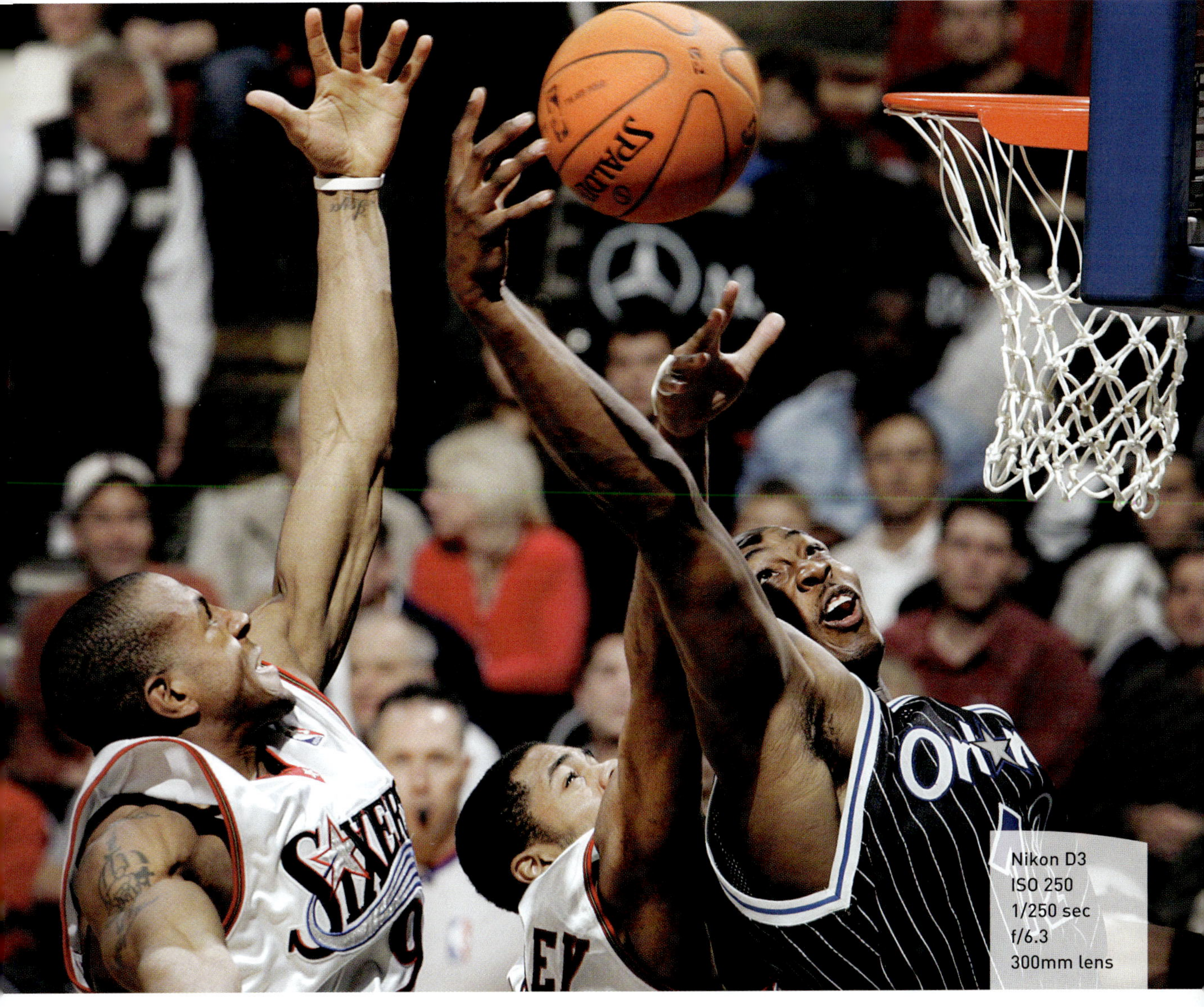

FIGURE 6.8
I made this image for a story about Dwight Howard—a big, physical player who makes his presence known at the hoop. I placed a 300mm lens over the entrance leading out to the court.

Because action at the hoop is a given at some point, I always try to find a spot in the stands where I can place a camera with a telephoto lens looking back across the basket from the side. This camera works only if the players are facing the right direction. But when they do, it makes a nice big rebound or dunk shot (**Figure 6.8**).

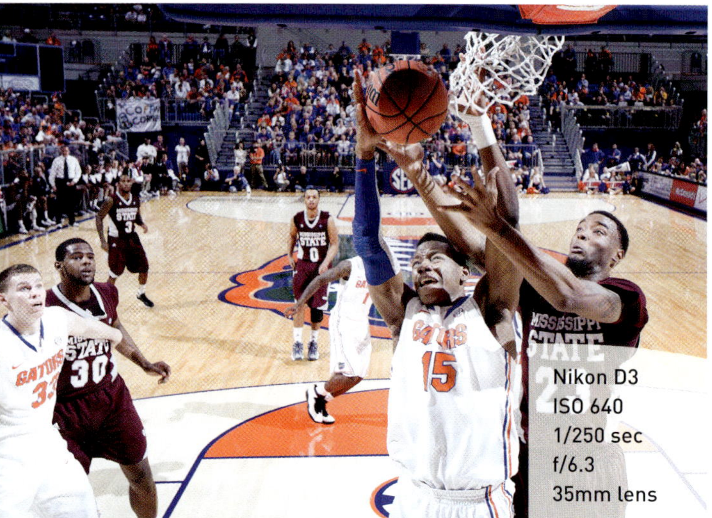

FIGURE 6.9
Because I don't know which way the players will turn their faces and bodies, I need cameras that can see them from all angles. Taking this image from my position on the floor would have blocked faces.

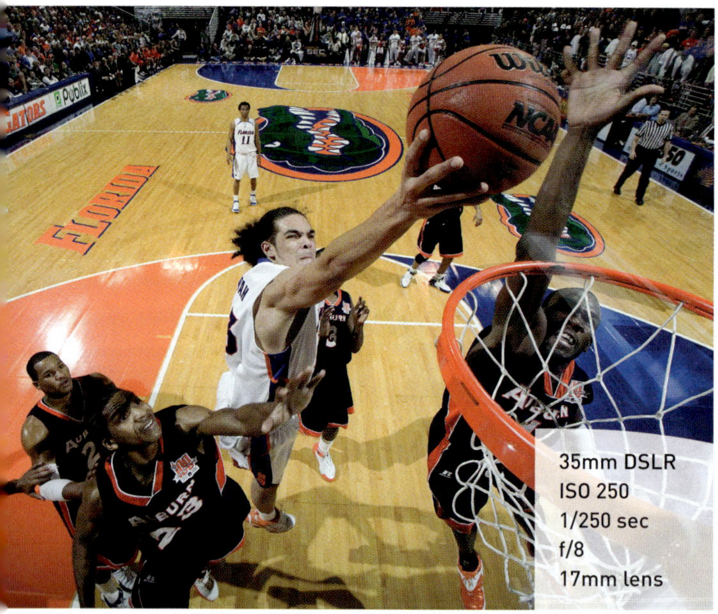

35mm DSLR
ISO 250
1/250 sec
f/8
17mm lens

FIGURE 6.10
Joakim Noah is over seven feet tall and has a massive wingspan. Placing a wide-angle lens behind the backboard allowed me to show that.

The stanchion of the basket is also a great spot for cameras. However, not all leagues, arenas, or tournaments allow cameras here. The view is an elevated version of the floor camera and is good for capturing layups and rebounds (**Figure 6.9**). This camera position allows me to get an elevated look at what I'm shooting on the floor.

Wide-angle lenses on cameras behind the glass create some of the most dynamic pictures from the game (**Figure 6.10**). A wide lens from that angle gives viewers a more complete look of the action at a particular moment than a tight shot from the side or a tight overhead shot, which is discussed next.

Remotes placed directly over the hoop create a very clean image with big impact. This angle is almost guaranteed to create great images. Generally, this position is hard to get to, and securing the camera properly is incredibly important (**Figure 6.11**).

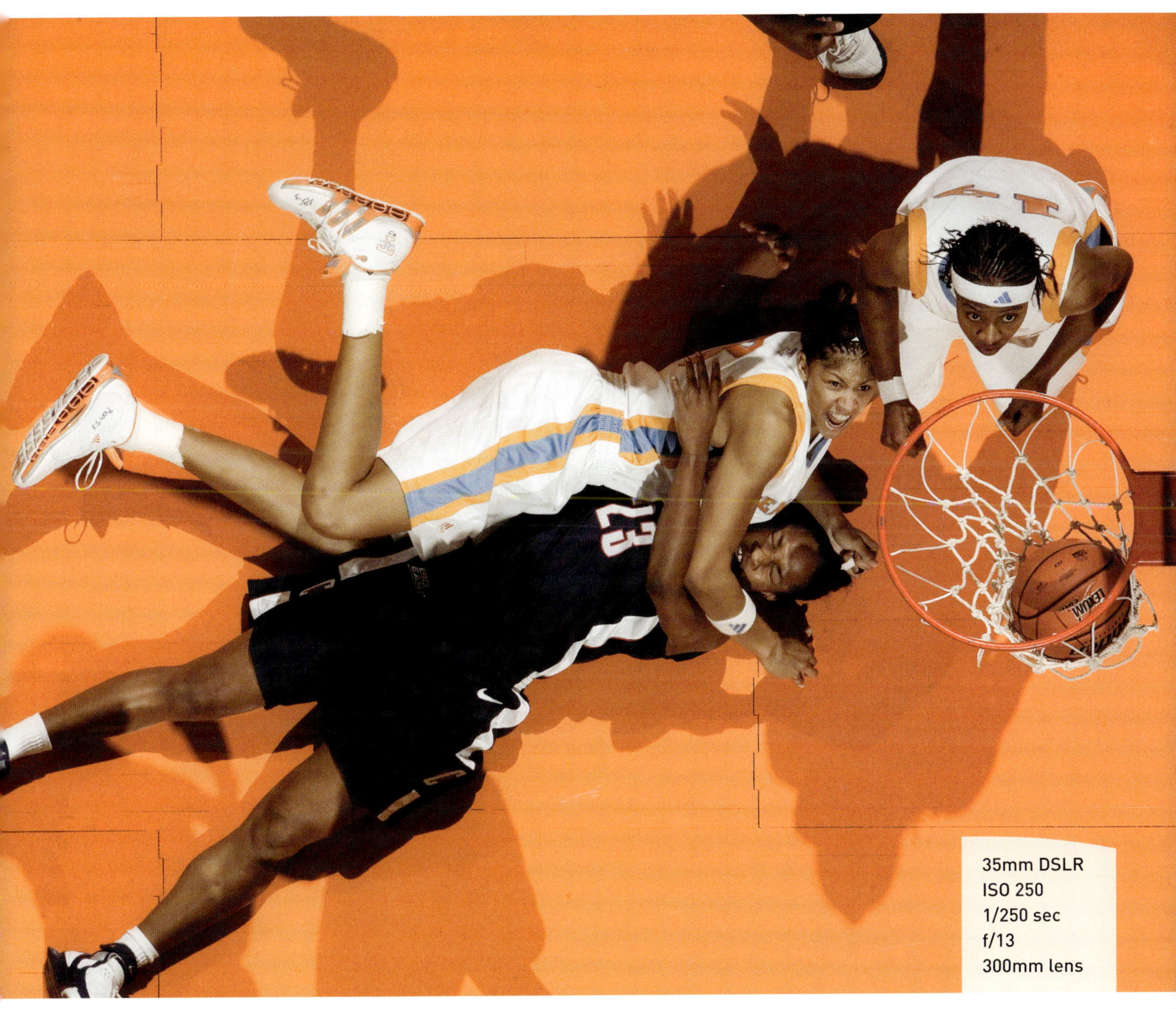

35mm DSLR
ISO 250
1/250 sec
f/13
300mm lens

FIGURE 6.11
Candace Parker falls to the court after making a layup against UConn. The overhead camera places the players over a clean background and is in prime position to capture peak action, like in this shot.

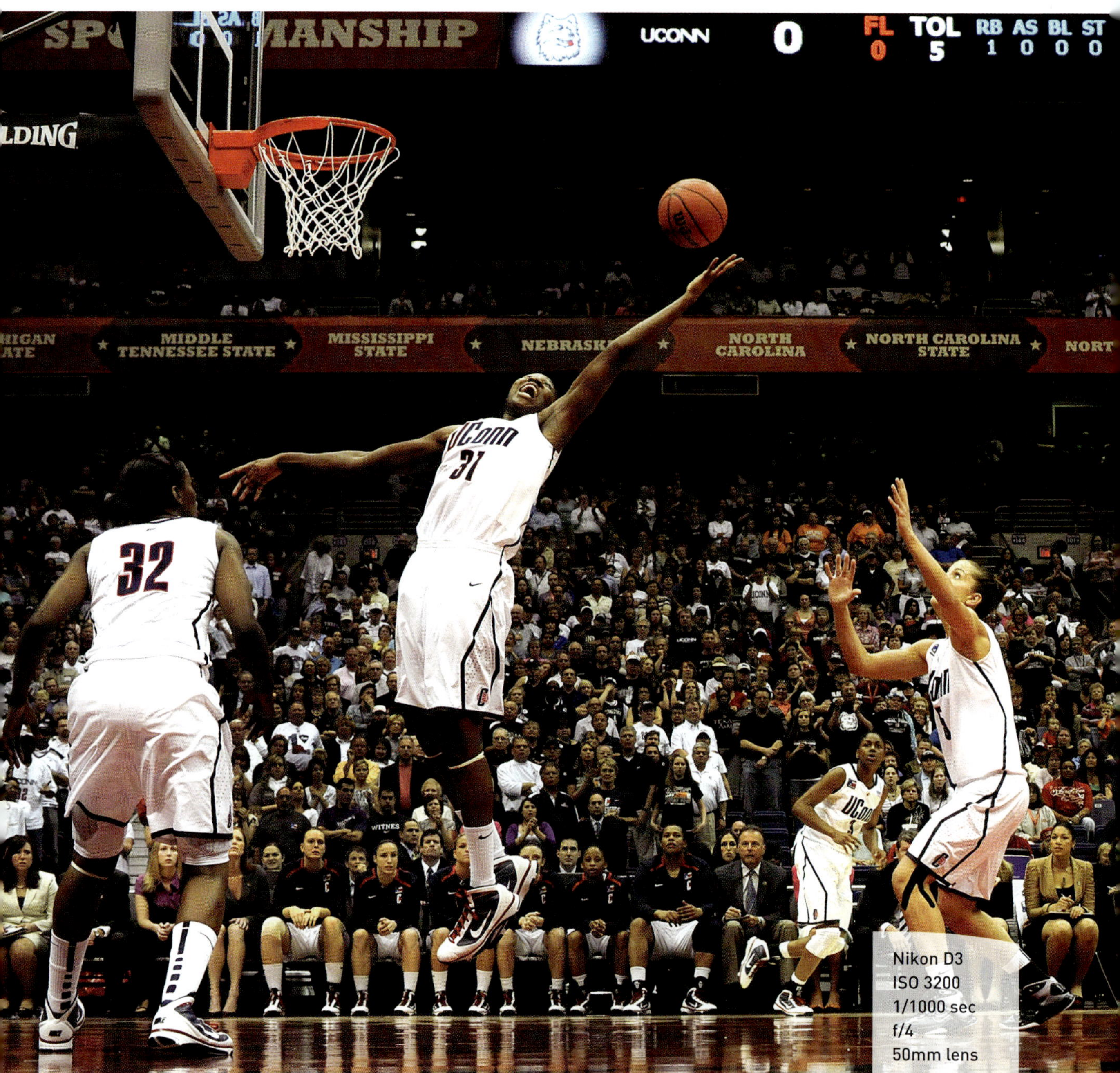

Nikon D3
ISO 3200
1/1000 sec
f/4
50mm lens

FIGURE 6.12

UConn vs. Stanford in the 2010 Women's NCAA National Championship Game. During the NCAA tournament, we are limited in where we can place remote cameras based on tournament rules and restrictions in the specific arena. This angle allowed me to show a lot of information, including the UConn bench, fans, and other players.

Media tables are always set up on the side of the court opposite the team benches. I typically set up under-the-table cams, which are wide-angle lens remotes on the floor to take shots from the side. This angle is especially good for women's basketball because the players generally play close to the floor, and cameras at this angle can focus on jump shots (**Figure 6.12**).

HANDHELD CAMERAS

I always have two cameras by my side for a basketball game—a telephoto (usually a 300mm f/2.8) and a wide to medium zoom (a 24–120mm f/4 or a 24–70mm f/2.8). I use the telephoto for down court action and the wide zoom for near court action. Both cameras are tethered into my remote system, so I can fire my remotes and the strobes from my handheld cameras (**Figure 6.13**). I explain this in detail in the next section, "Settings and Lighting."

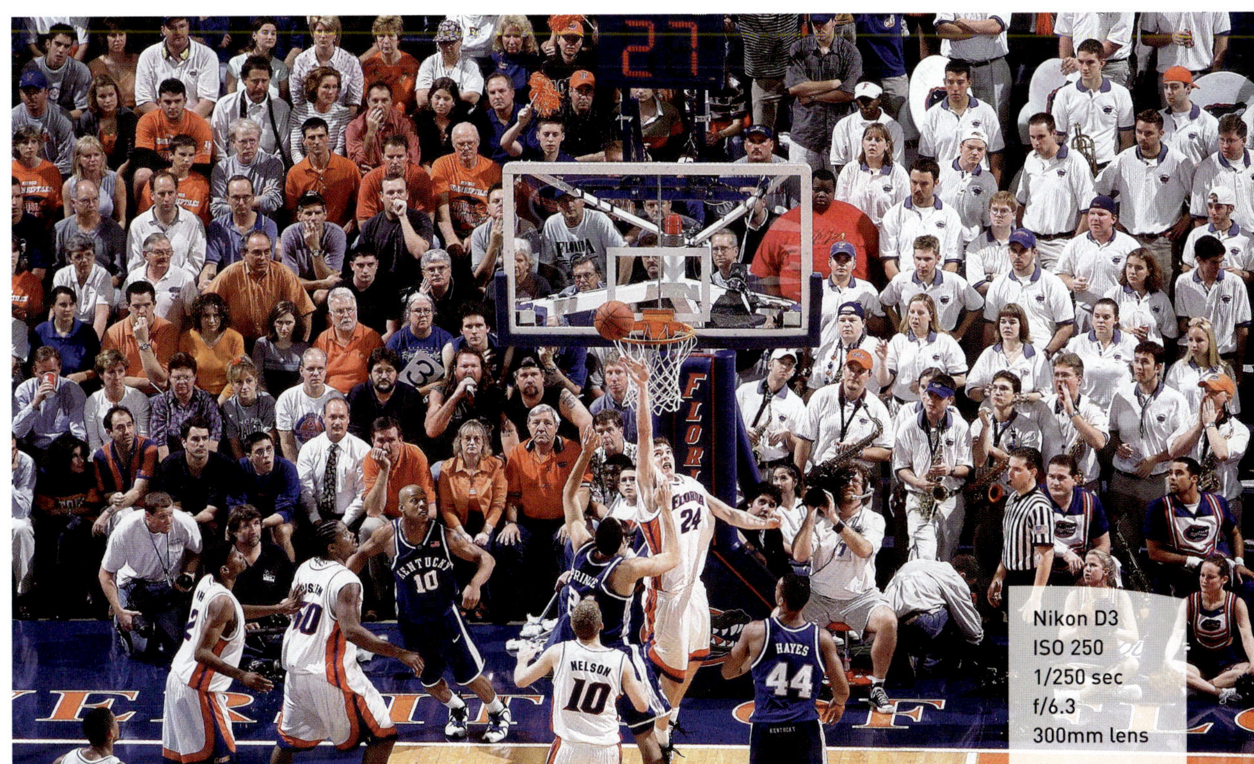

Nikon D3
ISO 250
1/250 sec
f/6.3
300mm lens

FIGURE 6.13
Can you spot me? I'm in black in the bottom-left corner. A wide angle is in front of me—a 400mm f/2.8 on a monopod on my lap—and I am firing my remotes, including the one that took this picture.

SETTINGS AND LIGHTING

Basketball is different from other action sports in that I almost always use a strobe to light the action. Even with the new DSLR cameras and their improved high ISO capabilities, images taken with a strobe look better. Many arenas that I work in at NBA or NCAA games have strobes already in place that *Sports Illustrated* either owns or rents.

The strobes I usually use are 2400 w/s units, and generally there are four of them, one in each corner of the arena. To connect them all, I run hundreds of feet of household 18 amp wire to each strobe and drop the line down to my spot on the floor.

The setup gets a bit technical because the strobes and cameras all have to fire at the same time. To make that happen, I have to use radio transmitters. PocketWizards are the most commonly used form of transmitter in the photo community. I use them frequently in other sports, but for basketball I use the PocketWizard's big brother, the LPA FlashWizard.

The FlashWizard is similar to the PocketWizard, but it is better at deflecting unwanted radio signals. This is important in basketball because I am in an enclosed space with literally thousands of conflicting signals. Scoreboards, Jumbotrons, radio, television, and every fan in the stands with a cell phone use radio signals, and sometimes those signals get crossed.

Each remote camera is connected to a FlashWizard, as are the strobes. When I plug my camera into the master FlashWizard, all of my cameras and strobes fire in sync with each other.

Shooting on strobe increases the quality of the photo, allowing for lower ISO settings, because the maximum shutter speed on strobe is 1/250 of a second. But strobes also reduce the frequency I can shoot. For the strobes to recycle their power, I can shoot only once every three seconds, which sometimes seems like an eternity, because cameras like the Nikon D4 can fire up to 11 frames per second. For this reason, I leave my down court camera off strobe. That allows me to shoot more action. To make sure I can still fire my remotes down court, I tape triggers to the side of my camera right next to the shutter release.

The settings on the cameras are fairly uniform, depending on the arena. On strobe, the exposure is always somewhere in the vicinity of ISO 400 and f/5.6, and the shutter speed is always 1/250 of a second.

Chapter 6 Assignments

Basketball requires you to shoot from fixed positions. These exercises will help you learn how to anticipate the action and respond quickly and accurately.

Learning How to Time Your Shots

Go to a basketball court where a game is in progress. Sit on the baseline, position yourself where you will not be stepped on by the players, and prefocus the camera on the hoop using the widest focal length lens you have at the widest aperture possible. Try to time your shots using single frame shutter advance. Practice until you can anticipate precisely when the ball will leave the player's hand. Be sure to keep the players' full bodies in the frame.

Learning How to Compose Your Camera

Go to a basketball court where a game is in progress. Sit on the baseline, position yourself where you will not be stepped on by the players, and place the camera on the floor/ground. Do this with the widest focal length lens you have. Tilt the camera up so you have the floor/ground in the foreground and the action completely within the frame. Shoot repeatedly and then look at the image review. Do this until you can confidently place the camera and make consistently well-composed images.

Positioning Yourself for Success

Go to a basketball court where a game is in progress, and find a high angle. Practice making images that show as much of the playing surface as possible. When courts are very dark and shooting positions are limited, making overall images may be the only option. Notice how being farther from the action allows you to use slightly slower shutter speeds than you use courtside and still stop the action.

Share your results with the book's Flickr group!
Join the group here: flickr.com/groups/sportsphotographyfromsnapshotstogreatshots.

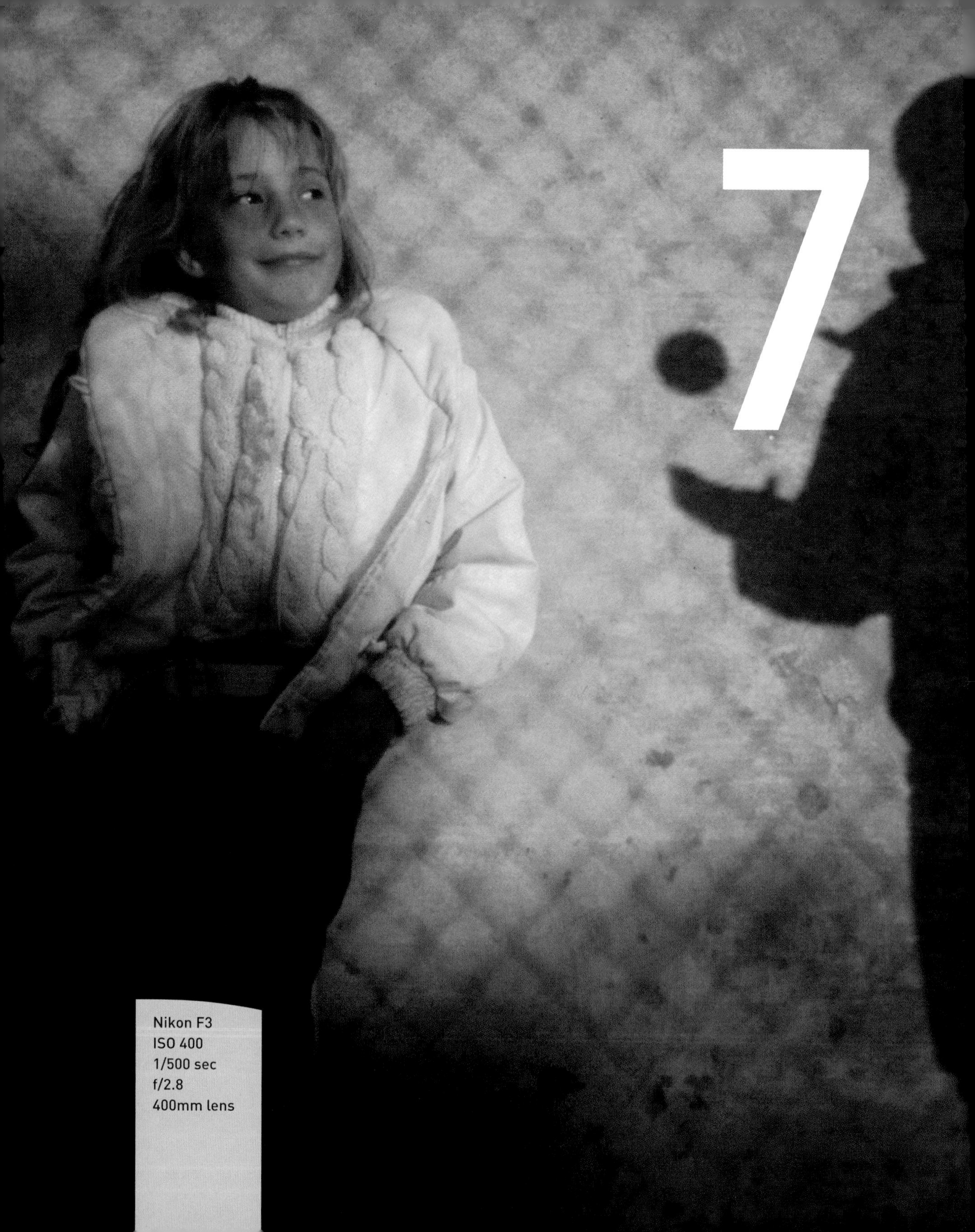

7

Nikon F3
ISO 400
1/500 sec
f/2.8
400mm lens

Baseball and Softball

SHOOTING AMERICA'S GAMES

Steve Busby, a former starting pitcher for the Kansas City Royals, summed up the sport of baseball nicely: "Baseball, to me, is still the national pastime because it is a summer game. I feel that almost all Americans are summer people; that summer is what they think of when they think of their childhood. I think it stirs up an incredible emotion within people" (*Washington Post*, 8 July 1974).

Baseball is played by children of all ages, and there are many variations of the game—from sandlot to stickball and little league to Major League. This chapter talks about the common ground and a few situations that are specific to baseball and softball on all levels.

Most of my favorite images of baseball are not of high action, but instead feature kids and fans playing and watching the game they love.

PORING OVER THE PICTURE

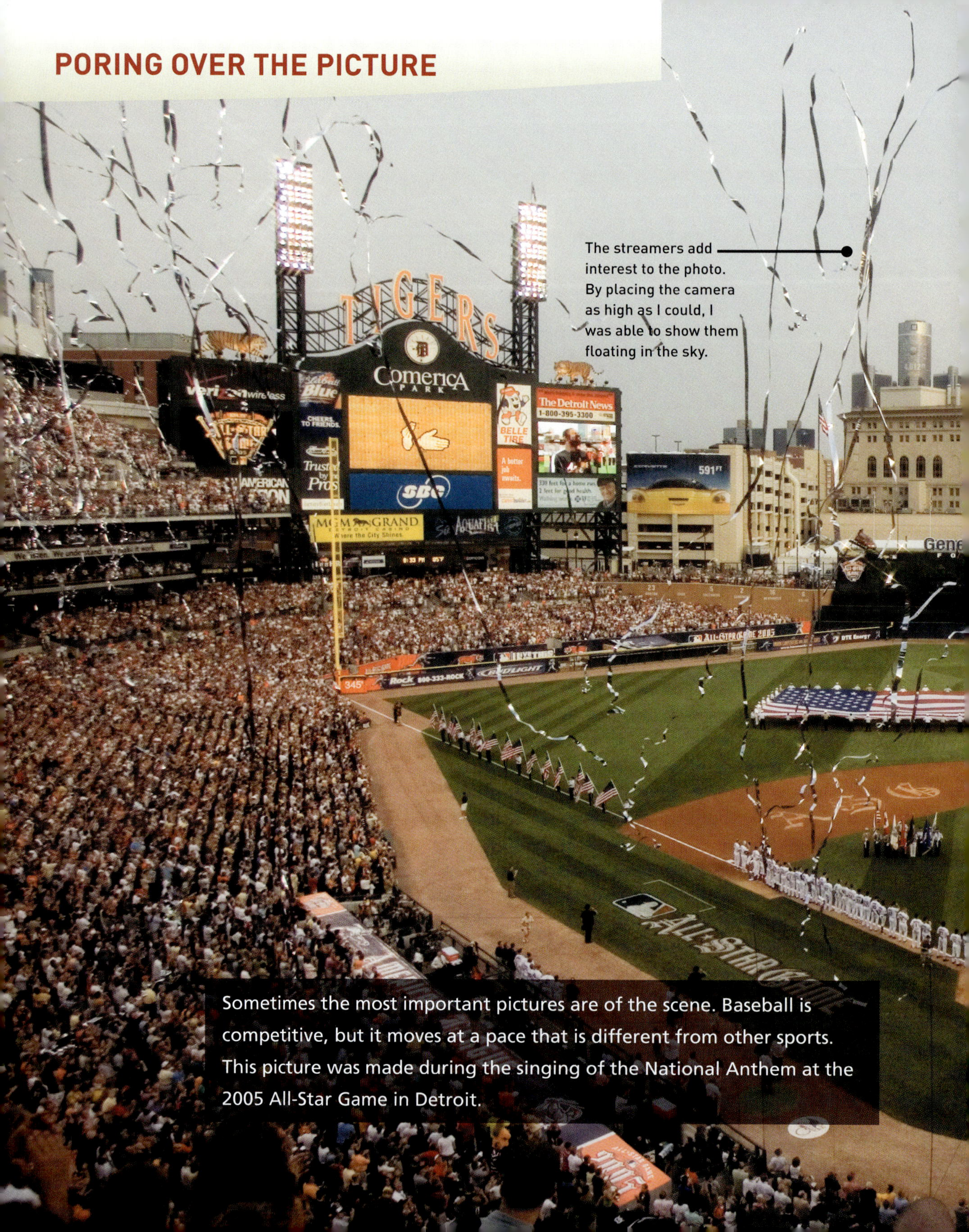

The streamers add interest to the photo. By placing the camera as high as I could, I was able to show them floating in the sky.

Sometimes the most important pictures are of the scene. Baseball is competitive, but it moves at a pace that is different from other sports. This picture was made during the singing of the National Anthem at the 2005 All-Star Game in Detroit.

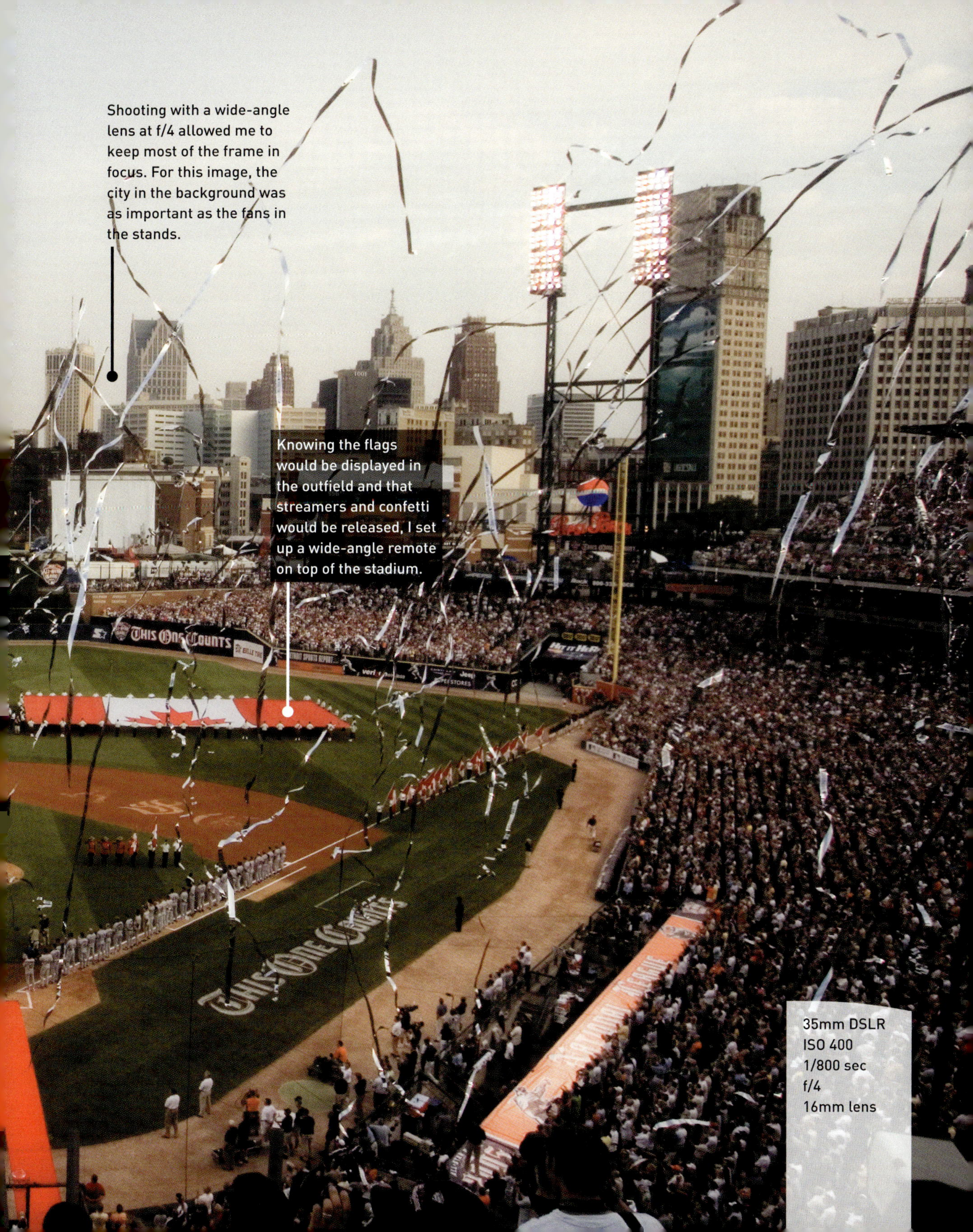

Shooting with a wide-angle lens at f/4 allowed me to keep most of the frame in focus. For this image, the city in the background was as important as the fans in the stands.

Knowing the flags would be displayed in the outfield and that streamers and confetti would be released, I set up a wide-angle remote on top of the stadium.

35mm DSLR
ISO 400
1/800 sec
f/4
16mm lens

BASEBALL: HOW TO GET THE BEST SHOTS

Dubbed "a baseball mastermind" by *Businessweek*, Bill Veeck—a franchise owner and innovator in Major League Baseball—described the essence of baseball nicely: "This is a game to be savored, not gulped. There's time to discuss everything between pitches or between innings."

Baseball fields are relatively big areas, so they offer you lots of shooting positions. And because the game moves relatively slowly, you have time to think, calculate, and move around the field to get the best shots.

WHERE TO POSITION YOURSELF

When you're covering baseball, you first need to decide where you can safely position yourself and not interfere with play.

Balls and bats fly in all directions. Because they are so hard, they can cause significant damage when they come in contact with people. Too many times I've seen fans and photographers get seriously hurt because they simply weren't paying attention.

FIRST BASE

First base is normally a prime position. If you are outside of the first base dugout, the side closest to the outfield, you'll have good sight lines to make photographs of the hitters and the pitchers—especially left-handed pitchers—because they will be facing you for part or all of their throwing motion. You'll be able to shoot the classic "double play" image of a runner sliding into second base and either the shortstop or the second baseman making a play. And you'll be in a terrific spot to make images of plays at the plate.

A high percentage of plays involve throws to first base. From your location outside first, you'll have the players throwing in your direction, which will allow you to make much better action images.

TIP

When a runner is on first base, prefocus on the bag. When the runner takes a lead, the pitcher will usually throw at least once to the first baseman to keep the runner close, reducing the runner's chances of advancing. If the runner dives back to base or is tagged out, or if the ball gets away from the first baseman, you'll be able to make a very nice image.

THIRD BASE

Third base is also a prime position. If you are outside of the third base dugout, the side closest to the outfield, you'll have good sight lines to make photographs of the hitters and the pitchers—especially right-handed pitchers—because they will be facing you for part or all of their throwing motion. As with the first base position, you'll be able to shoot the classic "double play" image of a runner sliding into second base and either the shortstop or the second baseman making a play.

You'll also be in a terrific spot to make images of plays at the plate, because you'll be looking down the line at the catcher as the play happens (**Figure 7.1**).

> **TIP**
>
> If you think there will be a play at the plate, swing your lens toward the plate immediately and focus quickly on the catcher. The action will almost always go to where the catcher is standing.

Additionally, you'll be facing first base, so this is a great position to show close plays there.

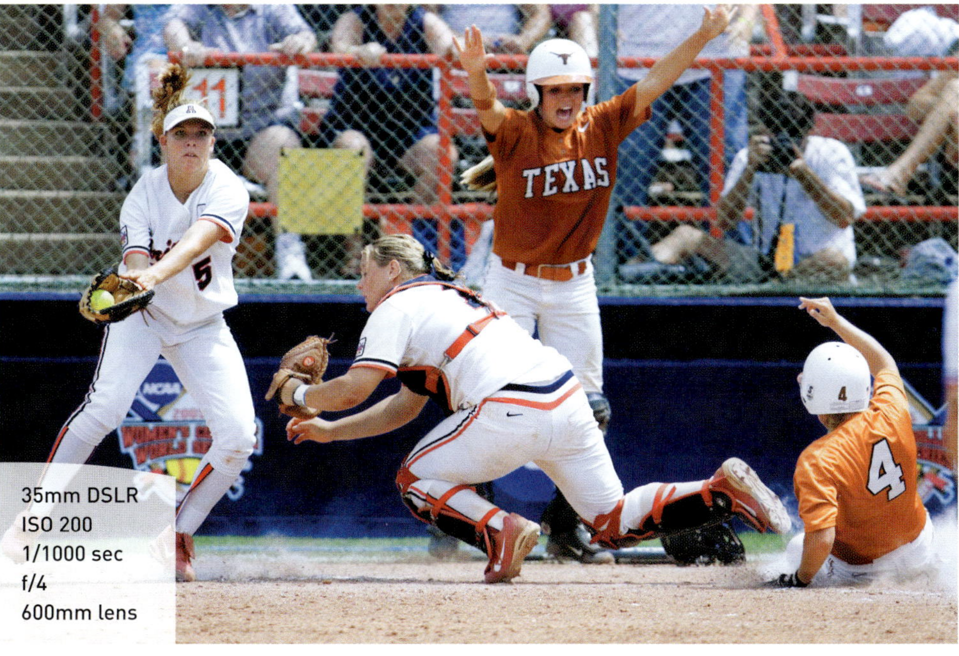

FIGURE 7.1 Shooting down the third base line put me in a prime location to capture this play at home plate.

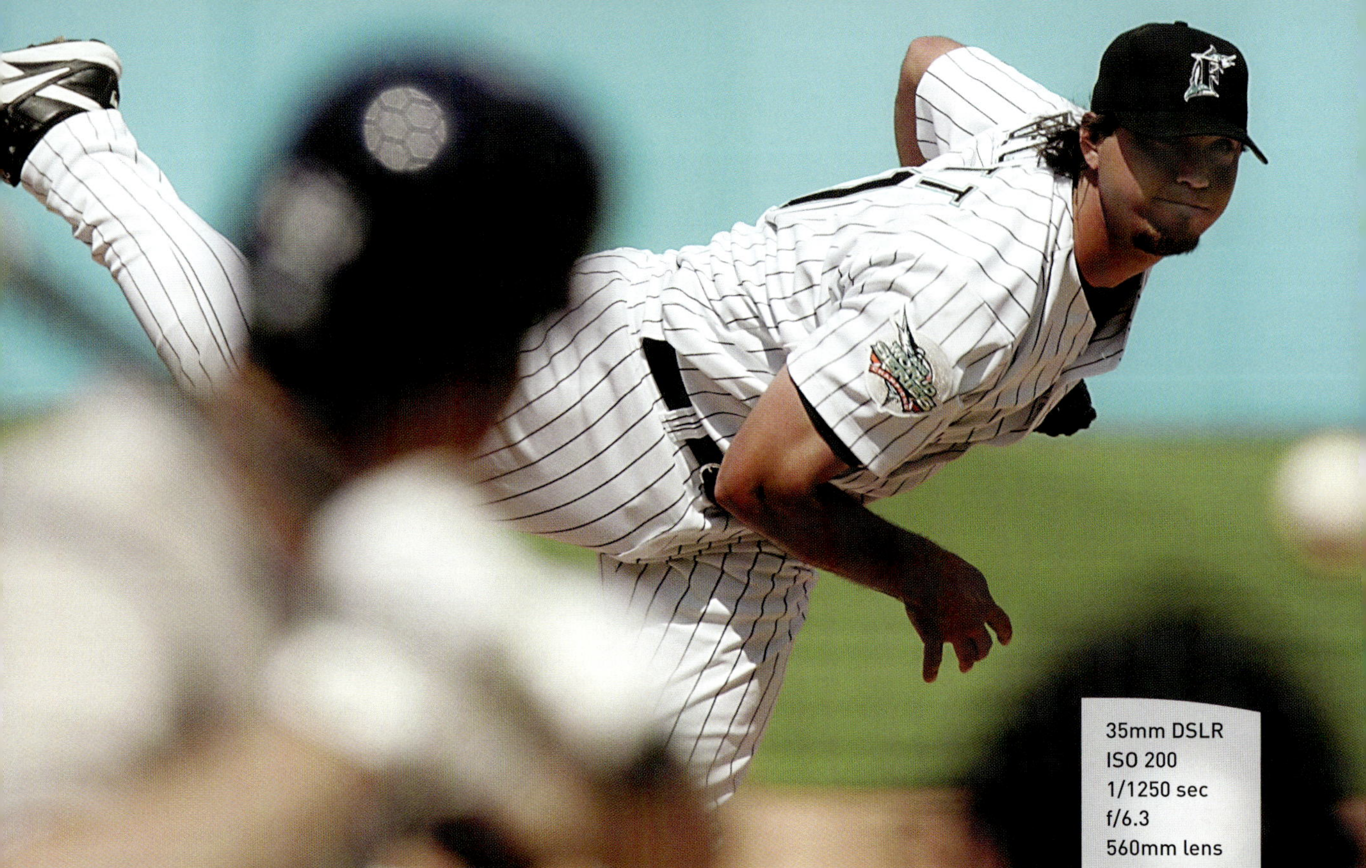

FIGURE 7.2
Shooting behind home plate gave me a great view of the pitcher as he released the ball.

TIP

When a runner on first base is trying to advance, you can prefocus your lens on second base and wait for the action to happen. When you're working with more than one camera, put one camera on a support, focus it on second base, and trigger it when the play happens. This lets you use the other camera to follow the action everywhere else on the field. This tip works for either the first base or third base dugout position.

BEHIND HOME PLATE

Taking a position directly behind home plate is as simple as it sounds. You need to line up your shot so you can see the pitcher head on, the hitter from behind, and the umpire looking over the catcher's shoulder. The backstop will be between you and the participants. You need to get as close to the actual backstop as possible. Put the front of your lens as close as you can to the physical backstop. A wide-angle lens will show the wires and will be a distraction in your image. With a longer lens, you'll be able to shoot through the wire without distortion or disruption (**Figure 7.2**).

TIP

The longer the lens, the easier it will be to shoot through the backstop without problems. The closer you can get the lens to the backstop, the better your image will be.

OUTFIELD LOOKING IN

Baseball is the only sport I know of in which the team on defense controls the ball. When you are in the outfield looking back toward home plate, you have an entirely different perspective on the game. You can see how the defense—the team on the field—is set up. You can see the face of the batter, and if the batter hits the ball, it should come in your direction.

You have several options for making images from the outfield: You can use a short lens and do overall images showing the field, the players, and the scene—both static and during the action (**Figure 7.3**).

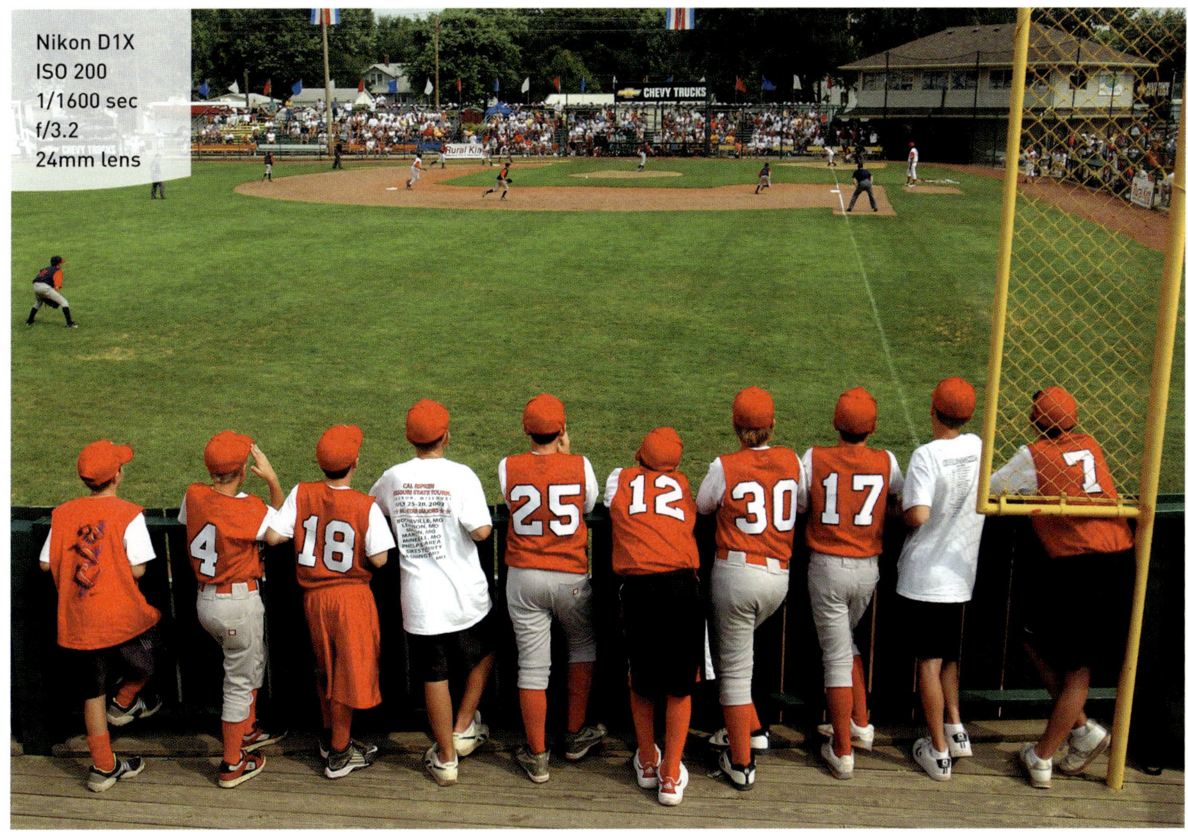

Nikon D1X
ISO 200
1/1600 sec
f/3.2
24mm lens

FIGURE 7.3 Shooting from the outfield with a wide-angle lens sets the scene of this game and gives the picture an element that a long lens from field level would not have.

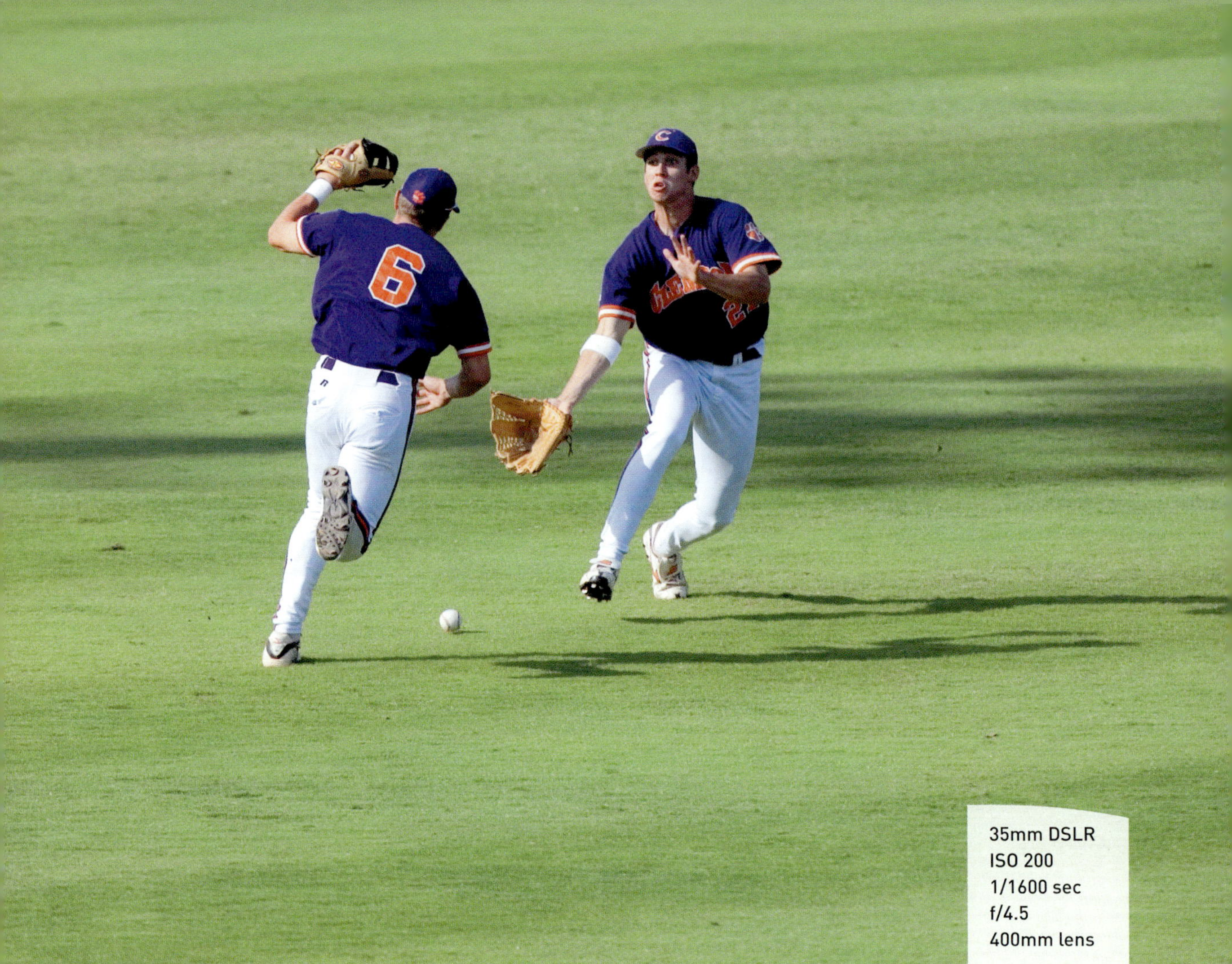

FIGURE 7.4
I took this picture from an elevated position behind first base. The higher position let me make a clean, fun image with an all grass background.

You can also use a long lens and isolate the action. If your lens is long enough—you can tell if it is only by looking through the camera, because every field differs in dimension—you'll be able to show the pitcher throwing the ball, the batter hitting it, and the home plate umpire watching intently.

You can concentrate on the individual bases and make very simple, easy-to-understand images of plays at the plate.

With a very long lens, 400mm to 600mm, you can make isolated action images of the hitters.

SHOOTING FROM ELEVATED POSITIONS

If you can find a higher location to work from, you can use all of your lenses to make interesting photographs of the players, the action, and the scene (**Figure 7.4**).

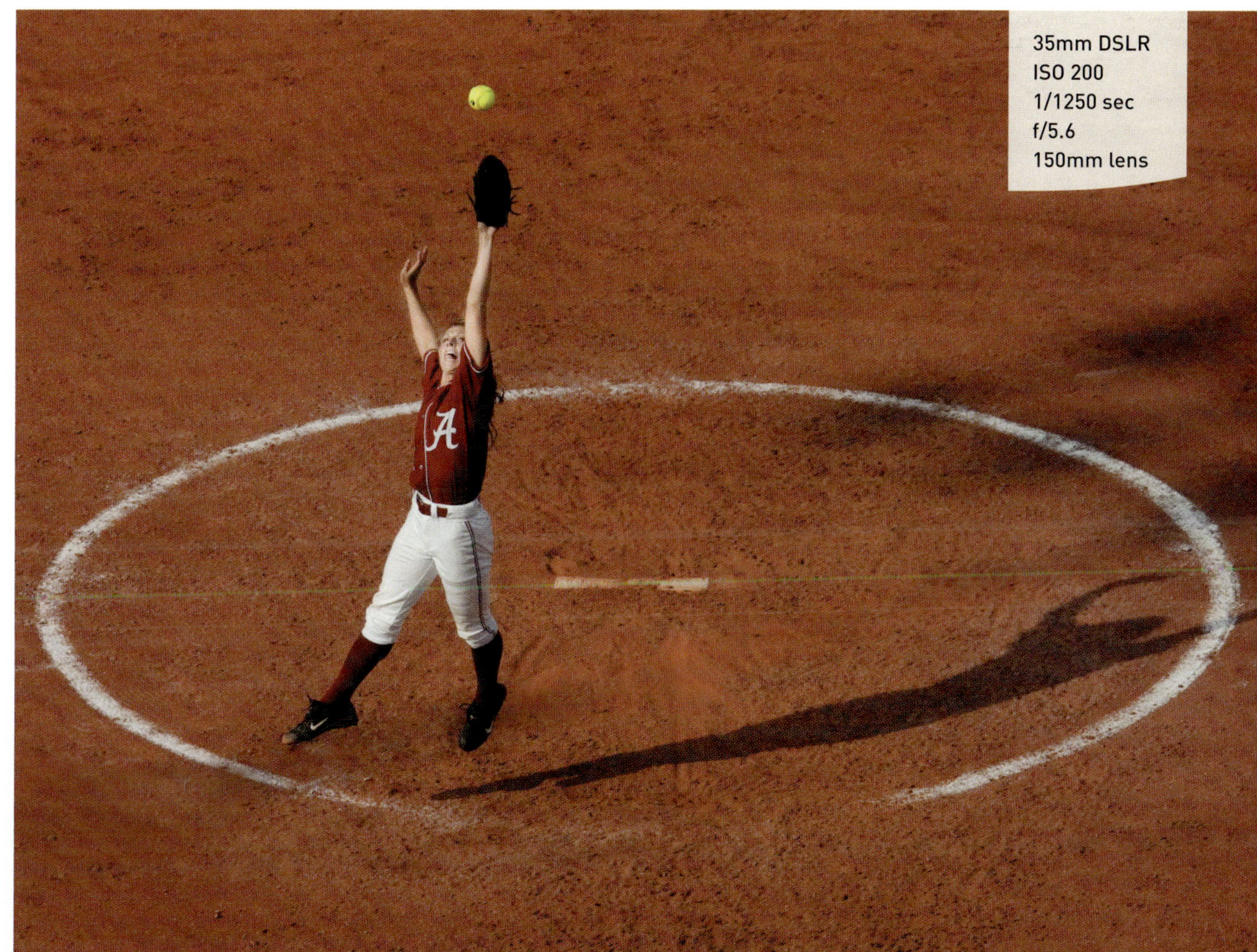

FIGURE 7.5
I shot this image elevated because of the way the light was falling. It was taken at about 7:30 at night, just as the sun was starting to set.

A DIFFERENT FEELING

Baseball enjoys a different tempo than other games. Because the action takes place in short spurts, you have time to change positions and plan your shots at a measured pace that's just not possible in many other sports.

Being above the field of play in an elevated position behind home plate allowed me to make the clean image in **Figure 7.5**.

Football, basketball, soccer, and boxing are all sports that involve constant action piled on more action, producing big play after big play. All of them move according to the constraints of a ticking clock. Baseball simply moves at a more leisurely pace, and it is almost always played in warm, dry weather and most often outdoors.

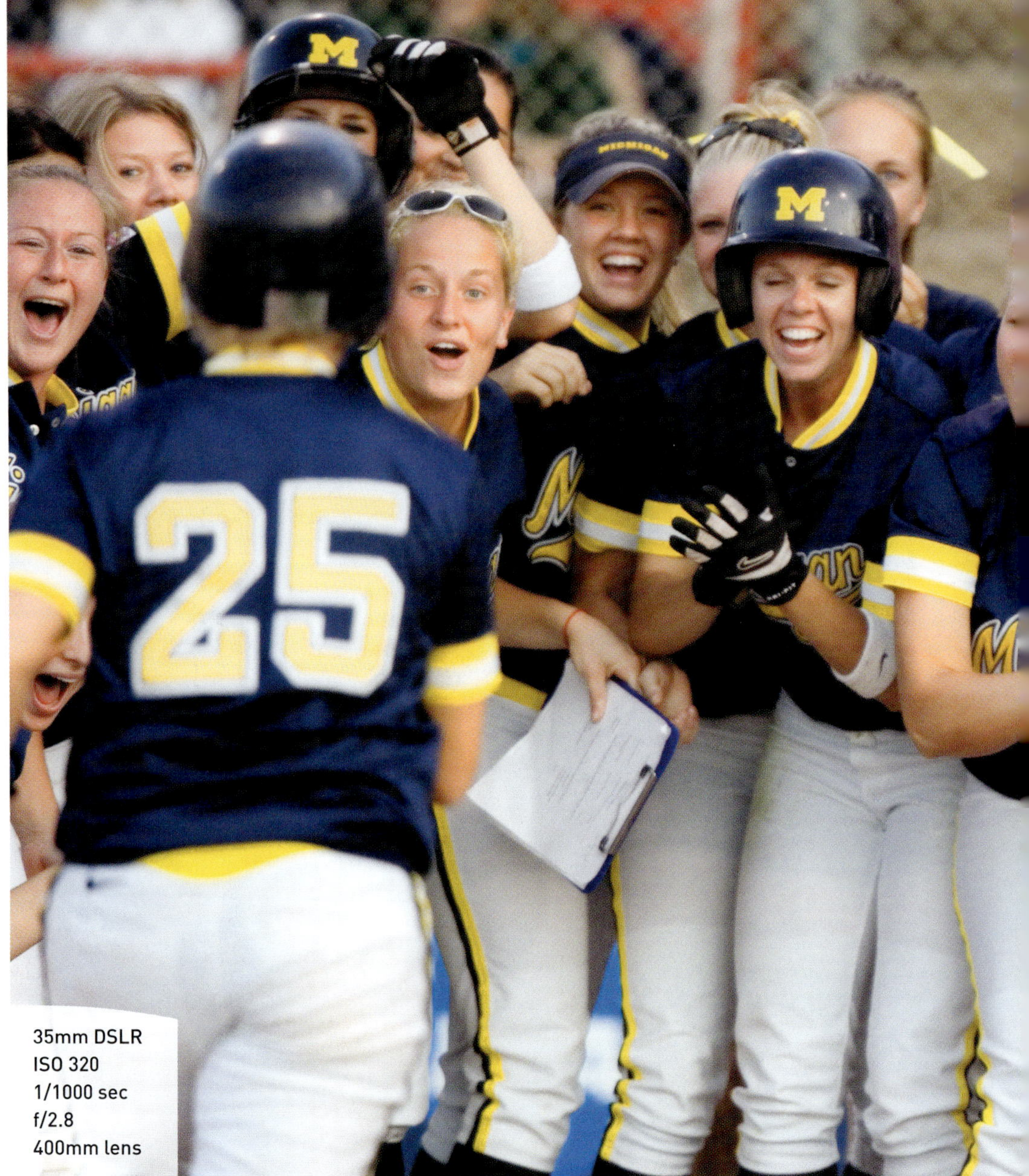

35mm DSLR
ISO 320
1/1000 sec
f/2.8
400mm lens

SHOOTING EMOTION

Baseball is a team sport, but often, relatively great distances separate the participants. They usually only come together during celebrations or fights. On both occasions, the bulk of the players will run out of the dugouts to the center of the field, making it easy to shoot the converging packs (**Figure 7.6**).

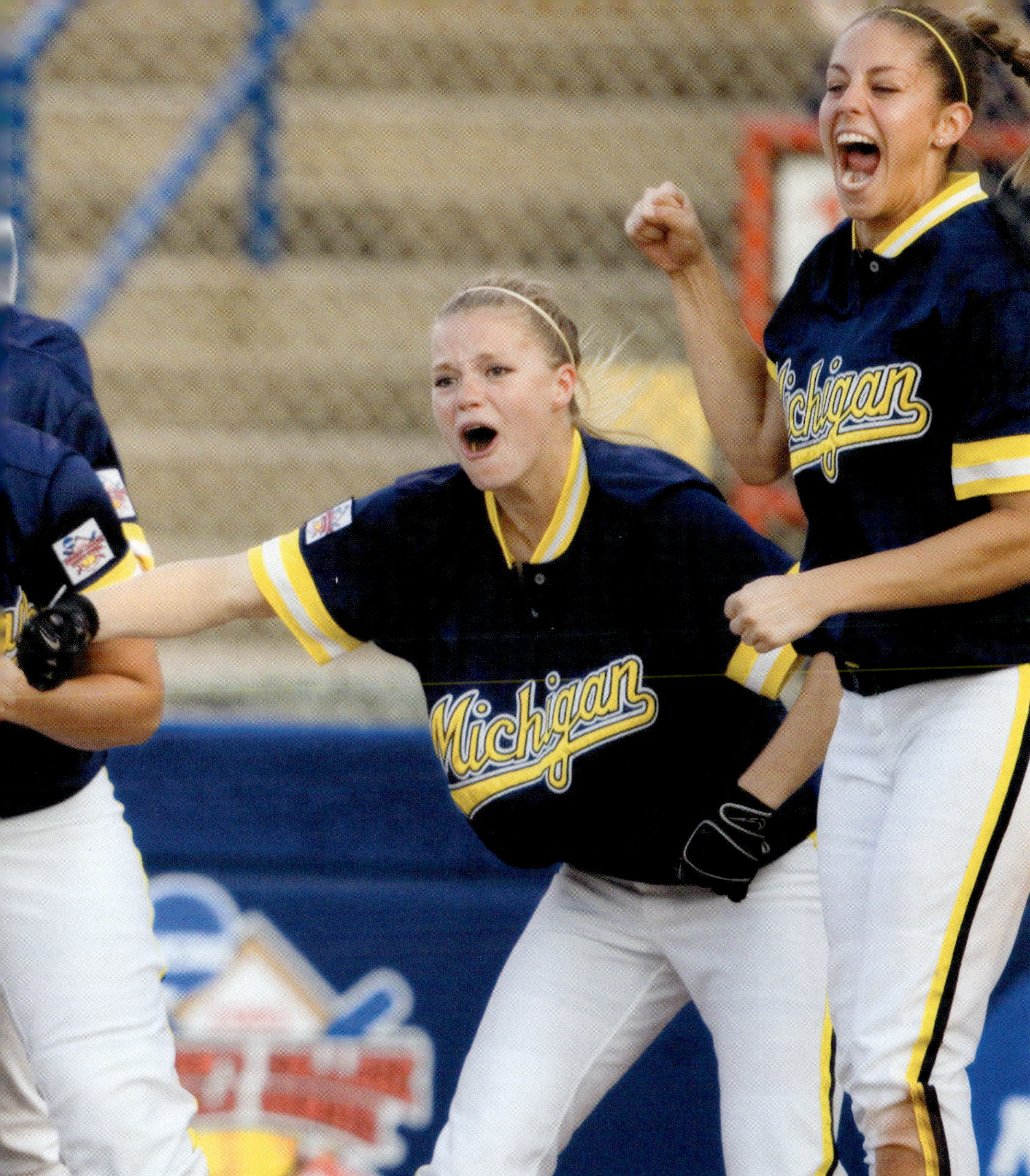

FIGURE 7.6
The Michigan Wolverines softball team celebrates a home run during the 2005 College World Series.

SPECIAL FEATURES OF BASEBALL

Baseball lends itself to great features: No masks obstruct players' faces—except the catchers'—and the game is played outside and frequently at the end of the day when you can shoot in the beautiful "golden hour" light. The golden hour refers to the hour before the sun sets when the light is rich, soft, and warm (or golden).

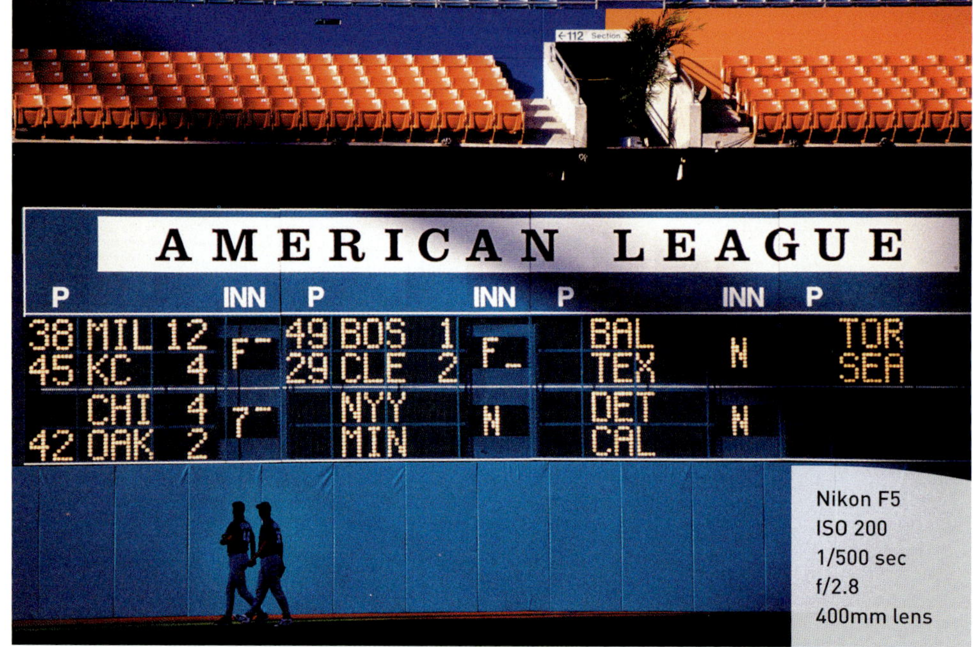

Nikon F5
ISO 200
1/500 sec
f/2.8
400mm lens

FIGURE 7.7
Using the "golden hour" light from sunset, I was able to use light and shadows to silhouette the outfielders against the blue of the wall.

The image in **Figure 7.7** has nothing and everything to do with baseball. It is not a peak action photo, yet it speaks to what baseball represents in America.

Also, because baseball is slower than other sports, you have time and freedom to look for pictures outside the field of play (**Figure 7.8**).

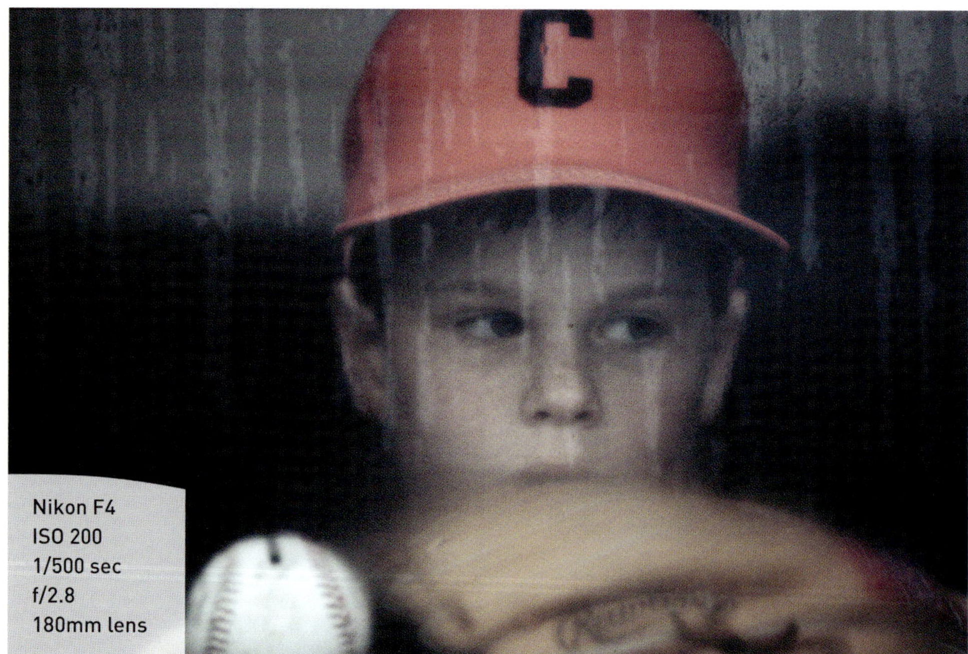

Nikon F4
ISO 200
1/500 sec
f/2.8
180mm lens

FIGURE 7.8
Sometimes a rain delay is the picture. This young player was waiting for a storm to blow over on the opening day of the little league season in Baxter Springs, Kansas, where Mickey Mantle played as a kid.

Chapter 7 Assignments

In the words of the Hall of Fame player, Yogi Berra, "Little league baseball is a very good thing. It keeps the parents off the street."

Go to a little league game and you'll find intense concentration, great emotion, and plenty of action. Although the field is smaller and the athletes are slower, the situations for getting great shots are every bit as much fun as any other level of the game.

Showing Emotion off the Field

Concentrate on making images involving emotion away from the field. Watch the fans especially. See how they react, relax, converse, and interact socially. Try to capture how this crowd is somehow different than the fans at other sports.

Working Behind the Backstop

Go behind home plate and use different lenses to shoot the action at different depth of field settings. Notice how the distance between the front of the lens and the backstop screen affects your ability to make clear, sharp photographs.

Timing the Ball for the Shot

Go behind home plate and set your camera to the highest shutter speed possible and maximum aperture. Focus on a spot part way between the pitcher and the hitter. Shoot the ball when it is in focus—which will not be easy. Keep trying until you can time it perfectly. Using a longer lens will help you accomplish this shot. When you can do it consistently, you'll be able to time the ball on the bat, the pitcher's throws, and plays in the infield easily.

Share your results with the book's Flickr group!
Join the group here: flickr.com/groups/sportsphotographyfromsnapshotstogreatshots.

8

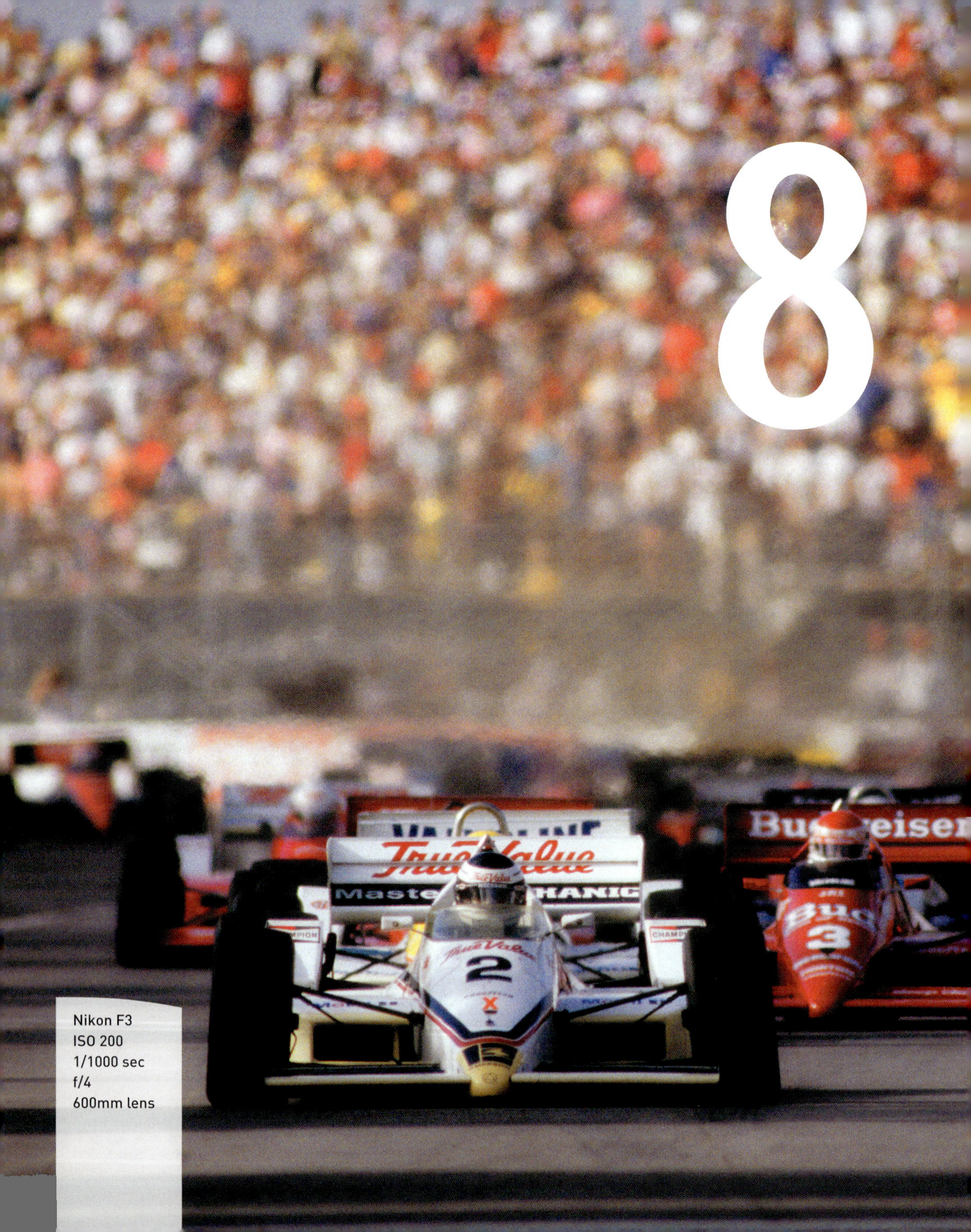

Nikon F3
ISO 200
1/1000 sec
f/4
600mm lens

Fast Tracks

HORSE RACING, TRACK AND FIELD, AND MOTOR SPORTS

Horse racing, track, and motor sports are some of the fastest sports in the world. The Kentucky Derby is often referred to as the Greatest Two Minutes in sports, the men's 100-meter dash determines the fastest man in the world, and the Daytona 500 is the "Super Bowl" of stock car racing.

In this chapter you'll learn my techniques for shooting each of these sports. Although there are certain similarities when it comes to coverage, each sport is vastly different.

Race cars blast down the front straightaway during an Indy Car race in Miami, Florida.

PORING OVER THE PICTURE

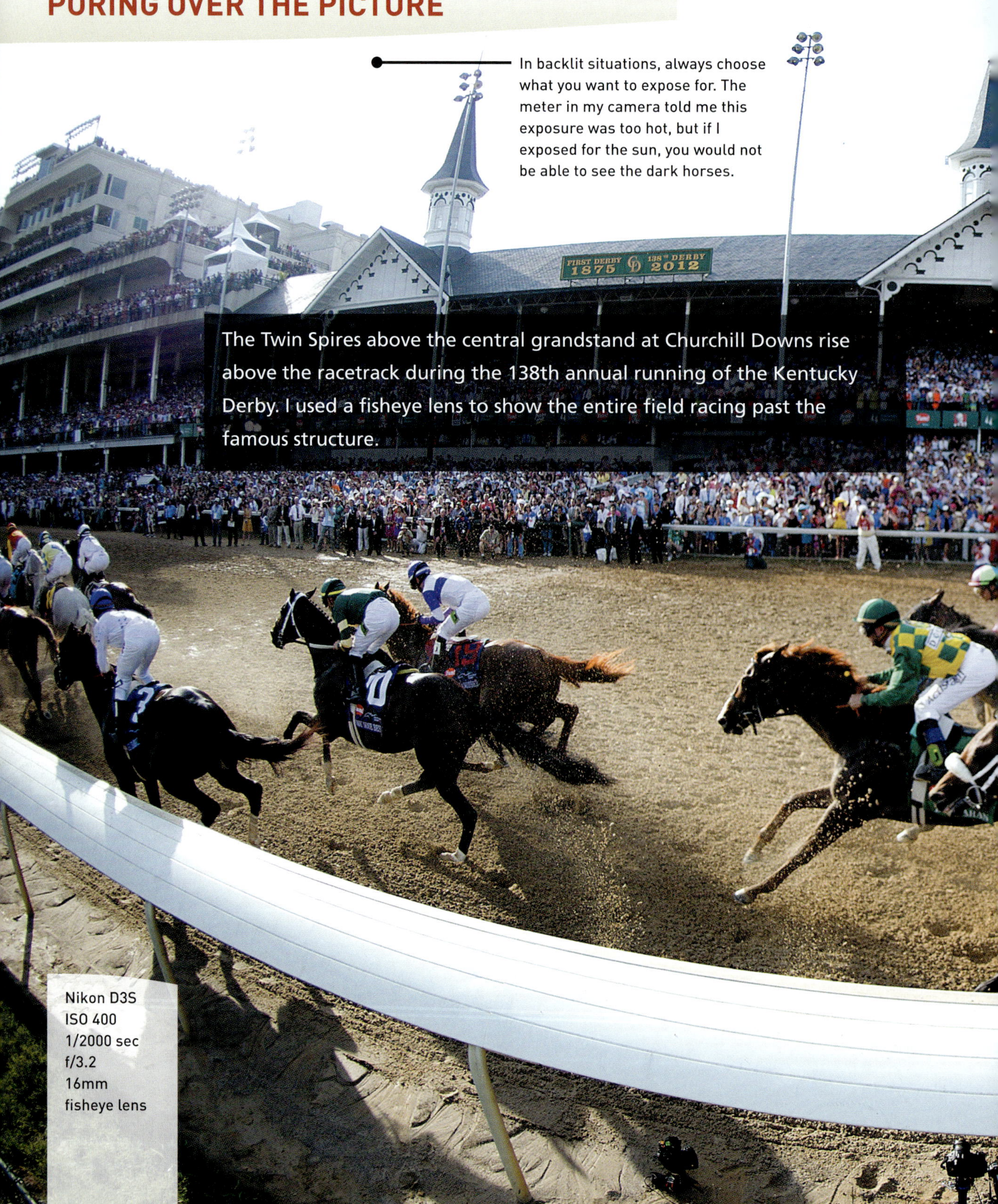

In backlit situations, always choose what you want to expose for. The meter in my camera told me this exposure was too hot, but if I exposed for the sun, you would not be able to see the dark horses.

The Twin Spires above the central grandstand at Churchill Downs rise above the racetrack during the 138th annual running of the Kentucky Derby. I used a fisheye lens to show the entire field racing past the famous structure.

Nikon D3S
ISO 400
1/2000 sec
f/3.2
16mm
fisheye lens

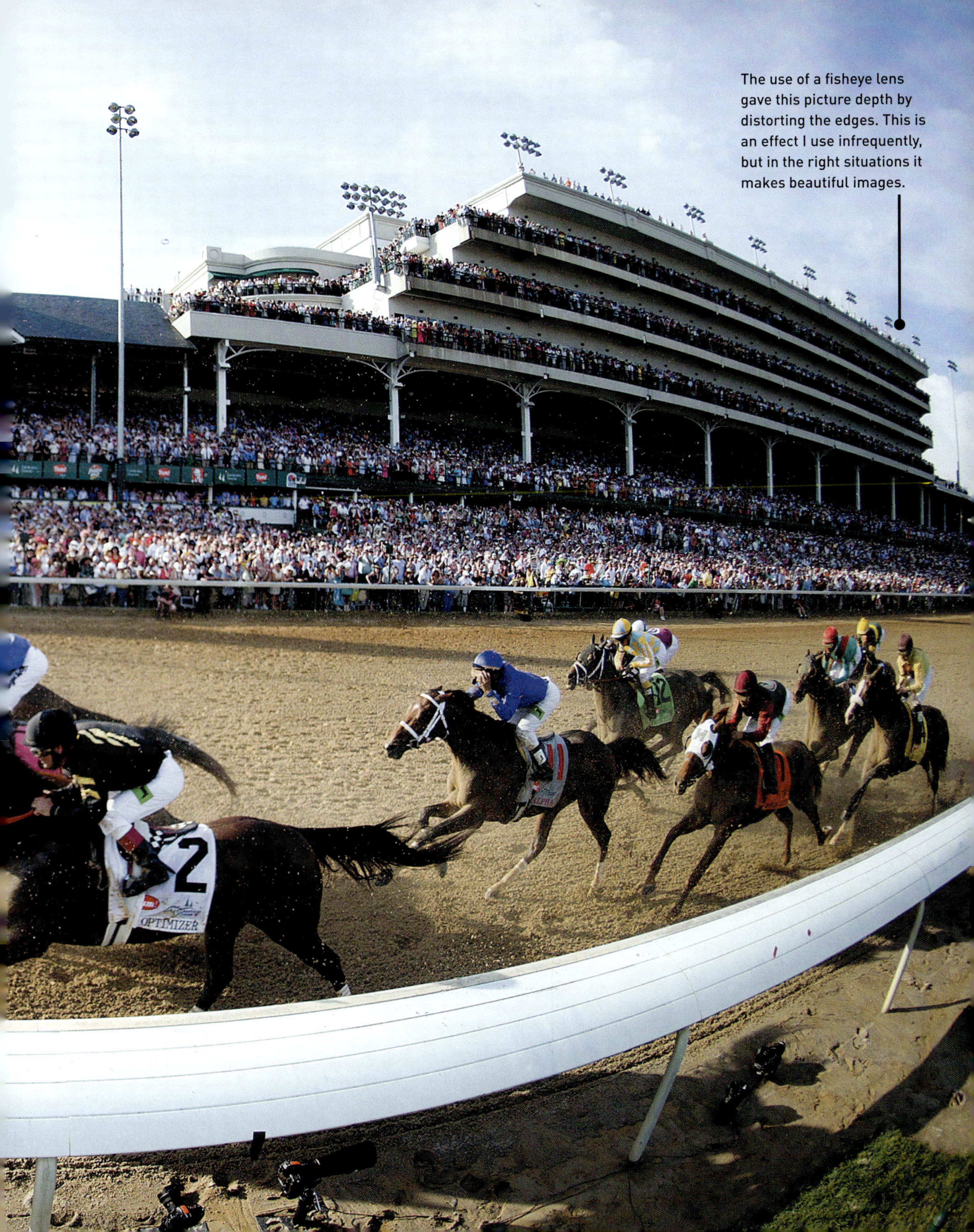

The use of a fisheye lens gave this picture depth by distorting the edges. This is an effect I use infrequently, but in the right situations it makes beautiful images.

HORSE RACING: HOW TO GET THE BEST SHOTS

Horse racing is one of my favorite sports to cover. It is also one of the most difficult. For a race like the Kentucky Derby, I'll put as many as 60 remote cameras around the track. I'll briefly discuss remote cameras and show some examples, but this chapter focuses mostly on how to cover the race with just the cameras in your hand.

WHERE TO POSITION YOURSELF

There are several excellent locations to shoot from when you're covering horse racing, depending on what you want to capture and what the track has to offer. My preferred places are head-on past the finish line, outside the track past the finish line, inside the rail past the finish line, overhead or from an elevated position past the finish line, the first and fourth turns, and at the finish line for a pan (panning was discussed in Chapter 2).

HEAD-ON POSITION

I almost always stand in the head-on position to shoot the finish of the race. For me, it's the best place to capture the peak action as the horses and jockeys sprint for the finish (**Figure 8.1**). If a jockey celebrates his or her victory, this is the best place to capture it. The only caveat is that you will invariably need a very long lens (400mm

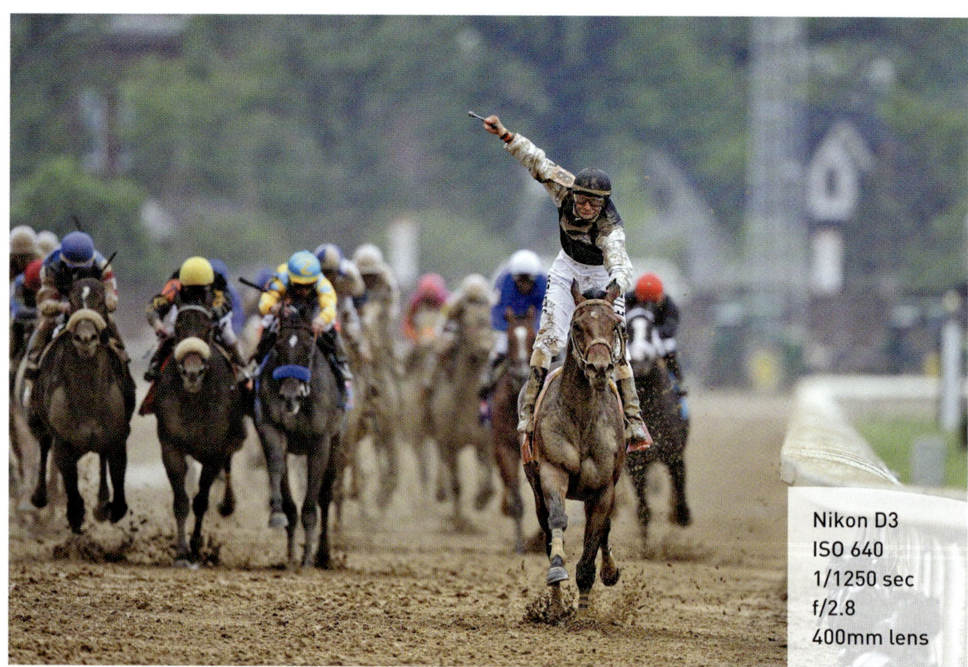

Nikon D3
ISO 640
1/1250 sec
f/2.8
400mm lens

FIGURE 8.1
Calvin Borel celebrates winning the 2009 Kentucky Derby with Mine That Bird. The race was a huge upset: Mine That Bird went into the race with 50-to-1 odds. This picture was the cover of *Sports Illustrated* that week.

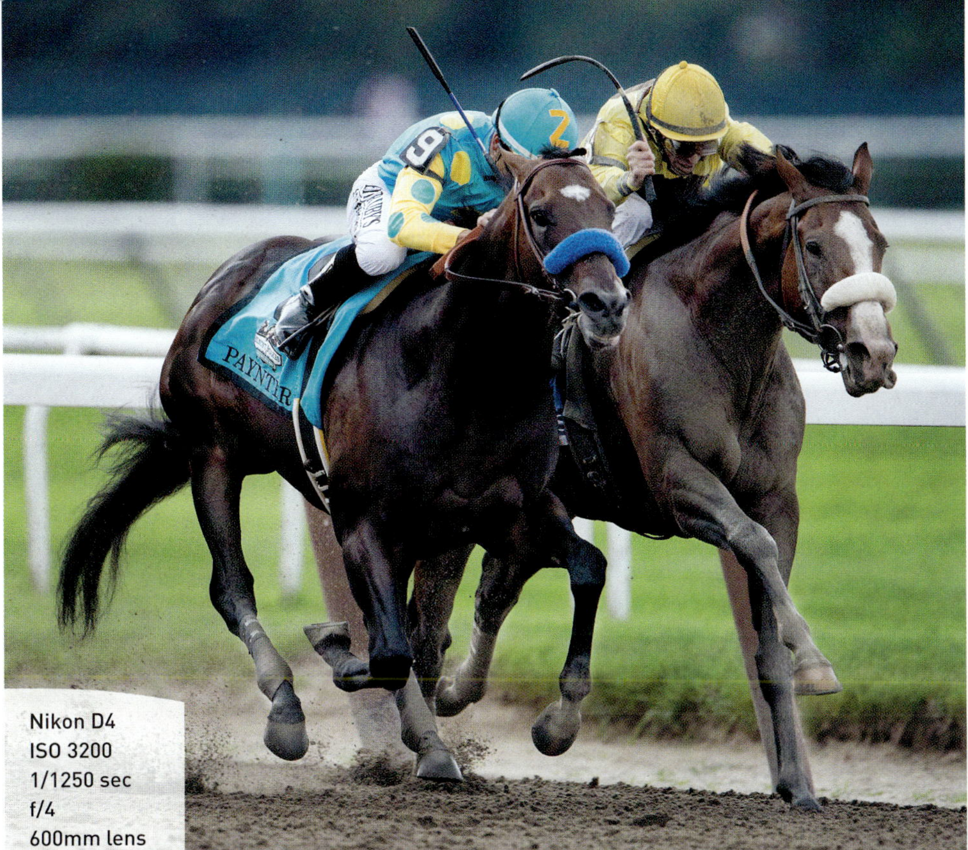

Nikon D4
ISO 3200
1/1250 sec
f/4
600mm lens

FIGURE 8.2
Union Rags outruns Paynter to win the 2012 Belmont Stakes in Elmont, New York.

to 600mm), because the head-on position is always located a significant distance from the finish line for safety reasons.

Notice the cameras underneath the rail on the right side of the frame in Figure 8.1. Those are remote cameras that I'll discuss later in the chapter.

OUTSIDE THE TRACK

If you don't have a super long telephoto, outside the track is a good place to stand. It allows you to get significantly closer to the finish line action. Your view from this angle will be to the right side of the horse and jockey as they cross the finish. This can also be a good place to capture reaction after the finish because if a jockey looks up, he usually looks toward the grandstands, which is where you will be standing (**Figure 8.2**).

TIP

Listen to the track announcer. The horses will be in your view only for a short time. It will help to know what's happening as they approach.

Digital SLR
ISO 800
1/1250 sec
f/8
96mm lens

FIGURE 8.3
Kent Desormeaux celebrates winning the 2008 Kentucky Derby with Big Brown.

INSIDE THE RAIL

Inside the rail is also a good place to stand if you don't have a super long telephoto. This location allows you to move closer than the head-on position. When I shoot from here, I like to include the rail, the grandstand, or both for graphically pleasing reasons. You can make a nice tight shot of the winner as he or she crosses the finish line, but I like to use this spot to make a looser photo that includes some scene. By shooting vertical in **Figure 8.3**, I was able to include the famous twin spires in the background, making this picture more than just a celebration shot. I also closed the aperture significantly to make sure the spires and the horse were in focus.

OVERHEAD POSITION

Overheads can be beautiful shots depending on the track. The elevated position is my favorite spot at Pimlico Racetrack in Baltimore, Maryland, home of the Preakness Stakes. At Pimlico you can get on top of the grandstand right across from the finish. There is always a bed of flowers at the Preakness Stakes that spells out P-I-M-L-I-C-O, which makes a really striking shot (**Figure 8.4**).

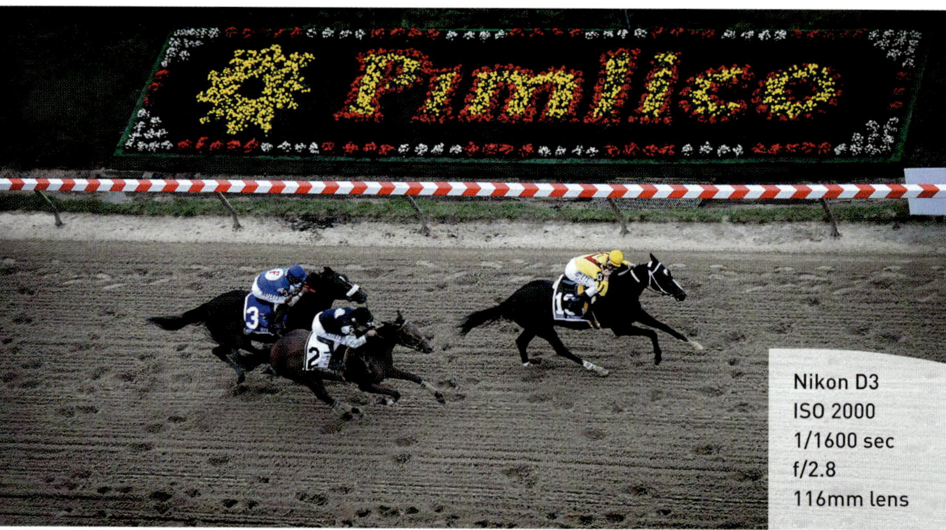

Nikon D3
ISO 2000
1/1600 sec
f/2.8
116mm lens

FIGURE 8.4
Calvin Borel points at the grandstands as he wins the Preakness Stakes with the filly Rachel Alexandra. After winning the Kentucky Derby with Mine That Bird, he abandoned hopes of a Triple Crown by switching horses.

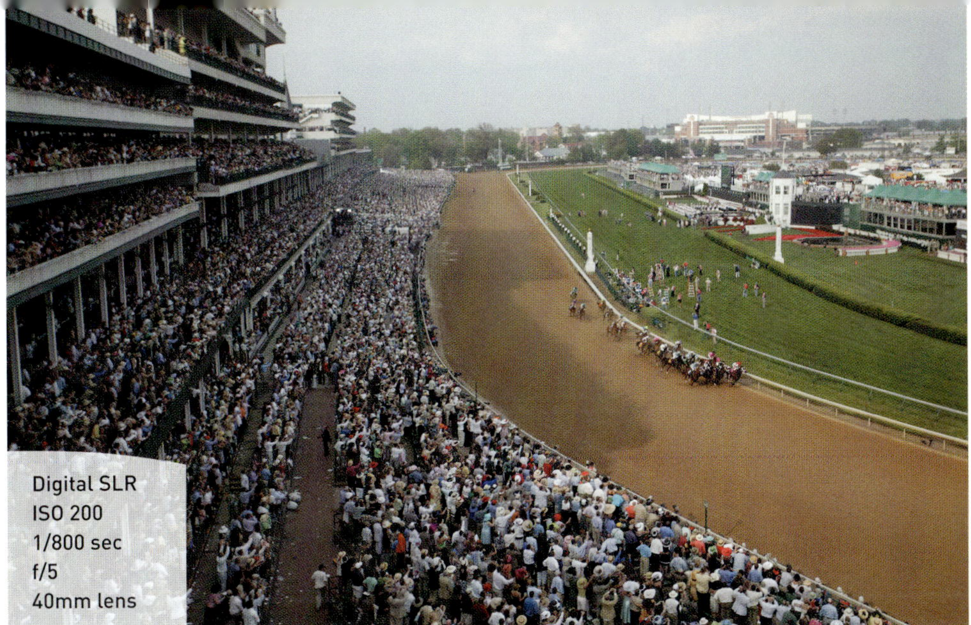

FIGURE 8.5
This shot was taken from overhead facing the finish line as the horses begin their loop of the track in the 2007 Kentucky Derby.

I also like the overhead position at Churchill Downs for the Kentucky Derby. The grandstands are always full for the Kentucky Oaks and the Kentucky Derby, so I like to make a wide shot of the grandstands with the horses and the track (**Figure 8.5** and **Figure 8.6**). It is especially nice on a sunny day.

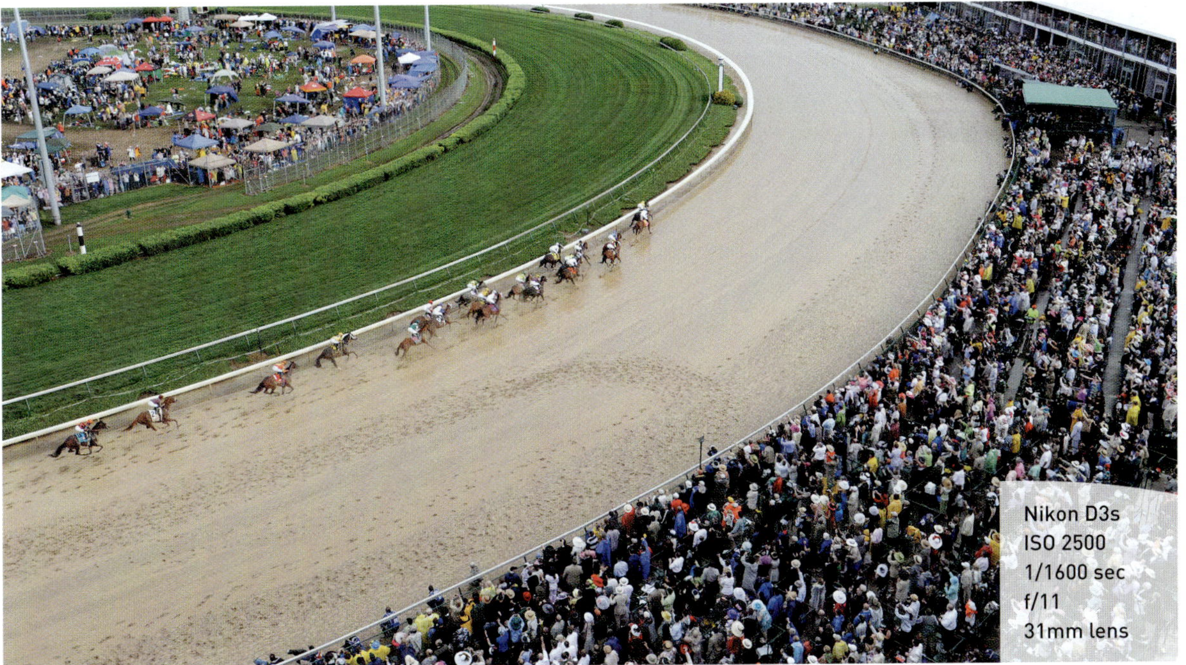

FIGURE 8.6
This shot was taken from overhead of the first turn during the 2010 Kentucky Derby.

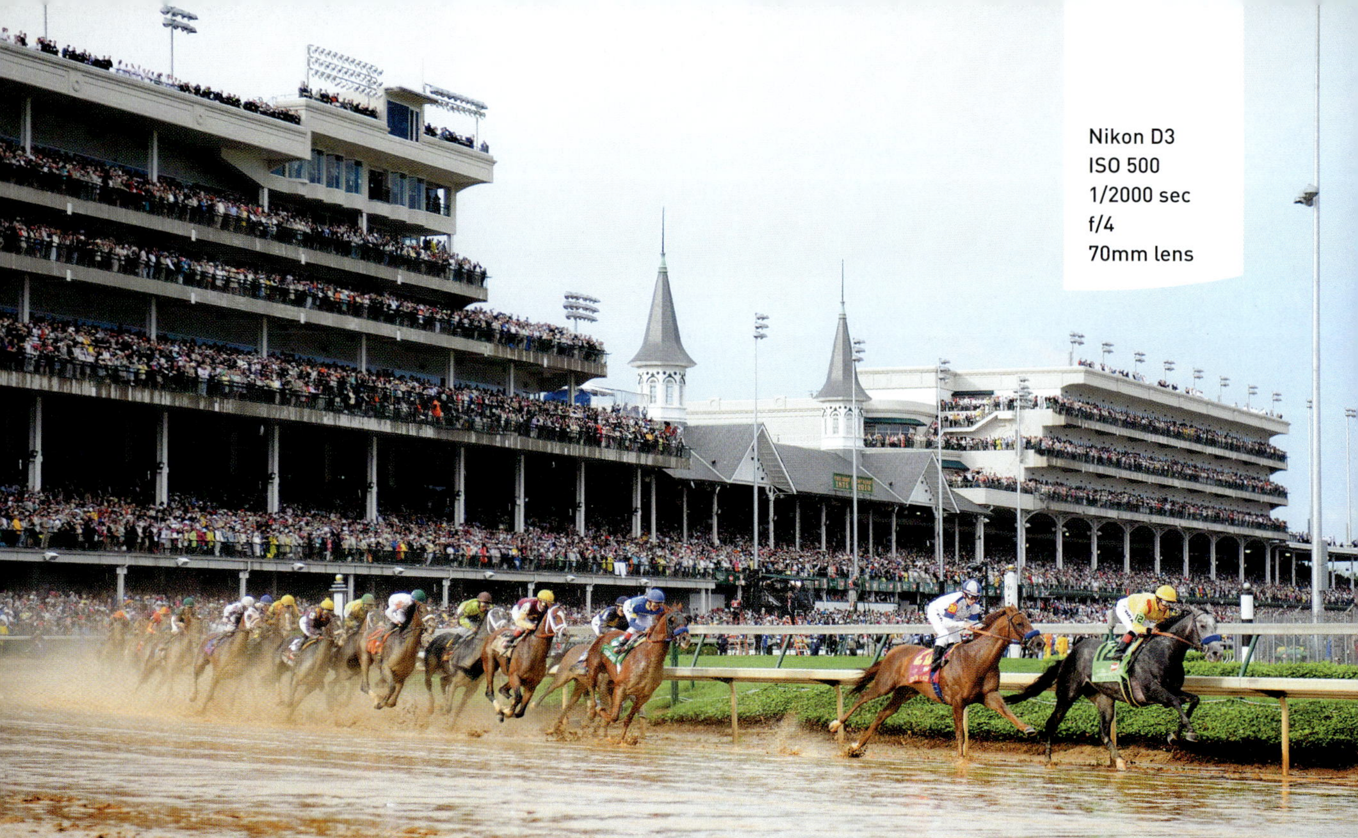

Nikon D3
ISO 500
1/2000 sec
f/4
70mm lens

FIGURE 8.7
The first turn of the 2010 Kentucky Derby (with a medium lens).

SHOOTING FROM THE TURNS

Shooting from the turns always results in a beautiful picture. Depending on which way the track faces and what time of day you are shooting, one of the turns will almost always give you beautiful light.

At the Kentucky Derby, one of my preferred shooting spots is at the first turn using a medium lens (**Figure 8.7**). This location allows you to shoot with a medium lens to include the grandstand or a telephoto to get a nice shot of the pack as it comes around the bend (**Figure 8.8**).

The fourth turn is also a very nice spot. At the Preakness Stakes, the horses and jockeys turn west around the fourth turn and into the late afternoon sun, which can make for truly stunning photographs.

TIP

Practice keeping the camera absolutely stable and moving constantly while panning.

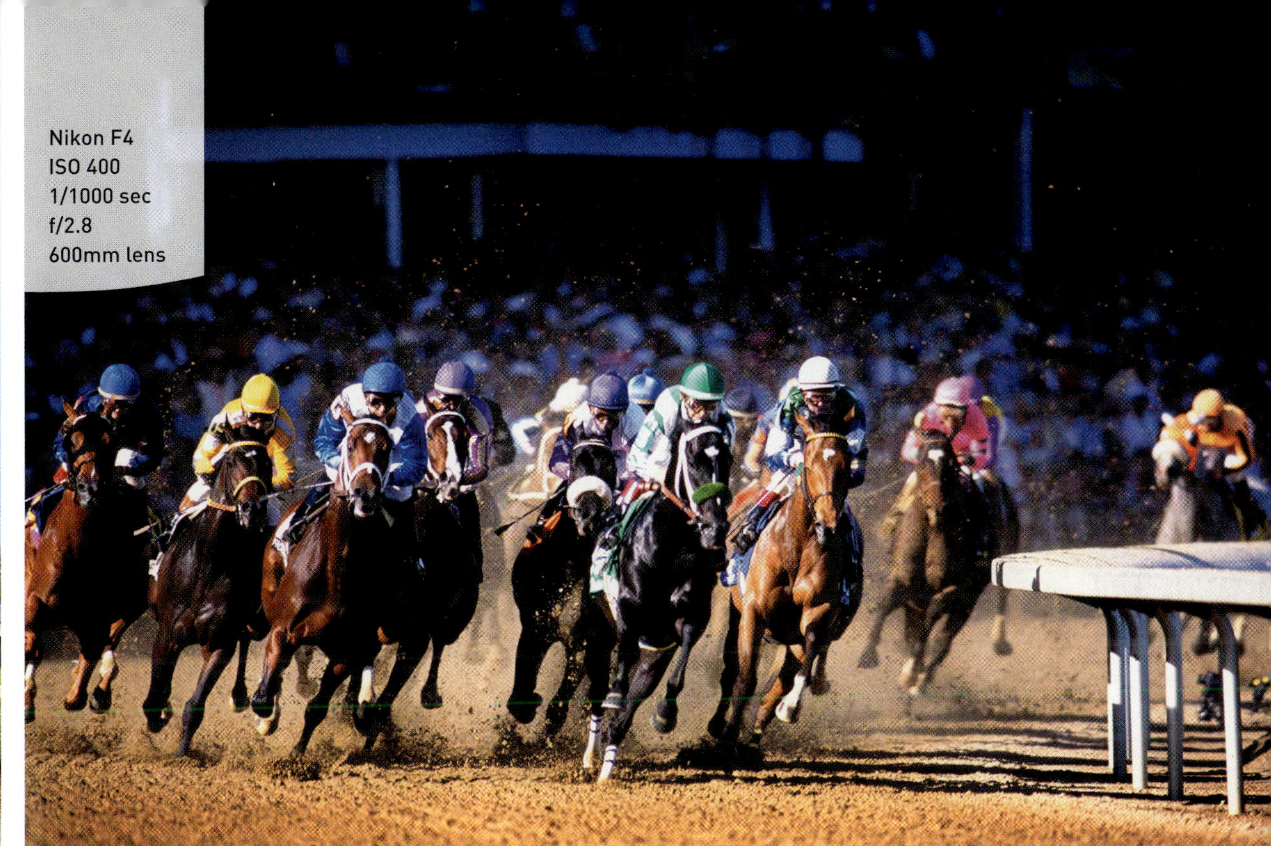

FIGURE 8.8 The first turn of the Kentucky Derby (with a telephoto lens).

Also, many jockeys make their move in the fourth turn, so it is a great place to shoot the winning horse as he makes his way into the lead. However, if you are covering a race alone and don't have any remote cameras, this can be a gamble, because you may choose the wrong horse as the winner. If your goal is only to make a beautiful picture, then this is a great spot.

TIP

All of the races will finish at approximately the same speed, just not the same position or with the same light. Knowing this will give you a chance to try various shutter speed and aperture combinations during the day so that when the big race happens—and it will almost always happen at the end of the day—you will be ready with the correct shutter speed and aperture combination.

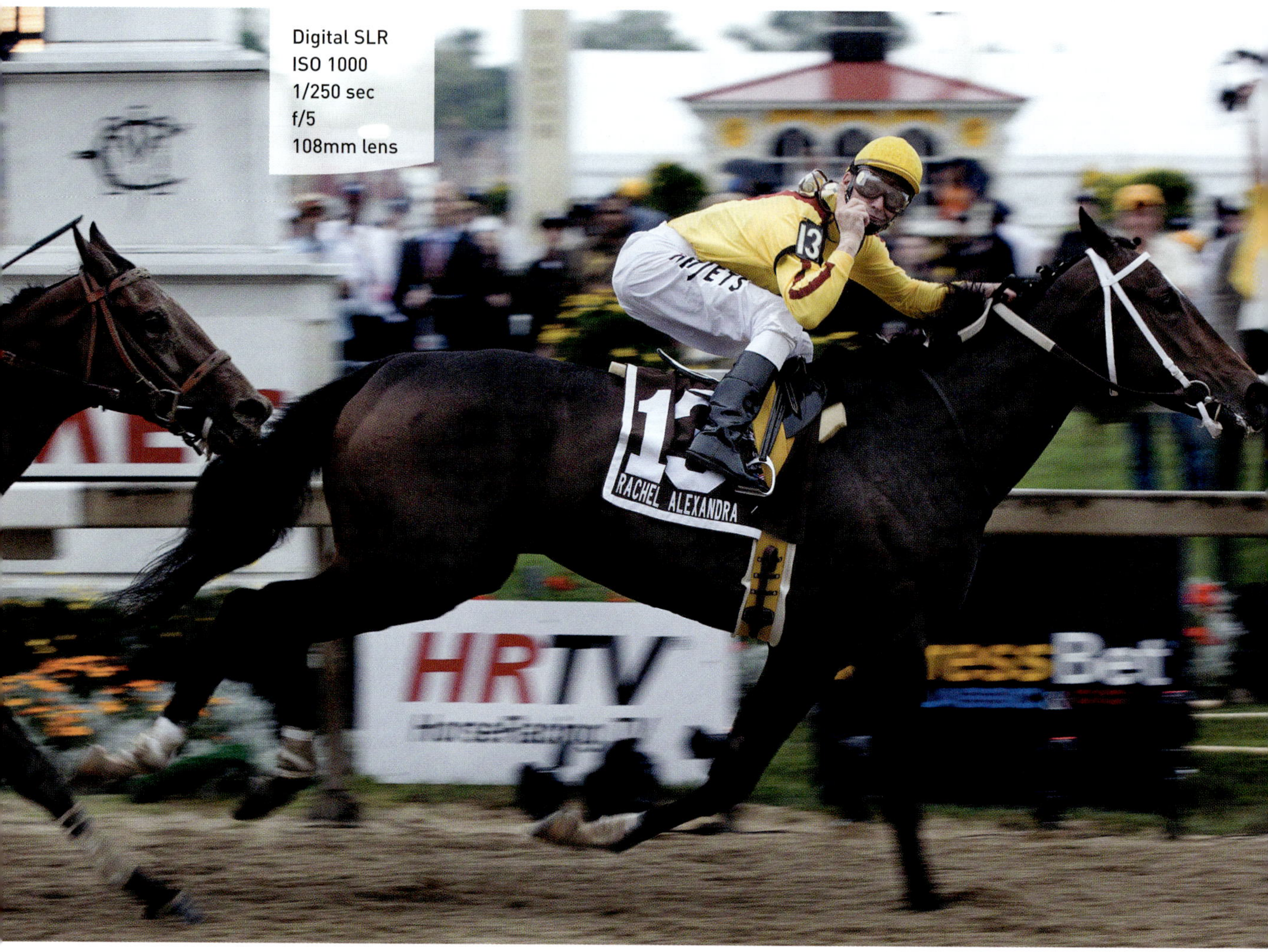

Digital SLR
ISO 1000
1/250 sec
f/5
108mm lens

FIGURE 8.9
Calvin Borel wins the 2009 Preakness Stakes with Rachel Alexandra. Using the pan technique, I was able to blur the unattractive background and focus only on Calvin and the horse.

FINISH LINE PAN

Horse racing is a sport that lends itself nicely to a pan. This is a great technique to try if you don't have a long or fast lens. I usually shoot a pan with either a 70–200mm f/2.8 or a 28–300mm f/3.5–5.6. I keep the focal length between 100 and 200mm, bump the shutter down to somewhere around 1/200 of a second, and decrease my aperture to increase my depth of field (**Figure 8.9**). I prefocus the lens on the finish line before the horses cross so that I am ready to pan when they approach the finish.

REMOTE CAMERAS

I use a lot of remote cameras when I'm covering horse racing. I always try to put cameras in places I can't be. Because I usually shoot from the head-on position, I use remote cameras to capture the other positions I listed (except for the pan; that has to be done manually). Using remote cameras allows me to be in multiple places at once, which increases my coverage significantly.

The best place to use remotes is under the rail (**Figure 8.10**). In horse racing an inner rail runs all the way around the track. This is a very dangerous place because many jockeys use the rail to squeeze in front of the other competitors. In the process, they frequently run up against the rail and sometimes get thrown from the horse while making their move. For this reason, tracks almost never let photographers stand flush against the rail, but they do allow remote cameras to be placed there instead.

There are several ways to fire remote cameras. I generally use PocketWizards with custom channels. You can also fire them by creating a circuit with a household power cord or through your computer with Ethernet cables.

FIGURE 8.10
This is an under-the-rail remote shot from the 2008 Kentucky Derby. This angle gives you a look at the race that you cannot capture with a handheld camera.

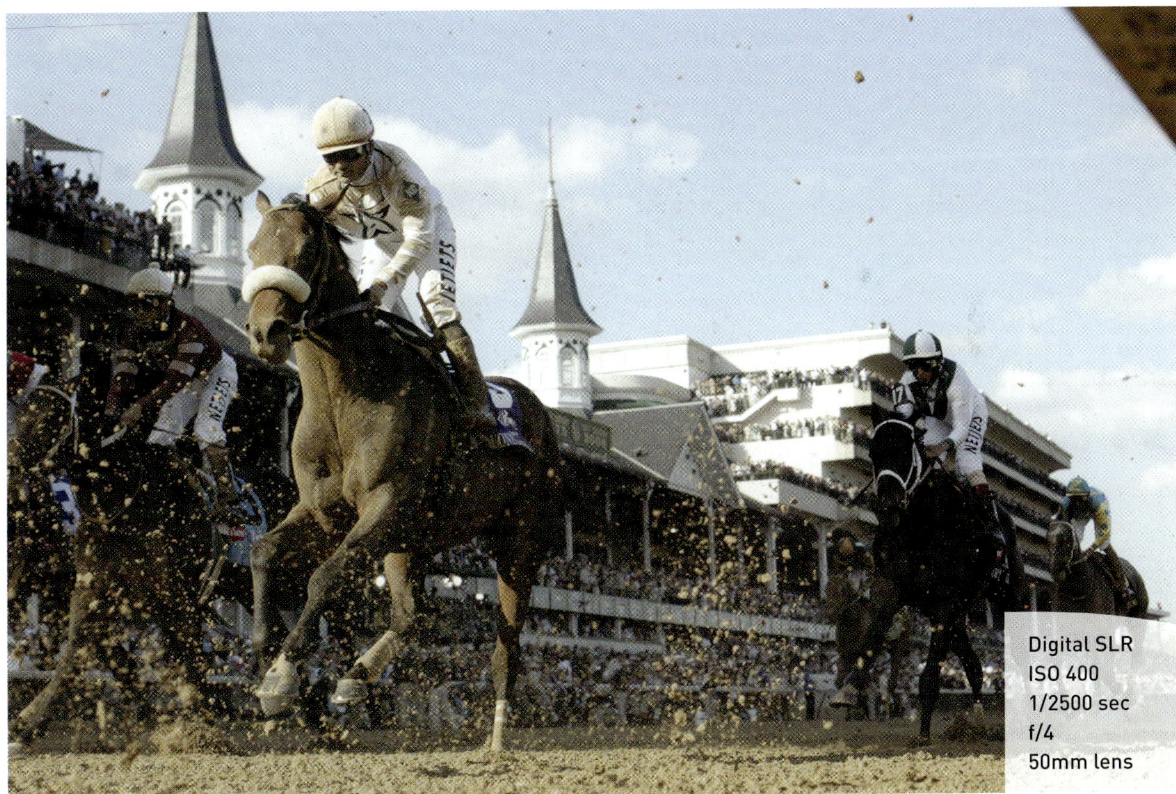

Digital SLR
ISO 400
1/2500 sec
f/4
50mm lens

TRACK AND FIELD: HOW TO GET THE BEST SHOTS

Track and field is probably the sport with the greatest variety of actions. There is always something happening at a track and field event, and men and women are also given equal prominence.

If your lens and DSLR body selection is limited, track and field events are ideal to cover because you can get close to the action for many of the events.

Because track events are so different from field events, I'll walk you through shooting at each event, starting with the track events and moving on to field events.

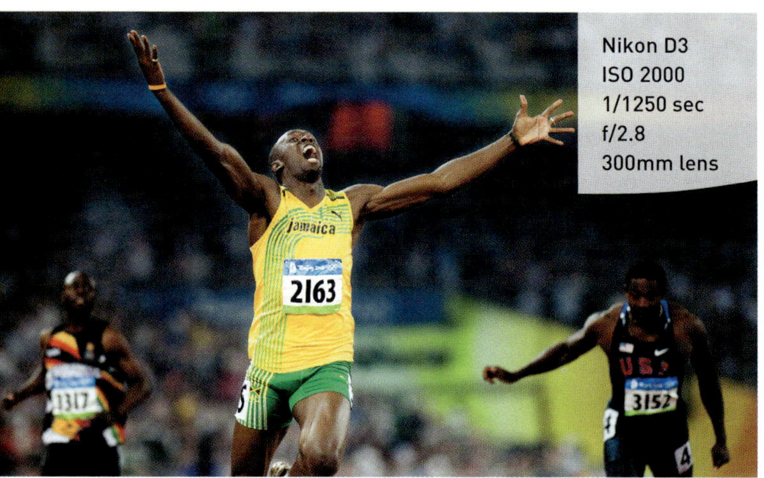

FIGURE 8.11
Usain Bolt celebrates after breaking the world record in the men's 100-meter dash during the 2008 Olympic Games in Beijing.

100M DASH

The 100-meter dash is always the most anticipated event in a track and field competition. Nothing gets a crowd excited like raw speed.

You have several position options when you're covering the 100-meter dash. My favorite position is the head-on position, located just off the track directly in front of the finish line (**Figure 8.11**). This position in track and field is not nearly as far from the finish as it is in horse racing. I generally shoot from this position with either a 300mm f/2.8 lens or a 400mm f/2.8 lens.

TIP

Shooting head-on allows you to use a slightly slower shutter speed while still stopping the action cleanly.

I also like to shoot the 100-meter finals from an elevated position behind and above the head-on position. This gives you a good look at the field as a whole and allows you to capture interesting shapes and patterns. Another popular position is at the finish line from the infield. From this position you are either at or right behind the finish from the infield looking back at the grandstands. This position is perfect for using a medium or wide-angle lens. It is also a nice spot to try a pan of the finish.

You can also shoot a pan from outside the track at the finish line. This is the best place for a pan, because there is nothing in the background that adds to the photo.

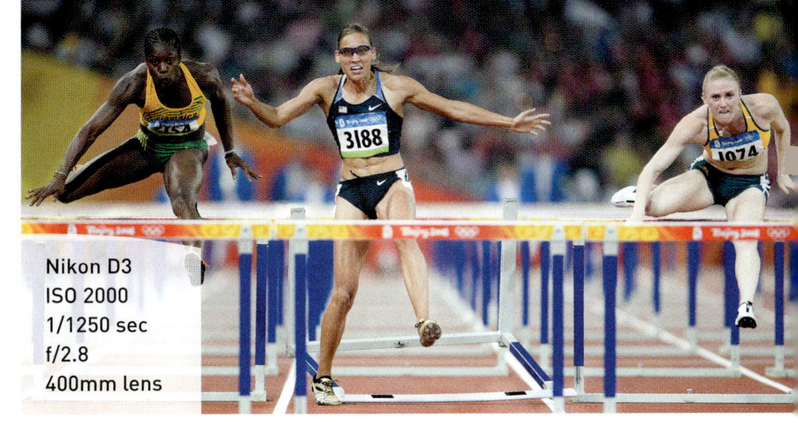

FIGURE 8.12 Lolo Jones reacts as she tries to keep from falling in the final of the women's 100-meter hurdles during the 2008 Olympics in Beijing. She was favored to win but stumbled over the last two hurdles and finished fourth.

110M AND 100M HURDLES

I love hurdle races because there is always the possibility for spectacular action. They sometimes feel faster—even though they aren't—than the 100-meter flat races. I usually shoot these races from the head-on position, and from that vantage point all I can see of the runners for the first half of the race is their feet between hurdles until suddenly they are in front of me and at the finish (**Figure 8.12**).

I also like to shoot these races from an elevated head-on position, because the hurdles provide very interesting patterns. Runners frequently fall over the hurdles, and above is the best place to capture that action and reaction (**Figure 8.13**).

> **TIP**
>
> Watch the runners' feet when they cross the hurdles. That will help you figure out who is winning before they reach the last hurdle.

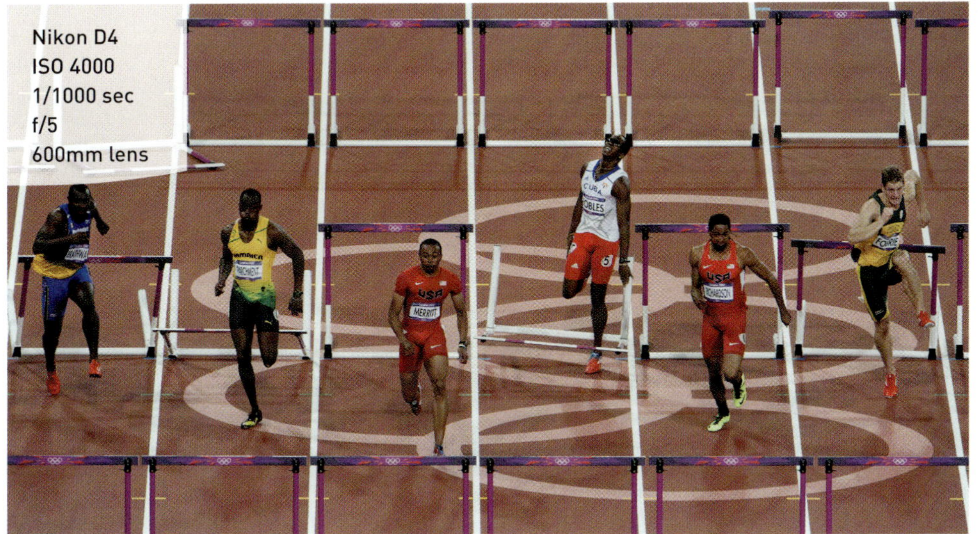

FIGURE 8.13 Dayron Robles pulls up halfway through the men's 110-meter hurdle final during the 2012 Olympic Games in London. He was the Olympic Champion in 2008 but pulled a hamstring and had to walk to the finish in 2012.

200M DASH

The shooting positions for the 200-meter dash are the same as the 100-meter dash with one exception: There is a turn in the 200-meter race. The turn in the 200-meter dash is a great place to shoot because it gives you a look at the start of the race. However, I prefer to shoot, the turn from the grandstands to use the pattern of the lane lines to make a more graphic image.

400M DASH AND HURDLES

My favorite place to shoot the 400-meter dash and hurdles is from the grandstands at the fourth turn. It makes a really nice graphic of the track and, depending on the weather and the time of day, the runners have long shadows running next to them (**Figure 8.14**).

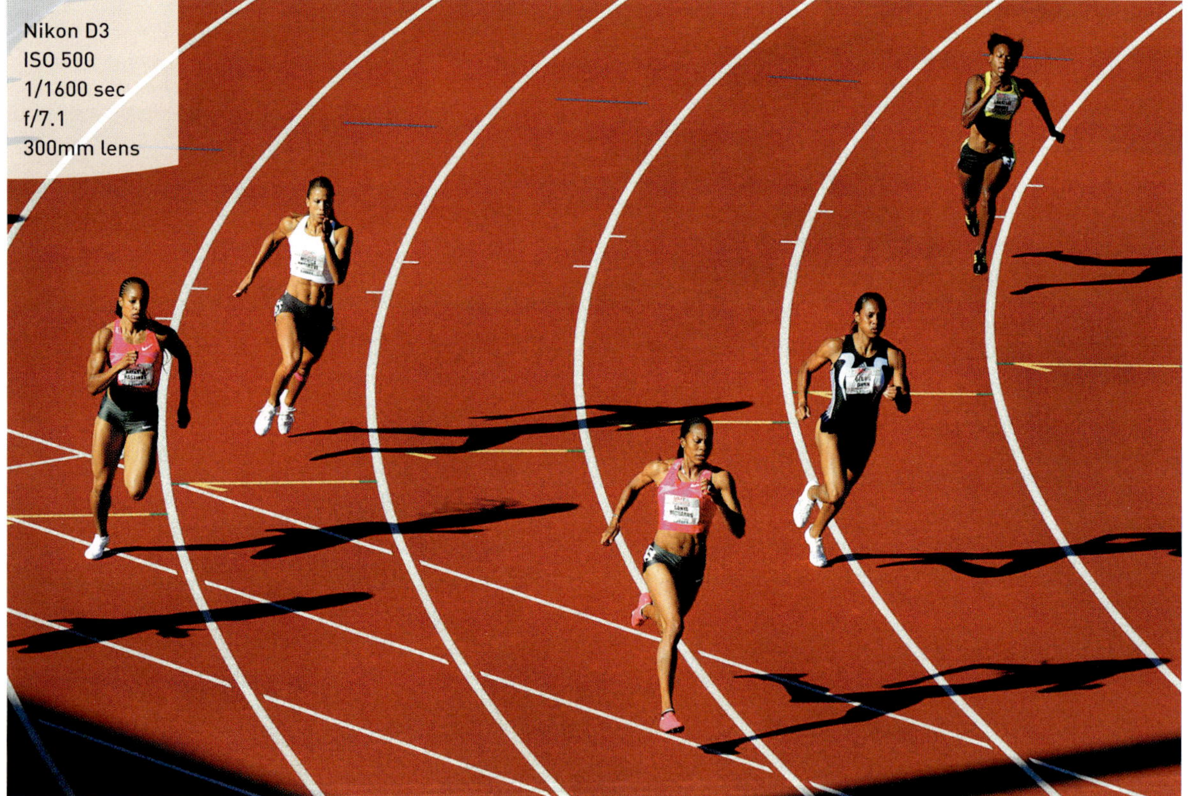
Nikon D3
ISO 500
1/1600 sec
f/7.1
300mm lens

FIGURE 8.14
Sonya Richards makes her way around the final turn of the women's 400-meter semifinal during the 2009 USATF Championships.

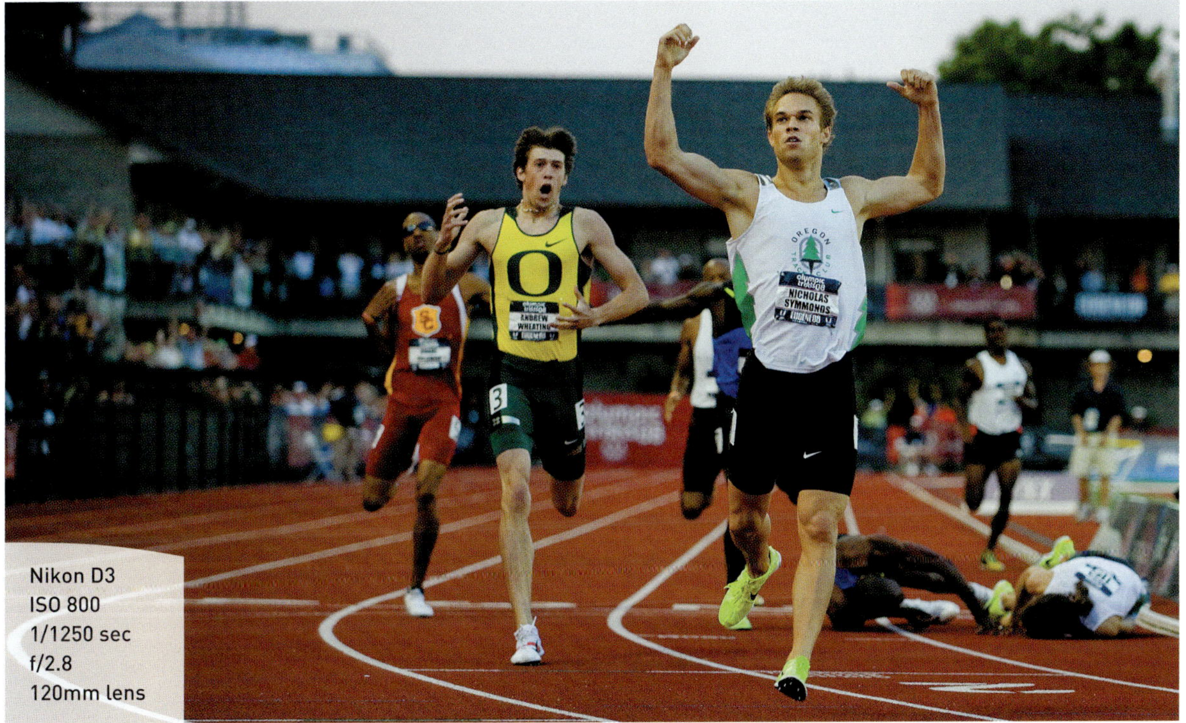

FIGURE 8.15
Nick Symmonds wins the men's 800-meter final during the 2008 USATF Olympic Trials in Eugene, Oregon.

800M EVENT

The 800-meter event can be characterized as a cross between a sprint and a distance race. This race is all about pace and timing. I like to shoot the 800-meter event from either the head-on position or from the fourth turn.

One of my prized track and field pictures was taken at the men's 800-meter final during the 2008 USATF Olympic Trials. Nick Symmonds flexed as he crossed the finish line, followed by a stunned Andrew Wheating, and third place was decided by a dive (**Figure 8.15**).

1500M RACE

The 1500-meter race is similar to the 800-meter race in that it's all about timing. Generally, the 1500-meter event is very paced until the last 100 meters. For that reason, I like to shoot from the head-on position.

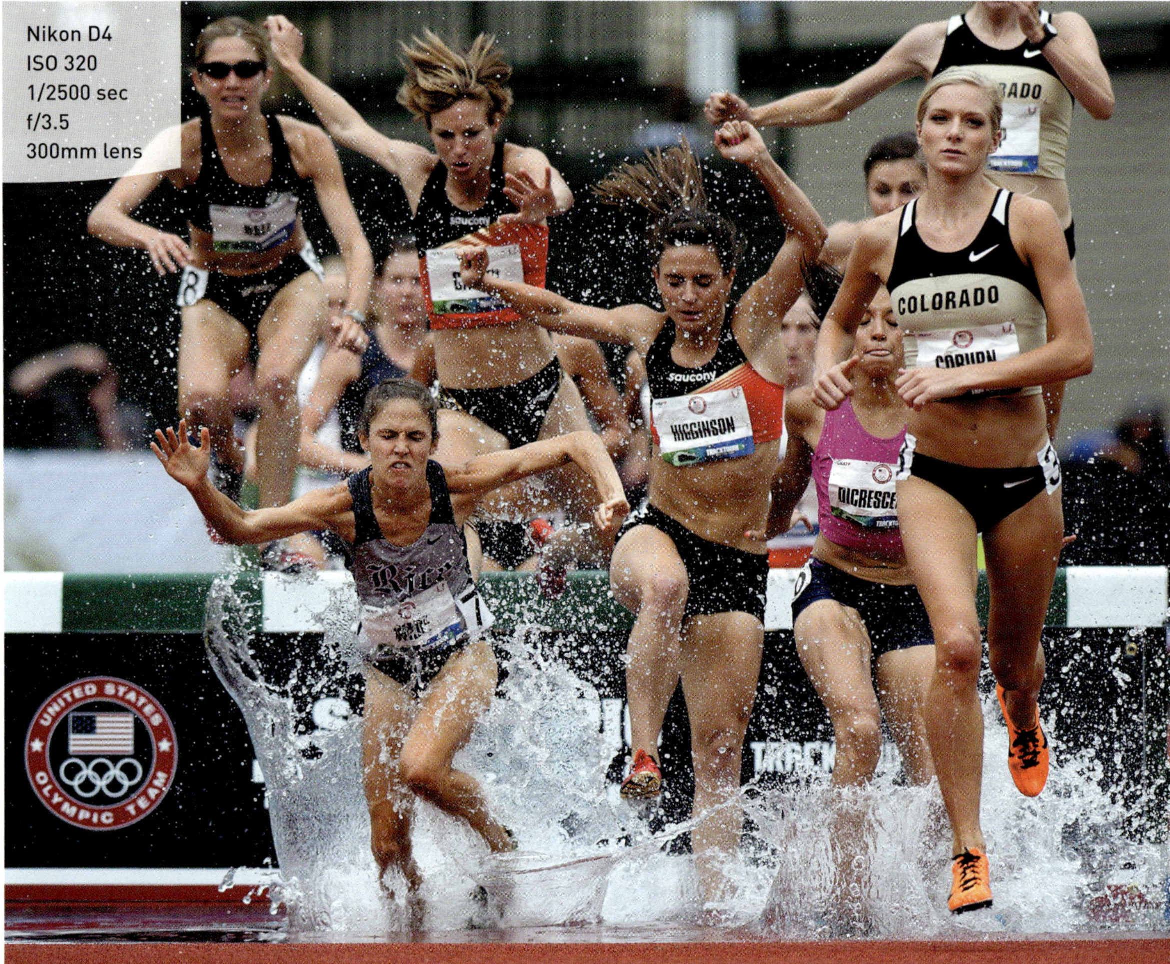

Nikon D4
ISO 320
1/2500 sec
f/3.5
300mm lens

FIGURE 8.16
The final of the women's 3000-meter steeplechase during the 2012 USATF Olympic Trials.

3000M STEEPLECHASE

The 3000-meter steeplechase is one of the strangest and most fun events to shoot in all of sports. It is a 3k race where once every 400 meters the athletes jump over a hurdle and into a pool of water (**Figure 8.16**).

This is one of the few races that I almost never shoot from the head-on position. The pool of water is located between the third and fourth turn, so I always position myself directly in front of the water pit and use a 300mm lens.

I also place a wide-angle remote camera (fired by a PocketWizard) next to the pool to capture the splash (**Figure 8.17**).

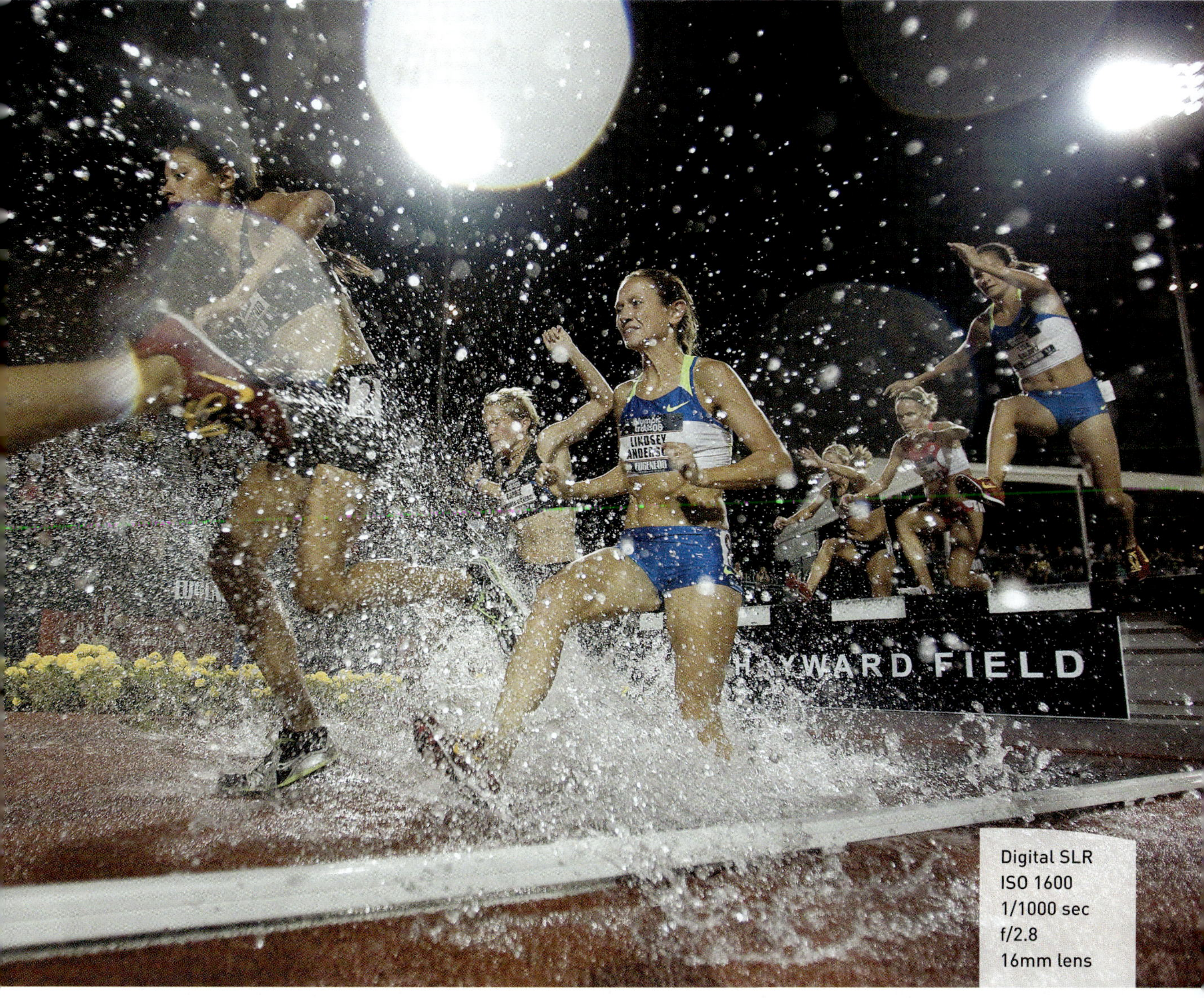

FIGURE 8.17
The competitors splash through the pit during the final of the women's 3000-meter steeplechase during the 2008 USATF Olympic Trials.

5000M AND 10,000M

The 5000-meter and 10,000-meter events are distance races, which give you, as a photographer, lots of time to work. I always shoot the finish from the head-on position. There is a foot race to the finish line every time, and foot races at the end of a long and steady distance race are always very strenuous and emotional. But as the race progresses, I like to take chances and try to make an artistic or graphic image. I play with my settings and move around the track (**Figure 8.18**). Photographically, there are no rules. Sometimes you come away with a surprising and beautiful image (**Figure 8.19**).

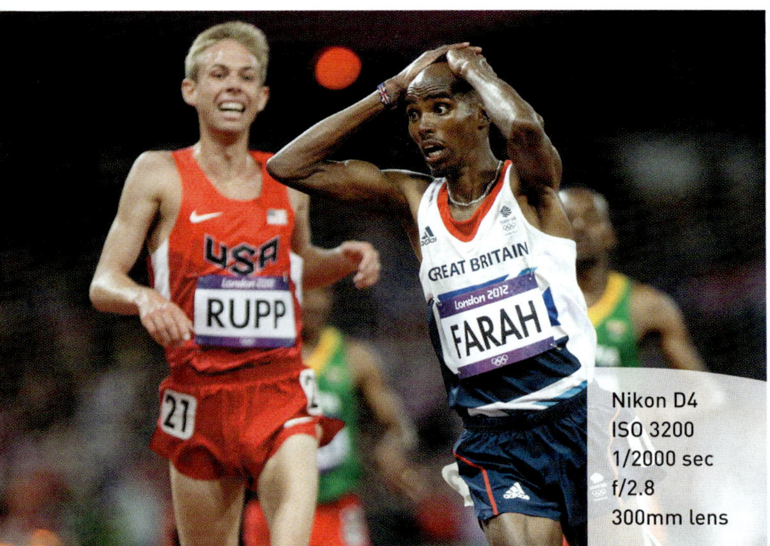

Nikon D4
ISO 3200
1/2000 sec
f/2.8
300mm lens

FIGURE 8.18
Mo Farah reacts to winning the men's 10,000-meter race, followed by his friend Galen Rupp. Farah is the first athlete from Britain ever to win the 10,000-meter event.

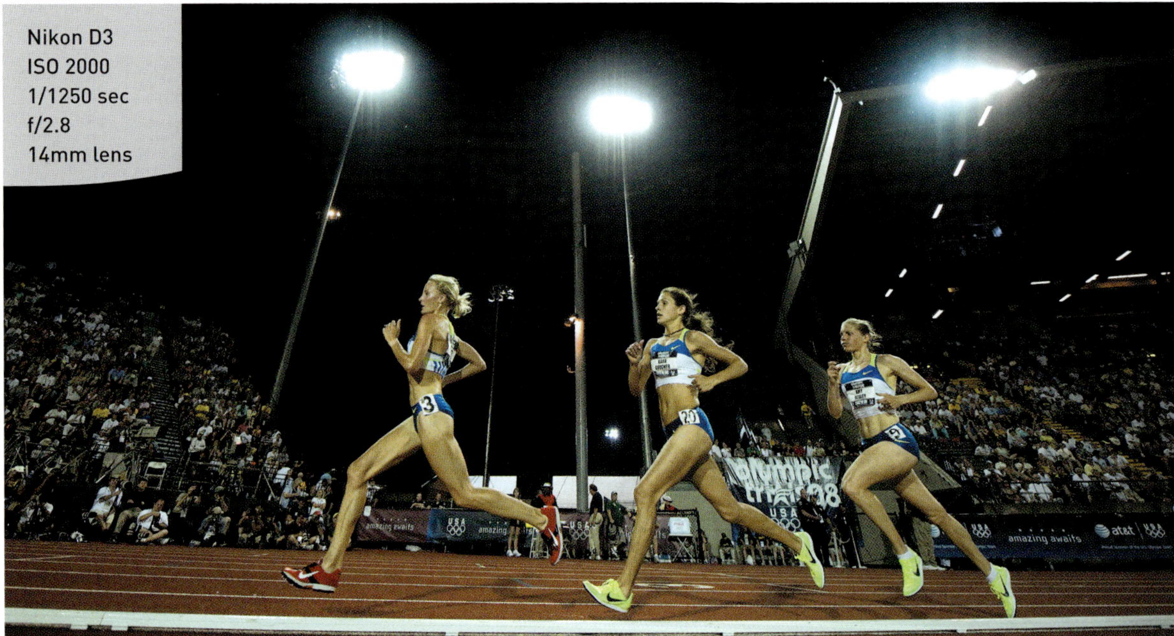

Nikon D3
ISO 2000
1/1250 sec
f/2.8
14mm lens

FIGURE 8.19
Shalane Flanagan, Kara Goucher, and Amy Begley—the top three finishers in the women's 10,000-meter final during the USATF Olympic Trials in 2008—make their way around the track.

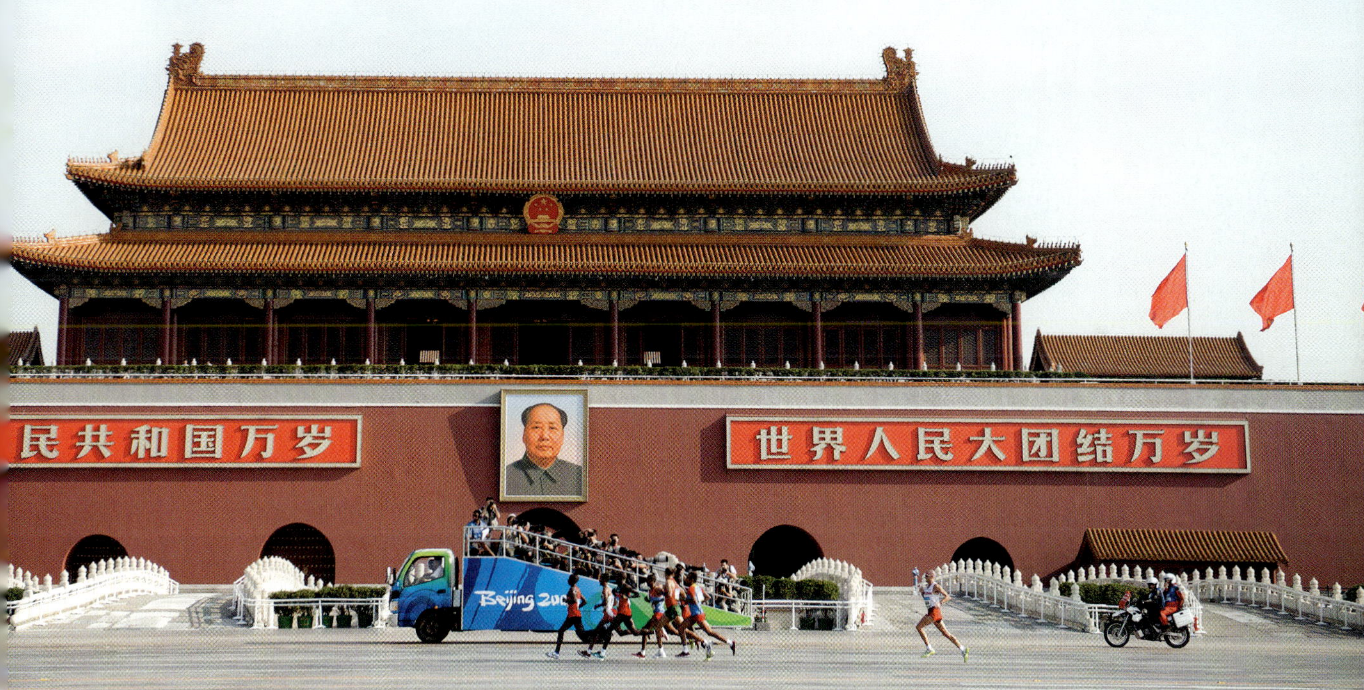

Nikon D3
ISO 200
1/1000 sec
f/4
56mm lens

FIGURE 8.20 The men's marathon at the 2008 Olympic Games in Beijing ran past the entrance to the Forbidden City.

MARATHONS AND RACEWALKS

Marathons and racewalks are almost always held on a road, meaning outside of a stadium. Therefore, the best location to cover these races depends entirely on where the race is taking place.

A position at the finish line is always a good location, but these races last several hours, and the best pictures are almost always somewhere else along the course (**Figure 8.20**).

For big events, the race organizers often provide a truck that travels just ahead of the first pack of runners.

FIGURE 8.21
An athlete fell down at the beginning of the men's race-walk final during the 2008 Olympic Games in Beijing.

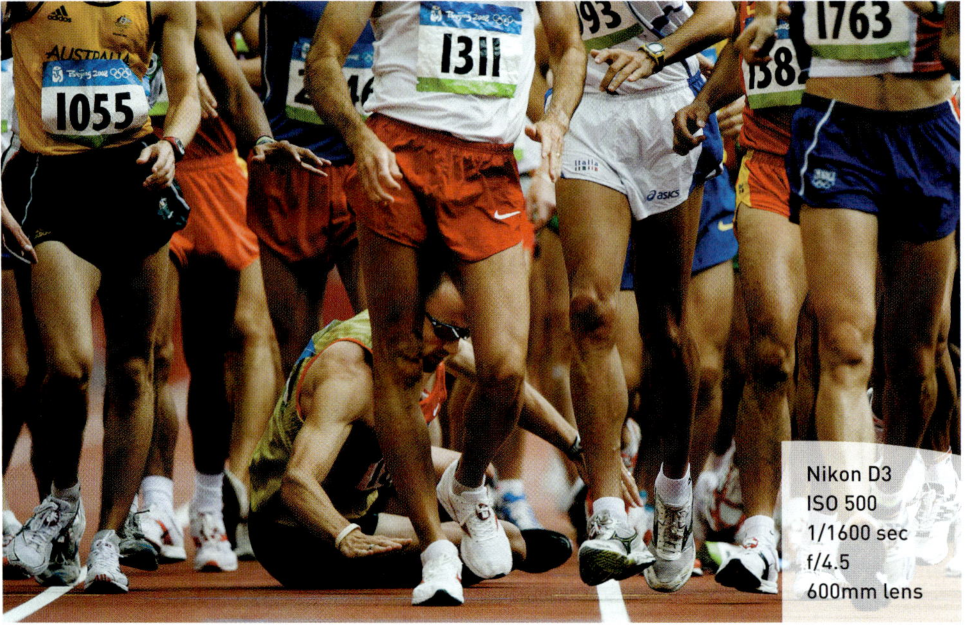

I like to shoot the start and finish at the start/finish line (**Figure 8.21**), but for the other two-plus hours of the race I try to find another interesting location to make a nice graphic or scenic photo.

HAMMER THROW AND DISCUS

Hammer and discus events are difficult to cover. For safety reasons, photographers are not allowed near the cage or the sidelines where a poorly thrown hammer or discus may fall. Photographers are very restricted as to where they can stand, so I like to place a wide-angle remote in the back of the cage. But be warned that a camera inside the cage is in a good position to get smashed. I've never had a camera destroyed in a cage, but I know people who have. A wide-angle remote creates a nice pattern picture that displays the thrower, the sky, and the netting (**Figure 8.22**).

JAVELIN

As with the hammer and discus events, you are restricted to where you can stand during the javelin event. Javelins aren't as wayward as a hammer or discus, but they are still weapons. Photographers are only allowed to stand to either side of the javelin thrower. If possible, I like to shoot from an elevated position behind the javelin thrower. This is only doable at certain venues. Most large stadiums, like those used during the Olympics, have a place to do this (**Figure 8.23**).

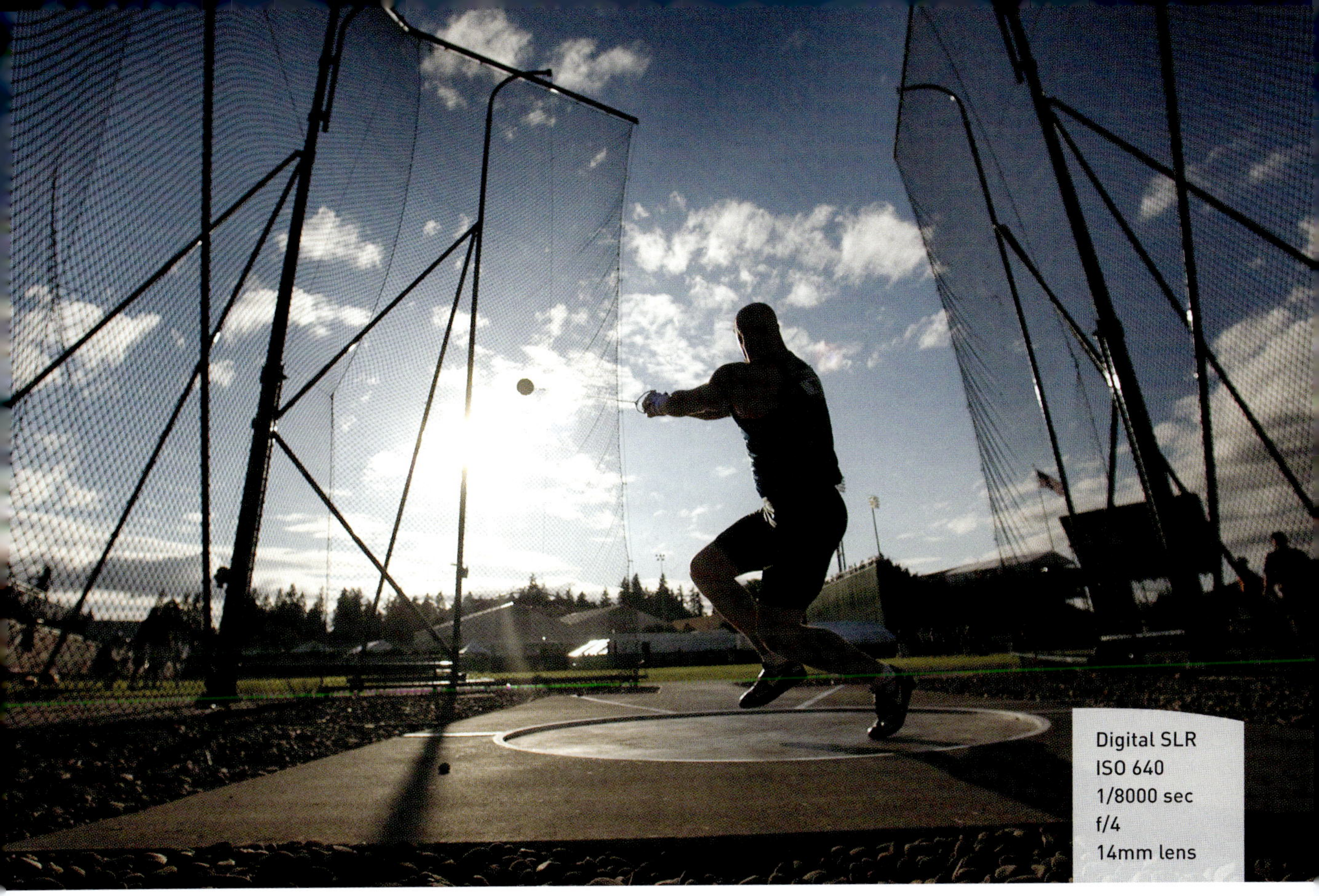

Digital SLR
ISO 640
1/8000 sec
f/4
14mm lens

FIGURE 8.22
The final of the men's hammer throw during the 2008 USATF Olympic Trials.

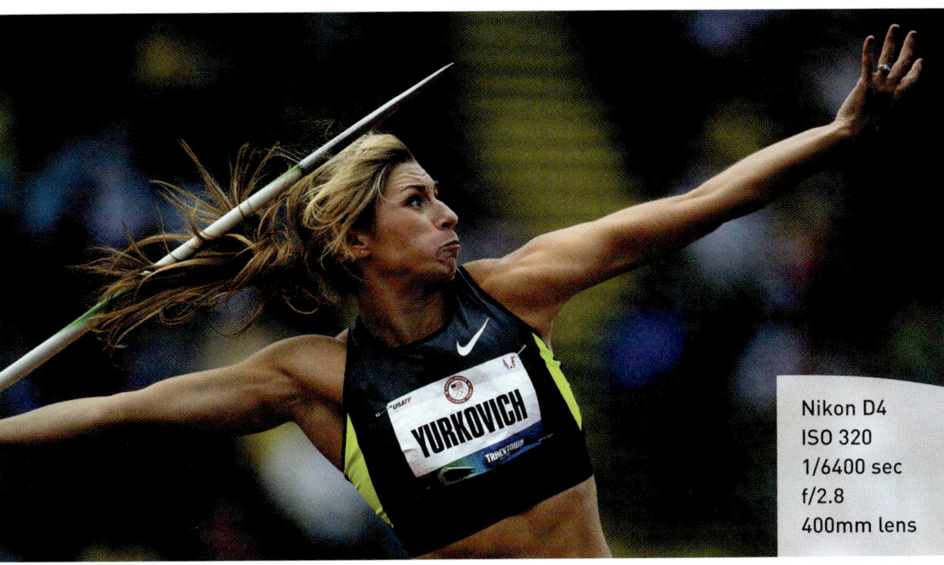

Nikon D4
ISO 320
1/6400 sec
f/2.8
400mm lens

FIGURE 8.23
Rachel Yurkovich throws the javelin during the 2012 USATF Olympic Trials.

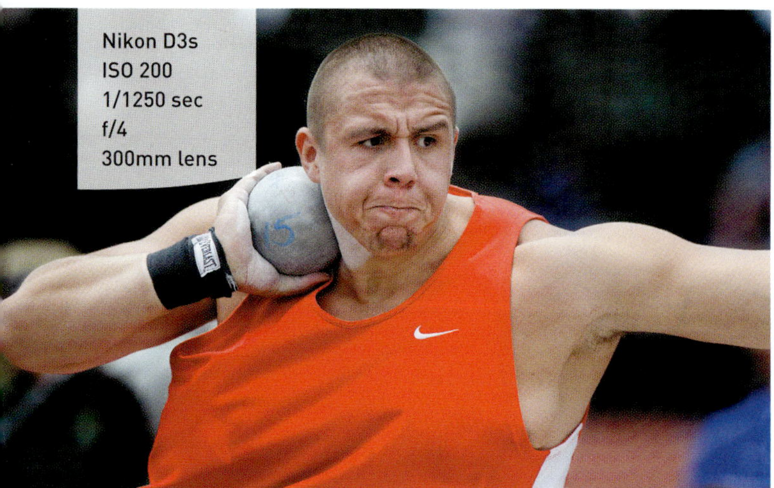

FIGURE 8.24
John Ybarra competes in the men's shot put during the 2011 USATF Championships.

SHOT PUT

Of the throwing events, shot put offers the best positions from which to shoot, in part because the object being thrown is not as dangerous as the other instruments. You still can't shoot from a head-on position easily, but you can shoot from an angled head-on position from the left or right (**Figure 8.24**).

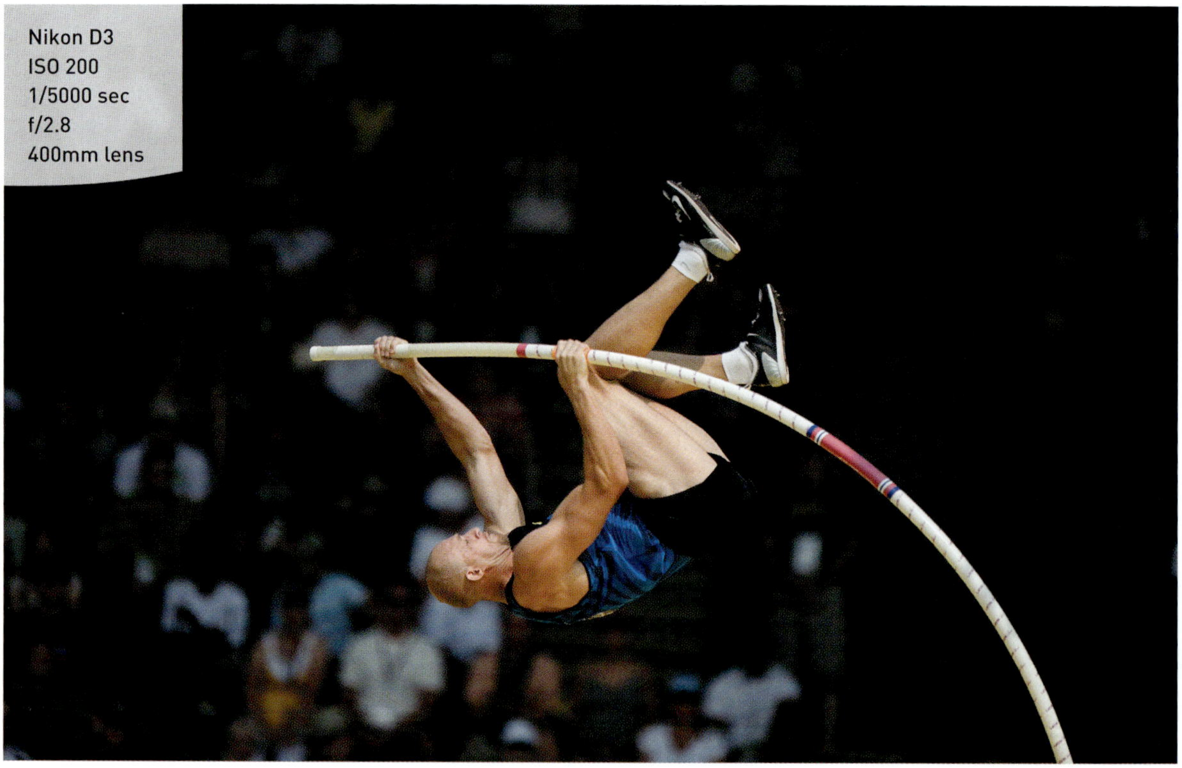

Nikon D3
ISO 200
1/5000 sec
f/2.8
400mm lens

FIGURE 8.25
The men's pole vault competition during the 2008 USATF Olympic Trials.

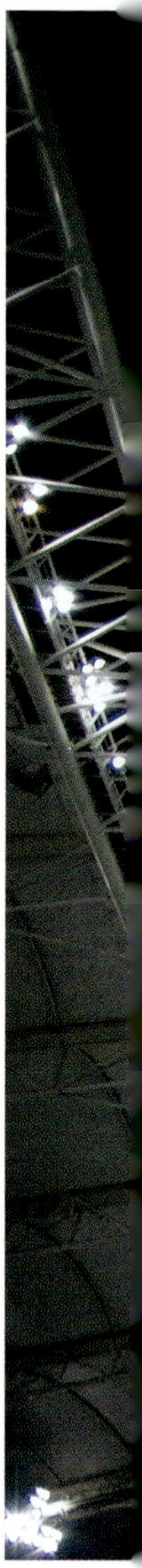

POLE VAULT

Pole vault is a beautiful and relatively simple event to shoot. You can shoot with a telephoto from several hundred feet away or with a wide-angle lens shooting up at the vaulter (**Figure 8.25**). Use a telephoto if you want to reduce the background. I like to shoot with a wide-angle lens looking up if there is a pretty sky to shoot into or an interesting graphic (**Figure 8.26**).

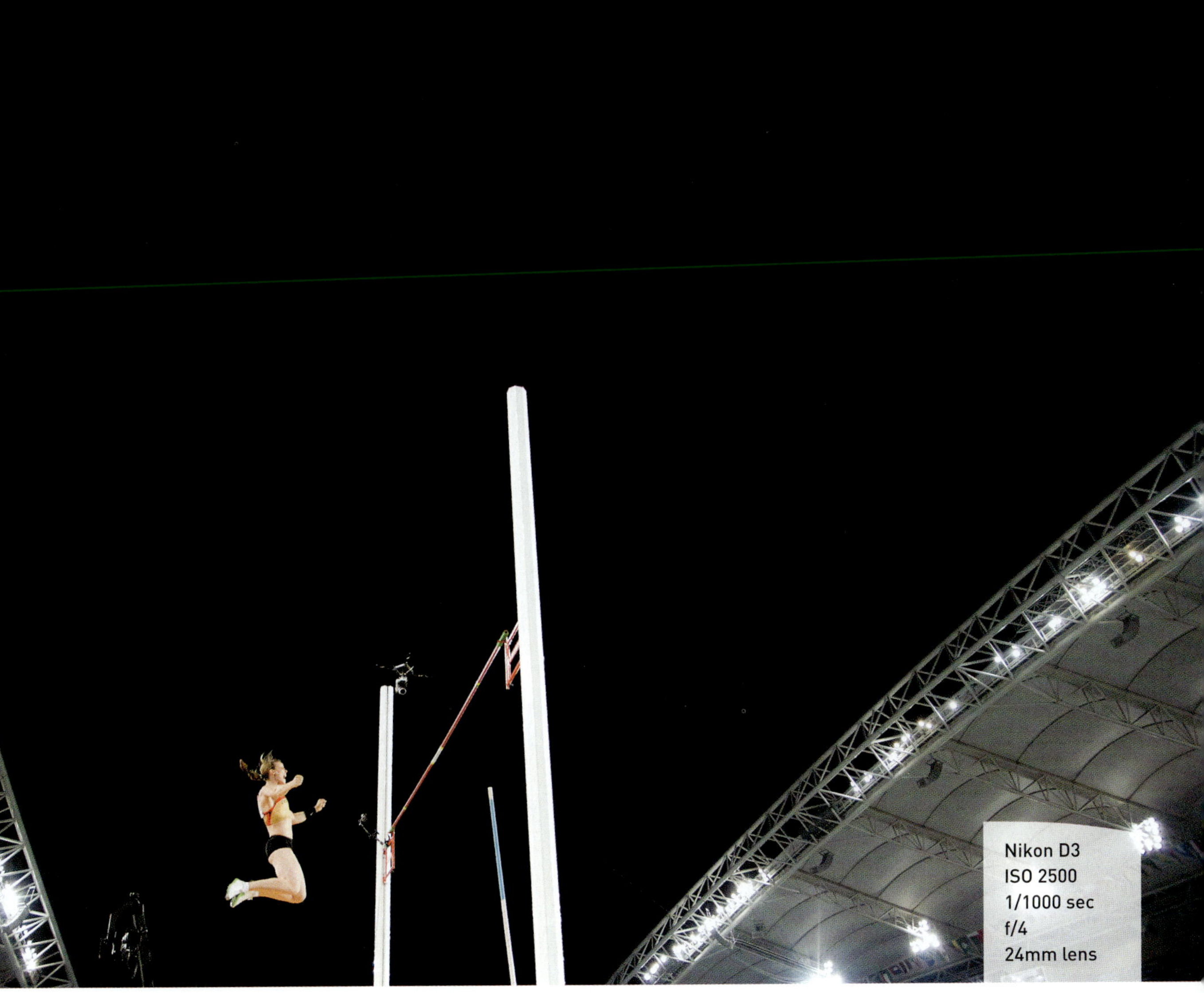

Nikon D3
ISO 2500
1/1000 sec
f/4
24mm lens

FIGURE 8.26
Silke Spiegelburg celebrates after clearing the bar during the 2011 IAAF World Championships in Daegu, South Korea.

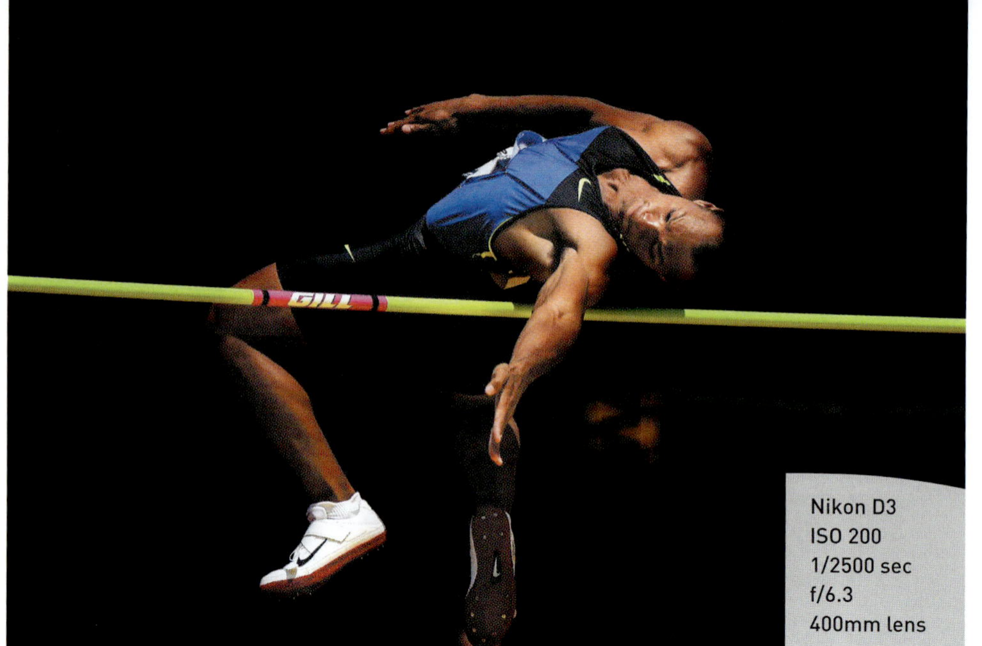

Nikon D3
ISO 200
1/2500 sec
f/6.3
400mm lens

FIGURE 8.27
Brian Clay clears the bar during the high jump portion of the men's decathlon during the 2008 USATF Olympic Trials. Clay went on to win the trials and the Olympic Gold in Beijing.

HIGH JUMP

The high jump is one of my favorite field events to cover. As the event progresses and the bar gets higher, the reactions get bigger. I always shoot the high jump with a telephoto lens in front of the high jump pad—that way I see the jumpers' faces as they cross the bar (**Figure 8.27**).

LONG JUMP AND TRIPLE JUMP

The long jump and triple jump are also terrific events to cover and can result in very dynamic pictures. My prime place to shoot this event is head on and as low as I can get with a telephoto lens. From this angle I can capture the explosion of sand as the jumpers land, along with the expressions on their faces.

If there is an elevated position above the sand pit, it is also an ideal place to shoot from (**Figure 8.28**). Many of the jumpers look up as they hit the ground, creating a dynamic graphic pattern.

MOTOR SPORTS: HOW TO GET THE BEST SHOTS

Formula One and stock car races are the most common motor sports, although go-cart, truck, and motorcycle races have gained popularity. There are heavy restrictions on where you can shoot during motor races for obvious safety reasons, and each track is different.

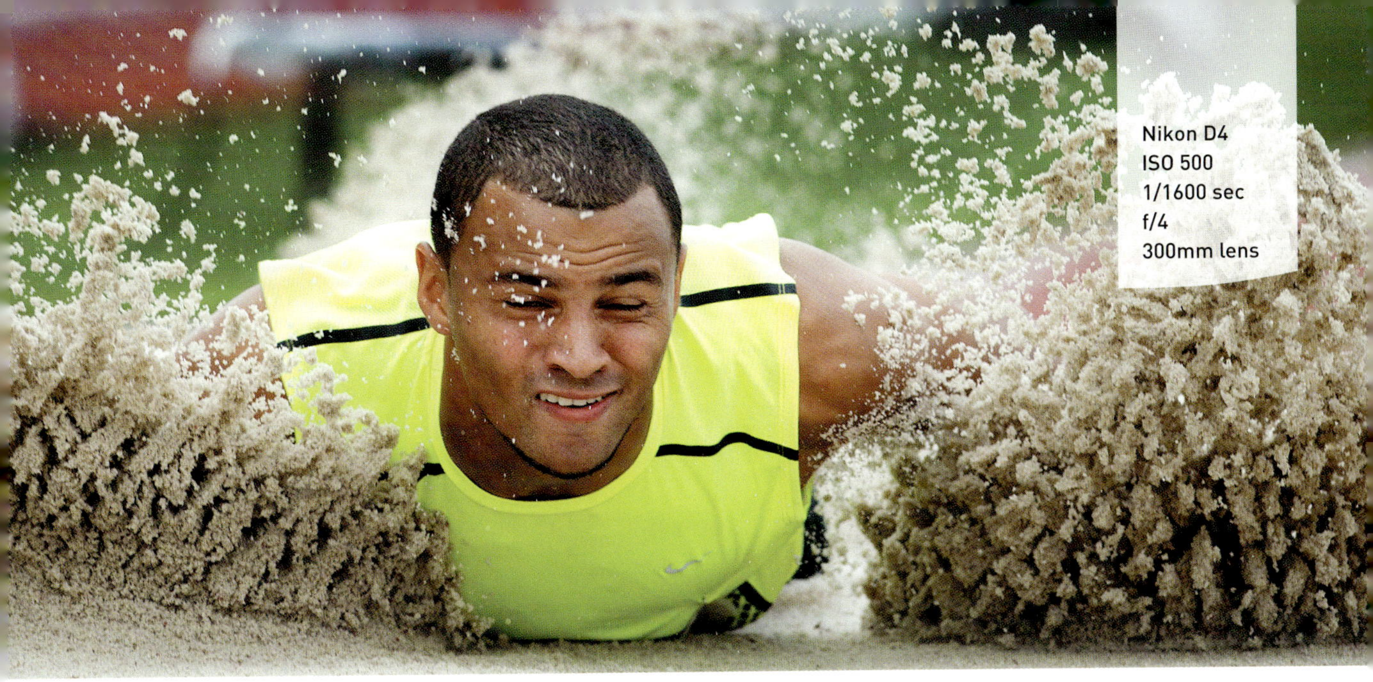

Nikon D4
ISO 500
1/1600 sec
f/4
300mm lens

FIGURE 8.28
Triple jumper Aarick Wilson does a face plant during competition for the U.S. Olympic team. He finished ninth in the competition. In 2008 he won the U.S. Olympic Trials.

WHERE TO POSITION YOURSELF

Even though every track is different, there are two places you can go to shoot from at almost every track: the turns and the grandstands.

TURNS

What turn to shoot depends on the track. Turn four is the most popular position at the Daytona 500, because that's where the most crashes happen. It was a crash in turn four that killed Dale Earnhardt in 2001, and the place has been hallowed ground in racing ever since. In **Figure 8.29** I chose to shoot turn four for this race through the fans. For effect, I lowered my shutter speed so the cars would blur in the background.

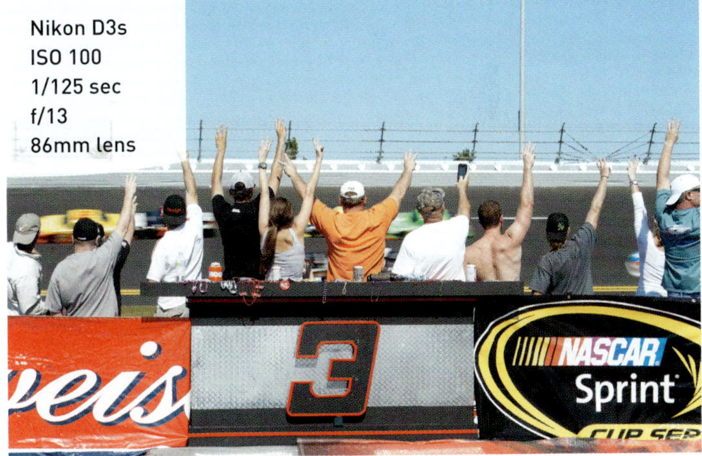

FIGURE 8.29
NASCAR fans hold up three fingers in their camping spot on turn four at the beginning of the 2011 Daytona 500. It was the tenth anniversary of Dale Earnhardt's (#3 car) death.

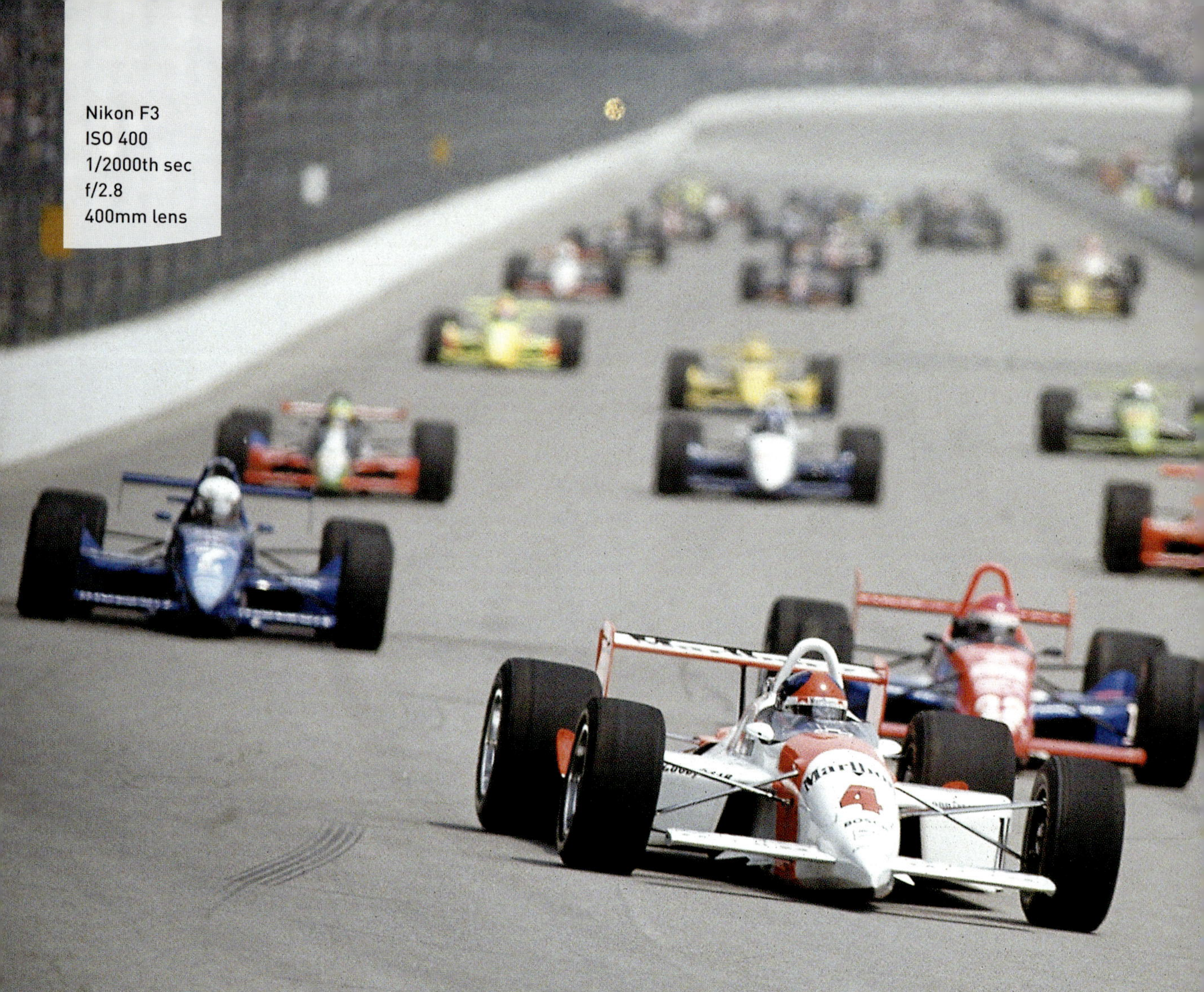

FIGURE 8.30
Emerson Fittipaldi (4) in action, leading during the 1993 Indianapolis 500 at the Indianapolis Motor Speedway.

Turn one is also a good place to position yourself at most tracks for a view of the finish line (**Figure 8.30**).

TIP

Shooting from the turn one position requires longer lenses, and for longer-distance races it is very helpful to work from a tripod. That way you can release the camera when the action gets closer to you and switch to a shorter lens.

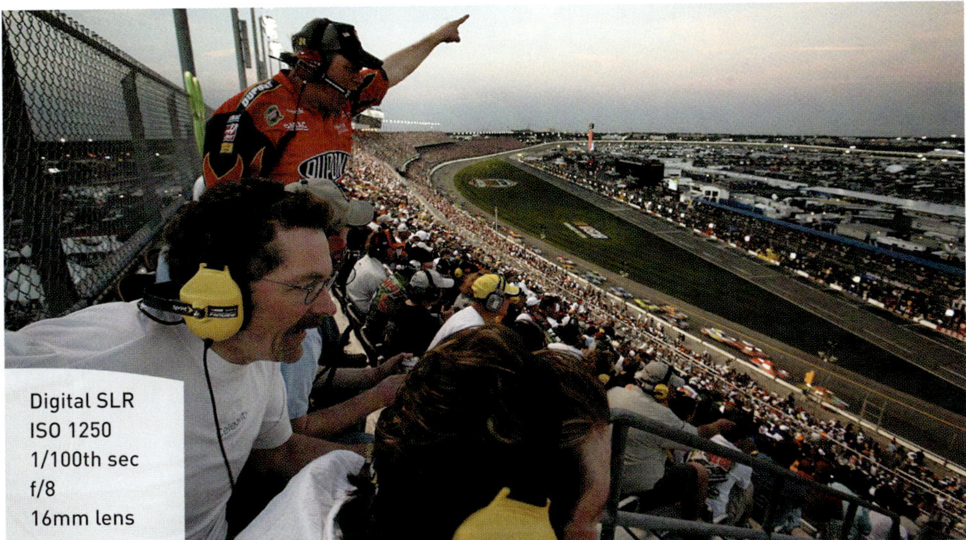

Digital SLR
ISO 1250
1/100th sec
f/8
16mm lens

FIGURE 8.31
Fans cheer during the 50th running of the Daytona 500.

GRANDSTANDS

Shooting from the grandstands gives you a nice view of the speedway as a whole, plus racing fans are just fun to be around. Of every sport I cover, I think racing fans are the most passionate (**Figure 8.31**).

MY GEAR

Racing shots require a very diverse set of gear. No matter the event—horse racing, track and field, or motor sports—you have a wide range of lenses to work with.

This is what I bring to every racing event:

- At least four Nikon D4 bodies
- At least four Nikon D3 or D3s bodies for remotes
- 600mm f/4 lens
- 400mm f/4 lens
- 300mm f/2.8 lens
- At least two 70–200mm f/2.8 lenses
- At least two 50mm f/2 lenses
- At least two 35mm f/1.4 lenses
- At least two 12–24mm f/2.8 lenses
- SB-910 small flash
- TC 1.4x teleconverter
- Eight PocketWizards and connectors

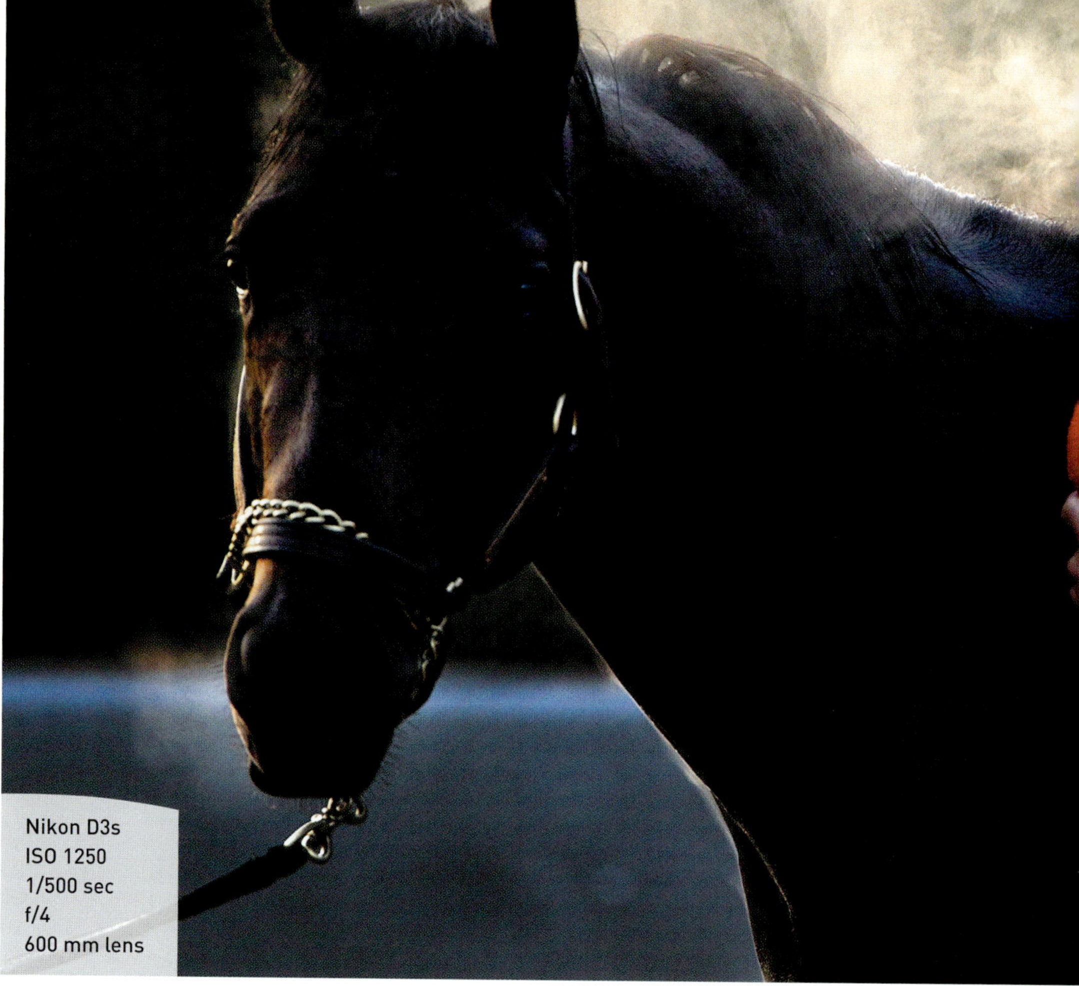

FIGURE 8.32 A horse gets washed at dawn after an early morning workout on the backside of Churchill Downs.

Nikon D3s
ISO 1250
1/500 sec
f/4
600 mm lens

My gear list is inflated greatly by the number of remotes I use at the various events. As mentioned earlier, I'll put up as many as 60 remotes for the Kentucky Derby. For the men's 100-meter final at the Olympics, I used 28 remotes. I work very differently from most photographers, because I have to be everywhere at once.

If you have only one camera, you can cover all of these events with one long lens and one wide-angle lens.

PAY CLOSE ATTENTION TO YOUR SETTINGS

With the exception of certain track and field competitions, all of the events mentioned in this chapter take place outdoors. Therefore, it is important to pay attention to changing weather conditions. Also, the grandstands at many venues cast shadows over large pieces of track, creating an exposure nightmare. Be sure to expose for the picture you want to make, not what your exposure meter or histogram is telling you.

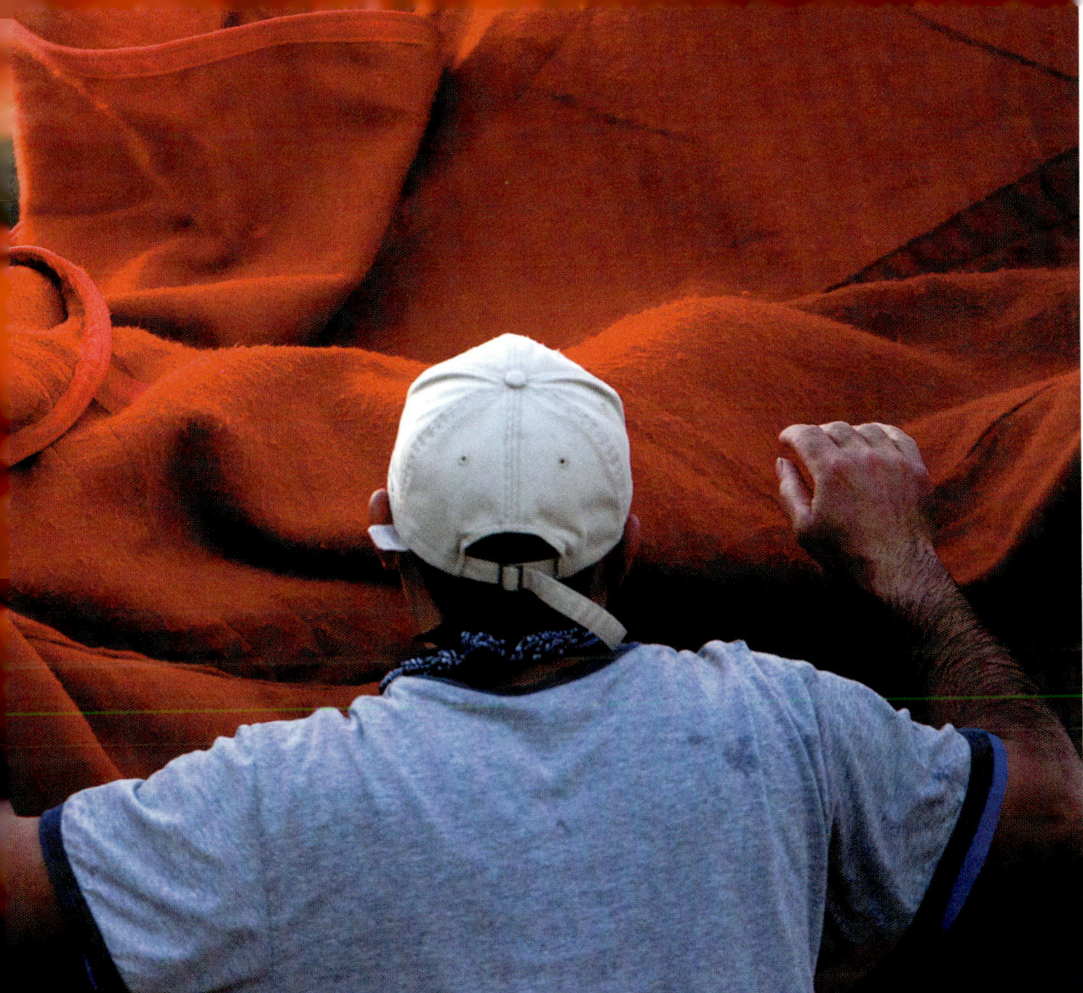

BEYOND THE RACE ITSELF

All of the events discussed have a lot of goings-on behind the scenes and off the track.

At horse races, I love to go to the barns in the morning while the horses are being breezed, fed, and bathed before the big races. The early morning light mixed with the cool morning air always makes for beautiful images (**Figure 8.32**).

At track and field events, focus on what happens after the race (**Figure 8.33**). Sometimes capturing the last person to cross the finish line results in the best picture. Athletic competition can be extremely emotional—in some cases just the act of finishing is more important to the athlete than winning anything.

Motor sport fans are some of the best people in all of sports. They are passionate about racing, loyal to their favorite drivers, and no one has more fun. The infield at the Daytona 500 is the place to be. **Figure 8.34** shows NASCAR fans camped in the infield of the Daytona International Speedway the night before the 50th anniversary of the Daytona 500.

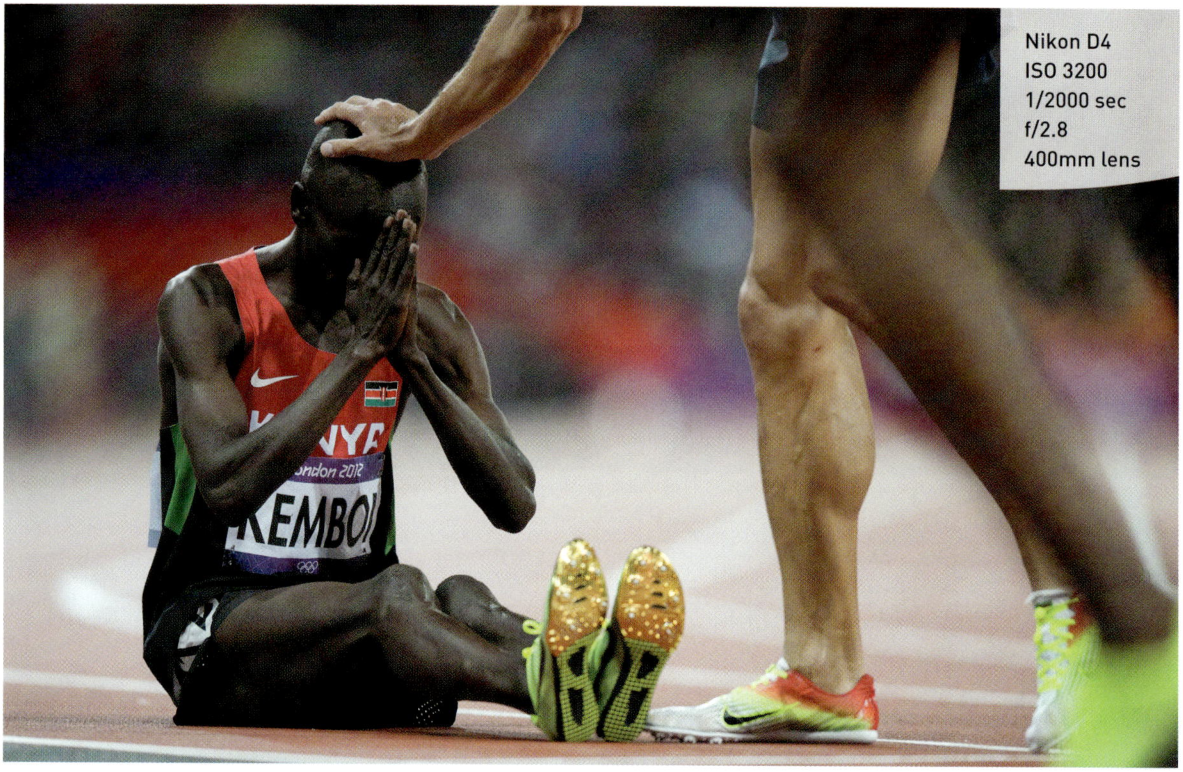

Nikon D4
ISO 3200
1/2000 sec
f/2.8
400mm lens

FIGURE 8.33
Ezekiel Kemboi Cheboi prays after winning the men's 3000-meter steeplechase at the 2012 Olympic Games.

FIGURE 8.34
By introducing a small flash into this situation, I was able to freeze action while slowing down my shutter speed significantly to allow more light to reach the sensor.

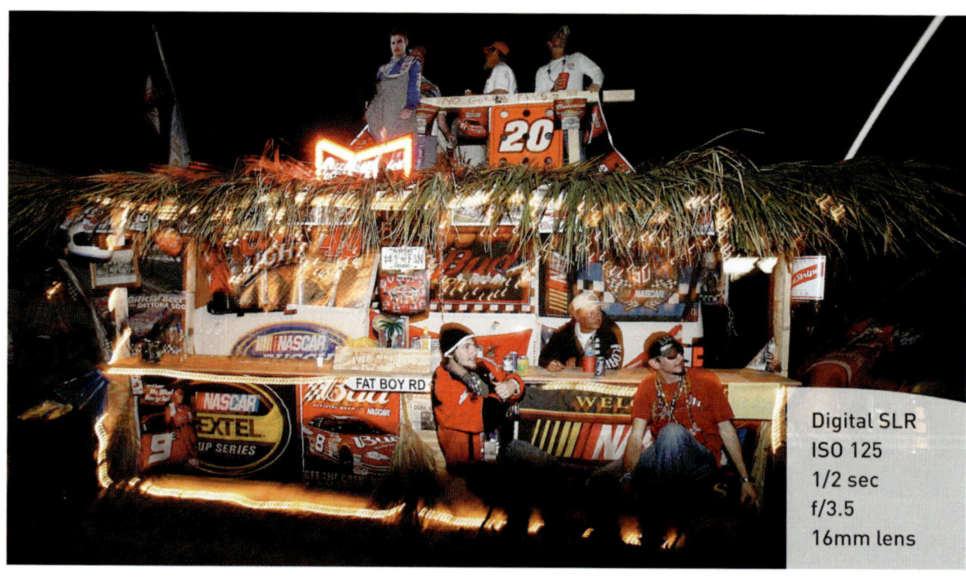

Digital SLR
ISO 125
1/2 sec
f/3.5
16mm lens

Chapter 8 Assignments

These assignments will help you learn to anticipate and capture fast-moving motion from head-on and side-on positions.

Shooting a Track Meet

Go to a high school track meet. Talk with the meet officials and get permission to photograph the event. Position yourself head-on to the finish line. Practice anticipating which athlete is in front and track that athlete into the finish line.

Then position yourself side-on to the finish line. Practice doing pans of the runners finishing the race.

At the track meet, also spend time shooting the throwing events. Learn how to position yourself directly behind the action, which allows for dramatic images, while offering the benefit of keeping you out of harm's way.

Capturing the Ponies

Go to a horse track and pay for general admission. Walk up to the rail next to the track as close as the track normally permits. Practice following the horses as they approach the finish line. You'll learn that horses move at a pace that appears to be more erratic than that of humans because of the length of their gait. Try changing your settings, both aperture and shutter speed, to see how that affects how the horses' legs are captured in your images.

Photographing Fast Cars

Auto racing will probably be the most difficult to gain access to in order to photograph from a close location. This is in large part because of the potential danger created by fast-moving cars. For now, it's best to simply stick to photographing humans and horses. When you are more comfortable covering sporting events, you can reach out to auto racing venues and publications to see what possibilities there may be.

Share your results with the book's Flickr group!
Join the group here: flickr.com/groups/sportsphotographyfromsnapshotstogreatshots.

9

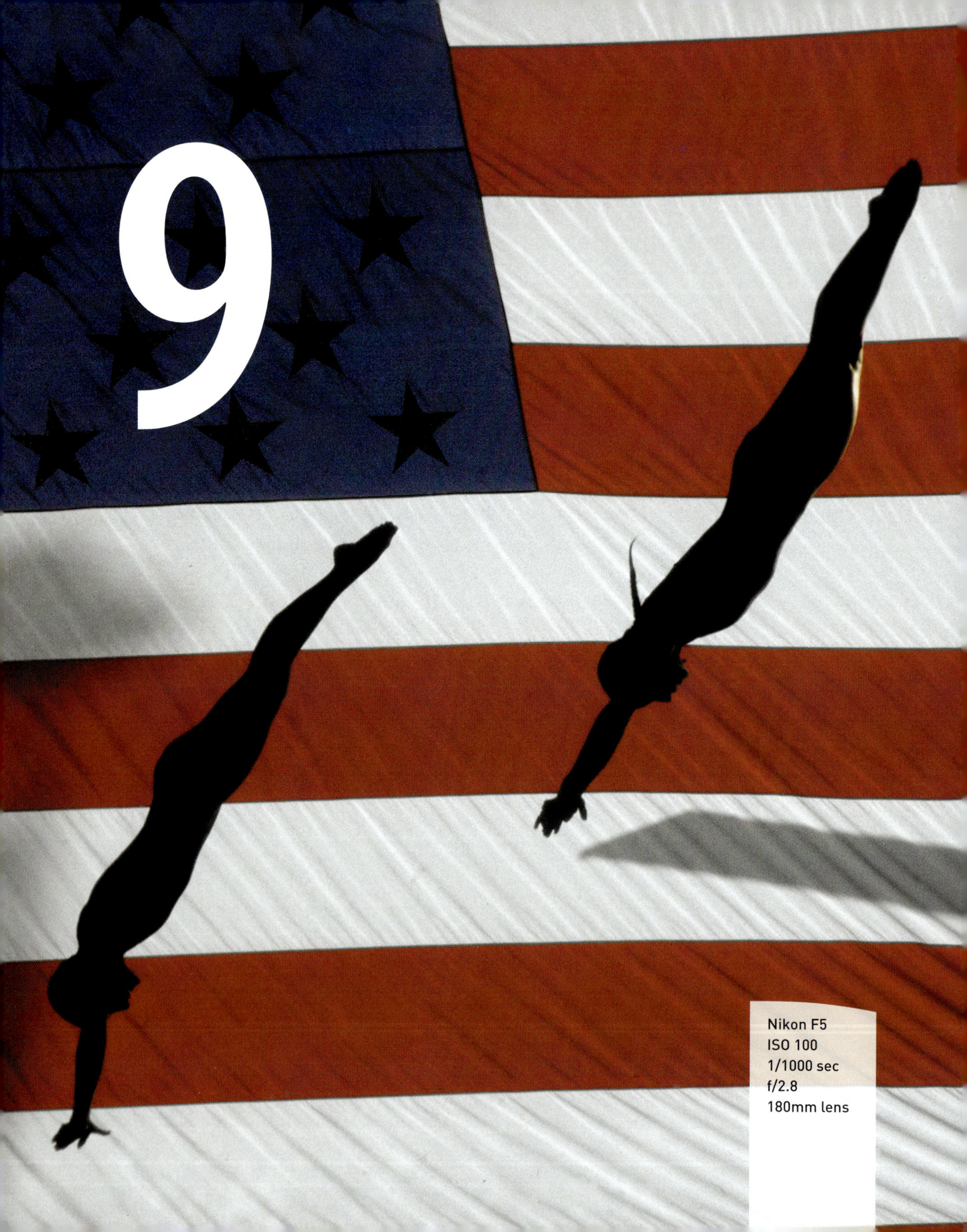

Nikon F5
ISO 100
1/1000 sec
f/2.8
180mm lens

Summer Olympic Sports

FROM THE GREEKS TO NOW

The sports described in this chapter—beach volleyball, boxing, cycling, diving, horse competitions, gymnastics, table tennis, swimming, weightlifting, and wrestling—are all part of Olympic competition. However, they are not just played during the Olympics. Each sport has stand-alone meetings and is very popular in its own right. For purposes of discussion, I have grouped them together.

Many common threads exist between all of these sports, so I'll start by explaining basic positioning and lens selection.

Olympic divers train in Coral Gables, Florida.

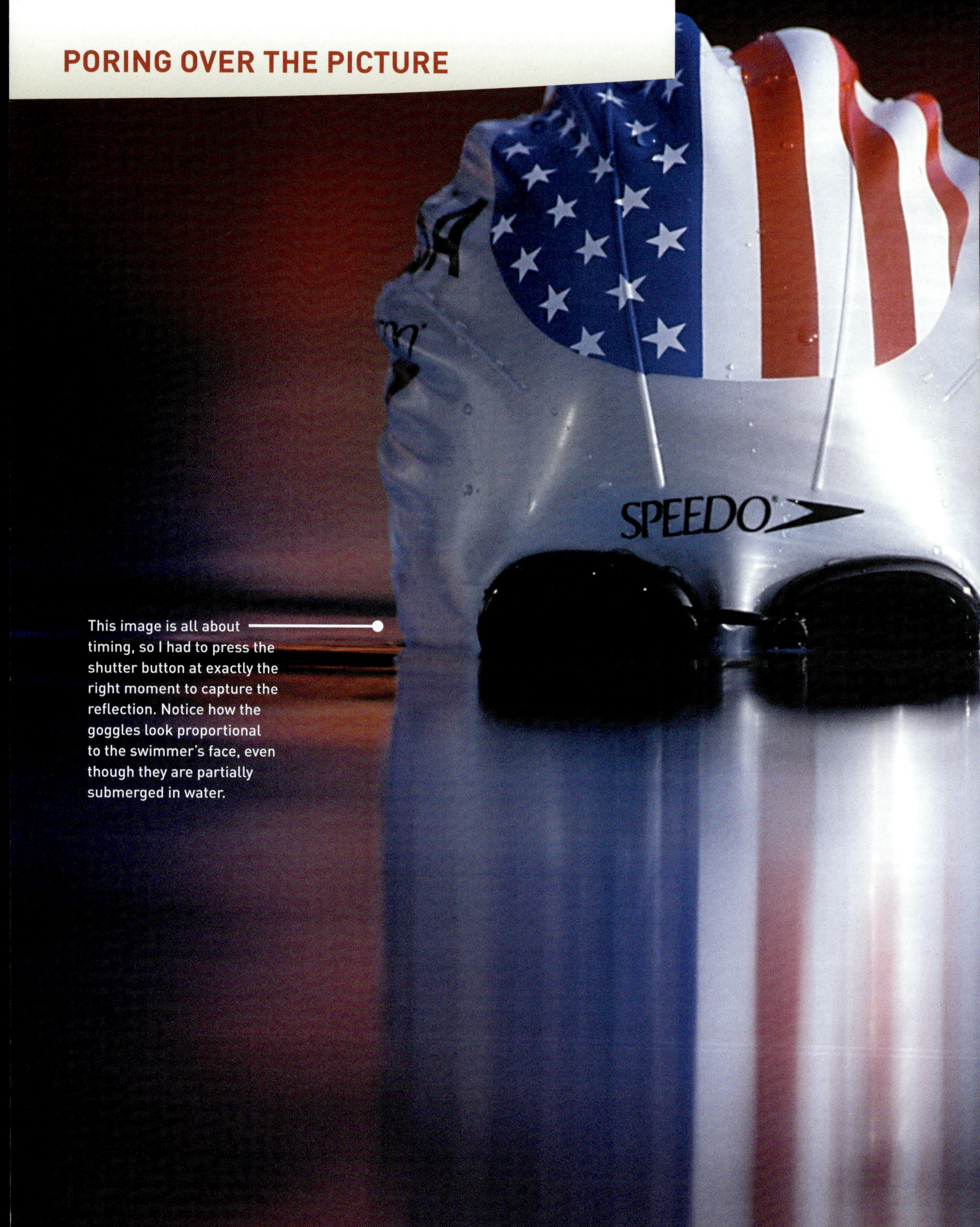

This image is all about timing, so I had to press the shutter button at exactly the right moment to capture the reflection. Notice how the goggles look proportional to the swimmer's face, even though they are partially submerged in water.

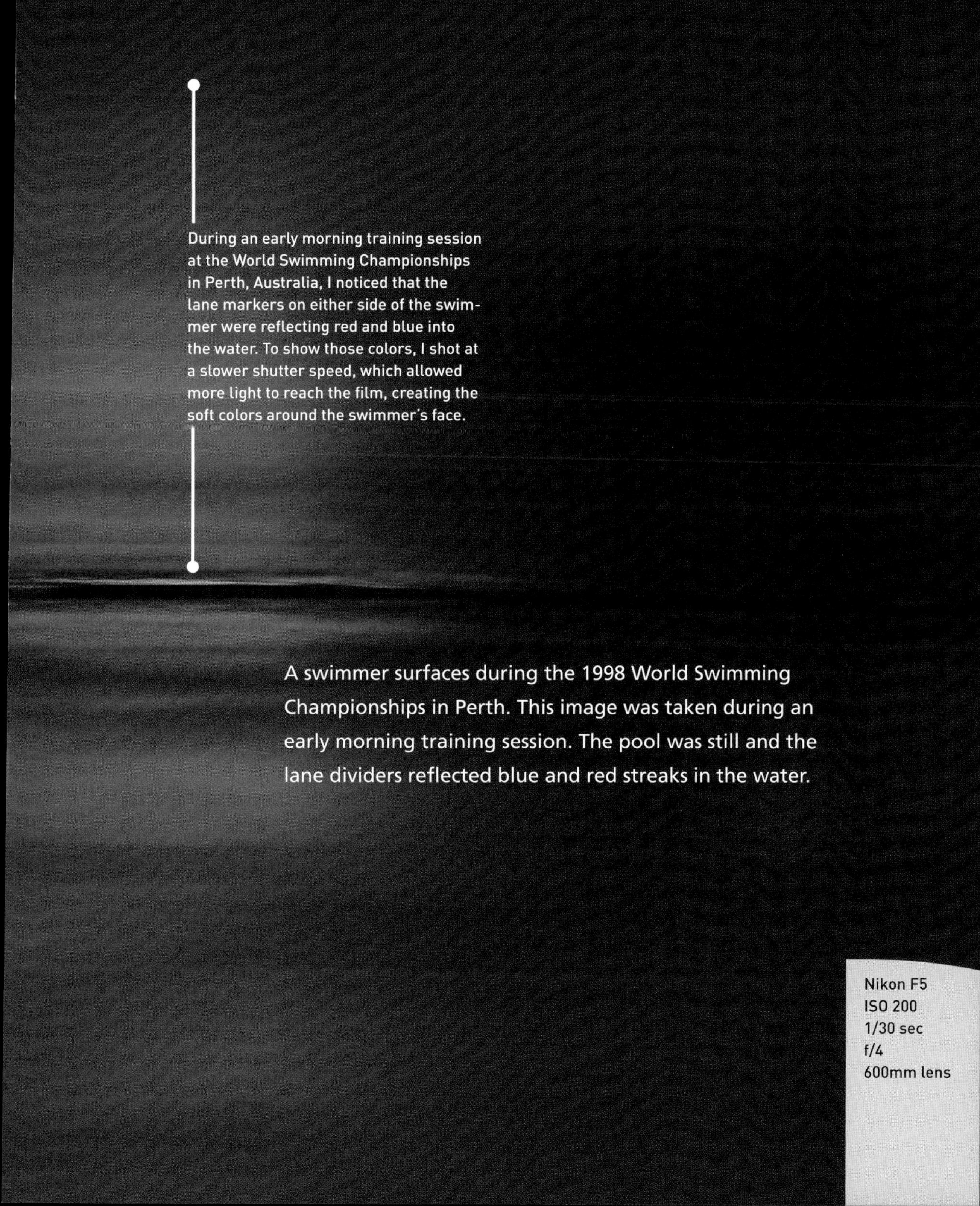

During an early morning training session at the World Swimming Championships in Perth, Australia, I noticed that the lane markers on either side of the swimmer were reflecting red and blue into the water. To show those colors, I shot at a slower shutter speed, which allowed more light to reach the film, creating the soft colors around the swimmer's face.

A swimmer surfaces during the 1998 World Swimming Championships in Perth. This image was taken during an early morning training session. The pool was still and the lane dividers reflected blue and red streaks in the water.

Nikon F5
ISO 200
1/30 sec
f/4
600mm lens

WHERE TO POSITION YOURSELF

For each of the summer Olympic sports, the venues are wide open. There may be assigned shooting positions, but basically it is important to find a position where you have a clean background, an unblocked view, and are out of the way. Many times shooting from the stands will yield the best view of the action.

LENS SELECTION

The lens you have available to use may determine where you can work.

In all things context is king. If you want to make tight action images, you'll need to be close enough to do that with the lens you are using. I am lucky to have a wide range of choices available to me now, so I figure out where I want to stand and then select the appropriate lens. That hasn't always been the case. When I started, I had one lens, and I let my legs do the zooming. That's still often the best solution.

The athletes competing in these summer sports don't wear masks, which makes it easier to capture facial expressions, especially reaction shots.

BEACH VOLLEYBALL: HOW TO GET THE BEST SHOTS

Played outdoors on a sand court, beach volleyball offers abundant opportunities for action and feature images. The action takes place between two teams made up of two players each.

Matches normally consist of the best of three sets. During the first two sets, the players change ends after every seven points, and in the third set they change ends after every five points. This allows you to photograph both teams on offense and defense during each set.

A lot of celebrating goes on during most matches. Most of the time the athlete at the net will turn toward the player in the backcourt and either gesticulate strongly or hug his or her partner. This sport offers a wealth of emotion to capture (**Figure 9.1**).

The players use a few basic skills: serving, digging, spiking, blocking, and attacking.

The court is divided by a net, and much of the action takes place within a few feet of the net, which makes it easy to track and anticipate what will happen (**Figure 9.2**).

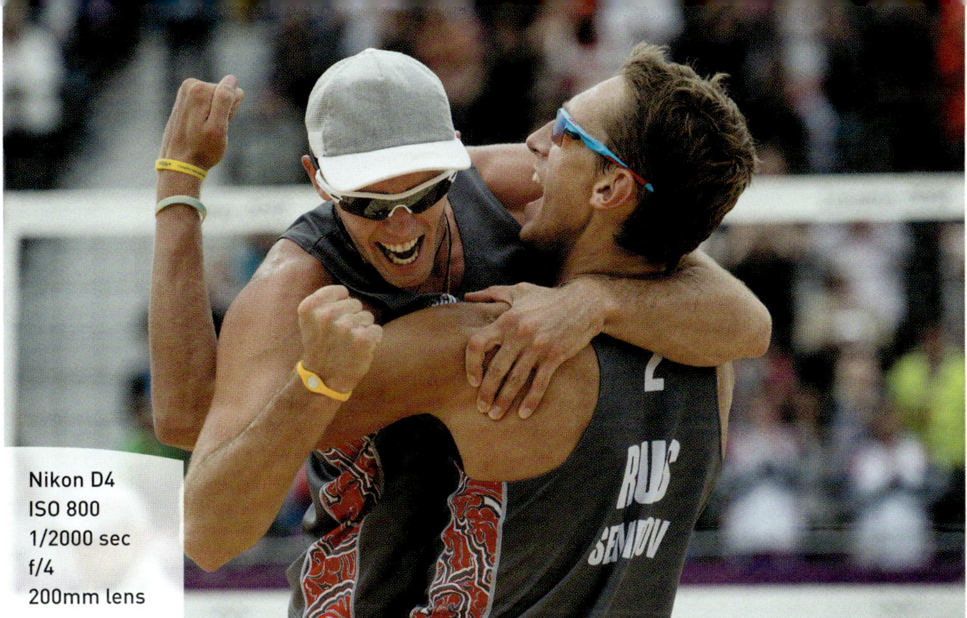

Nikon D4
ISO 800
1/2000 sec
f/4
200mm lens

FIGURE 9.1
The Russian men's beach volleyball team celebrates after beating China during the 2012 Olympic Games in London.

FIGURE 9.2
The women's beach volleyball teams from Switzerland and Russia face off during the 2012 Olympic Games in London.

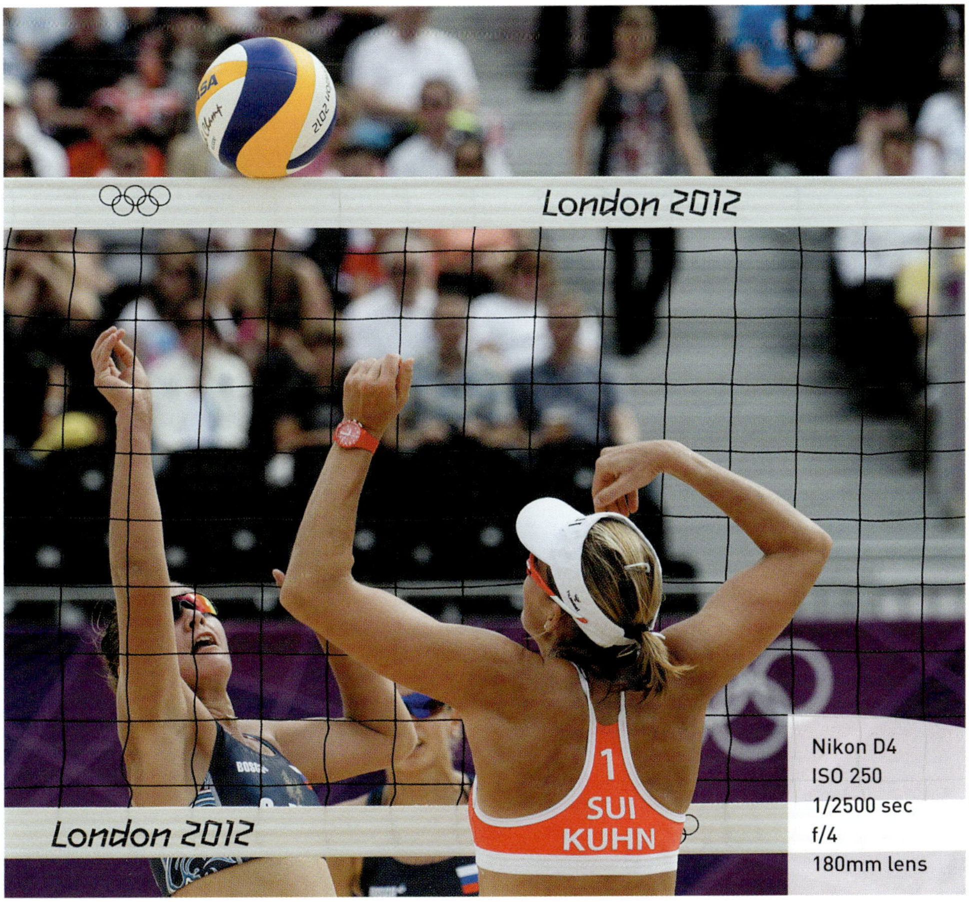

Nikon D4
ISO 250
1/2500 sec
f/4
180mm lens

FIGURE 9.3
The Australian player at the net signals her teammate during the 2004 Olympic Games in Athens.

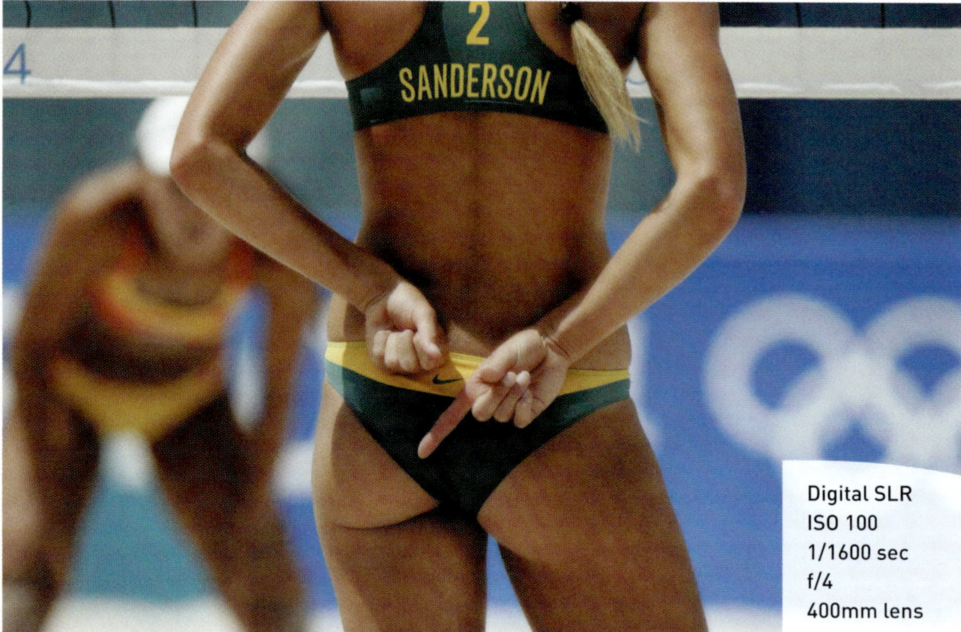

Digital SLR
ISO 100
1/1600 sec
f/4
400mm lens

Access is normally very good. The entire baseline on both ends and the sides of the court all provide excellent shooting positions. If an overhead position is available and it is possible to shoot down on the action, the sand provides an interesting but simple background to make the action stand out.

The player at the net will signal the other partner in the backcourt to indicate which direction to move right before the ball is served (**Figure 9.3**). The act of signaling can make for a very nice detail image. When you're positioned behind the serving team, paying attention to the signal allows you to know in advance how the serving team hopes the play will go. As a result, you'll have the advantage of knowing where to focus and how to quickly compose your shot.

Following the return of the serve, the action sets up, most often at the net. The setter positions the ball so that the attacker can spike the ball. When the attacker comes to the net, the receiving team will attempt to block the ball. These head-to-head confrontations at the net are easy to shoot and make unfailingly good images. The other action that frequently happens when the players are at the net is that the attacker will lightly tap the ball—the action is called a *dink*—and attempt to tip the ball over the overstretched arms of the blocker.

TIP

Use enough depth of field to keep the attacker and the defender in focus.

TIP

Prefocus on the net when you know there is going to be a spike. It will help you react quickly because you won't be searching for focus while you are trying to compose the image.

During day matches, the sand reflects a lot of light; it's like having a giant reflector underneath the players. This does two things: It changes the direction of the light in a way not normally seen in action images, and it increases the quantity of the light available. The result is wonderfully lit images, which gives you the ability to use extremely fast shutter speeds at fairly low ISOs (**Figure 9.4**).

Deep blue skies, flying sand, and constant action make beach volleyball a terrific sport to photograph.

FIGURE 9.4
A player from Brazil dives for the ball during a match with Russia in the 2012 Olympic Games in London.

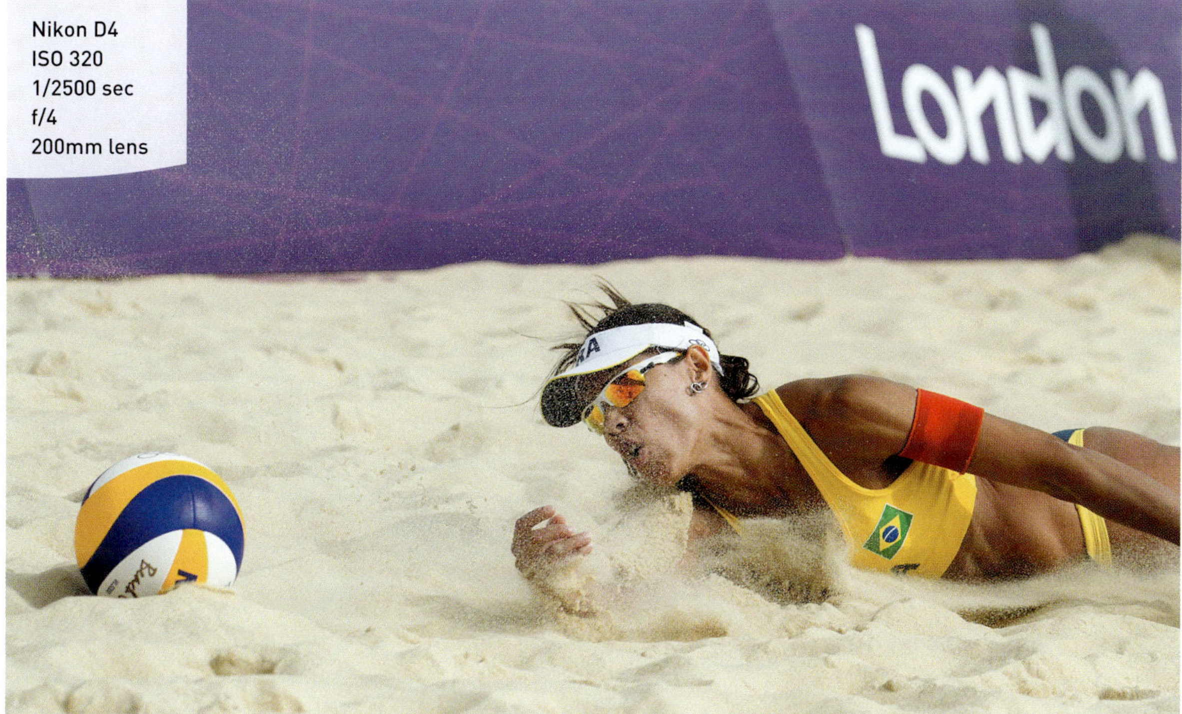

BOXING: HOW TO GET THE BEST SHOTS

Often called the "sweet science," boxing takes place in a ring where two athletes fight. The bout is decided when one fighter is ruled unable to proceed by a referee, quits, is disqualified for rule breaking, or is declared the winner based on the judges' scorecards at the end of the fight (**Figure 9.5**).

From ringside positions, you'll be shooting up at the fighters while they dance around the ring and throw punches. Wide-angle lenses work best here. A medium telephoto is important if you want to get in tight on the boxers' faces between rounds while they are resting and receiving medical attention in their respective corners.

Slightly elevated positions allow you to shoot over the ropes that surround the ring. Don't get so focused on the action that you ignore the scene. A wide angle from up high can be an important storytelling element, capturing the scene around as well as in the ring.

For capturing peak action, a very fast shutter speed is necessary. A minimum of 1/1600 is preferable.

Boxing is frequently lit "theatre style," meaning the lights are concentrated on the ring, making it look like the scene is illuminated by a giant spotlight. This makes for dramatic images. The backlighting will help freeze the water droplets flying from the athletes when a punch is landed.

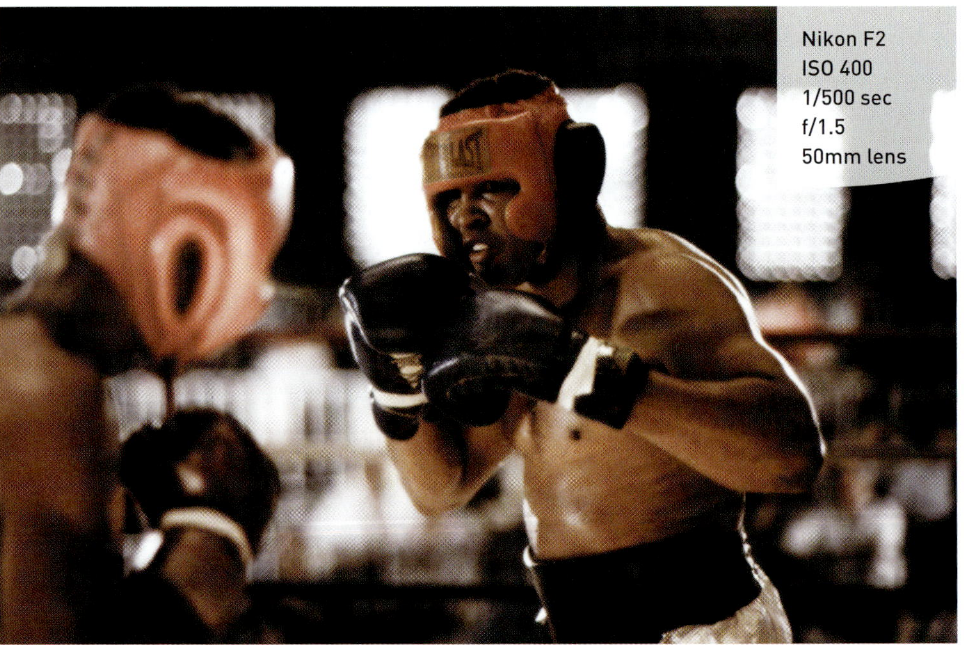

Nikon F2
ISO 400
1/500 sec
f/1.5
50mm lens

FIGURE 9.5 Muhammad Ali trains in the Bahamas for his last fight.

TIP

Bodily fluids spew from the athletes. Be prepared to deal with that.

TIP

You will be working in a hunched over position most of the night, so dress appropriately.

CYCLING: HOW TO GET THE BEST SHOTS

Cycling, like many of the other Olympic sports, has a number of different divisions. The sport has been contested in every one of the modern Summer Olympic Games since 1896. The only other Olympic sports that have been in every Olympics are athletics, artistic gymnastics, fencing, and swimming.

Road cycling takes place on a course laid out over normal roads. Typically, the cyclists compete in two road cycling events: time trials, which are basically a sprint competition, and road races where cyclists compete in packs.

For road cycling races, I try to concentrate on two positions. One is a scenic location out on the course where I can place the racers in an environment that defines the race (**Figure 9.6**). After the pack has passed, I then move to the finish line to capture the winner crossing it.

There are literally thousands of cycling road races held every year that have nothing to do with the Olympics. The most famous of these is the Tour de France, which is held over three grueling weeks, normally in July. The race consists of 21 one-day stages. The Tour is an amazing event to cover; it is part race, part carnival (**Figure 9.7**). Covering the tour is a difficult challenge because the peleton (the main group of riders) moves very quickly, and the leader, wearing the coveted yellow jersey, is frequently difficult to spot until the very finish of the stage. But the scenery is spectacular, the competition fierce, and the emotions high.

TIP

Drive the course backwards when you're looking for shooting positions so you are looking in the direction you will likely be photographing. It makes scouting much more precise.

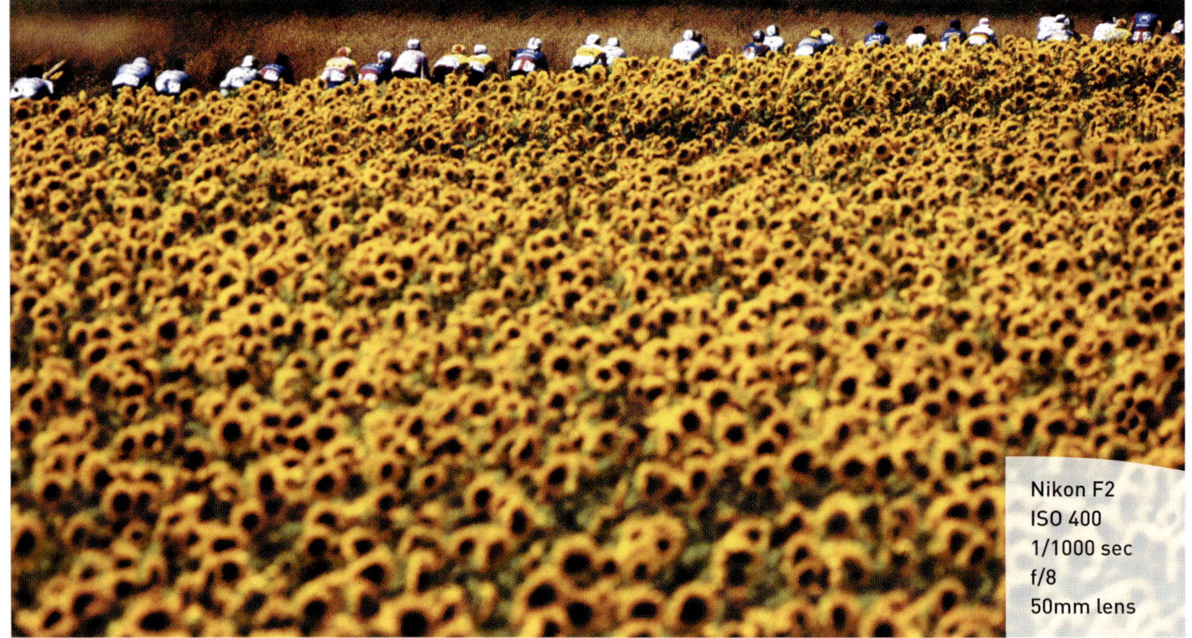

Nikon F2
ISO 400
1/1000 sec
f/8
50mm lens

FIGURE 9.6
Before shooting the Tour de France for *Sports Illustrated*, I carefully scouted the course to try to find a nice scenic shot. While the race was taking place, I moved ahead of the riders so I could photograph the pack as the riders moved through the field.

FIGURE 9.7
Fans cheer the bikers on during the Tour de France.

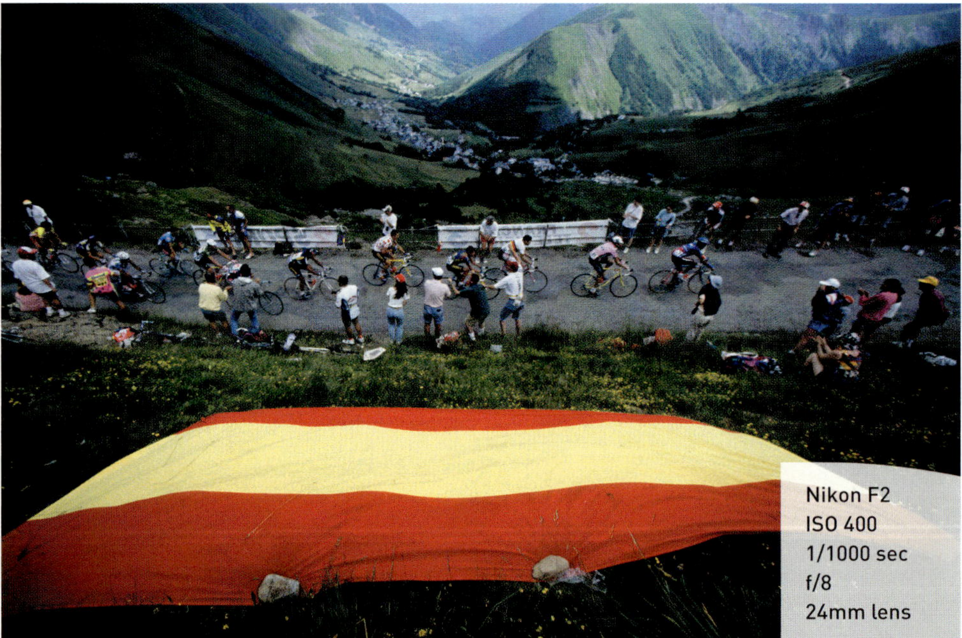

Nikon F2
ISO 400
1/1000 sec
f/8
24mm lens

Track cycling consists of various events: Sprint, Team Sprint, Keirin, Team Pursuit, and Omnium. Each of the events has slightly different rules and vastly different strategies. For the purposes of this book, I'll discuss the general shooting considerations that apply to all of them.

Track cycling races take place on banked oval courses, which may be indoors or out. As with most of the other sports discussed, there are many different combinations that will work to make spectacular images.

I like to shoot head on from the end of one of the straightaways, normally facing the start/finish line. To capture the action as the cyclists come out of the far turn and head toward me, I use the longest lens possible. As they power through the turn right in front of me, I switch to a wide-angle lens. If I'm able to place a wide-angle remote to capture the cyclists going through the turn, I'll often use a short telephoto and do pans as the racers pass in front of me. Because the cyclists in most of the races do multiple laps, I have time to try a number of different lens and setting combinations (**Figure 9.8**).

TIP

Use a very fast shutter speed, at least 1/1250 of a second, when the cyclists are moving parallel to you. If you don't, the image will blur.

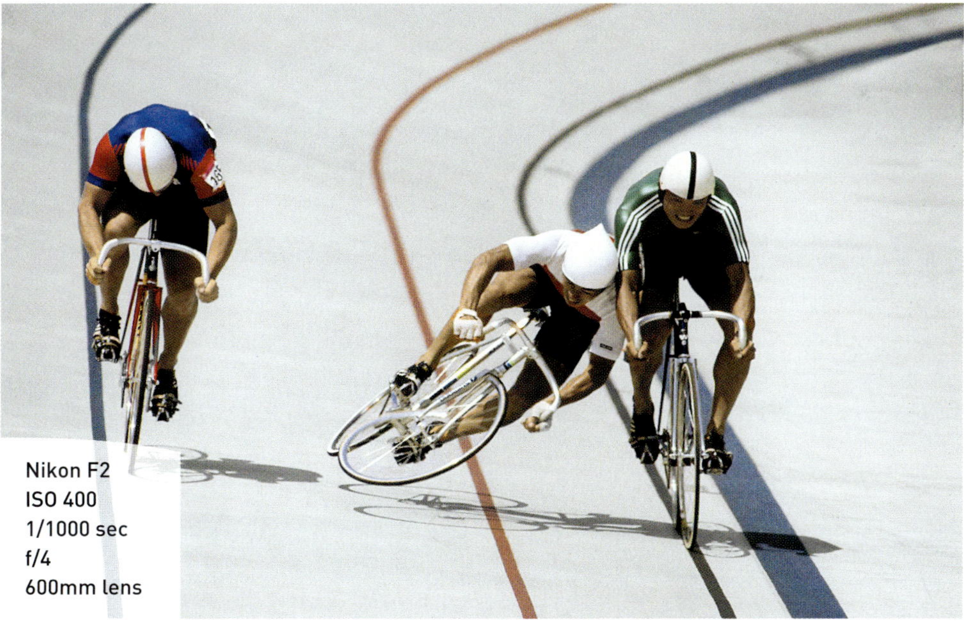

Nikon F2
ISO 400
1/1000 sec
f/4
600mm lens

FIGURE 9.8
A biker falls into the rider next to him during the 1984 Olympic Games in Los Angeles.

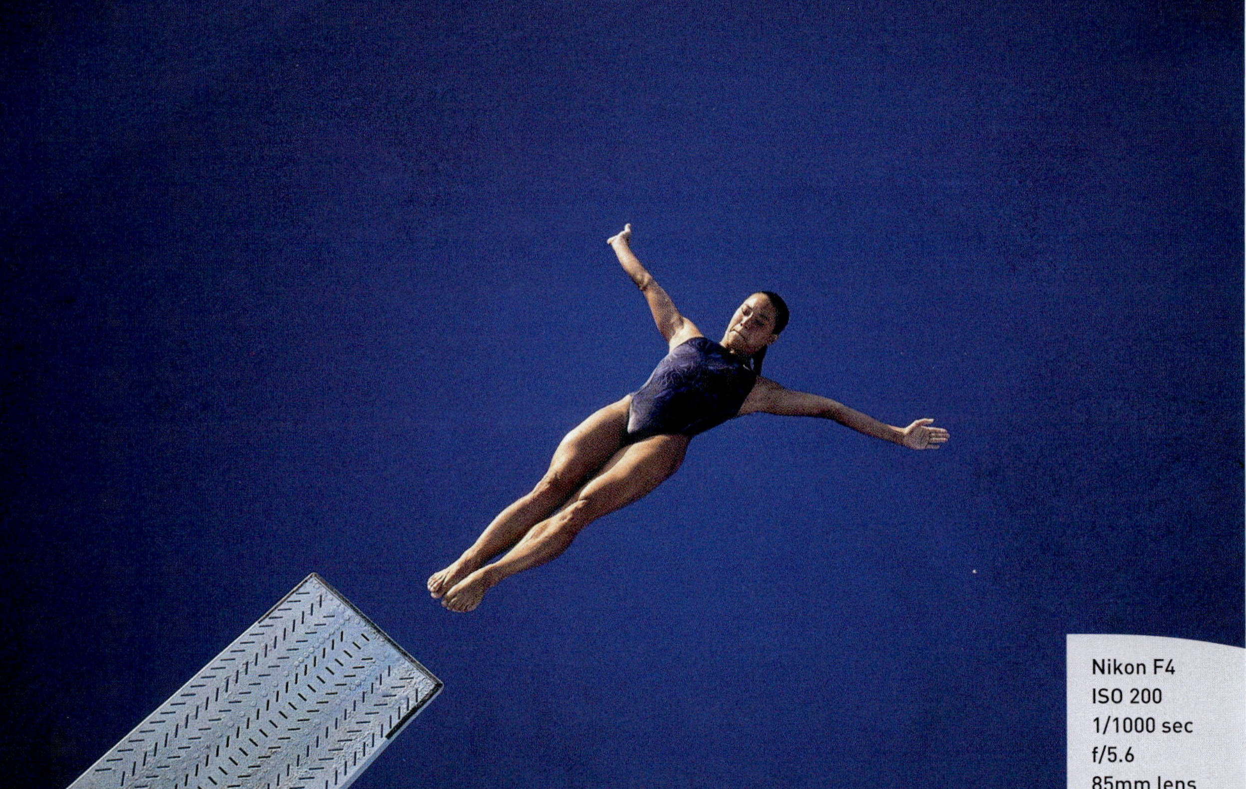

Nikon F4
ISO 200
1/1000 sec
f/5.6
85mm lens

FIGURE 9.9
By positioning myself above the diver, I was able to capture her midflight above the pool, creating a very clean, simple, and beautiful image.

DIVING: HOW TO GET THE BEST IMAGES

Diving consists of a number of events, each with its own unique characteristics. There are two types of launching pads for the divers: springboards and platforms, and each has a different height.

Usually, every event requires the athletes to perform six different dives. As in gymnastics, each diver will practice his or her routines during a warm-up period. Pay close attention to practice and take notes; you'll then be ready for the actual competition.

Generally, you'll need a telephoto lens to photograph diving because access is normally very limited to the pool deck for safety reasons.

Find a position that gives you an open sight line from the start of the dive to the finish. Be careful to select a clean background (**Figure 9.9**). Diving is a very beautiful sport, and you want to be sure that the diver dominates the image (**Figure 9.10**).

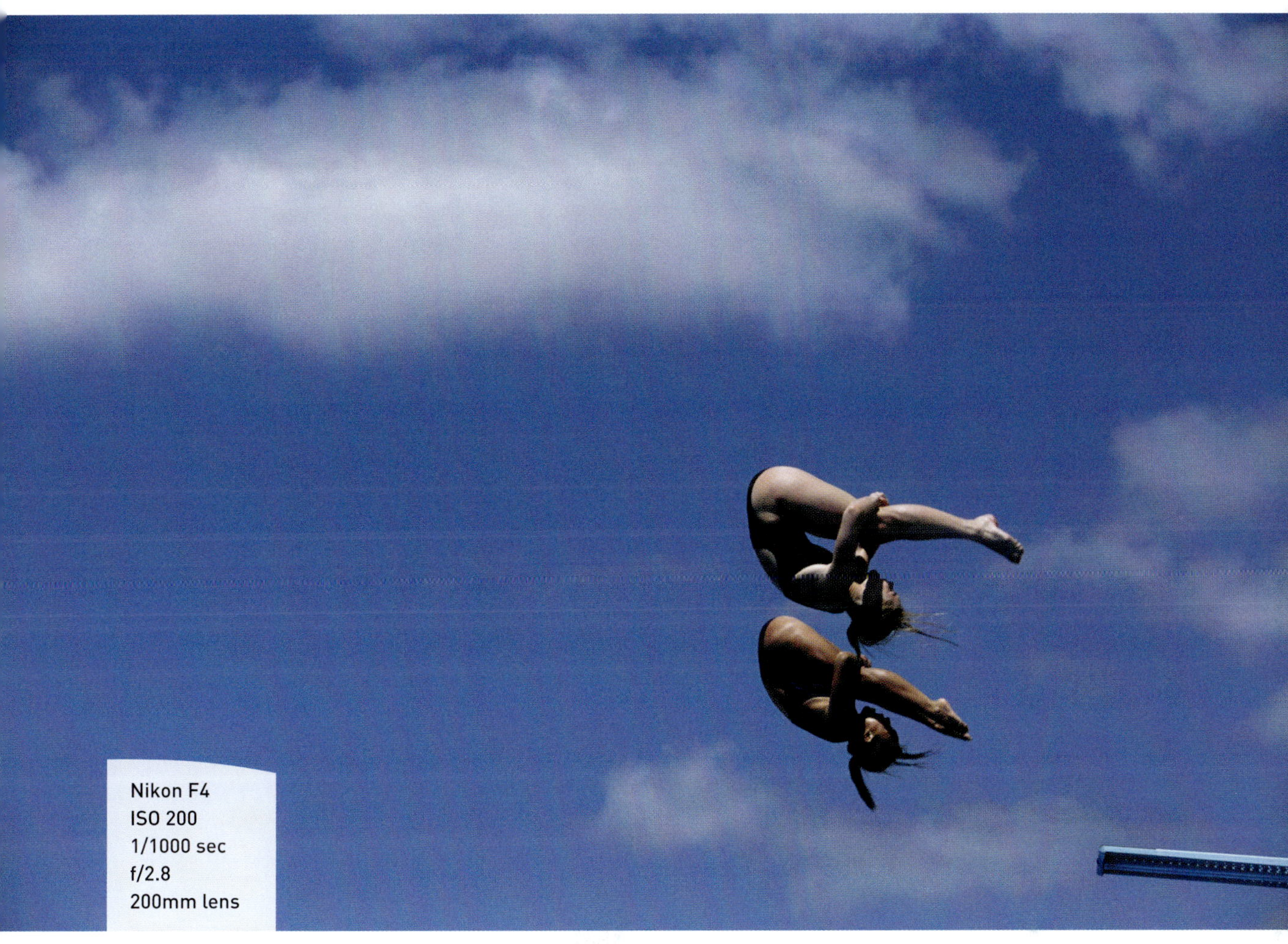

Nikon F4
ISO 200
1/1000 sec
f/2.8
200mm lens

FIGURE 9.10
I shot this from the stands to the side of the diving platforms. From an elevated position, I was able to shoot the divers against the sky.

TIP

A tripod will allow you to do long exposures, letting the divers blur while they are in motion. If you shoot from the side of the diving board, the divers will remain in focus because their motion is up and down, not side to side.

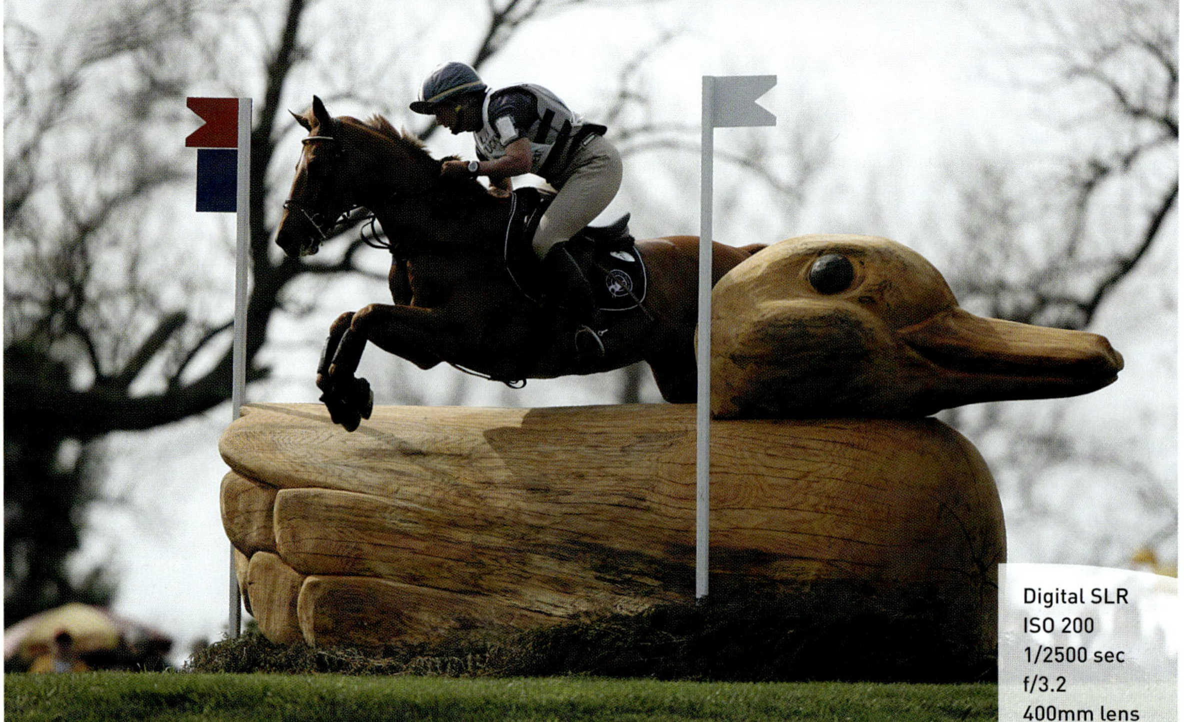

Digital SLR
ISO 200
1/2500 sec
f/3.2
400mm lens

FIGURE 9.11
A rider clears a jump during the 2007 Equestrian Games.

DRESSAGE, EVENTING, AND JUMPING: HOW TO GET THE BEST IMAGES

Dressage, eventing, and jumping are the various horse competitions held at the Olympics and in non-Olympic competitions. Each of the events has slightly different rules and vastly different strategies. Here I'll discuss the general shooting considerations that apply to all of them.

TIP

Using a flash near the horses is not acceptable.

Each competition features three components: the riders, the horses, and the course.

TIP

You will need to use a fast shutter speed—1/2000 of a second or more—when the horses are moving parallel to you.

These events are routinely held during the day, and many shooting positions are available. It's best to spend time scouting the field of play and determine well in advance of the event where you can get clean, straight-on, and side-on views of the horses and riders.

Figure 9.11 shows that by shooting with a telephoto lens and getting low to the ground, I was able to make a clean image of the horse jumping over the duck.

TIP

Remote cameras placed low and next to the jumps and obstacles make dramatic images.

High vantage points are important as well, because they allow you to show the beauty and the difficulty of the competition. My position at a high vantage point allowed me to take advantage of the location of the course in Greenwich and to show the cloudy London sky in **Figure 9.12**.

FIGURE 9.12
A rider from the British Eventing team makes his way around the course during the 2012 Olympic Games in London.

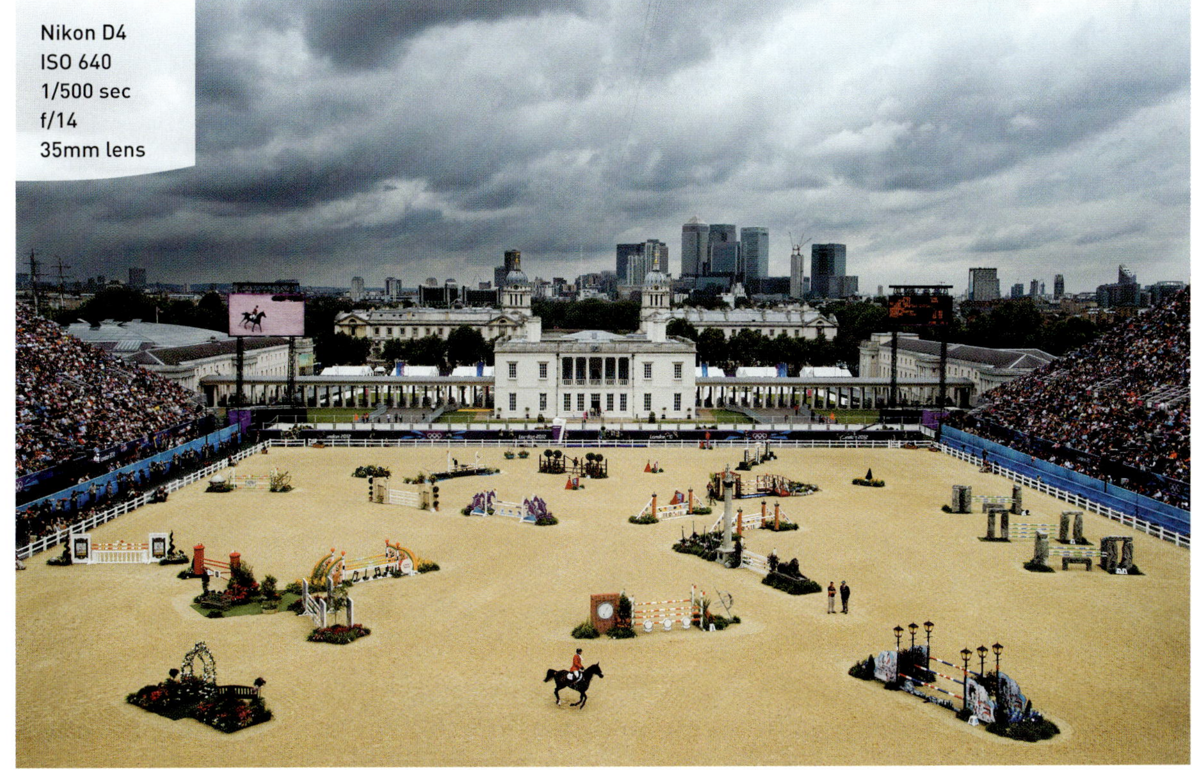

Nikon D4
ISO 640
1/500 sec
f/14
35mm lens

These horse competitions are more about stamina and grace than they are about power and speed. All four elements are certainly present, but style is the most important aspect of these images.

TIP

Use enough depth of field to capture the entire horse and the rider. The horse will move quickly and cover ground very fast. Be sure to leave yourself enough room to include both.

GYMNASTICS: HOW TO GET THE BEST SHOTS

Gymnastics consists of multiple events, and each has slightly different rules and unique movements (**Figure 9.13**). Both men and women compete in floor exercise and vault. Women also compete in balance beam and uneven bars. Men compete in parallel bars, horizontal bars, and pommel horse.

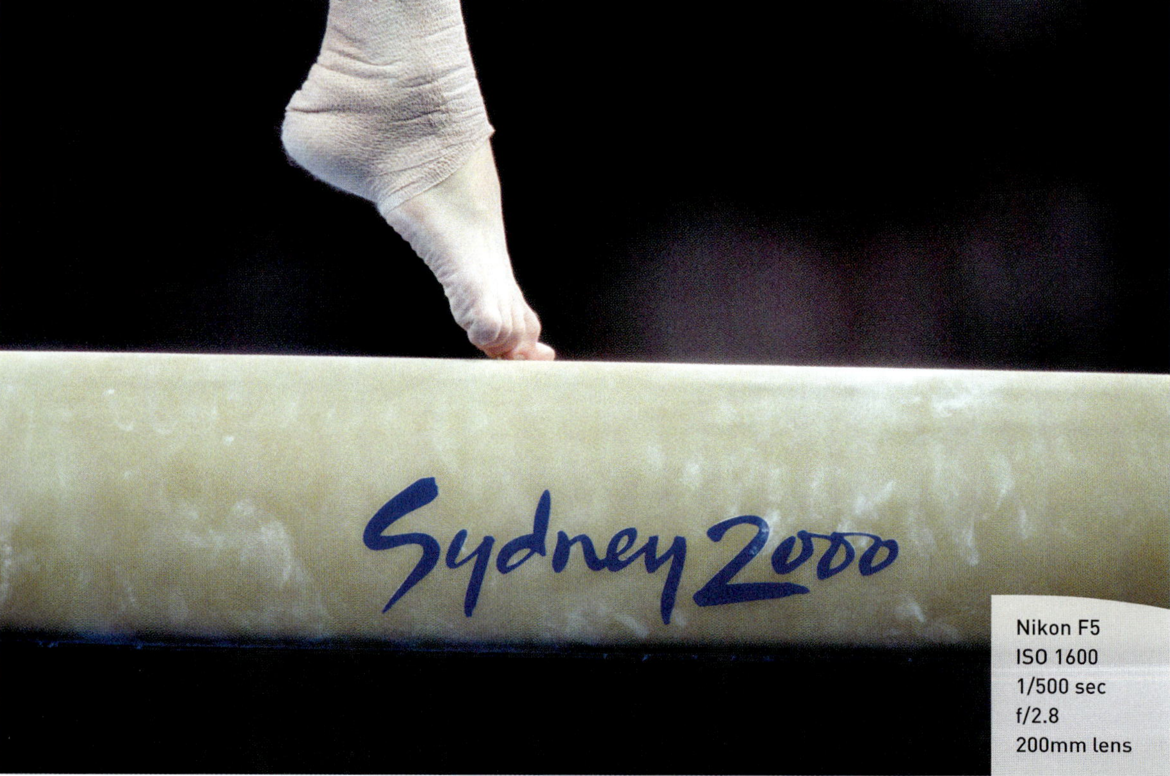

Nikon F5
ISO 1600
1/500 sec
f/2.8
200mm lens

FIGURE 9.13 This is a detail shot I made during the 2000 Olympic Games in Sydney.

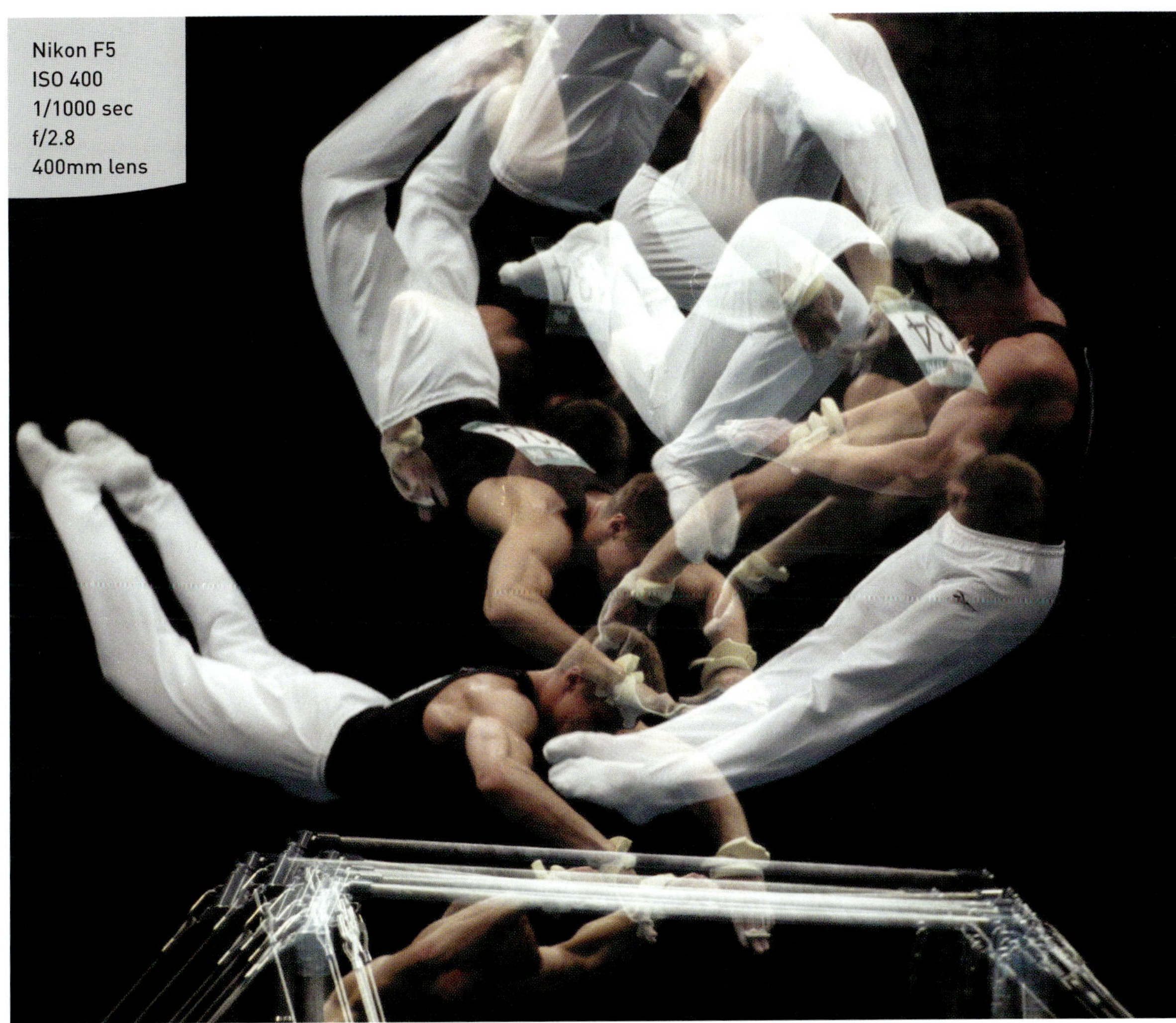

FIGURE 9.14
This is a multiple exposure of Alexei Nemov on the horizontal bars during the 1996 Olympic Games in Atlanta.

This is another sport that is more about beauty than about speed or power, but speed and power are necessary to achieve the beauty. Showing the combination of the three elements and demonstrating how they work together is critical.

I had one chance to make the image in **Figure 9.14**. Alexei Nemov was expected to win the gold in the 1996 Olympic Games, so I wanted to make a special, different picture of him in action. Because you are not allowed to use tripods or strobe during the Olympics, I arrived at the location hours in advance to give myself time to find my spot and figure out how to steady my camera. I then set up with a long lens, camera, and monopod in a small space that would allow me to capture Nemov against a black background. The ten exposures show the strength, speed, and accuracy of Nemov's performance that day.

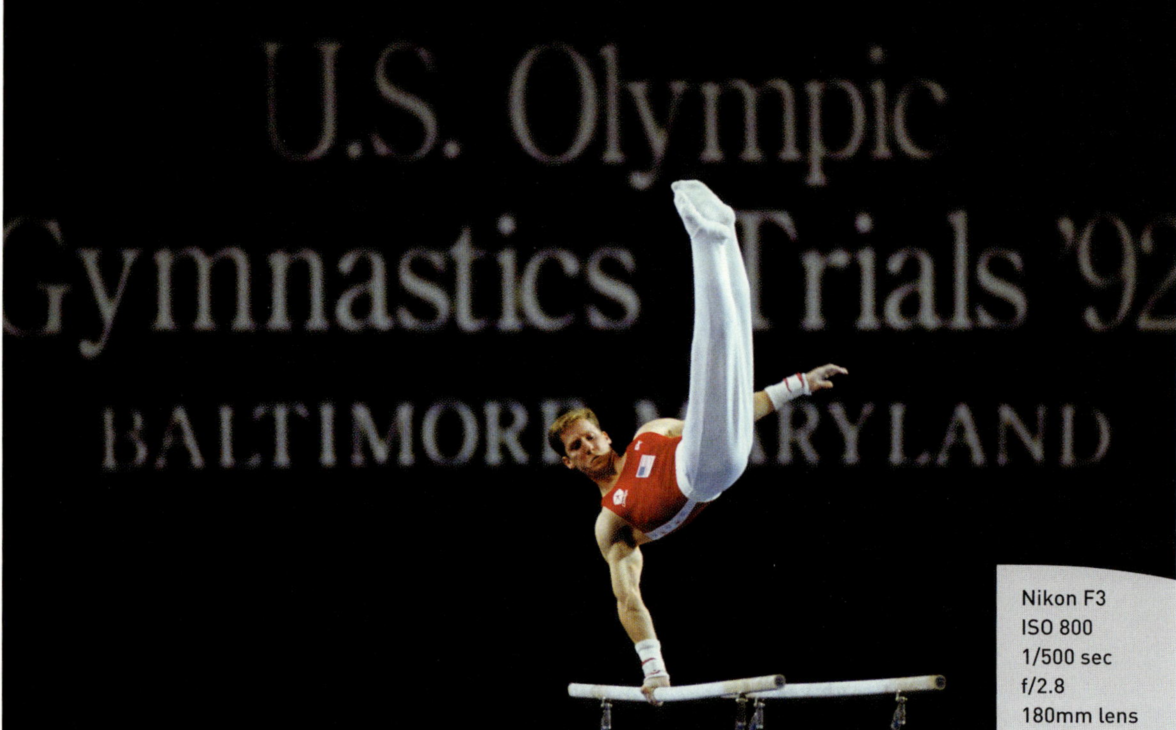

FIGURE 9.15
A gymnast performs on the balance beam during the 1992 United States Olympic Trials.

With each of the disciplines, you'll need to work with the organizers of the meet to be sure you are shooting from a place that is safe for the athletes and for you, and does not cause a distraction. Flash is strictly forbidden. In addition, you should not move once the athlete starts a routine. Motion can create a distraction and cause an athlete to lose concentration while in motion, which can result in a poor performance, or worse, an injury.

Clean sight lines are tough to find because multiple events will be going on at the same time. For the image in **Figure 9.15**, I positioned myself carefully to include the background. By using a shorter lens and slightly more depth of field, I was able to include more information in the photo.

Also, the gymnastic apparatuses clutter up the backgrounds, so shooting wide open with the longest lens possible will help reduce the clutter (**Figure 9.16**).

TIP

Watch the athletes carefully while they warm up. Almost always they will go through all of their motions in practice. That will help you know where to position yourself and how to anticipate what they will do during their routines.

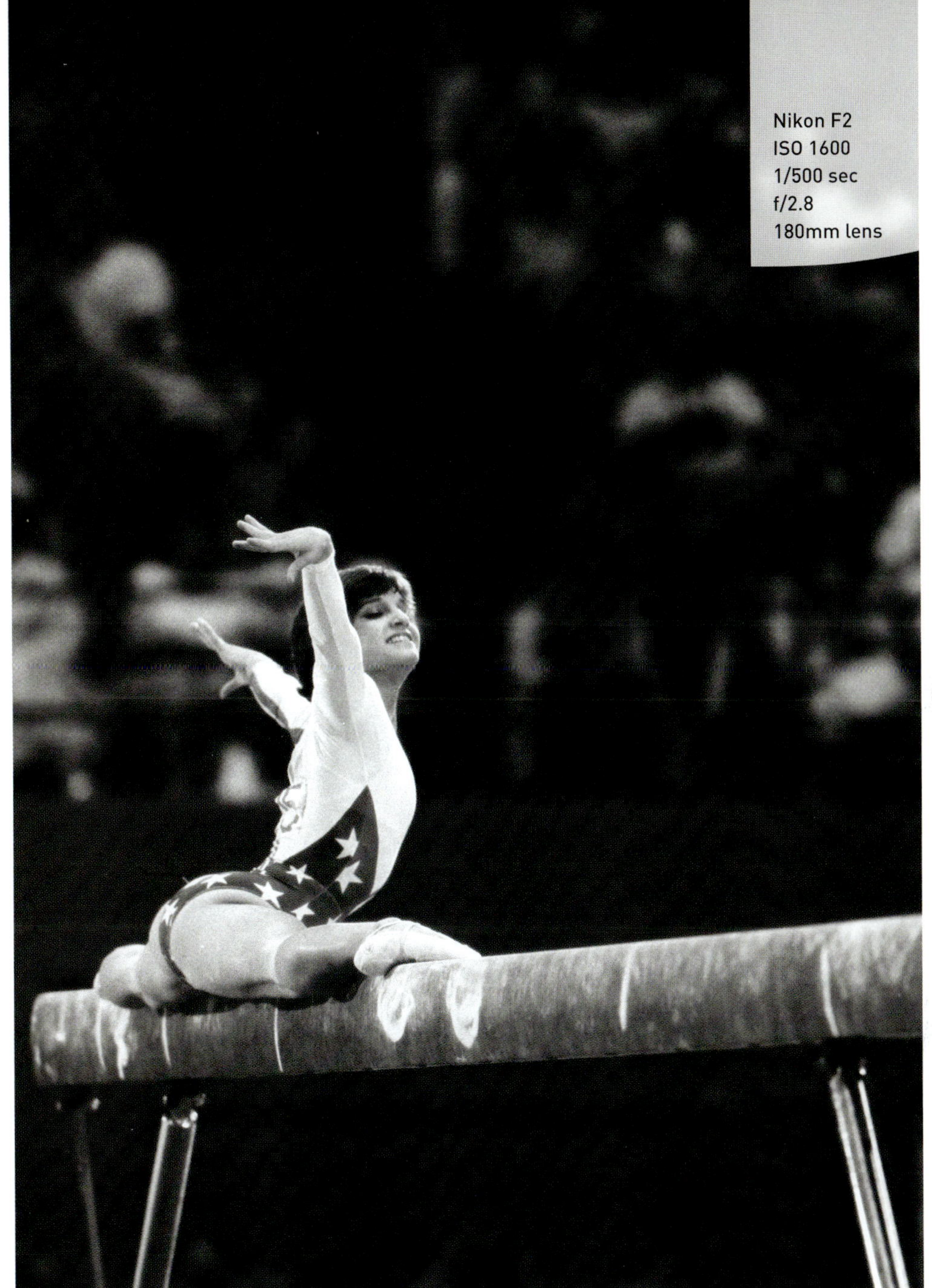

FIGURE 9.16
Mary Lou Retton performs on the balance beam during the 1984 Olympic Games in Los Angeles.

TABLE TENNIS: GETTING THE BEST SHOTS

Table tennis is played indoors in a tightly controlled environment and can be played by two or four players.

TIP

Because the action takes place indoors around a relatively small surface, the table, it is easy to mount a camera on a tripod and do multiple exposures. The light and therefore the depth of field will be consistent, so you can easily calculate the exposure.

This is a wonderful sport to experiment with. The games are frequently long with repetitive action, they take place on a small surface, and they have very few key moments. This gives you a chance to try blurs, pans, and multiple exposures.

I love photographing table tennis, because it allows me to make images I simply can't make in other sports (**Figure 9.17**). The courts are full of color and graphic lines.

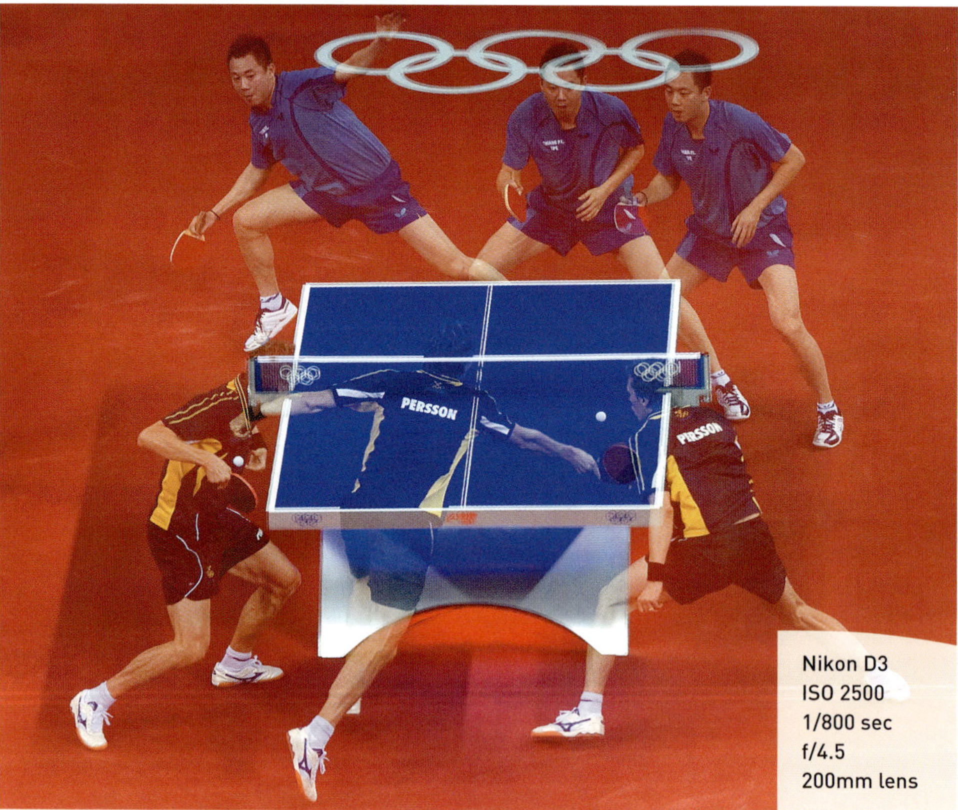

FIGURE 9.17
I made this multiple exposure during the 2008 Olympic Games in Beijing.

Nikon D3
ISO 2500
1/800 sec
f/4.5
200mm lens

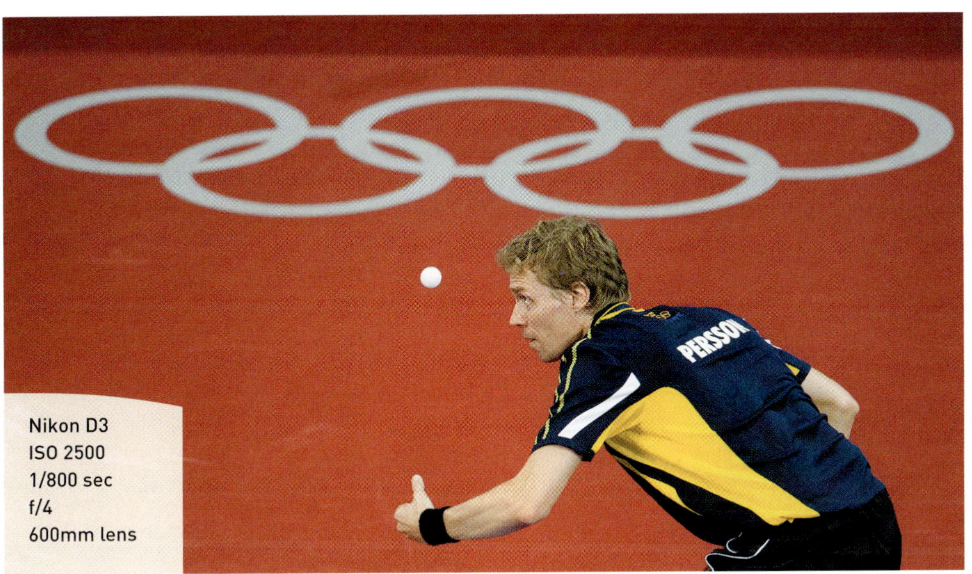

Nikon D3
ISO 2500
1/800 sec
f/4
600mm lens

FIGURE 9.18
Jörgen Persson of Sweden sets up to serve during the 2008 Olympic Games in Beijing.

Multiple exposures and blurs work really well in table tennis, because everything but the athletes is stationary.

TIP

The athletes change sides during the match, allowing you to photograph both players equally without changing positions.

Using a long lens to isolate the athletes' expressions as they serve can lead to intense and humorous photographs (**Figure 9.18** and **Figure 9.19**). Also, backgrounds can be very cluttered and ugly during table tennis tournaments. By shooting with a telephoto lens at a limited depth of field, I was able to concentrate all action on the athlete and reduce the background in Figure 9.19.

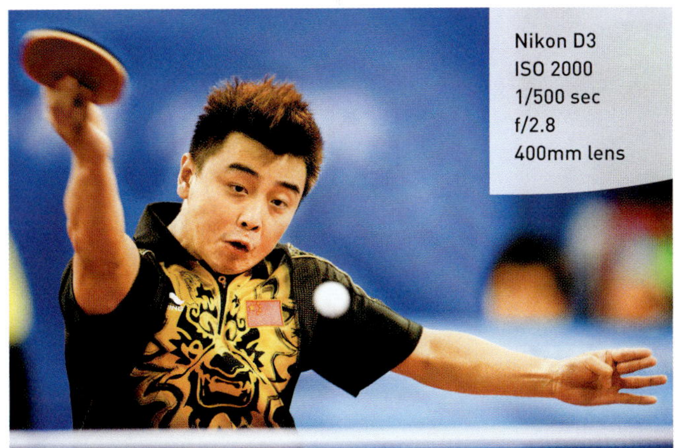

Nikon D3
ISO 2000
1/500 sec
f/2.8
400mm lens

FIGURE 9.19
An athlete from China returns a serve during the 2008 Olympic Games in Beijing.

SWIMMING: GETTING THE BEST SHOTS

Each of the various swimming strokes requires you to shoot from different angles and positions. Because of the arm motions, you need to analyze each stroke before you select a position from which to shoot. You should be able to see the swimmers' faces when they breathe (**Figure 9.20**). Having the face visible in every frame is not mandatory, but for the most part it is very important.

> **TIP**
>
> Use a very fast shutter speed to freeze the water droplets. That will create motion in an otherwise very still frame.

By getting as close to water level as possible, you should be able to get a good look at the swimmer's face as he moves toward you.

> **TIP**
>
> For the butterfly stroke, it is critical to shoot head on; otherwise, all you will see is splash.

FIGURE 9.20
A University of Florida swimmer practices his butterfly stroke.

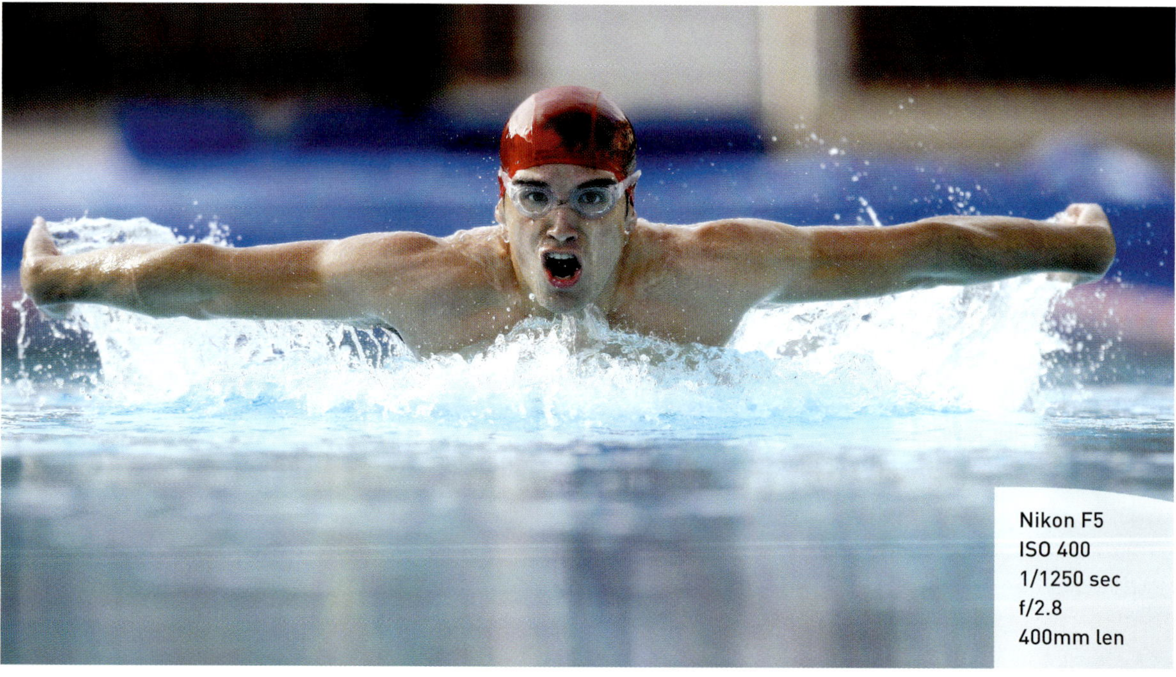

Nikon F5
ISO 400
1/1250 sec
f/2.8
400mm len

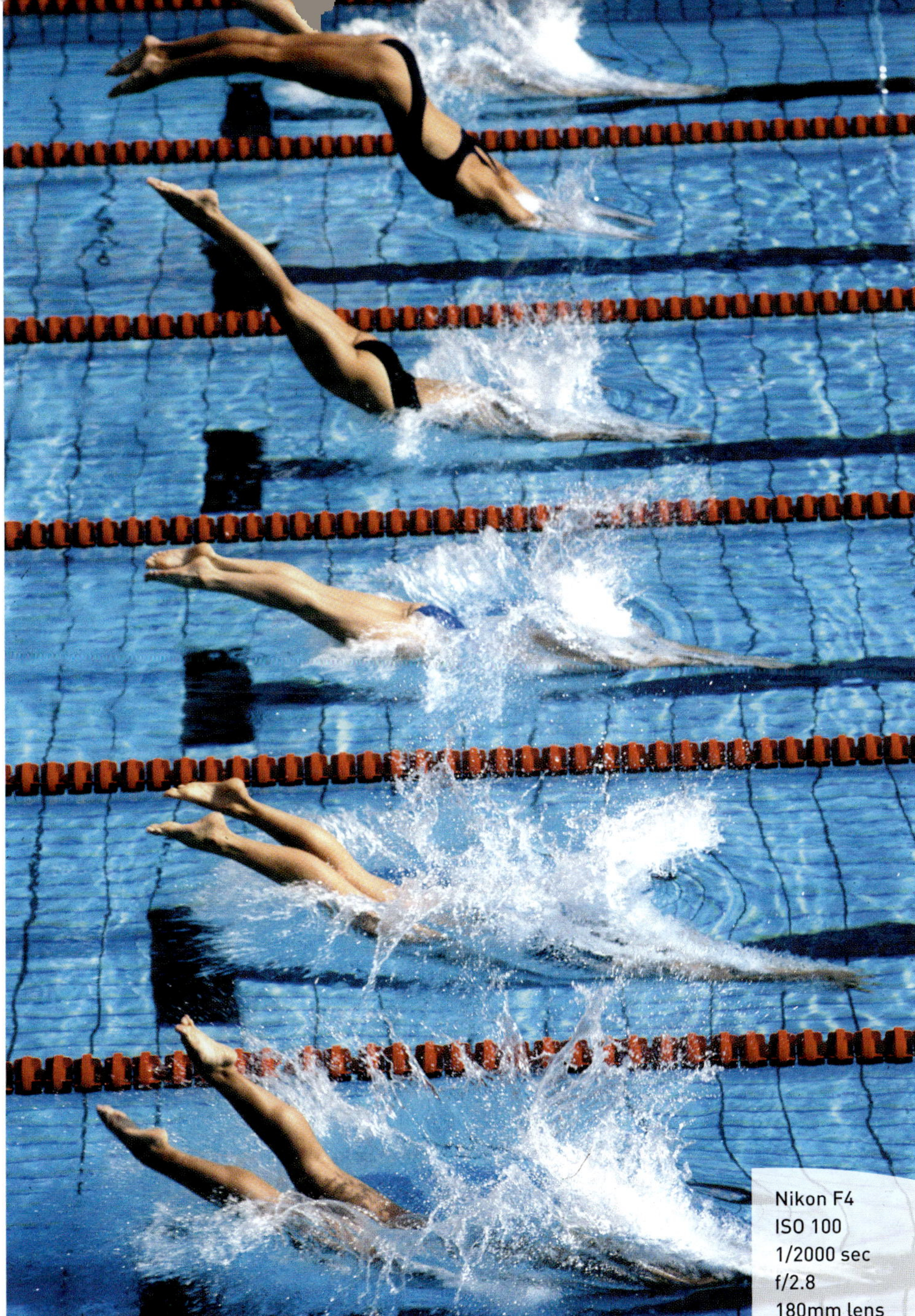

FIGURE 9.21
Swimmers dive into the pool.

Being elevated is often an advantage because not only can use the lane markers as graphic elements in your composition, but you can also easily see who is in front. Shooting from the side at pool level, you can only see the leader because the splash will obscure the other swimmers (**Figure 9.21**).

FIGURE 9.22
Nelson Diebel celebrates winning a gold medal in the 100-meter breast stroke during 1992 Olympic Games in Barcelona.

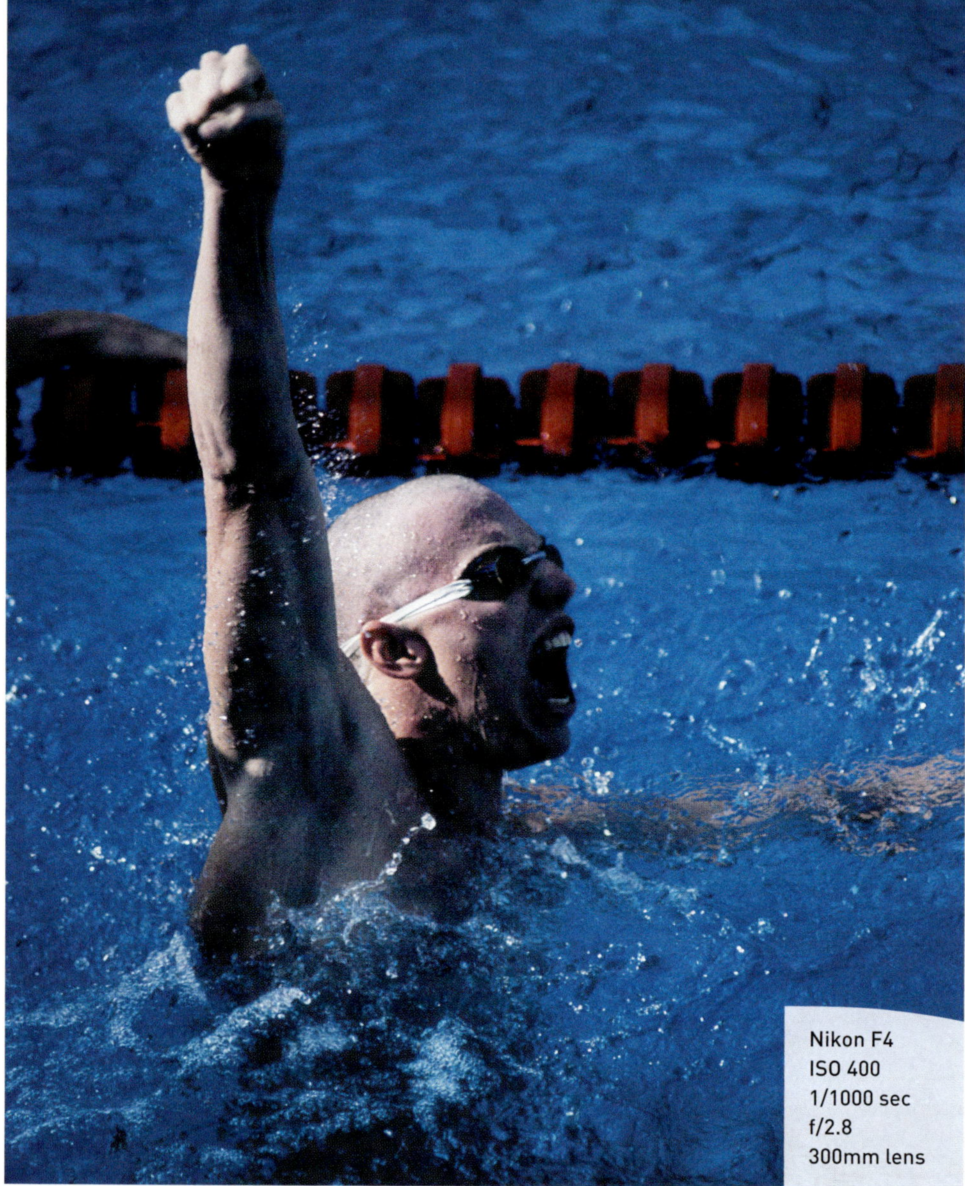

Nikon F4
ISO 400
1/1000 sec
f/2.8
300mm lens

If you want to get emotional reactions in pictures, look for the timing clock that is visible from the pool. The swimmers will turn to look at the clock to see theirs and others' times, and often the order of finish. Then they'll react. You need to position yourself so that you can see their faces when they see the clock (**Figure 9.22**).

TIP

Many pools have viewing windows underneath the water. Shooting from that vantage point will give you a much different look.

WEIGHTLIFTING: GETTING THE BEST SHOTS

Competitors are ordered by their body weight in weightlifting events. Like boxing and wrestling, weightlifters are grouped together by size. The lifters compete in the snatch and the clean and jerk.

The object of the competition is to lift the most weight. It's very straightforward. Usually, you will have great shooting positions on both sides and the front of the athlete. Because it is a solitary sport, the sight lines will be direct and typically very clean—nothing will get in the way (**Figure 9.23**).

TIP

Use a long lens and stand to the side of the athlete. A profile shot can be very graphic and emphasize the weights in the foreground.

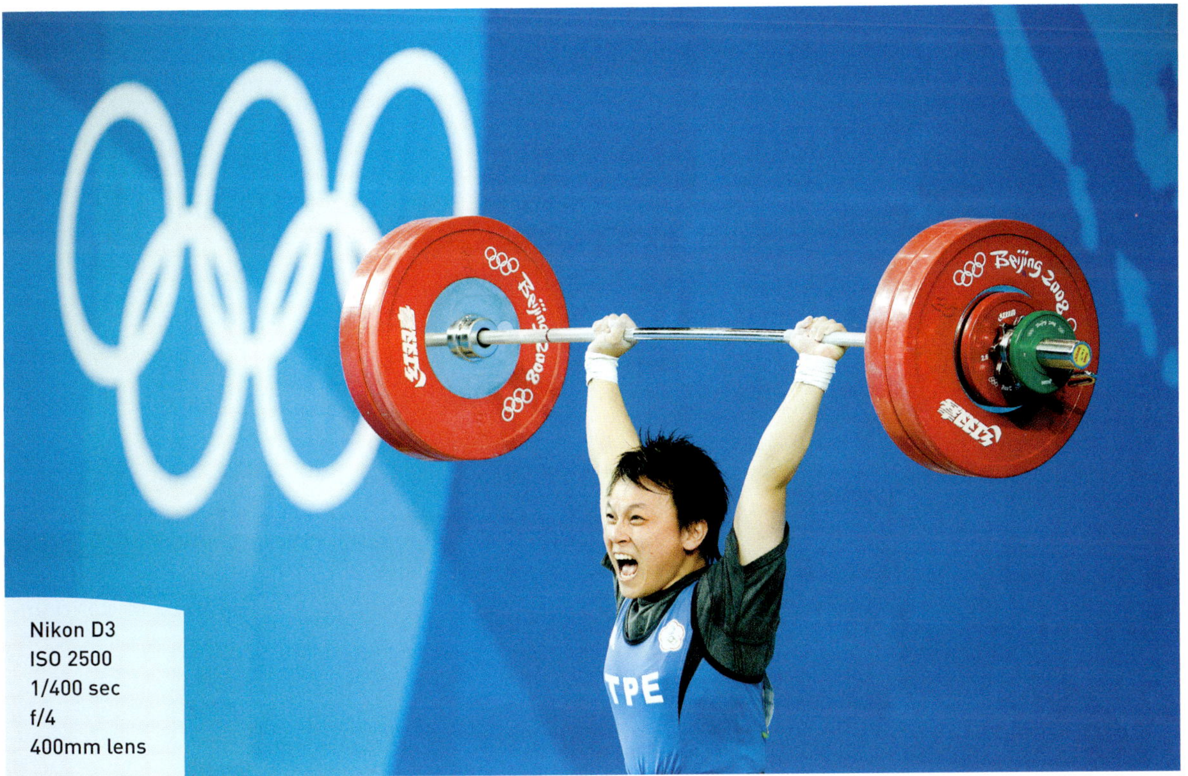

Nikon D3
ISO 2500
1/400 sec
f/4
400mm lens

FIGURE 9.23 A female weightlifter from Taipei competes in the clean and jerk during the 2008 Olympic Games in Beijing.

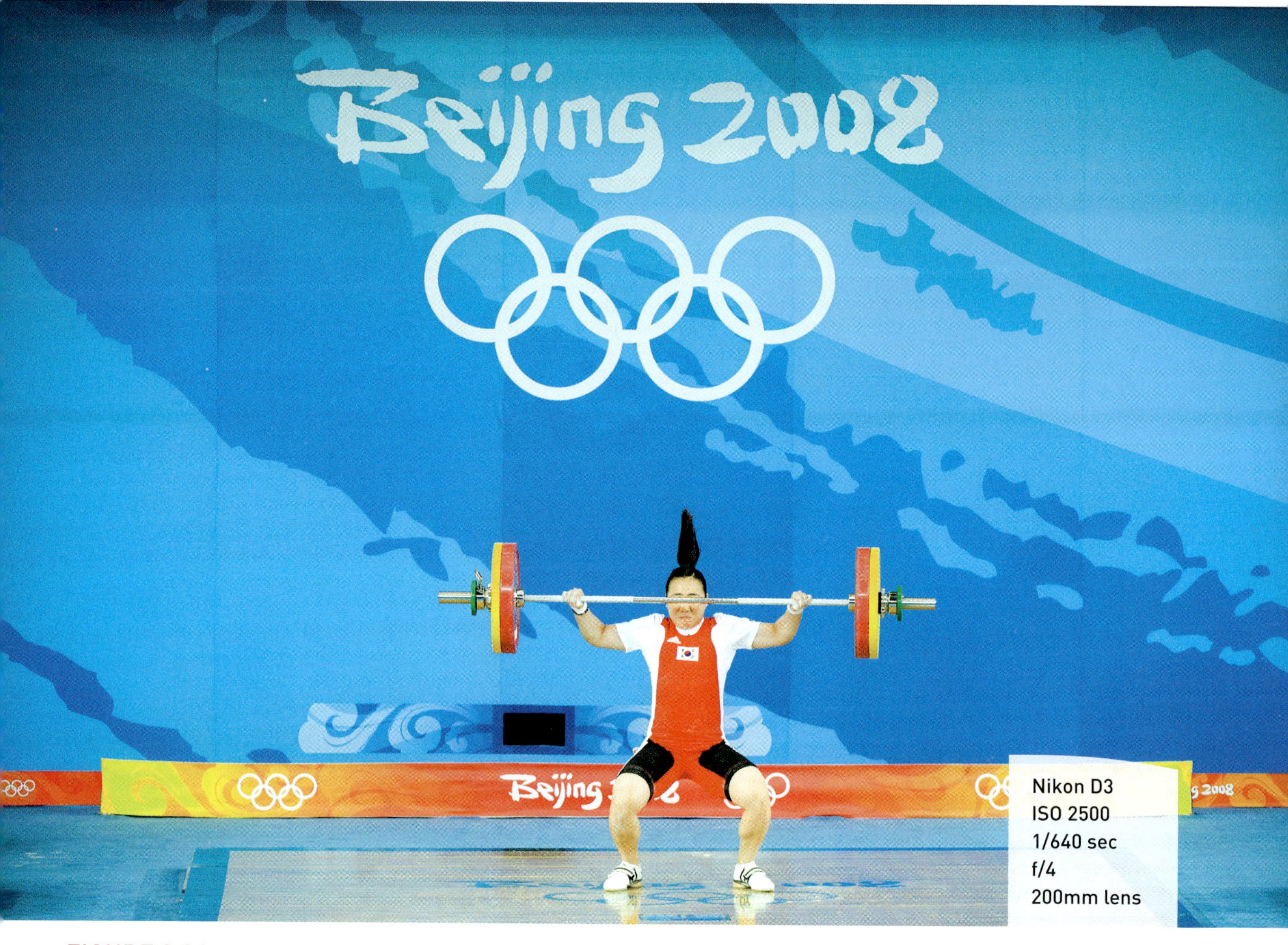

FIGURE 9.24
A female weight-lifter competes in the 2008 Olympic Games in Beijing.

When the weight is lifted quickly, you will see explosive ballistic movement. But there is very little side-to-side or front to back movement, so focus will be easy. These athletes exhibit great grace even under maximum exertion (**Figure 9.24**). In addition, the light will be consistent, making exposure simple.

TIP

Often, the best images happen at the end of the lift. Don't look away until the weight is safely back on the ground and the athlete reacts.

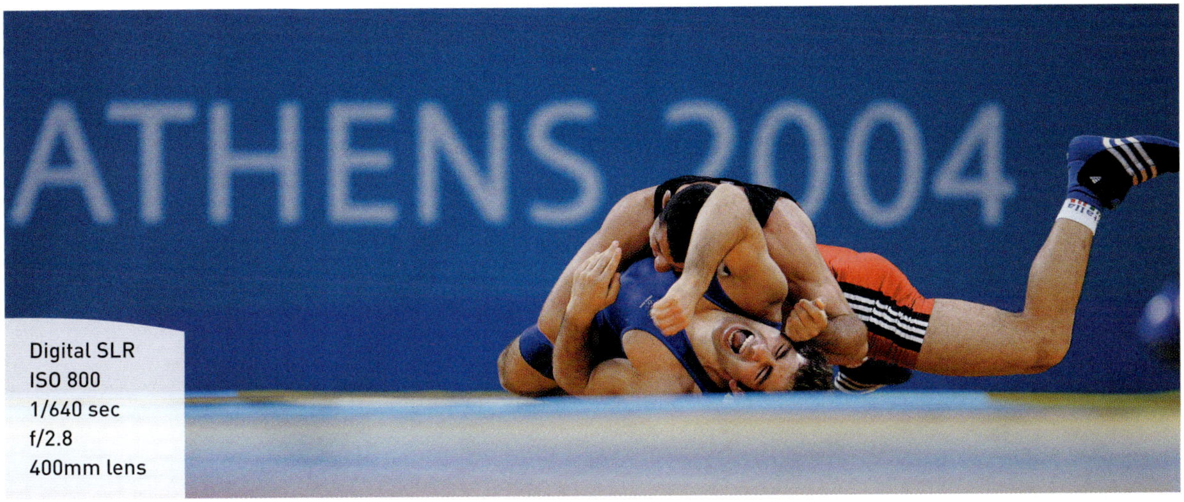

Digital SLR
ISO 800
1/640 sec
f/2.8
400mm lens

FIGURE 9.25
Two wrestlers compete during the 2004 Olympic Games in Athens.

WRESTLING: GETTING THE BEST SHOTS

Wrestlers compete in weight classes. Wrestling is an individual and team sport, but only two athletes wrestle at a time. They grapple with each other in an attempt to gain a superior position (**Figure 9.25**).

TIP

The action does not move as fast as in many other sports, but there will be moments of explosiveness, so try to keep your shutter speed at 1/1000 or higher.

The two athletes compete on a mat. Most mats are colorful, and the center ring provides opportunities for pattern pictures. Elevated positions are very important when you're shooting wrestling matches.

Wrestling almost always takes place indoors, so the weather and the light are not factors.

TIP

In wrestling the most dramatic action frequently takes place when one of the athletes is about to be pinned. To capture that action, the two best places are as low and close to the floor as you can get so that you can see the face of the athlete doing the pinning and from as high as possible so that you can see the face of the athlete being pinned.

CAPTURING THE SCENE AROUND THE EVENTS

Each of the aforementioned sports has a significant and dedicated fan base. Although many of them are team sports, the athletes compete on a solitary basis. Pay close attention to the different way the fans interact with the athletes as opposed to how the fans interact with athletes in team sports.

Because the athletes are often alone, it is easier to compose portraits while they are on the field of play.

GEAR

These sports are all best covered with a wide range of lenses. That said, if you have only one camera, you can cover all of these events with one long lens and one wide-angle lens. For many of the Olympic sports—when the competition is on a local level—using a 50mm lens is perfect.

This is what I bring to every Olympic sport discussed earlier:

- At least two Nikon D4 bodies to use as handheld cameras
- At least two Nikon D4 bodies for remotes
- 600mm f/4 lens
- 400mm f/4 lens
- 300mm f/2.8 lens
- 200mm f/2.0 lens
- 50 mm f/1.4 lens
- 35mm f/1.4 lens
- 12–24mm f/2.8 lens
- TC 1.4x teleconverter
- Four PocketWizards and connectors

My gear list is inflated greatly by the number of remotes I use at the various events.

SETTINGS

With the exception of some swimming and cycling competitions, all of these events normally take place indoors. Therefore, the light should remain constant, which will help you concentrate on focus and composition. Unless you are trying to create a special effect—a blur or a pan—it is always best to use the highest possible shutter speed.

Chapter 9 Assignments

The following assignments are designed to teach you skills that you can transfer from sport to sport. For example, the techniques that you learn while doing blurs during the table tennis assignment you can apply to the other sports. The same is true as you master panning speed and settings during the cycling assignment.

Blurring the Action

Find a table tennis table. Put your camera on a tripod, and ask two players to volley back and forth. Try different shutter speed and aperture combinations until you can anticipate the best way to let the action blur while retaining enough of the players' shape that you can tell what is happening. You are looking for the intersection of art and action.

Panning and Stopping Action

Find a cyclist who will ride past you at varying distances and at different speeds. Practice panning. Keep the camera very stable and your motion consistent. Observe how the distance from the subject to the camera changes the speed necessary to stop action. Also, consider how the distance from the subject to the camera changes the shapes recorded during the pan.

Comparing the Direction and Color of Light

Find a piece of white fabric. With the sun overhead, stretch out the white cloth on the ground. Have your subject do different exercises while standing on the cloth. Pay attention to the amount of light that is reflected up from the cloth and what the color of the light is. Next, do the same assignment with a brightly colored piece of fabric. Then repeat the assignment using a black piece of fabric. When you are finished making photographs using all three pieces of fabric, compare the results and determine how the direction and the color of light reflected affects the results of your images.

Share your results with the book's Flickr group!
Join the group here: flickr.com/groups/sportsphotographyfromsnapshotstogreatshots.

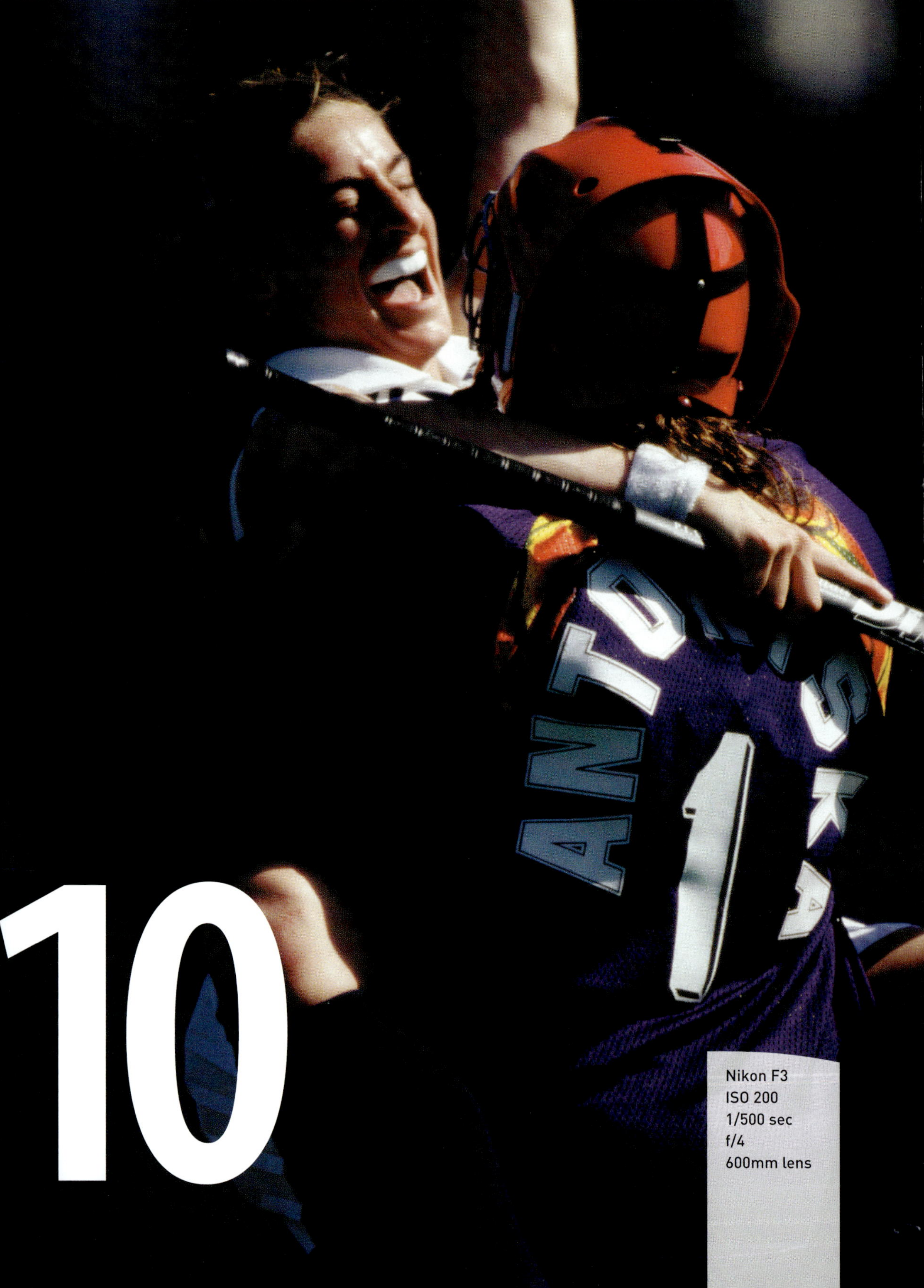

10

Nikon F3
ISO 200
1/500 sec
f/4
600mm lens

Quick Action

SOCCER, LACROSSE, AND FIELD HOCKEY

Soccer, lacrosse, and field hockey are all very fast-paced games played on large fields. This changes how you cover these sports. For example, in basketball you are limited by space. In football, the action is broken up, giving you time to decide where to go next. But in the three sports discussed in this chapter your space is not restricted and you have very little time to react to the pace.

This chapter looks at each sport—soccer, lacrosse, and field hockey—separately to show you what works best. I'll discuss the best shooting positions for each, and then describe the gear and settings I recommend for photographing these sports.

Women celebrate winning a field hockey game. Using the late afternoon light, I was able to expose for only the face of the athlete and draw it out of the dark background.

PORING OVER THE PICTURE

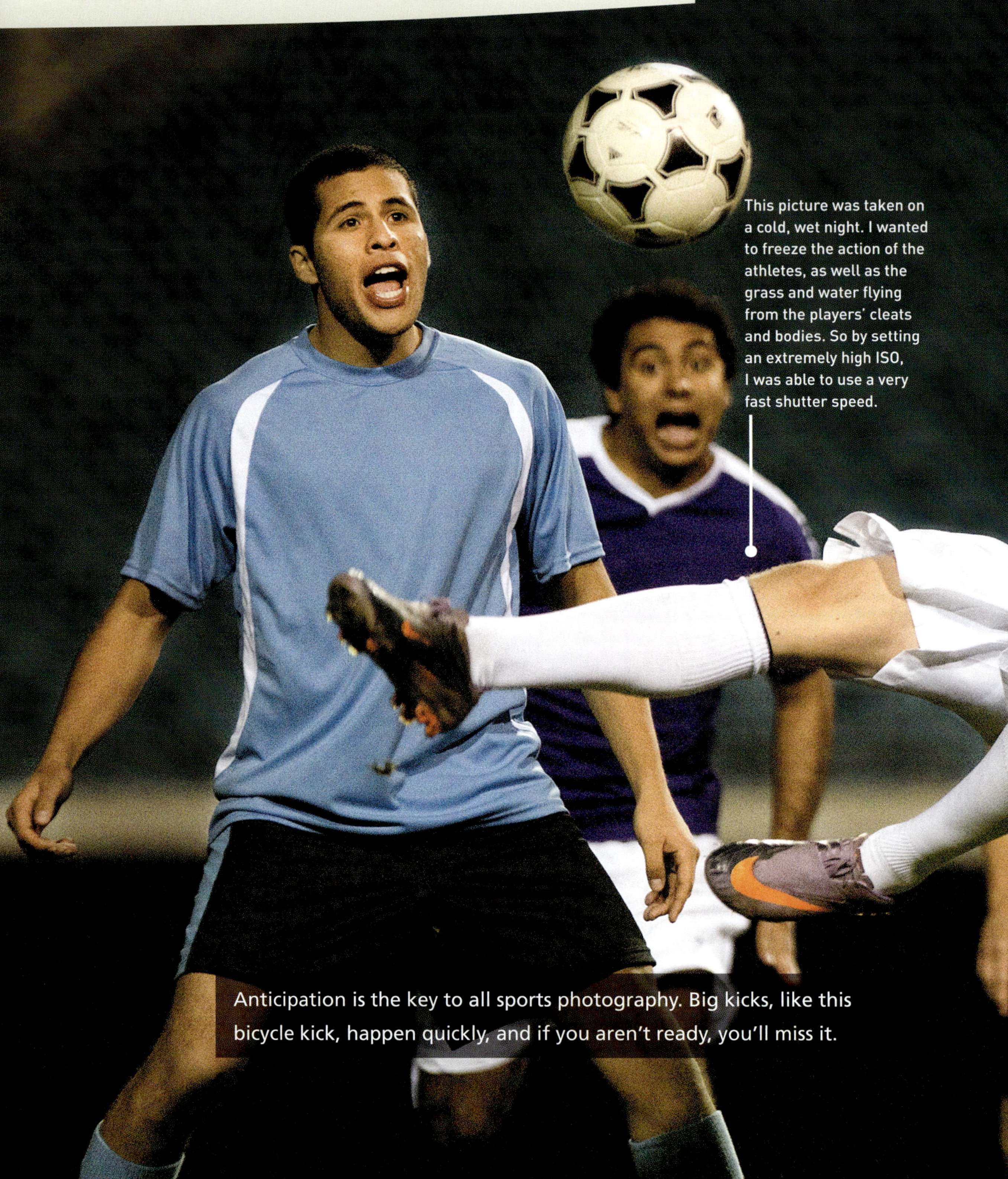

This picture was taken on a cold, wet night. I wanted to freeze the action of the athletes, as well as the grass and water flying from the players' cleats and bodies. So by setting an extremely high ISO, I was able to use a very fast shutter speed.

Anticipation is the key to all sports photography. Big kicks, like this bicycle kick, happen quickly, and if you aren't ready, you'll miss it.

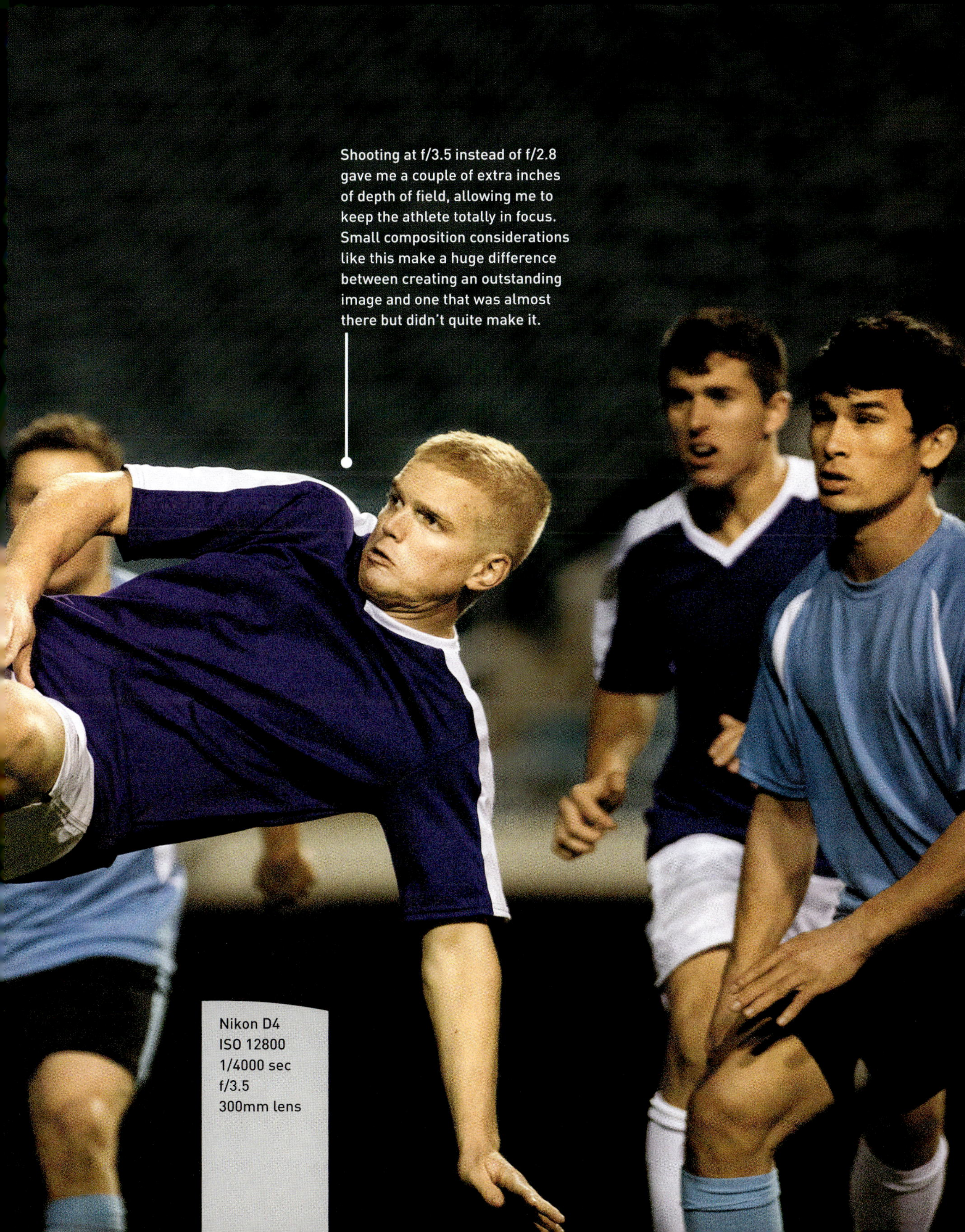

Shooting at f/3.5 instead of f/2.8 gave me a couple of extra inches of depth of field, allowing me to keep the athlete totally in focus. Small composition considerations like this make a huge difference between creating an outstanding image and one that was almost there but didn't quite make it.

Nikon D4
ISO 12800
1/4000 sec
f/3.5
300mm lens

SOCCER: HOW TO GET THE BEST SHOTS

Soccer is the most popular international sport. From the World Cup to little league, the game moves fast, and finding the best shots needs to be a quick process. Getting great shots of the athletes is easier than in some other sports because they are uninhibited by padding, allowing you to capture a lot of emotion in their faces.

WHERE TO POSITION YOURSELF

Because soccer players and the game move so quickly, you cannot follow the action from one end of the field to the other with any precision. Therefore, I focus on two areas during soccer games: the sidelines by the corner arc and behind the goal line. Note that you are not allowed to stand behind the actual goal in NCAA and professional soccer for safety reasons. In addition to describing how to shoot from these two areas, I'll explain how to use one simple, wide-angle remote camera in the goal.

CORNER ARC

The sidelines by the corner arc are great spots to get action shots around the goal. Going into a game I'm usually asked to follow a team or player and unless I am focusing on a defensive player, I'll always shoot that team and/or player on offense. Shooting from the sidelines gives you a clean side look (**Figure 10.1**). They are also great places to capture slides and hits.

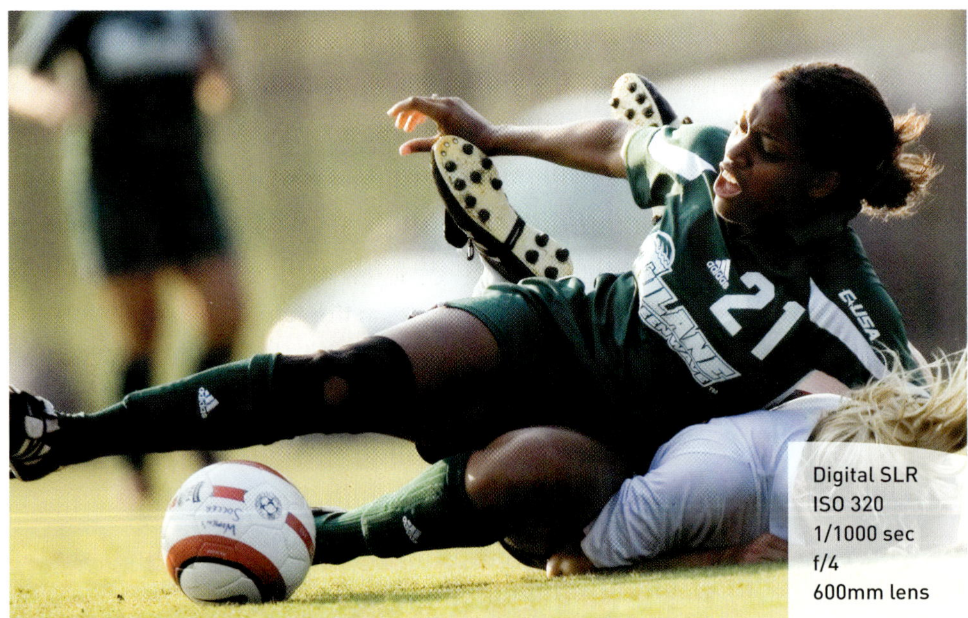

Digital SLR
ISO 320
1/1000 sec
f/4
600mm lens

FIGURE 10.1
A player from Tulane University's women's soccer team fights an opposing player for the ball. Shooting low from the sidelines with a long lens allowed me to make a tight, clean shot of the action.

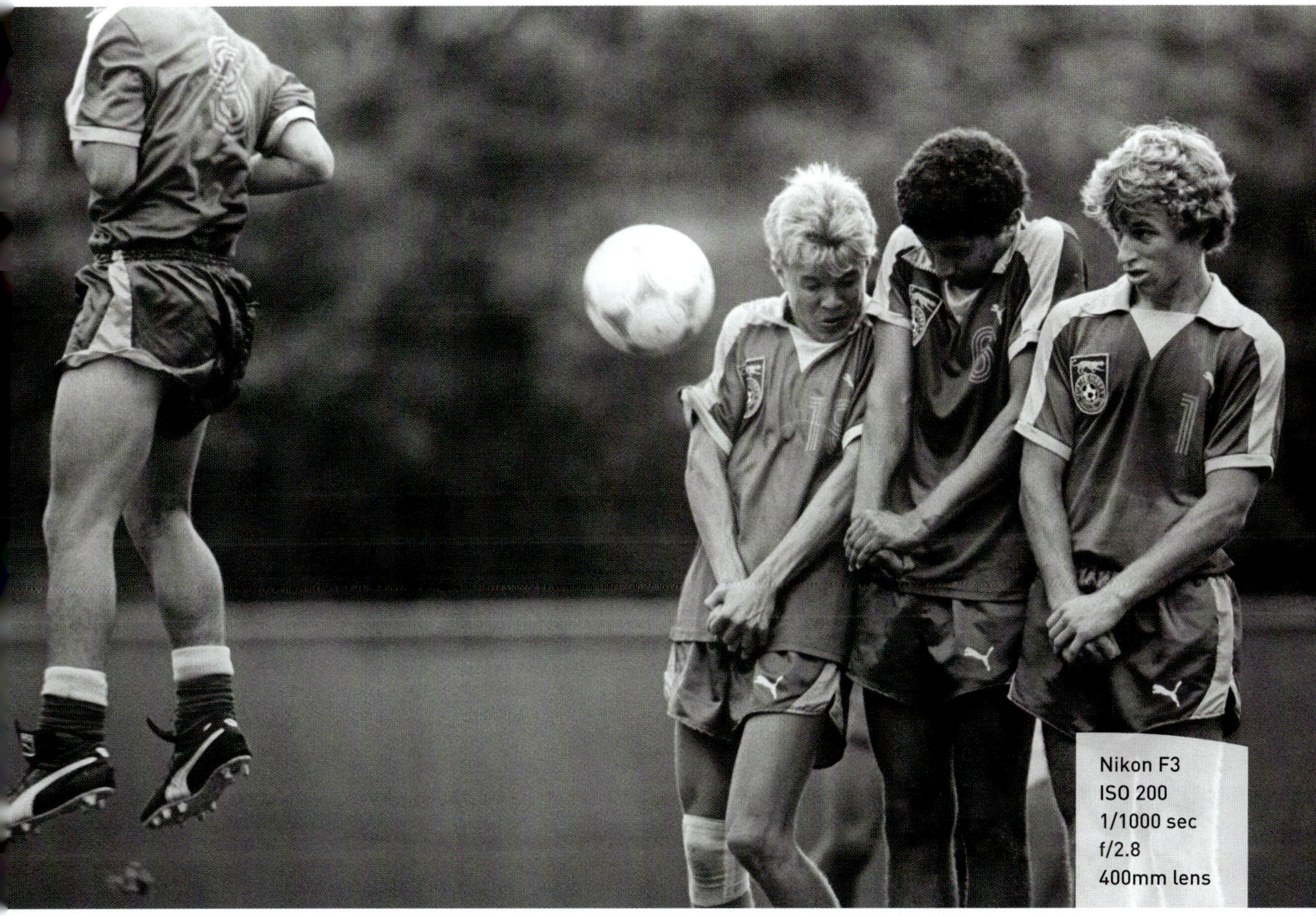

FIGURE 10.2
Boys brace for a penalty kick.

GOAL LINE

Shooting behind the goal line is also ideal to get action around the goal. This position gives you a more head-on look at the action than the corner arc. I always shoot from as close to the goal as possible for penalty kicks and kicks from the corner arc (**Figure 10.2**).

TIP

Penalty kicks make for interesting photographs almost every time. You can concentrate on the players preparing to block the kick. It's a simple and often evocative shot to make.

FIELD HOCKEY: HOW TO GET THE BEST SHOTS

Field hockey, like soccer, is a great sport to cover because the athletes do not wear anything to obstruct their faces, like helmets or hats. Field hockey is fast, low to the ground, and a fun sport to shoot.

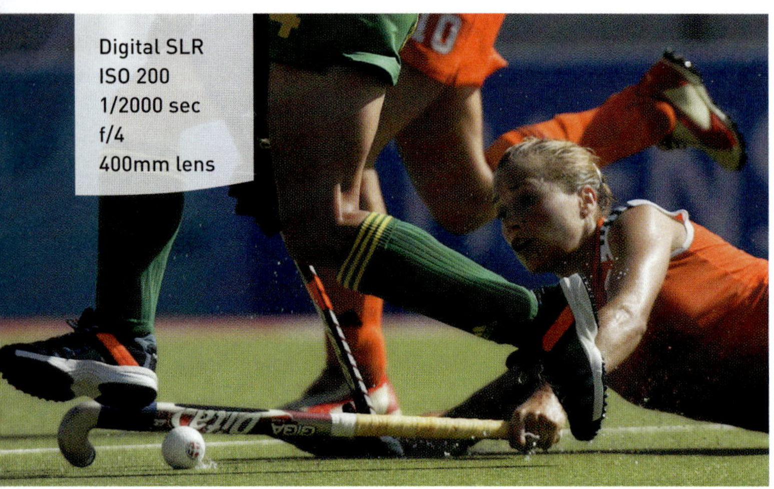

FIGURE 10.3
This photo was taken during a game between the Netherlands and Australia during the 2004 Olympics.

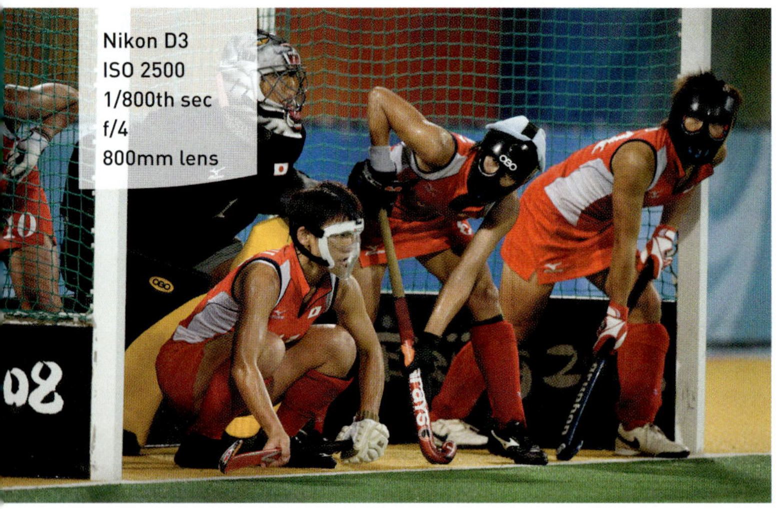

FIGURE 10.4
In this photo Japan is bracing for a shot from Argentina during the 2008 Olympic Games.

WHERE TO POSITION YOURSELF

When I cover field hockey, I generally work from three locations: the sidelines, behind the goal line, and in an elevated position. For safety reasons, you are not allowed to stand behind the goals.

SIDELINES

The sidelines in field hockey give you a great look at the action. Because field hockey is played low to the ground, the athletes usually spend a lot of time on the ground, either diving for the ball or getting knocked down by other players.

By getting low on the sidelines with a long lens, I was able to capture a high-action moment in **Figure 10.3**. I wanted to make sure the athlete and the sticks were in focus, so I shot with a slightly greater depth of field.

The sidelines are also good places to shoot penalty shots. Penalty shots in field hockey are visually appealing because of the face masks the players wear (**Figure 10.4**).

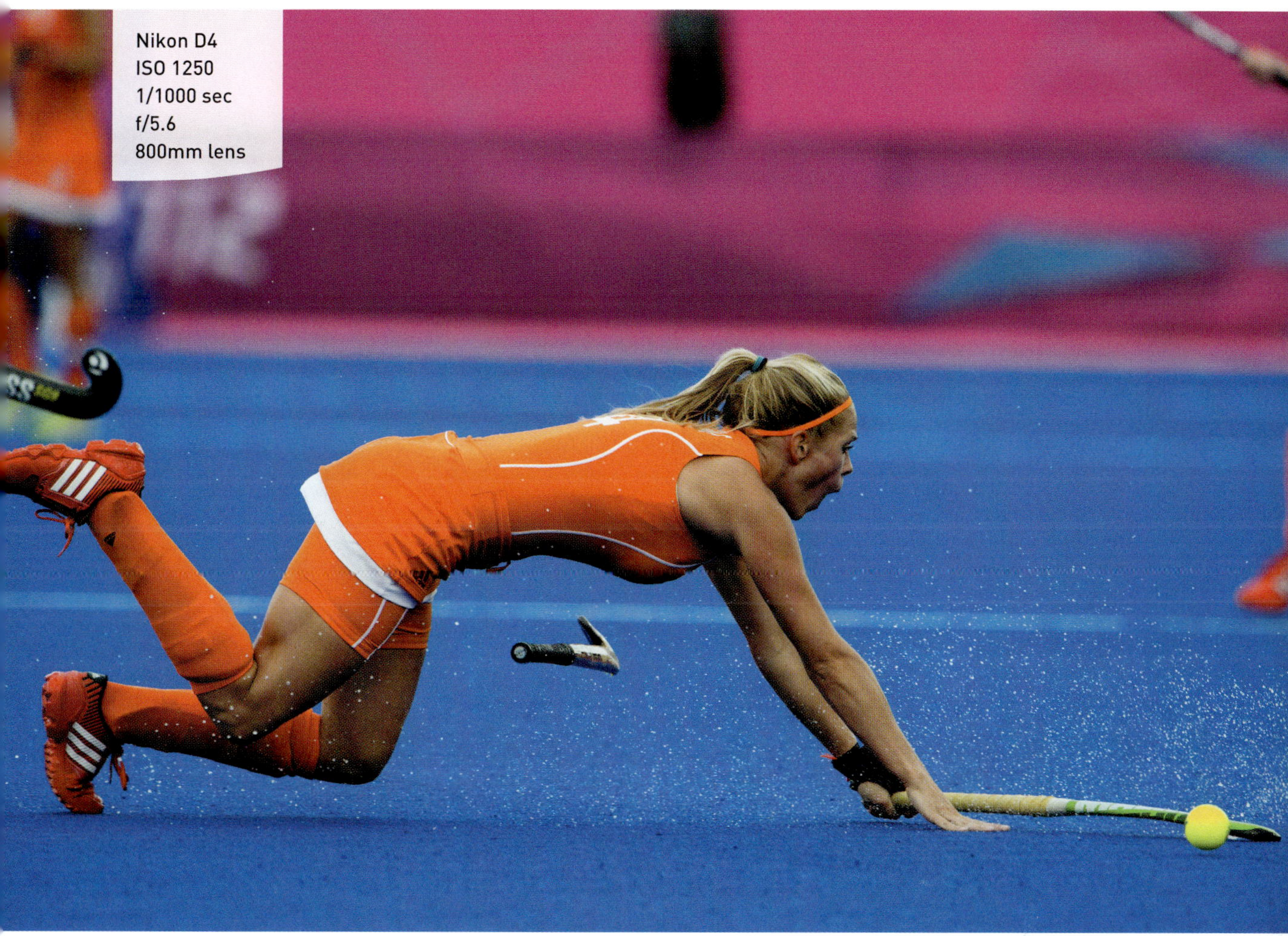

FIGURE 10.5 The Netherlands plays team Great Britain during the 2012 Olympic Games.

TIP

If a goal is scored, the players will run to the player who scored the goal. It happens every time and is the best chance to make a celebration image.

GOAL LINE

I also spend a lot of time behind the goal line during field hockey games. It's a good place to shoot the action around the goal and coming down the field. I made the image in **Figure 10.5** with the longest lens I could find and sat behind the goal line to capture the action.

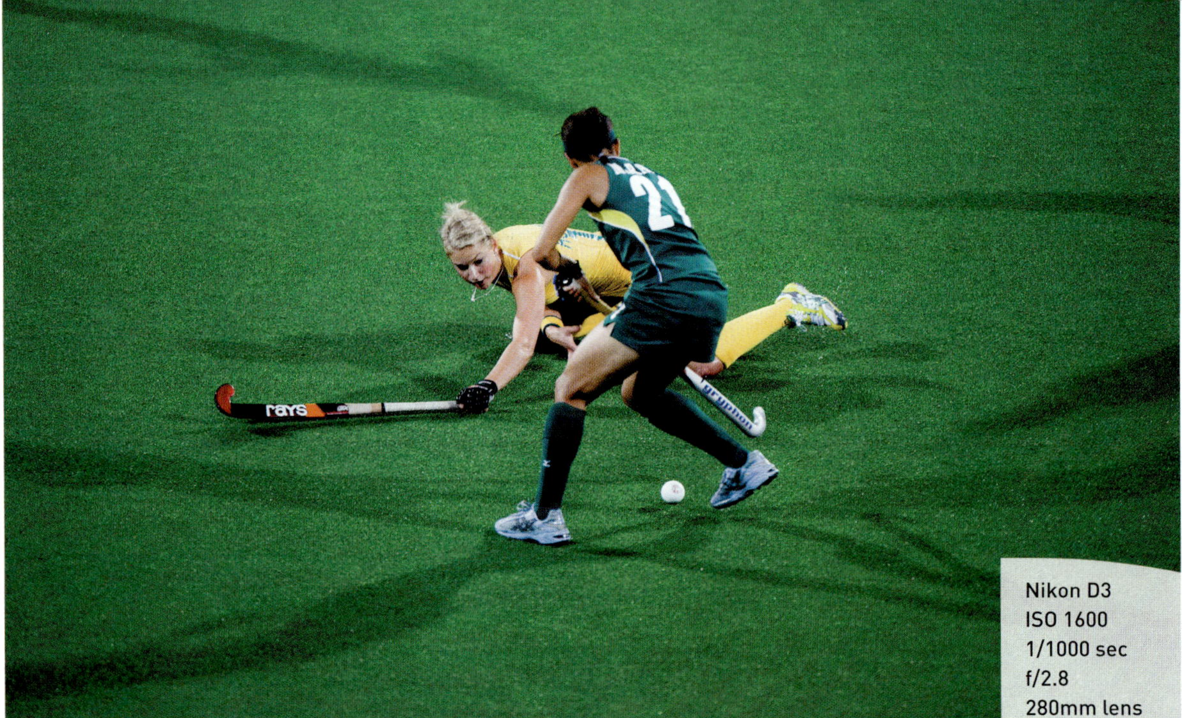

FIGURE 10.6
Australia plays New Zealand during the 2008 Olympic Games.

ELEVATED POSITION

Shooting from elevated positions is a great way to get a more encompassing look at the action. Because field hockey is played outside, an elevated position allows you to take advantage of light and shadows in a way that isn't possible from ground level.

The game in **Figure 10.6** was played at night, so shooting from an elevated position allowed me to use higher shutter speeds because there was more light. It also allowed me to take advantage of the shadows created by the artificial lights.

Figure 3.5 in Chapter 3 shows one of my favorite images from this position.

LACROSSE: HOW TO GET THE BEST SHOTS

Lacrosse has gained huge popularity in the United States over the last several years. The NCAA men's lacrosse tournament is a terrific event to cover, because the game is fast-paced and fun to watch.

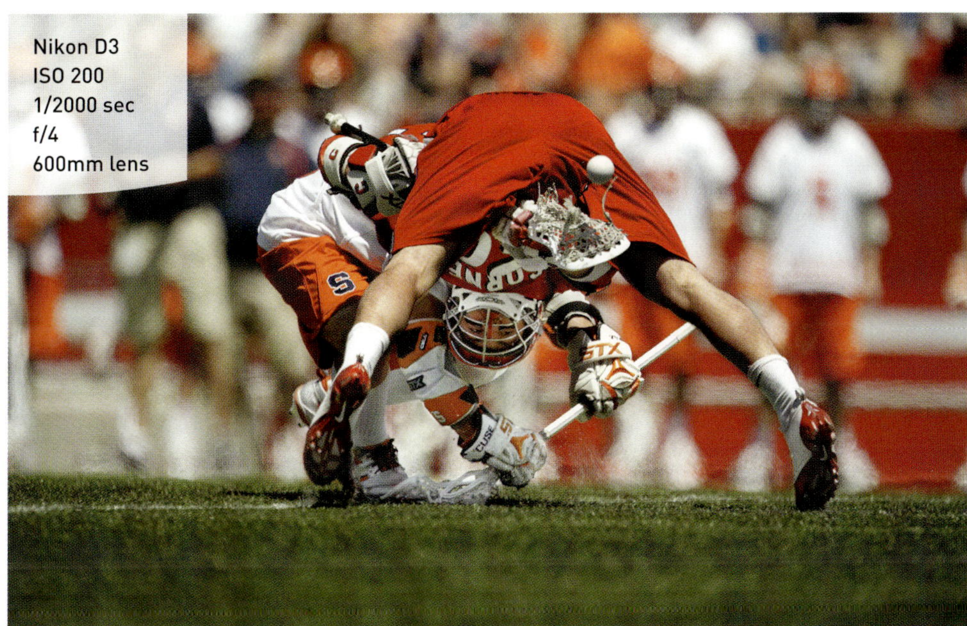
Nikon D3
ISO 200
1/2000 sec
f/4
600mm lens

FIGURE 10.7
Syracuse plays Cornell during the 2009 NCAA Lacrosse Championship.

WHERE TO POSITION YOURSELF

While shooting lacrosse games, I work from three main areas: the sidelines at the center line, the sidelines at the attack/defense areas, and in an elevated position.

CENTER LINE

The center line is the best place to be for the face-off, which always creates great images. Lacrosse moves very quickly, but the face-off is the one time in every game when you are guaranteed to have two players in the same place at the same time. It is one shot you can prepare for.

Lining up on the sidelines by the center line for the face-off shown in **Figure 10.7** allowed me to capture the moment the game started. The image is different from a sports perspective because of the position of the players.

TIP

Shooting the face-off shot with a long lens from a low angle makes a very interesting and often funny picture.

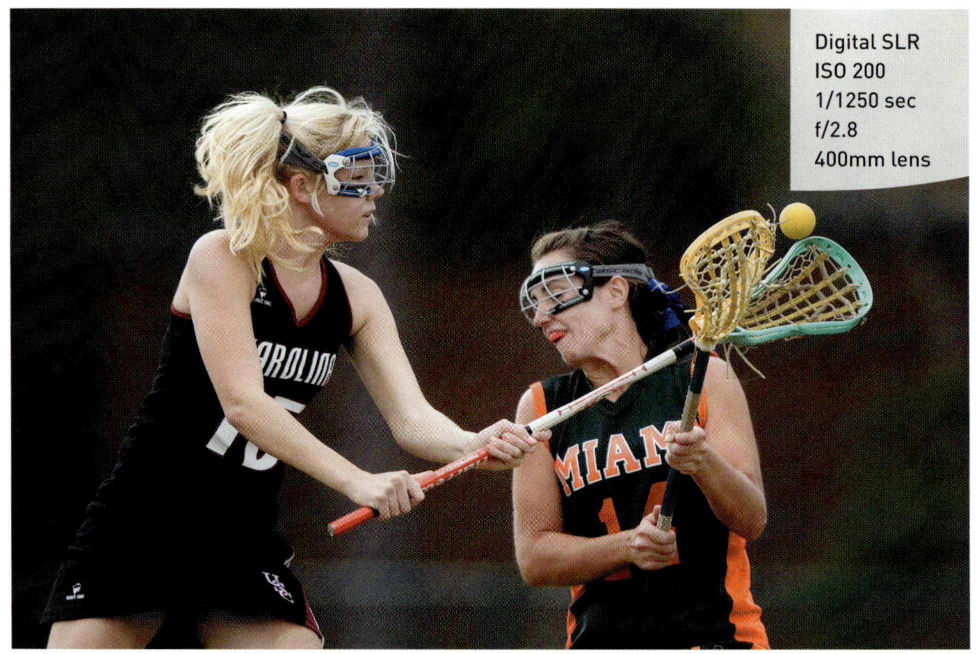
Digital SLR
ISO 200
1/1250 sec
f/2.8
400mm lens

FIGURE 10.8
Miami plays South Carolina during a game in 2006. Shooting from the sidelines gave me a clean view of the athletes' faces at they attacked each other.

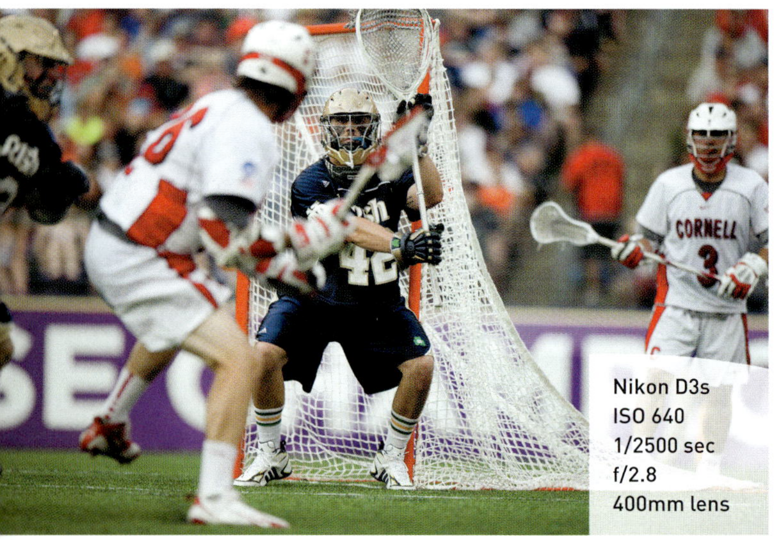

Nikon D3s
ISO 640
1/2500 sec
f/2.8
400mm lens

FIGURE 10.9
The Notre Dame goalie braces for a shot from Cornell during the 2010 NCAA Championship. Shooting from the sidelines gives you a clean view of the goal and the action around it.

ATTACK/DEFENSE AREA SIDELINES

The attack/defense area sidelines are my favored positions to cover lacrosse. The goal is not located on the base line, like soccer or field hockey, so being on the sidelines actually is the best place to capture the action around the goal (**Figure 10.8** and **Figure 10.9**).

ELEVATED POSITION

Again, an elevated position gives you a different look at the action on the field. Lacrosse fields have lots of lines and shapes, so elevated positions allow you to take advantage of color and shapes, and make action photos with a unique look (**Figure 10.10**).

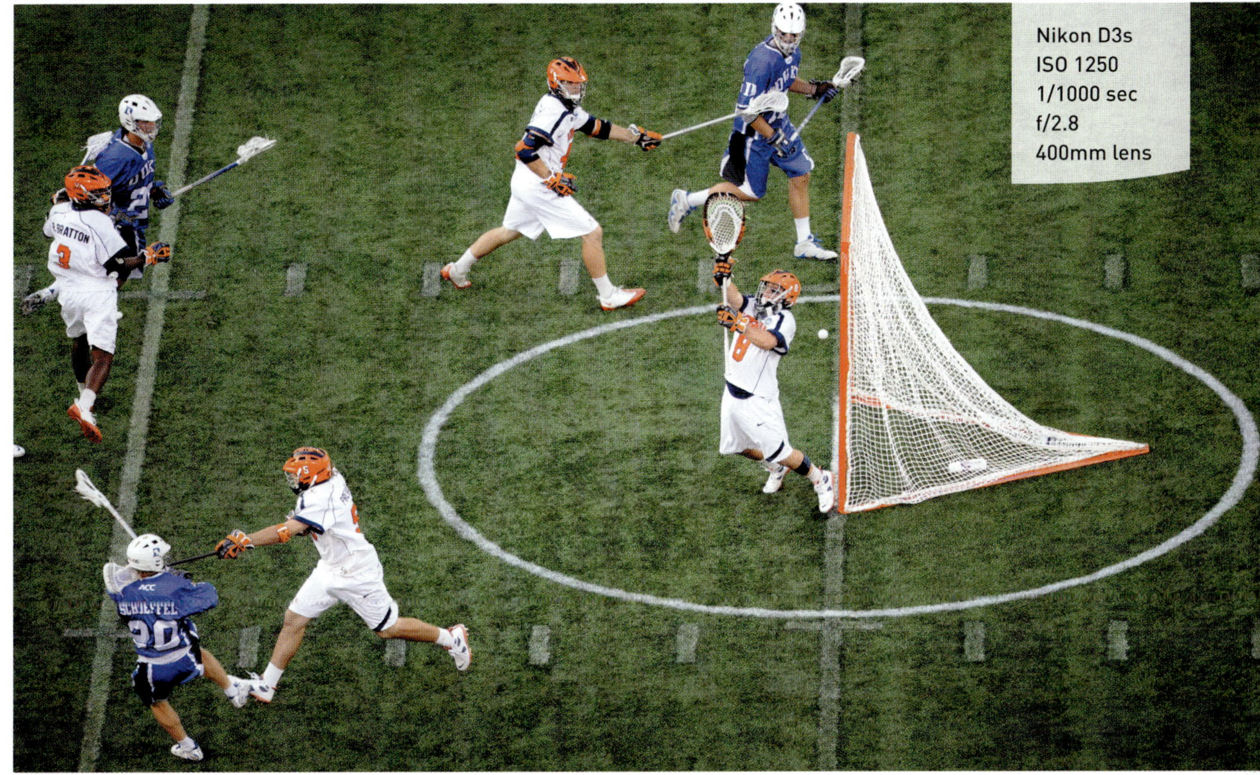

Nikon D3s
ISO 1250
1/1000 sec
f/2.8
400mm lens

FIGURE 10.10
Duke plays Syracuse during the 2009 NCAA Championship.

MY GEAR

The nature of soccer, lacrosse, and field hockey lends them to being photographed using extremely long glass. I love to shoot these sports with the Nikkor 800mm f/5.6, but that lens is rare and very expensive. Here is my gear list that I would absolutely bring to a soccer, field hockey, or lacrosse game:

- Three Nikon D4 bodies
- One Nikon D800
- 800mm f/5.6 lens
- 600mm f/4 lens
- 400mm f/2.8 lens
- 70–200mm f/2.8 lens
- 14–24mm f/2.8 lens
- TC 1.4x teleconverter
- Two Gitzo monopods

If you have only one camera, bring the longest lens you have or can get. Teleconverters are great for these sports also. I recommend the TC 1.4x because it will normally be the sharpest teleconverter, but if you have a good TC 2x, the extra length could be very helpful. It is important to have as much reach as possible, because so much of the game will be played far from where your position will be.

THE CAMERA SETTINGS

Because soccer, field hockey, and lacrosse are outdoor sports, it is more difficult to calculate exposure. Images taken at a noon game will look very different from those taken at a game played at 9:00 at night.

Always consider how much of the frame you want to be in focus. People tend to put their cameras on the widest aperture possible for photographing sports, but that isn't always the best way to go. However, sometimes you must allow as much light into the sensor as possible, like at night. Once you decide your depth of field, set your shutter speed at a high enough speed to stop action, and then set your ISO to fit your other two calculations.

I like to freeze action, so I always shoot using a shutter speed of at least 1/1000 of a second.

COVERING THE MOMENTS BEFORE THE GAME

Be aware of extenuating circumstances when you cover any sport. There is always a compelling story outside of the game, whether it is a personal feat that a coach or player has overcome or achieved, or a traumatic experience the team has come through.

I covered a Nebraska women's soccer game after one of the team's star players was killed randomly at a party the weekend before. She had been at the wrong place at the wrong time and was killed by a stray bullet. Before the game the team players lined up for the national anthem as they always did, leaving a space where she stood and filling it only with the joined hands of two teammates (**Figure 10.11**).

COVERING THE ACTION

As mentioned earlier, shooting soccer, field hockey, and lacrosse is all about anticipation. The more you know about the sport you are shooting, the easier you can anticipate what will happen next. The first time I shot lacrosse—even after doing research on the rules of the game beforehand—I was lost. It took half of a game to begin to understand the action happening in front of me. It made shooting that first game very difficult, but it was also fun to learn.

In these fast-paced games, it is important to know where the ball is at all times (**Figure 10.12**). Following the ball is hard work because the players are so fast, but it allows you more chances to make great images and also keeps you safe.

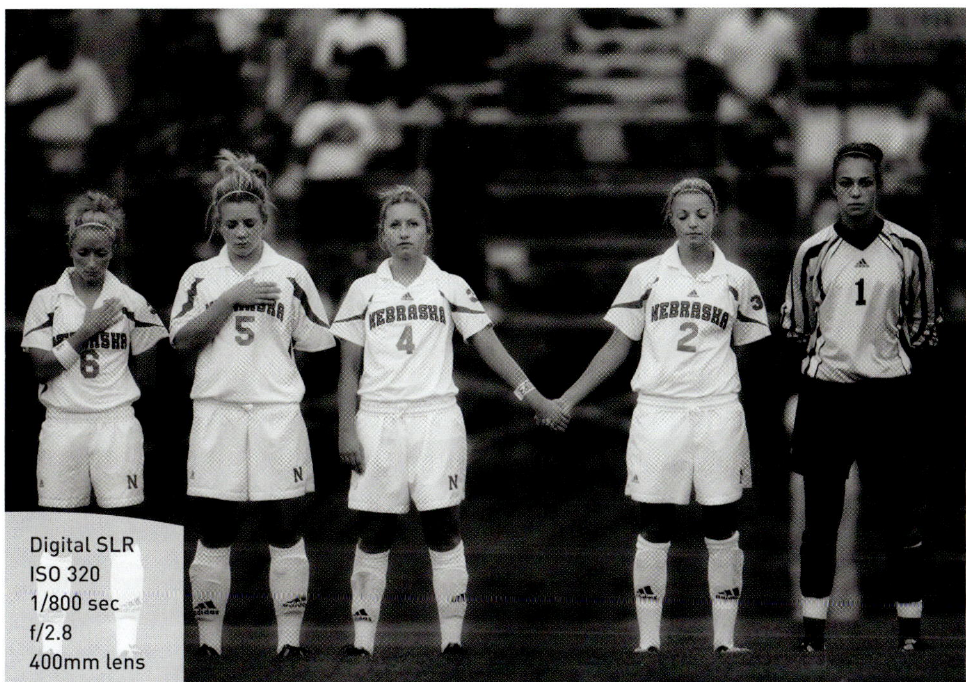

Digital SLR
ISO 320
1/800 sec
f/2.8
400mm lens

FIGURE 10.11
The Nebraska women's soccer team pays a solemn tribute to a beloved team member.

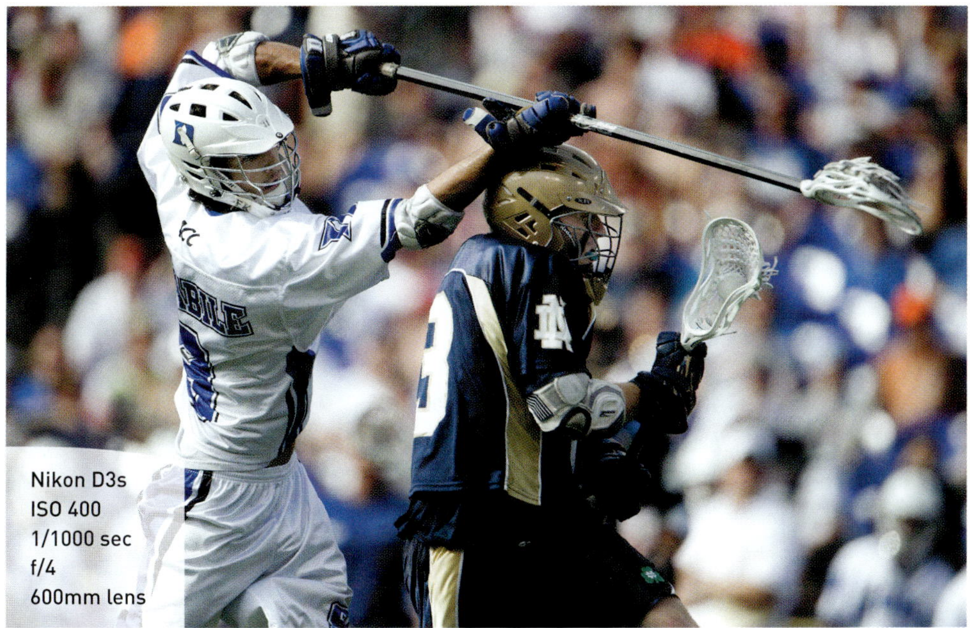

Nikon D3s
ISO 400
1/1000 sec
f/4
600mm lens

FIGURE 10.12
Notre Dame plays Duke in the final of the 2010 NCAA Lacrosse Championship.

COVERING THE MOMENTS AFTER THE GAME

As discussed in previous chapters, reaction photos can be as important as action photos. Always keep an eye out for celebration after a big game (**Figure 10.13** and **Figure 10.14**).

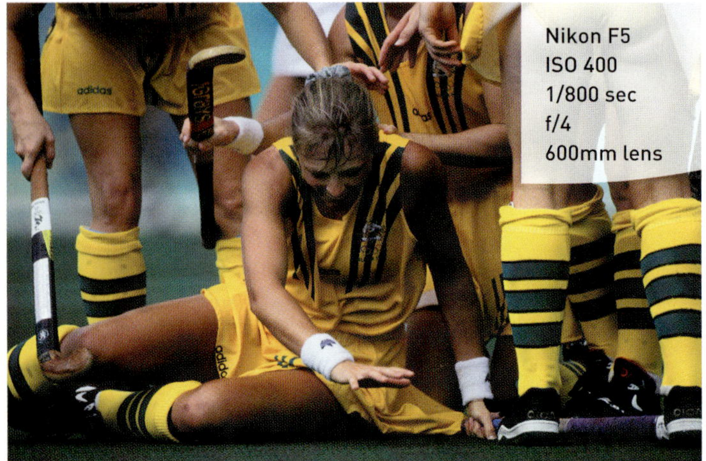

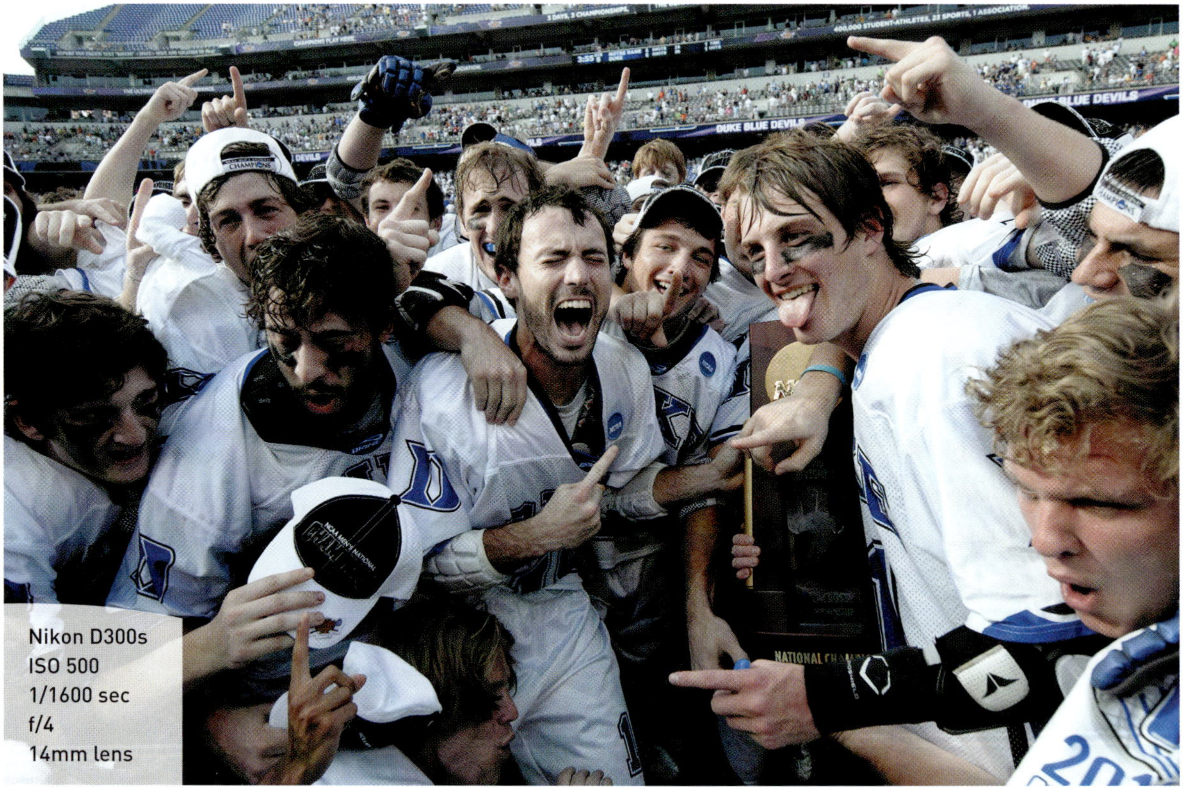

Nikon F5
ISO 400
1/800 sec
f/4
600mm lens

FIGURE 10.13
The Australian field hockey team celebrates after winning a game during the 2004 Olympic Games.

Nikon D300s
ISO 500
1/1600 sec
f/4
14mm lens

FIGURE 10.14
The Duke men's lacrosse team celebrates after winning the 2010 NCAA Lacrosse Championship.

Chapter 10 Assignments

All of the sports discussed in this chapter have very similar motions and concepts. The assignments are thus fairly interchangeable. The lessons learned from one sport transfer easily to another.

Creating Portraits

Go to a little league soccer game before it starts. Spend time shooting the athletes getting ready for the game. Practice making feature pictures and portraits before the game begins. Work on making interesting images showing the relationships between the players and coaches.

Anticipating the Action

Go to a lacrosse game. Try to find a high angle to shoot from and watch the patterns of colors and shapes develop to make unique images. Learn to anticipate when the ball will change teams and the movement will switch quickly from one end of the field to the other.

Timing the Ball

Go to a field hockey game and position yourself side on to the goal. Before the game begins, the athletes will spend significant time taking shots on goal. Learn to time the ball leaving the stick and then the goalie stopping the ball from entering the goal. During an actual game this will not happen often, but during warm-ups you will have many chances to practice taking these images.

Share your results with the book's Flickr group!
Join the group here: flickr.com/groups/sportsphotographyfromsnapshotstogreatshots.

11

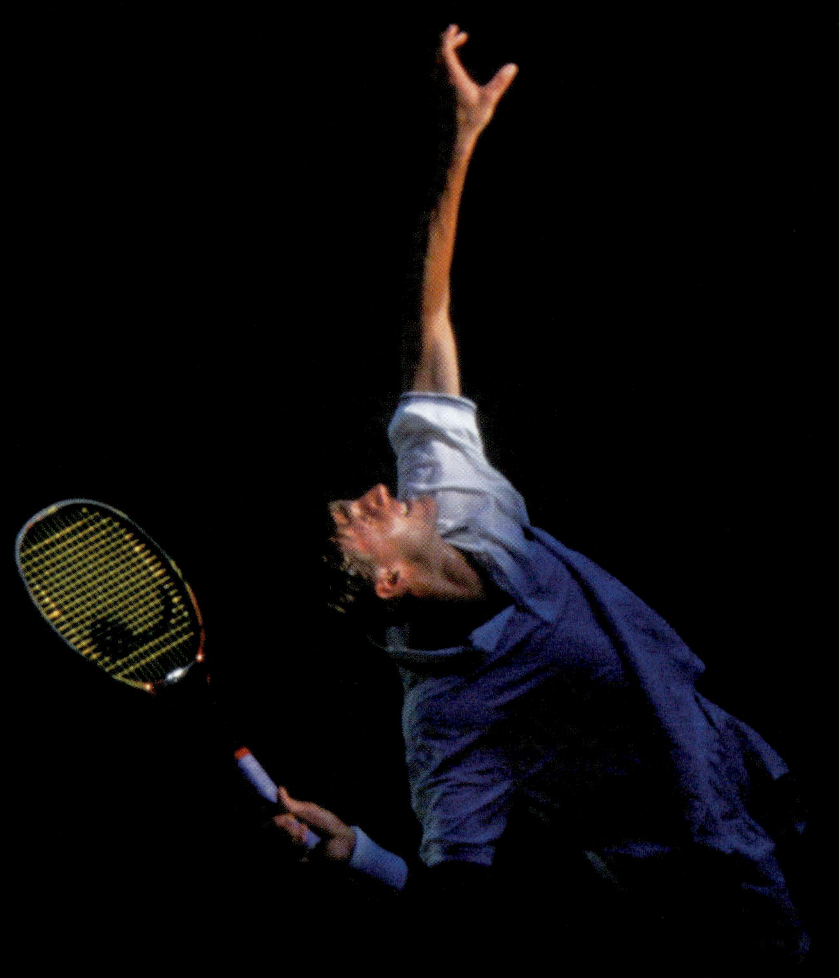

Nikon F3
ISO 400
1/1600 sec
f/2.8
180mm lens

Golf and Tennis

THE SILENT SPORTS

Golf and tennis are hugely popular, especially as leisurely or amateur sports. For the most part, they are played during the day in beautiful areas. Therefore, shooting these sports is very different than shooting other sports. Golf is played on a wide open field; tennis is played on an enclosed court.

In this chapter I'll discuss how to cover each sport to make great shots.

Shooting from an elevated position allowed me to capture this athlete with only the court behind him. Because this image was shot at sunset, I was able to expose so that he would pop out of the background.

PORING OVER THE PICTURE

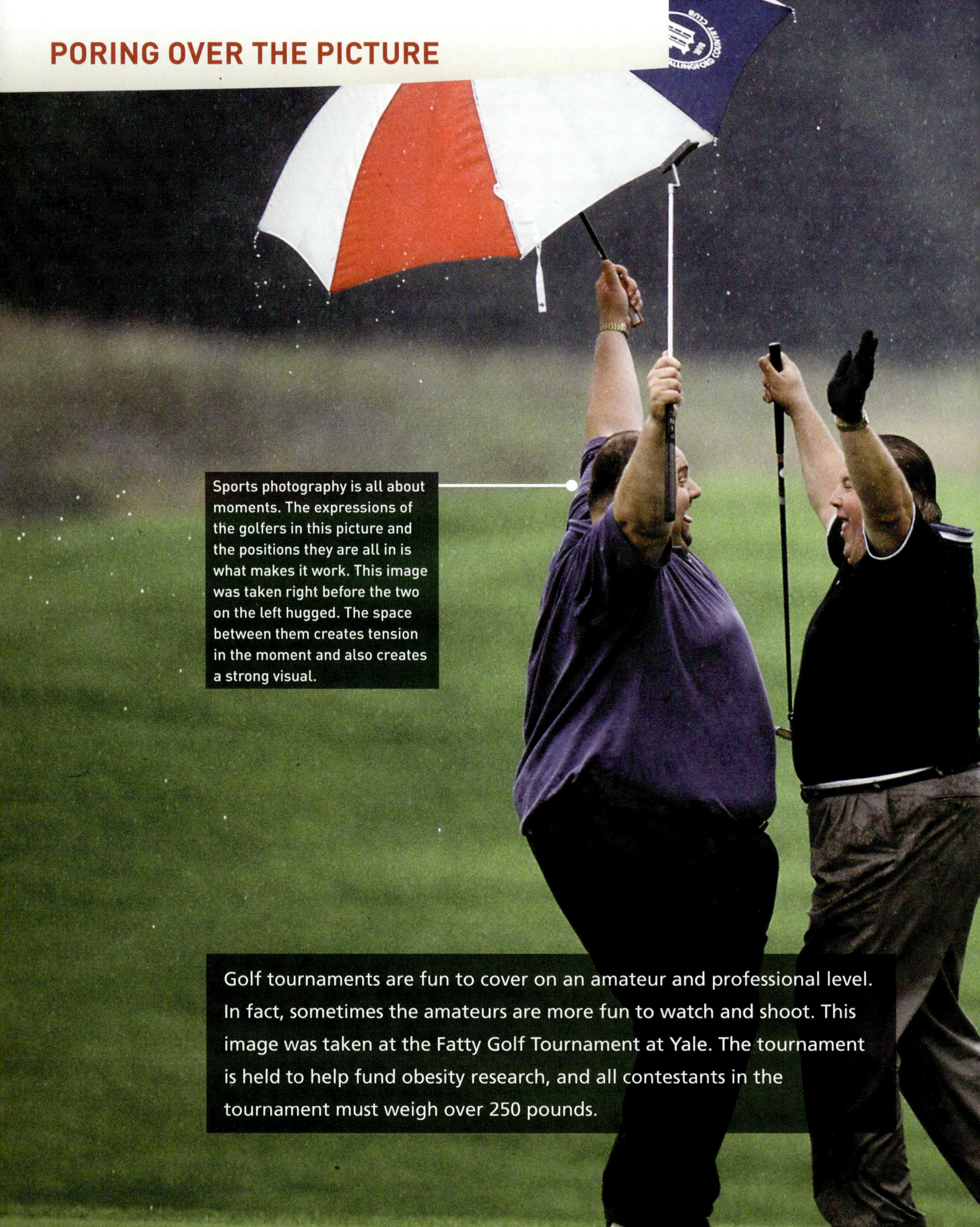

Sports photography is all about moments. The expressions of the golfers in this picture and the positions they are all in is what makes it work. This image was taken right before the two on the left hugged. The space between them creates tension in the moment and also creates a strong visual.

Golf tournaments are fun to cover on an amateur and professional level. In fact, sometimes the amateurs are more fun to watch and shoot. This image was taken at the Fatty Golf Tournament at Yale. The tournament is held to help fund obesity research, and all contestants in the tournament must weigh over 250 pounds.

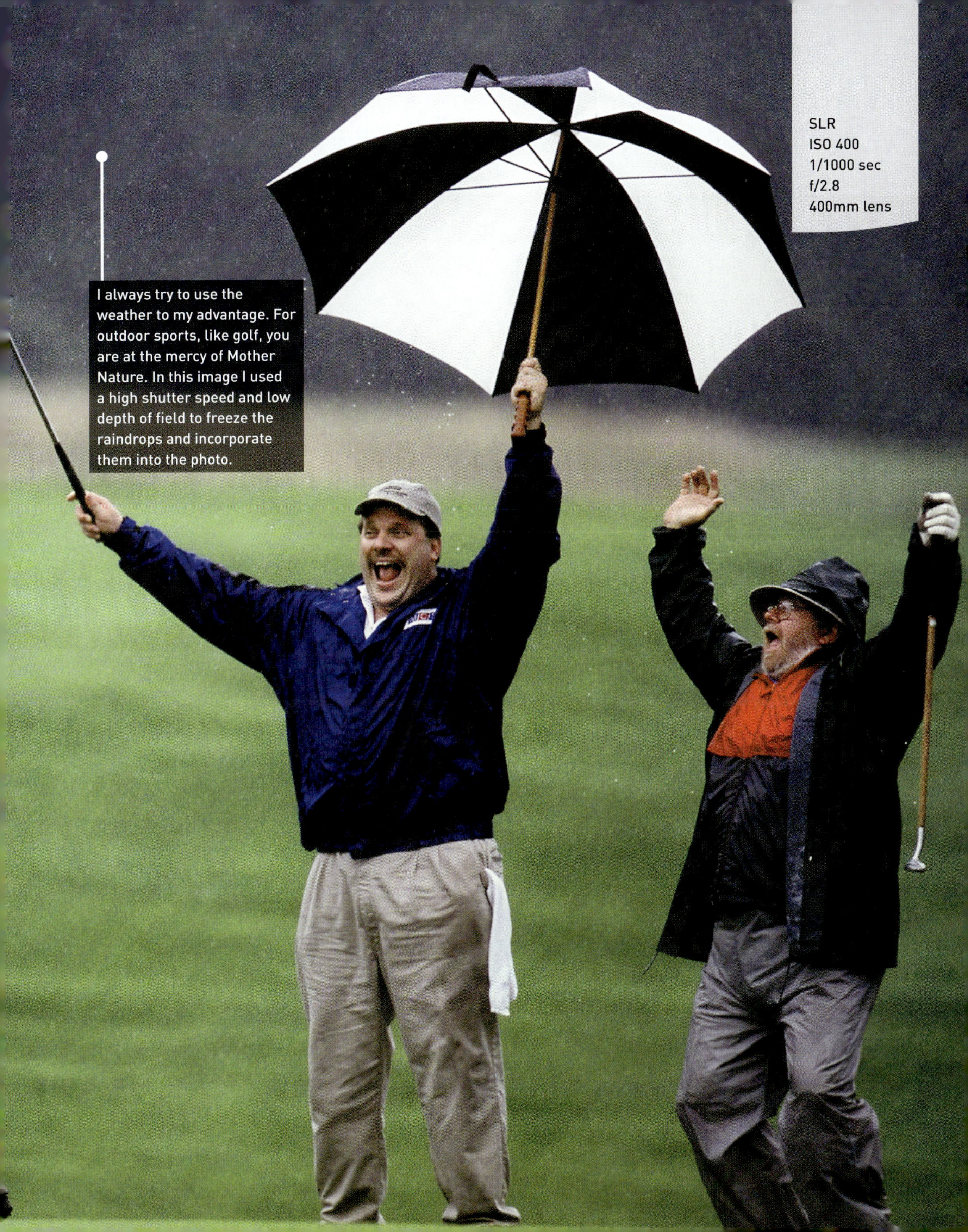

I always try to use the weather to my advantage. For outdoor sports, like golf, you are at the mercy of Mother Nature. In this image I used a high shutter speed and low depth of field to freeze the raindrops and incorporate them into the photo.

SLR
ISO 400
1/1000 sec
f/2.8
400mm lens

GOLF: A NICE LONG WALK

Golf likely enjoys the largest fields of play of any sport. This makes finding good angles relatively easy. On the other hand, it is important not to disturb the golfers, so never shoot during a golfer's backswing, and stay out of their direct field of vision.

Almost by definition, golf courses are lovely. They are like giant, well-kept parks where the game is played.

Because golf is played all day long in a wide range of weather conditions, it's important to be prepared for long walks in weather good and bad. I never know what kind of conditions I'll find, but I always try to make the best of whatever the weather offers me.

TIP

Covering golf means long walks. So wear good shoes, carry only the equipment you need, and take water with you.

WHERE TO POSITION YOURSELF

To stay well away from the golfers, the longer the lens you can use the better. Wide angles are of course effective when you want to show the scenic nature of the surroundings, but again, you have to remember to be very conscious of any noise you make.

TIP

Don't be afraid to shoot loose and include the grounds. Golf is a scenic sport, and the environment is important.

The object of the game of golf is to cover the course hitting the ball as few times as possible while still finishing each hole (**Figure 11.1**). Golf is a game of precision, not speed.

TIP

On important putts stay focused on the golfer. The reaction will come after the ball drops into the cup, or misses.

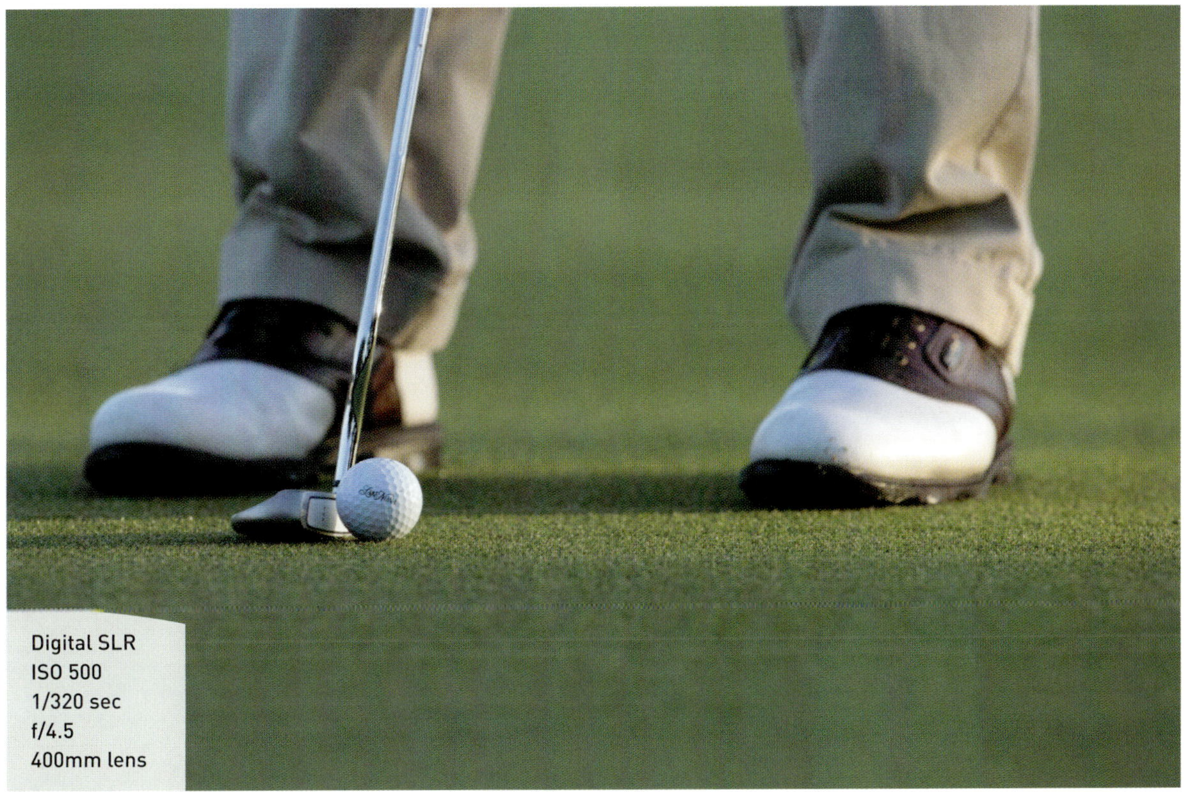

FIGURE 11.1 I like to make detail shots—close-ups of certain elements of the game—throughout the course of a round or tournament.

GEAR

I use two cameras and three lenses when I cover golf. To show the beauty of the course while play is going on, I like to carry a very wide-angle lens. When the players are on the green and I can approach, discreetly, while they are putting, I use a medium zoom. To photograph golfers on the fairway and while they are hitting drives, it's very important to use a long telephoto. When I'm working on tour events, I'll often use a camera blimp to deaden the sound so I can shoot without bothering the players.

You can also make good images with a normal lens or a short zoom. Position yourself out of the golfer's sight line, and shoot only after contact is made with the ball.

Here is the equipment I use to shoot golf:

- 2 Nikon D4 cameras
- 14–24 f/2.8 lens
- 24–120 f/4 lens
- 600 f/4 lens
- TC 1.4x teleconverter

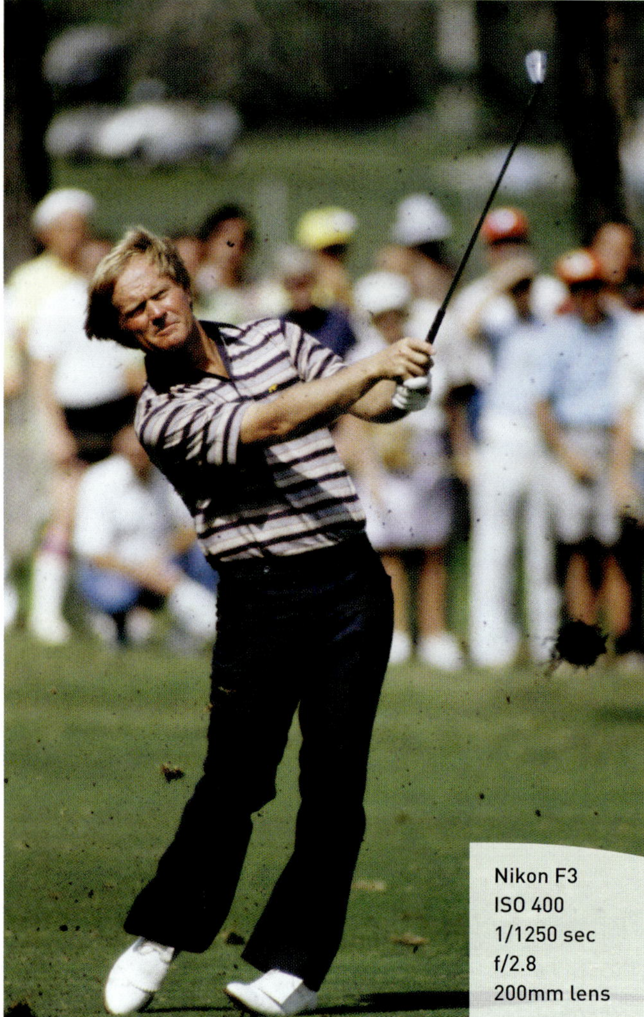

FIGURE 11.2
Jack Nicklaus chips onto the green.

SETTINGS

Golf is played outdoors and is almost always played during the day. To stop the movement of the ball when it is hit, it's best to use a shutter speed of 1/2000 of a second or higher.

When you're isolating a golfer, you should use the maximum aperture to decrease depth of field. For example, by shooting at a low depth of field and a high shutter speed in **Figure 11.2**, I was able to isolate Jack Nicklaus from the background and freeze the dirt as it flew around him.

But when you're using a wide-angle lens to do an overall, scenic image, more depth of field is desirable to increase sharpness and add interest to the image.

TENNIS: NET GAIN

In tennis, each player uses a racket to hit a rubber ball covered with felt over a net and safely into the opponent's court. The goal of the game is to place the ball where it cannot be returned by your opponent.

Pete Sampras sums up the game best: "It's one on one out there man. There's no hiding. I can't pass the ball" (**Figure 11.3**).

WHERE TO POSITION YOURSELF

Tennis is played both indoors and outdoors during the day and under lights at night. In addition, the action takes place all over the court, so it's important to get a sense of how the players in the match play the game.

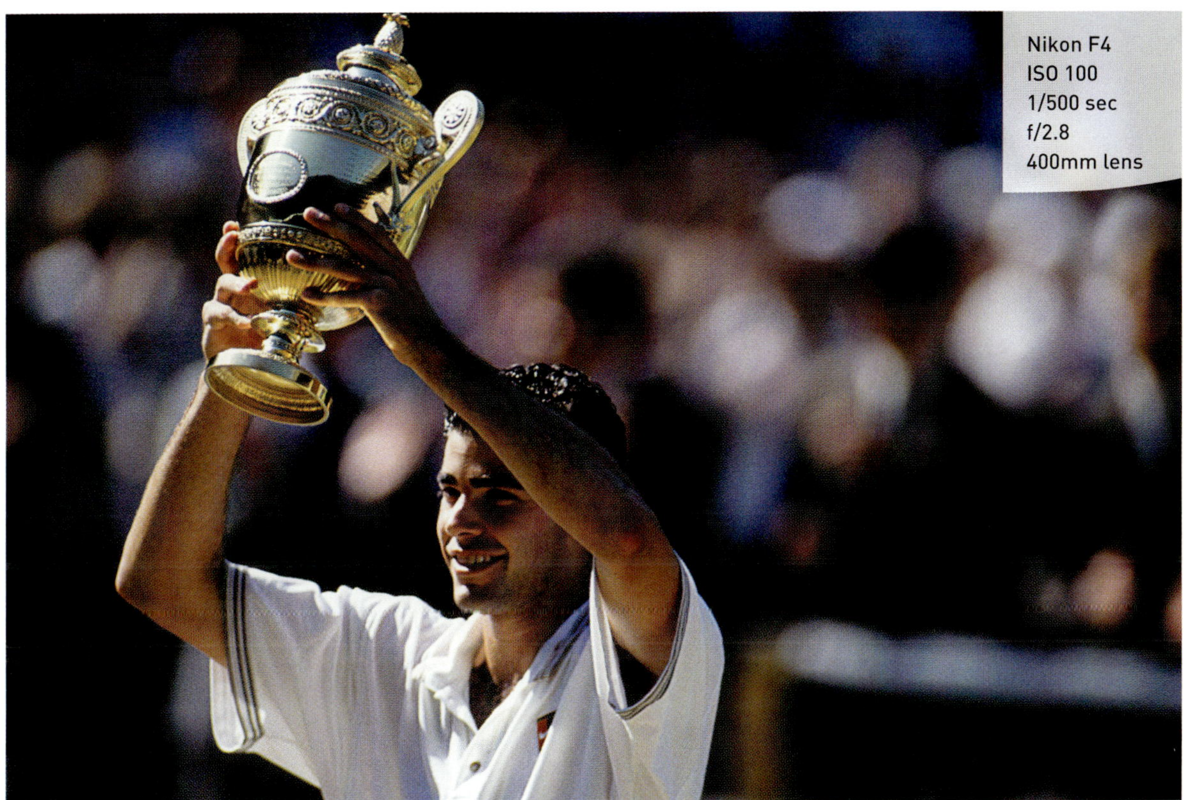

Nikon F4
ISO 100
1/500 sec
f/2.8
400mm lens

FIGURE 11.3
Pete Sampras holds up his trophy after winning Wimbledon in 1996.

Good places to shoot will be along the sides and ends of the court. Usually, you don't want to be on the same side of the court where the players sit during breaks. You can change positions when the players change ends of the court.

Tennis is a game of acute angles—for the players and also for photographers covering the action. It's important to keep the ball in the picture as much as possible, and that means you need impeccable timing. It's critical to compose and focus before the ball hits the racket. That way you are ready to shoot in the split second the ball is in the frame.

TIP

Use manual focus when you're shooting through the net. If you use auto-focus the camera will not know what element you want to focus on and will likely as not select the net.

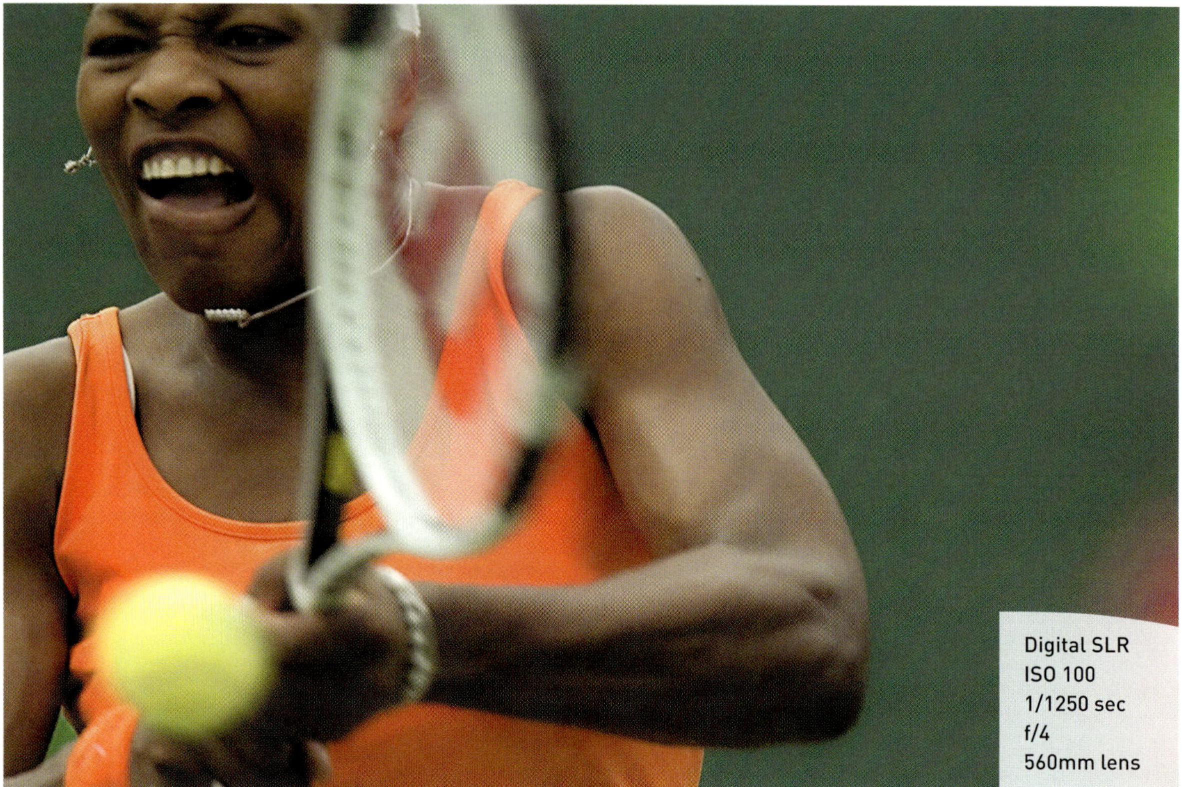

FIGURE 11.4
Serena Williams returns a serve.

Serena Williams is one of the most powerful players in the game today. By shooting extremely tight on her at the moment of impact in **Figure 11.4**, I was able to show her strength and concentration as she attacked the ball.

Andre Agassi was one of the game's most dominant players. I went tight in **Figure 11.5** to show his intensity.

TIP

Serves are good times to practice making images with the ball in the frame. Tennis moves very quickly, and it can be difficult to follow with precision when you first start covering it. However, it is important not to make much noise when the serve is happening.

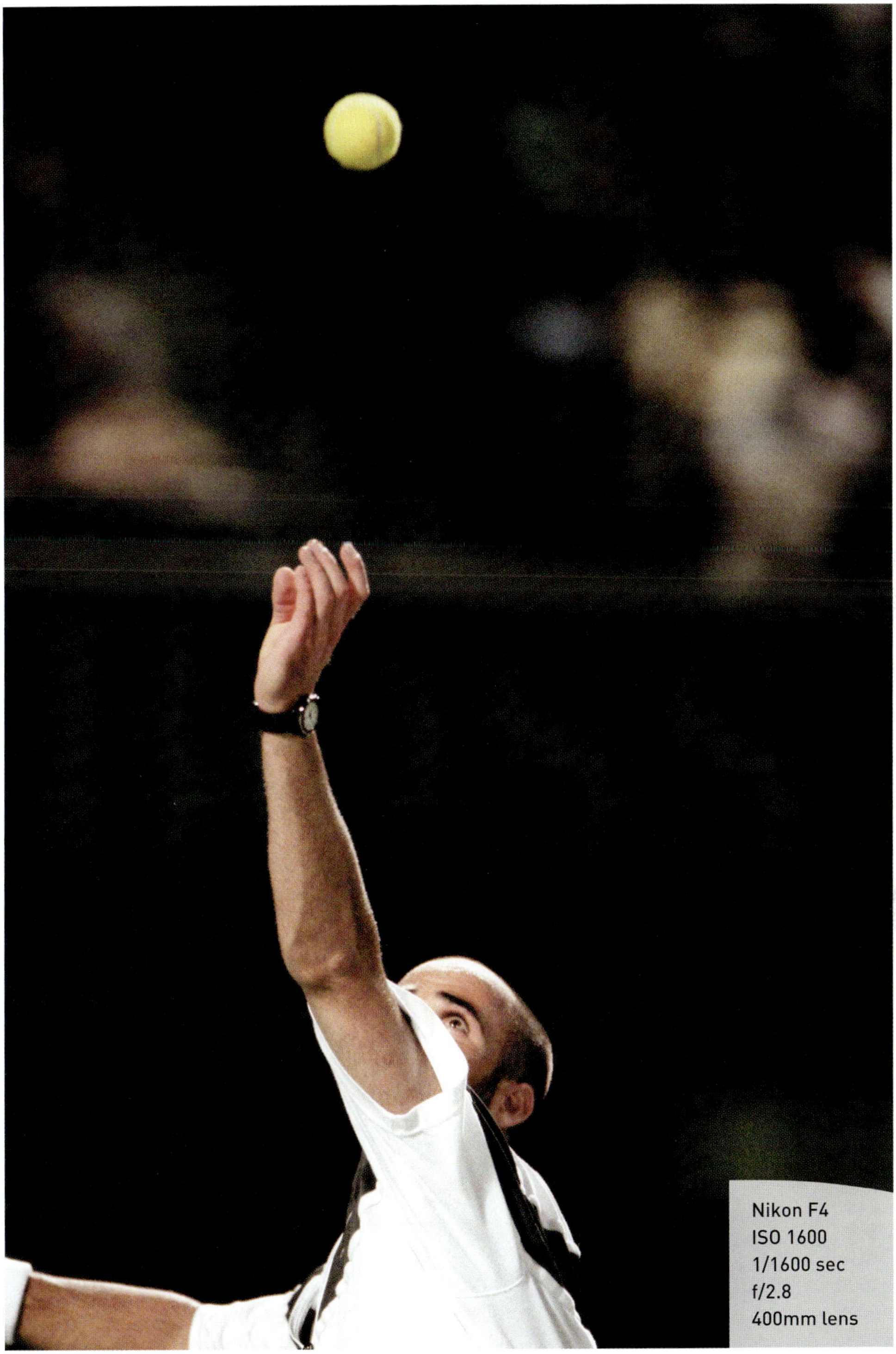

FIGURE 11.5
Andre Agassi gets ready to serve the ball.

Nikon F4
ISO 1600
1/1600 sec
f/2.8
400mm lens

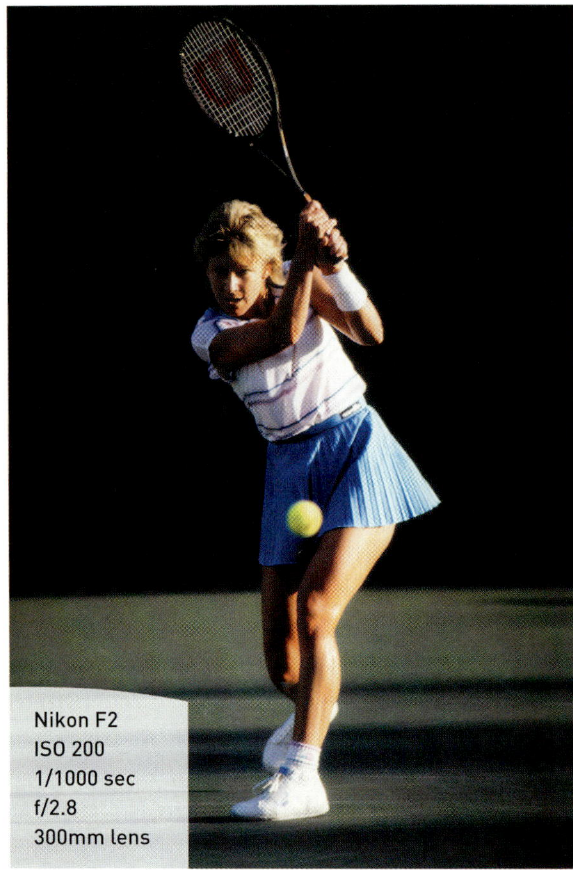

FIGURE 11.6
Chris Evert, winner of 18 Grand Slam events, shows the backhand shot she was famous for at the Lipton.

Nikon F2
ISO 100
1/1000 sec
f3.5
.400mm lens

FIGURE 11.7
Taking advantage of strong cross lighting, I made this portrait of Steffi Graf, one of the greatest tennis players of all time.

Tennis courts are virtually all the same size. However, singles courts are slightly more narrow than doubles courts.

Clay, grass, and synthetic courts are all used as playing surfaces in the major championships. Which you will be shooting is important to know because it will not only determine the color of the light that is reflected back up into the players, but also because it will help regulate the speed at which the ball travels and how it bounces (**Figure 11.6**).

As with golf, it is essential not to make noise, especially when the players are serving (**Figure 11.7**).

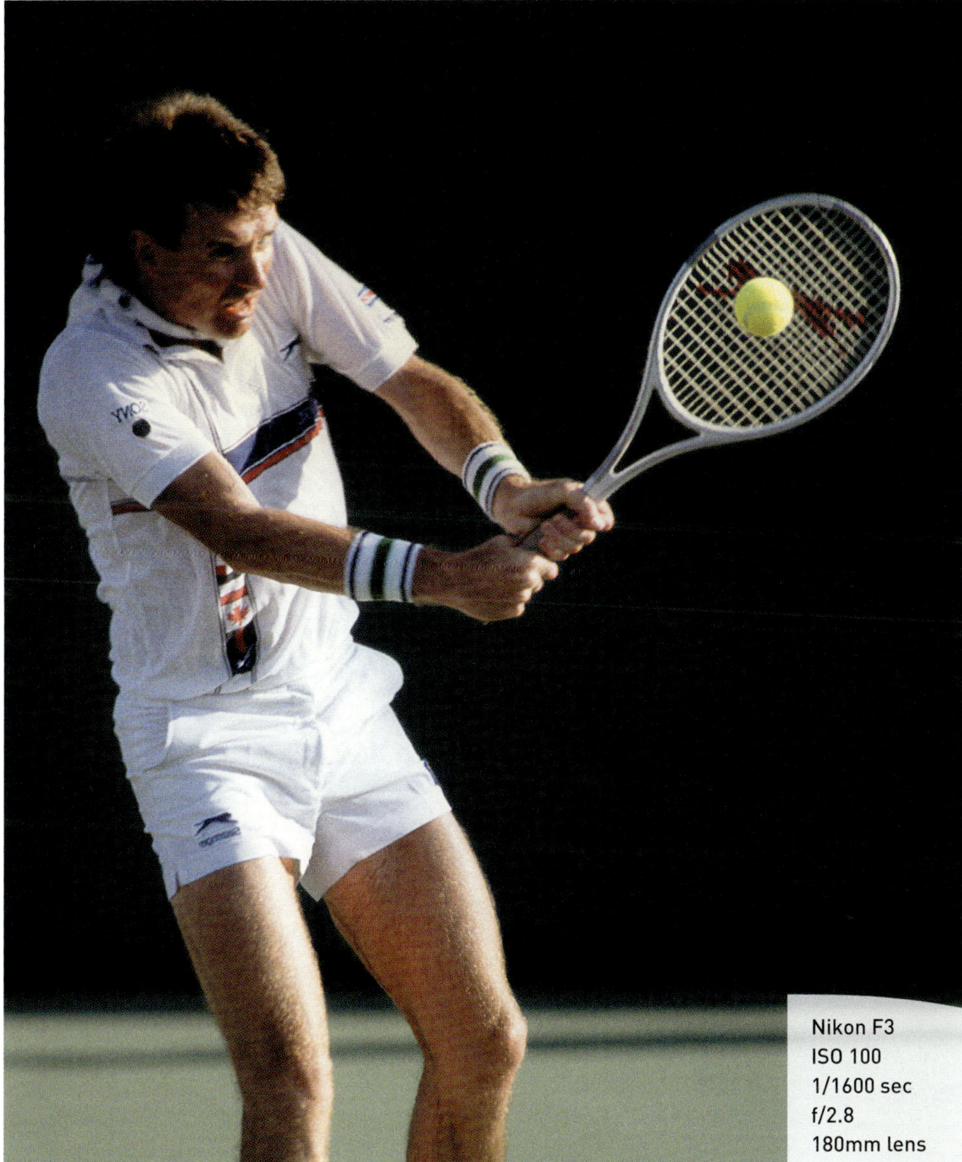

Nikon F3
ISO 100
1/1600 sec
f/2.8
180mm lens

FIGURE 11.8
Tennis is very fast paced; therefore, high shutter speeds are imperative to stop the motion and capture crisp images.

SETTINGS

The ball moves very quickly, as do the rackets. To freeze those actions, you need to use a fast shutter speed of at least 1/1600 of a second (**Figure 11.8**).

GEAR

This is the gear I normally take to a tennis match, but the most important piece of equipment is a telephoto lens:

- 3 Nikon D4 cameras
- 35 f/1.4 lens
- 200 f/2.0 lens
- v400 f/2.8 lens

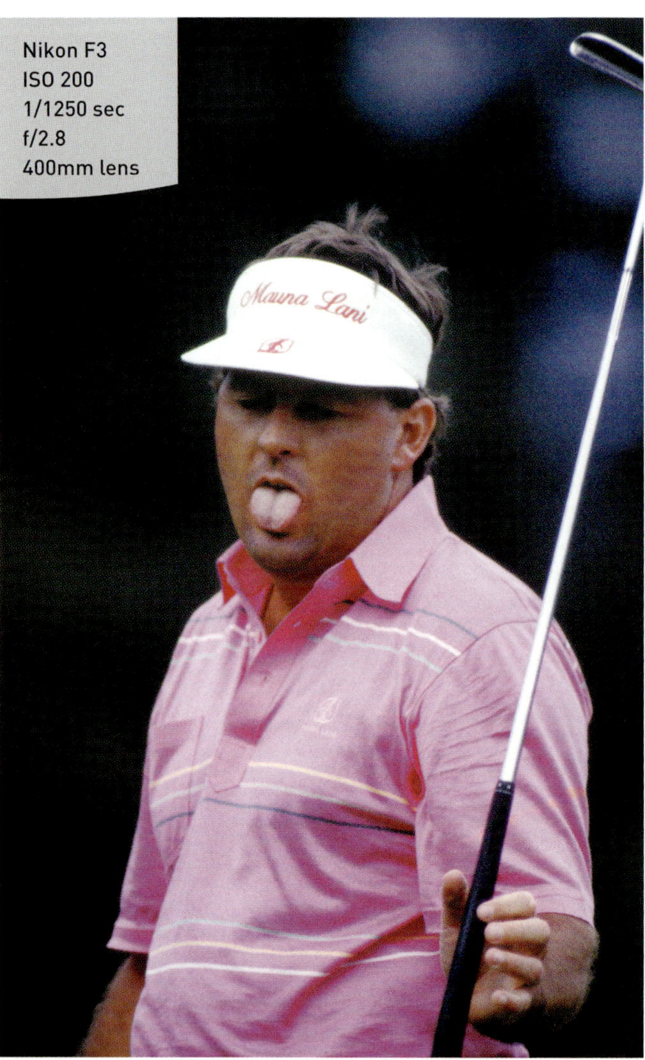

FIGURE 11.9
Lanny Wadkins reacts after a bad putt at Doral.

COVERING MOMENTS AROUND THE ACTION

As with the other sports discussed in this book, golf and tennis produce high-emotion moments, especially in the finals of big tournaments. The level and cause of a reaction varies greatly depending on the athlete (**Figure 11.9**).

John McEnroe was always one of my favorite players to cover. He would get upset over a bad bounce in practice. Photographing him in big tournaments always led to great reaction images (**Figure 11.10**).

In **Figure 11.11** Conchita Martínez shows her reaction to becoming the first Spaniard to win Wimbledon, the world's most prestigious tennis tournament.

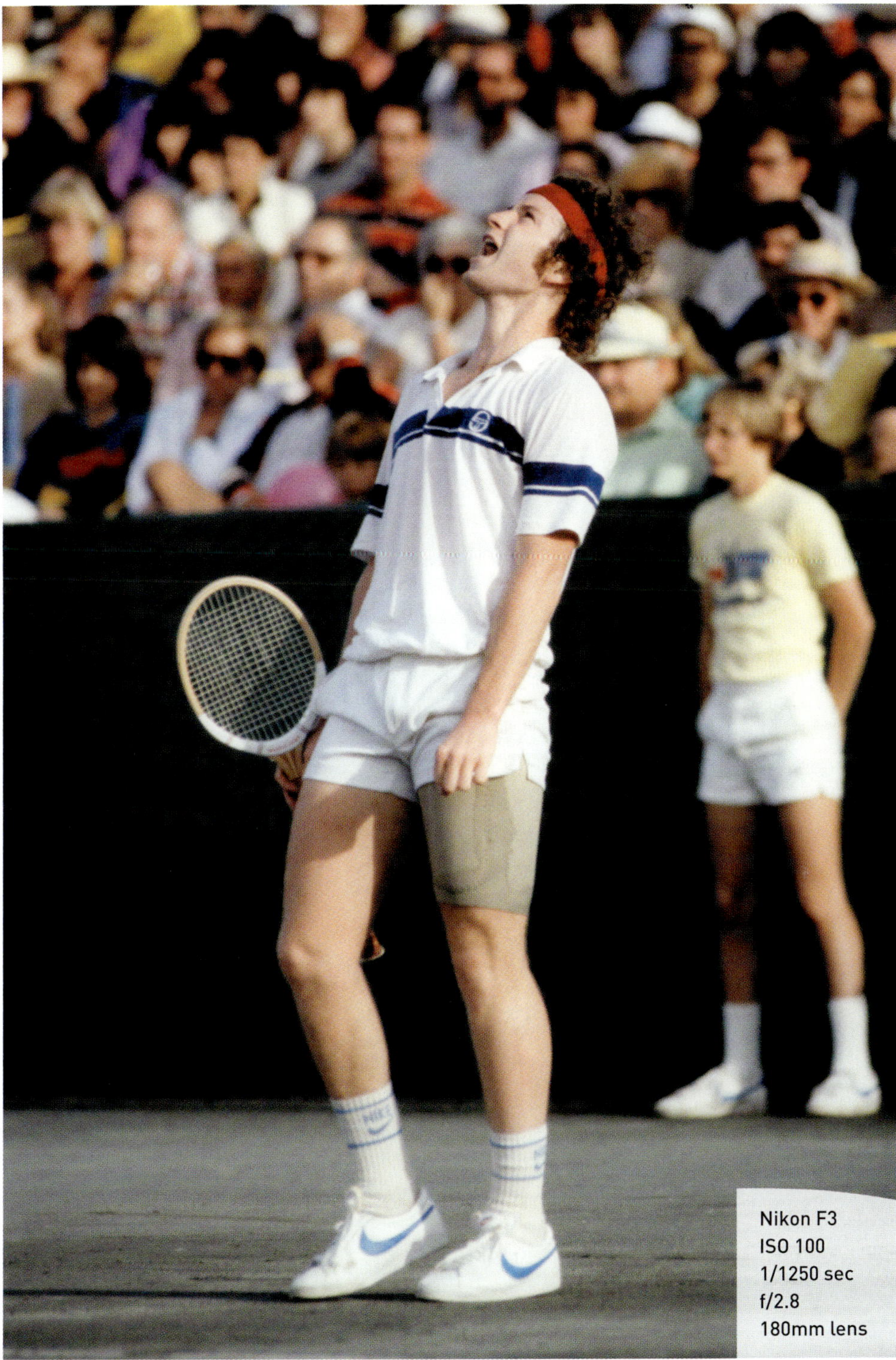

FIGURE 11.10
John McEnroe reacts after losing a point at Lipton.

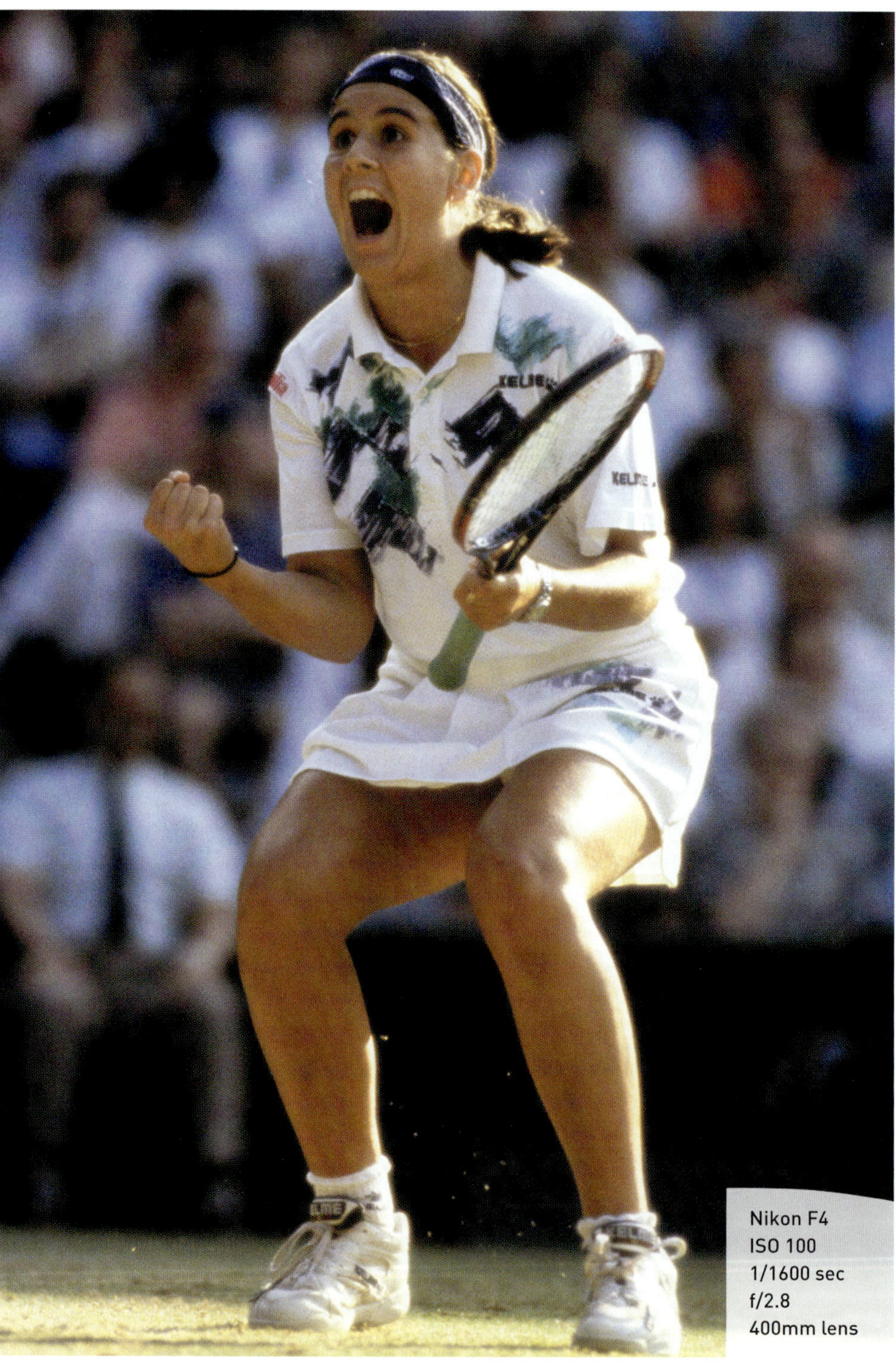

FIGURE 11.11
Conchita Martínez is ecstatic after defeating nine time champion Martina Navratilova to win Wimbledon in 1994.

Nikon F4
ISO 100
1/1600 sec
f/2.8
400mm lens

Chapter 11 Assignments

The goal for each of the following assignments is to practice timing your shots.

Anticipating the Peak Moment

Set your motor drive to single frame advance. Have someone bounce a tennis ball and try to capture the ball hitting the ground. Keep practicing until six times out of every ten bounces the ball is touching the ground in the photograph. This will help you learn to anticipate the peak moment.

Focusing and Composing for Movement

Go to a golf course putting green, but be careful not to disturb anyone who wants to practice putting. Take the longest lens you have and get as close to the ground as you can. Have someone roll a golf ball toward you. Practice focusing on the moving ball. Do this so that your composition is not in the center of the frame side-to-side and top to bottom but rather in a corner of the frame. You need to learn to focus and compose in this manner so that you can capture a player and the moving ball in the same frame while still filling the frame with your composition.

Timing the Hit

At the golf course, find someone who is on the driving range and ask if you can stand to the side and practice timing that person hitting drives. Do this until you can anticipate the moment of impact when the club strikes the ball. Then move slightly to the front, taking care not to be in harm's way, and repeat the drill.

Share your results with the book's Flickr group!
Join the group here: flickr.com/groups/sportsphotographyfromsnapshotstogreatshots.

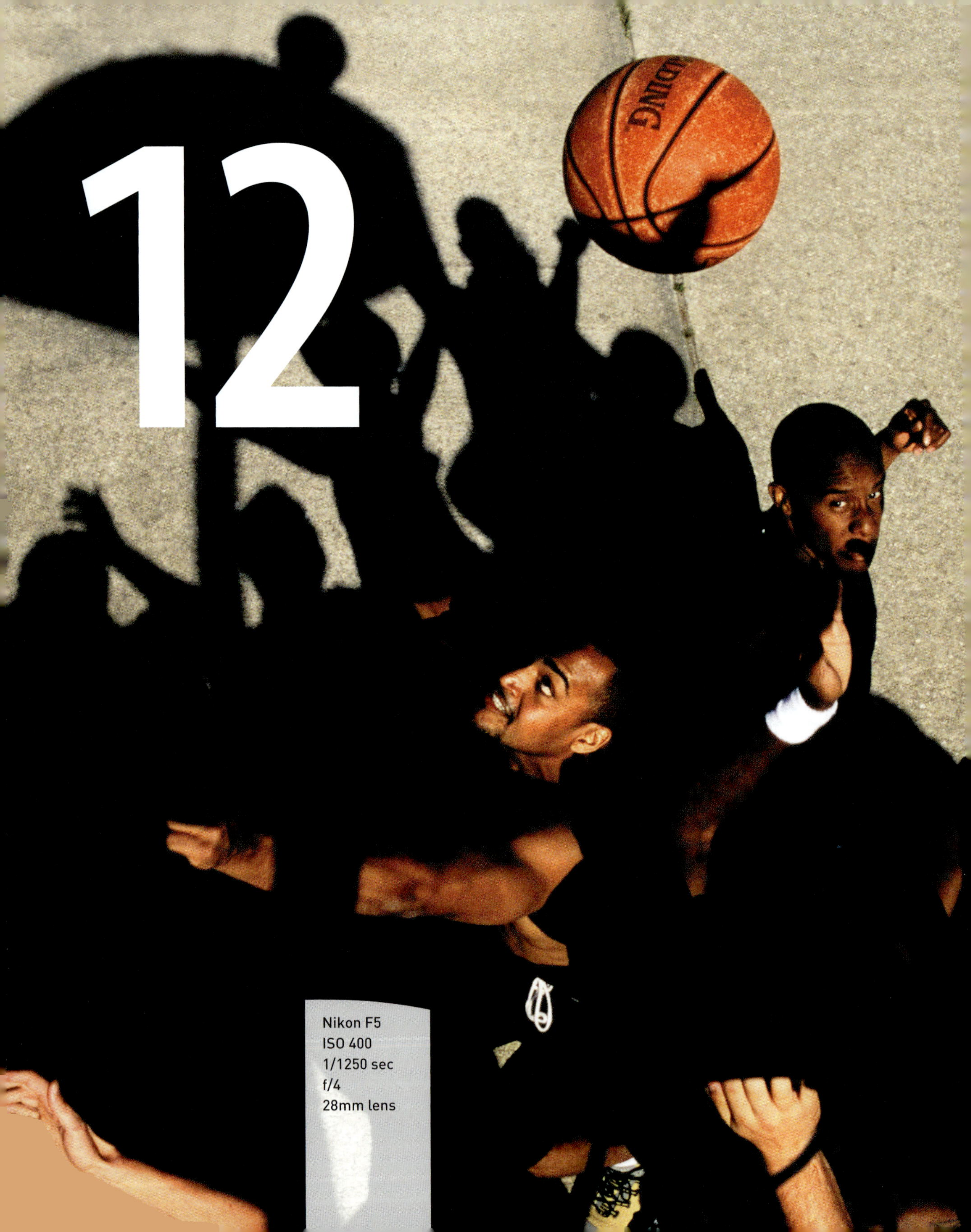

12

Nikon F5
ISO 400
1/1250 sec
f/4
28mm lens

Personal and Professional Growth

BEYOND THE SHOOT

The most important thing you can do as a photographer is continue to grow. My desire to be better and learn more is what has gotten me this far in the industry. If I am not taking a picture, I am studying new ways to create images and solve technical problems. There is no off position on the visual switch. I am always working and always thinking.

This chapter provides you with some suggestions to help you grow photographically on a personal and professional level.

A group of men play a pick-up game of basketball in Gainesville, Florida. Usually, I'm shooting NCAA sports in Gainesville, because it is the home of the University of Florida. But after teaching a class one evening, I saw this game on a neighborhood court.

PORING OVER THE PICTURE

I chose to compose this image to show the tension of the moment. You will notice I did not include the bow in the picture; I included only the end of the arrow and his arm, lifted to shoot. This composition creates strong angles and makes the image visually appealing.

People frequently ask me if I have any "personal" projects. For me, everything I shoot is personal. I give every image my best effort and undivided attention. This photo was taken during the archery competition at the Olympic Games in Athens in 2004.

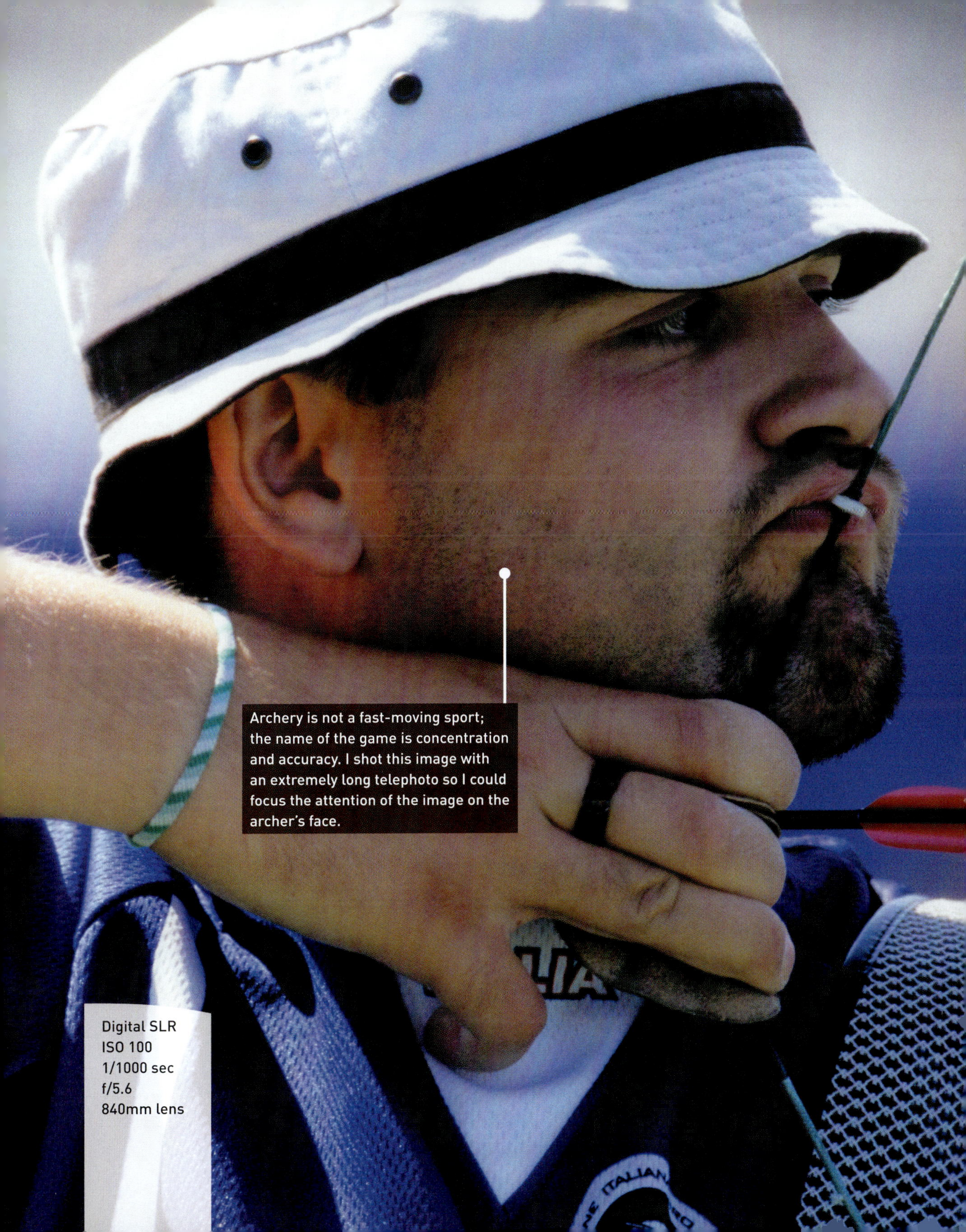

Archery is not a fast-moving sport; the name of the game is concentration and accuracy. I shot this image with an extremely long telephoto so I could focus the attention of the image on the archer's face.

Digital SLR
ISO 100
1/1000 sec
f/5.6
840mm lens

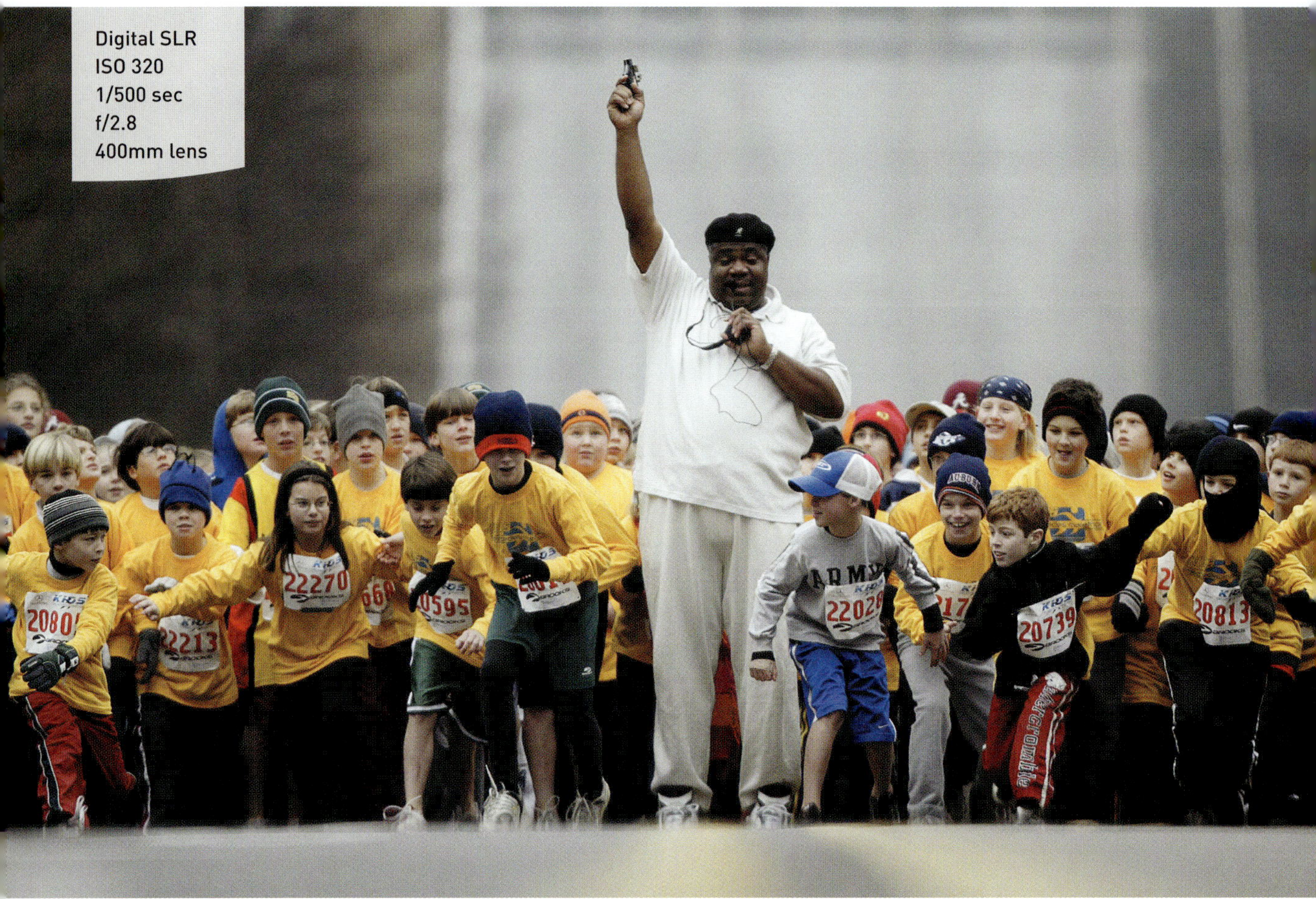

FIGURE 12.1
A group of kids line up for the start of the Kids 5k that ran before the Olympic Marathon Trials in 2004.

EXPANDING YOUR BUSINESS

People always ask me how I got to where I am. The answer is simple: I work harder and longer than anyone else. And I'm lucky that my vocation and avocation are the same. They say if you can do something you love, you never work a day in your life, and that has definitely been true for me.

With that said, I've worked arduously throughout the years to grow my business and my list of clients. Most important, I diversified the range of sports I covered. Not only do I photograph major professional sports, but I also spend a lot of time photographing kids in neighborhoods playing and competing in community events (**Figure 12.1**). As discussed throughout this book, sports photography isn't all about big hits and big games. Instead, it is a cultural experience. Treat every event you attend with that in mind, and you'll find a plethora of unique and compelling images.

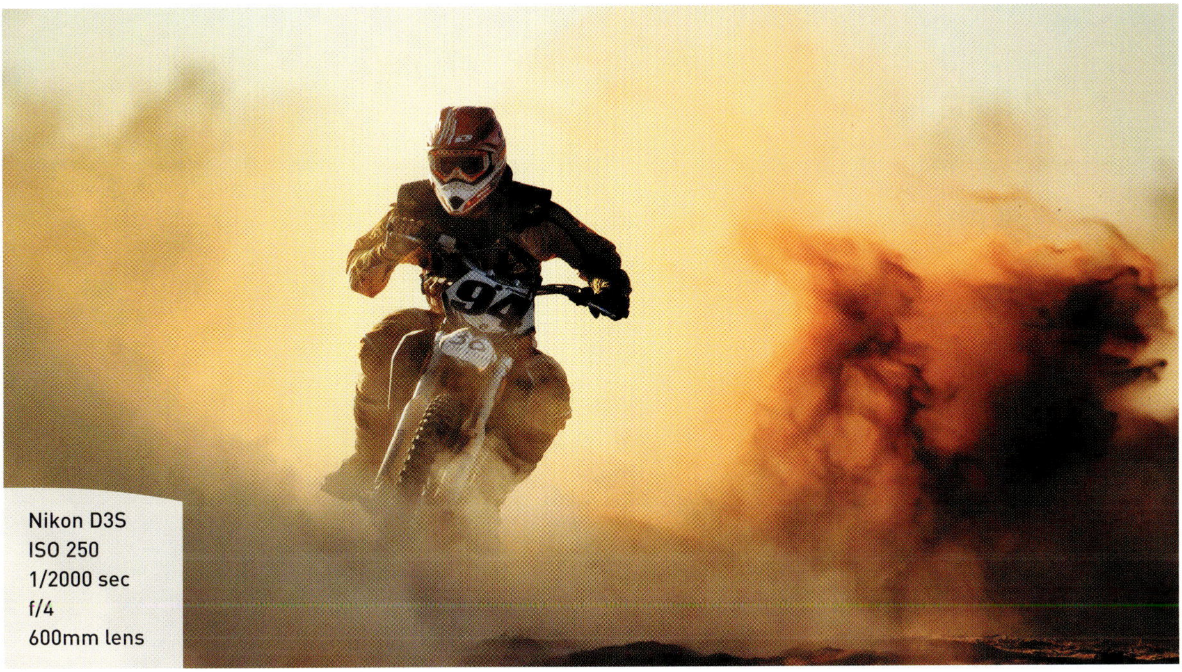

Nikon D3S
ISO 250
1/2000 sec
f/4
600mm lens

FIGURE 12.2
The dust and sunset light allowed me to create an image I had not previously considered.

For example, I was supposed to shoot an ad in the Australian outback and, as happens frequently, the shoot I had traveled to the middle of the earth for fell through. The picture in **Figure 12.2** happened because I didn't panic. Fortunately, I recalled passing a motocross park on our drive out, so I turned the car around and drove back confident that I could salvage the assignment. I did.

YOUR PORTFOLIO

You don't need a large portfolio. That is a common misconception. Editors and art directors look for good images whether you have 5 or 50. My advice is to have a diverse set of images. Mix it up. Don't include only one kind of image in your portfolio. You want to show that you can do anything. Therefore, include images of multiple sports, more than one focal length, and various angles.

WHERE TO INVEST

It is important to constantly invest in yourself with both time and money. Camera gear is expensive, which prevents many people from growing their business. The gear doesn't take the picture, the photographer does, but having what you need for the job is still essential.

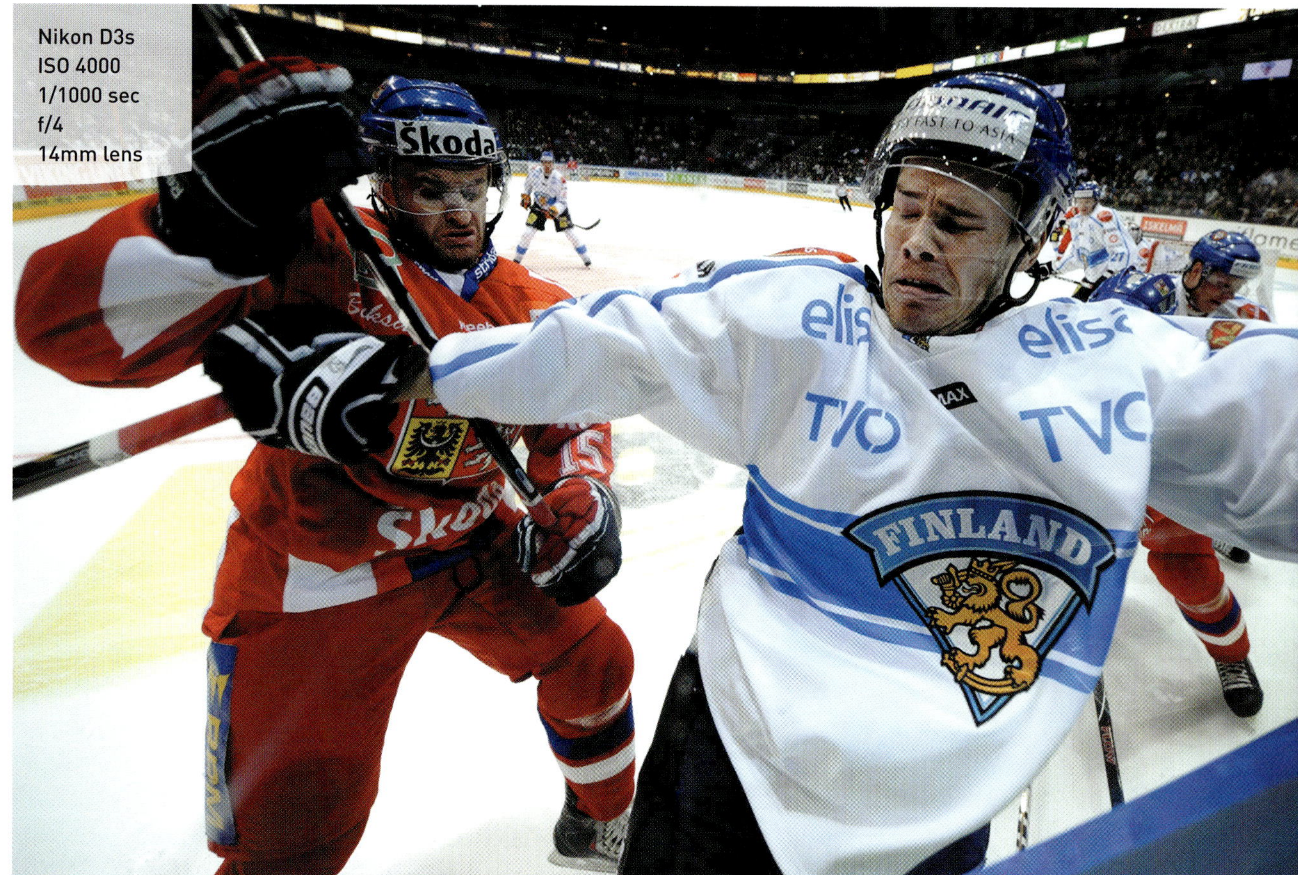

Nikon D3s
ISO 4000
1/1000 sec
f/4
14mm lens

FIGURE 12.3
Before cameras like the Nikon D3s, I would have spent two days lighting this hockey arena with 4800w/s strobes to illuminate the players and freeze the action.

Technological advances influence sports photography more than any other photographic discipline. The camera manufacturers are constantly raising the bar in terms of what the cameras can do, but you have to be prepared to use them to their fullest potential. Better sensors in the new DSLR cameras allow you to use faster shutter speeds in lower light with amazing results. The new sensors also allow you to use ISOs that were previously unimaginable (**Figure 12.3**). Faster and more sensitive auto-focus allows you to track subjects better and more easily than before. Prior to auto-focus sports photography was extremely difficult. Manually focusing a 600mm lens required incredible concentration and a lot of hand-eye coordination (**Figure 12.4**). In addition, new sophisticated triggers allow you to fire cameras remotely from greater distances with better accuracy.

I've never bought a piece of equipment that hasn't paid for itself. Be smart in your investments, but don't be afraid to make them.

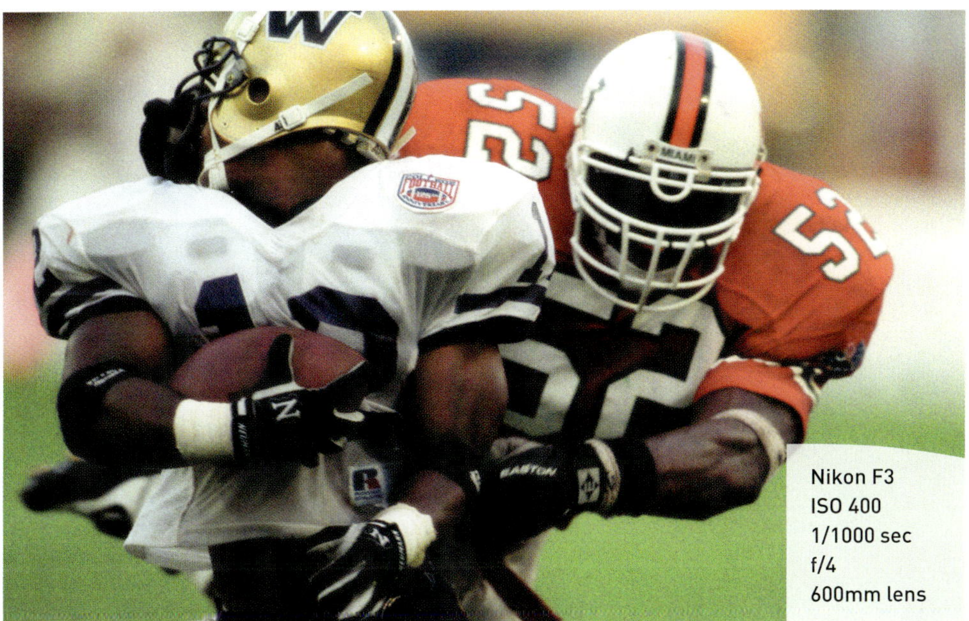

Nikon F3
ISO 400
1/1000 sec
f/4
600mm lens

FIGURE 12.4 This picture of a University of Miami linebacker tackling a University of Washington running back was taken in the late 1980s when cameras were nothing more than the box that held film and lenses.

SHARPEN YOUR SKILLS

The best way to improve your skills and increase your chances of making consistently good images is to work hard, practice constantly, and study. Practice makes perfect.

When I was a young newspaper photographer in Miami, I went to every assignment eager to make good images (**Figure 12.5**). There is no such thing as a bad assignment. You can make images of anything, anywhere. You never know when the muse will strike and the photographic stars will align.

Find subjects to shoot. In every community in the world something is going on every week. Whether it is a high school track meet or a little league baseball tournament, somewhere people are playing sports. In fact, **Figure 12.6** is a perfect example. I was looking for something fun to shoot and did a quick search online to find kids' go-kart racing at the Daytona International Speedway, which is only a short drive from my house.

Approach everything with a goal in mind, such as what kind of image you want to take away from the event (**Figure 12.7**).

FIGURE 12.5
Kids toss a baseball back and forth as they walk home after a little league game in Scottsbluff, Nebraska.

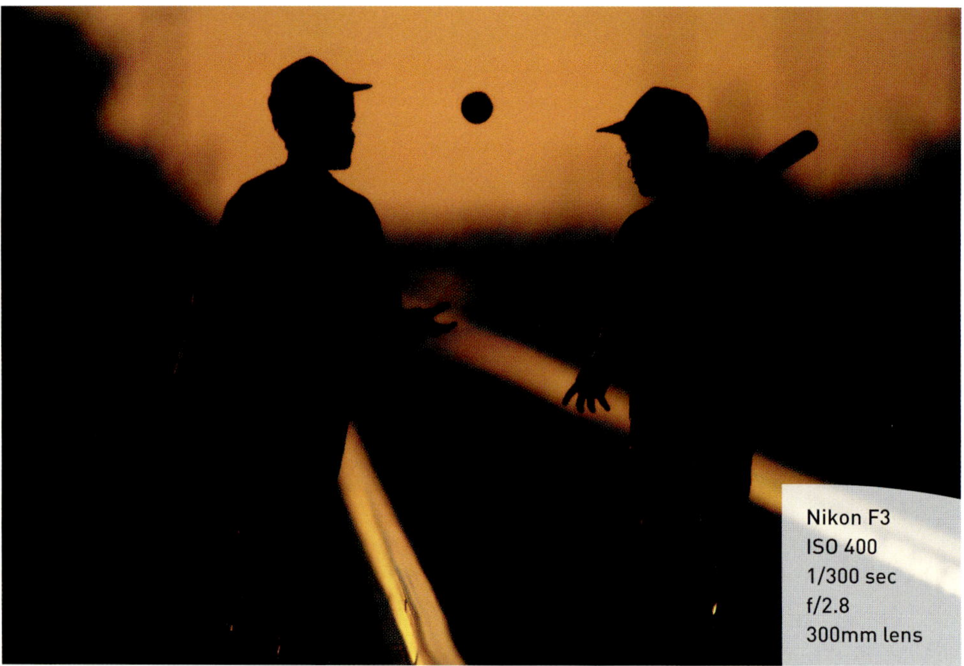

Nikon F3
ISO 400
1/300 sec
f/2.8
300mm lens

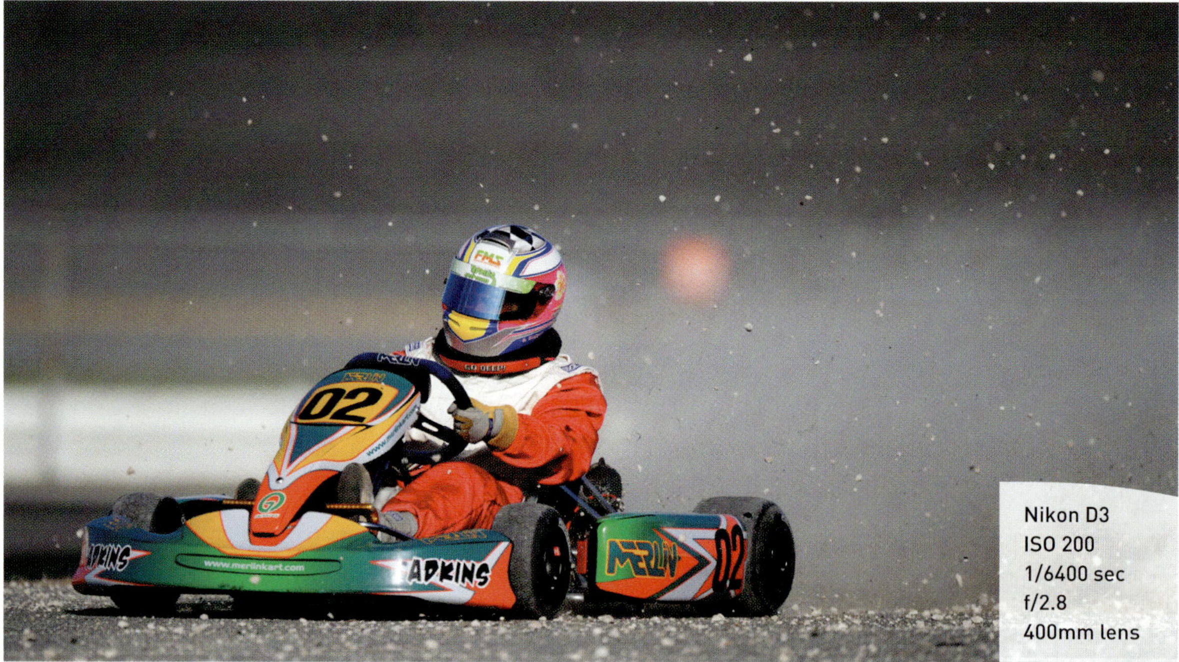

Nikon D3
ISO 200
1/6400 sec
f/2.8
400mm lens

FIGURE 12.6
I took this image on an off week in late December 2008.

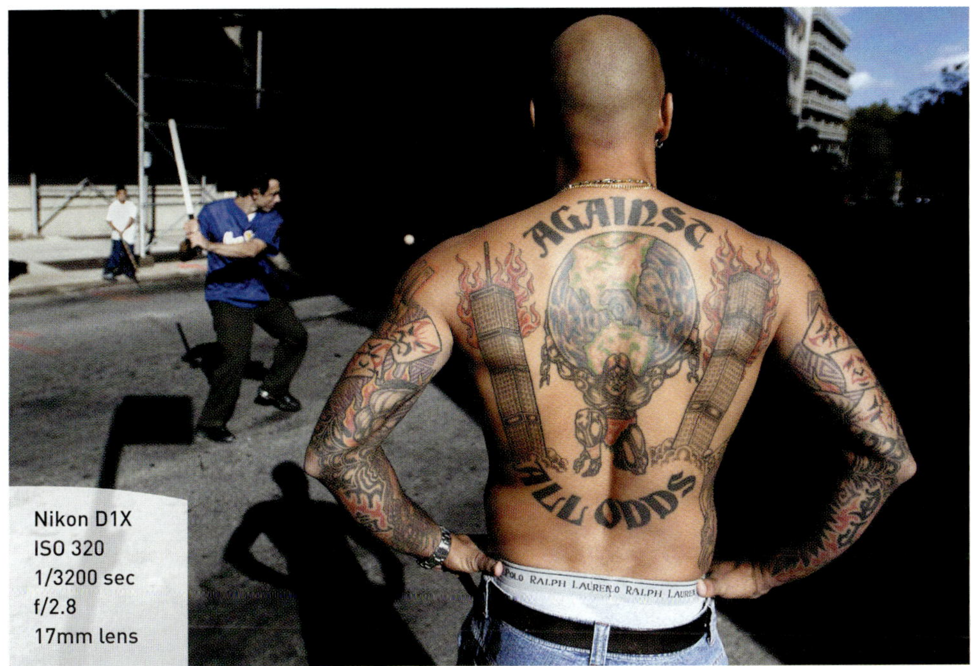

Nikon D1X
ISO 320
1/3200 sec
f/2.8
17mm lens

FIGURE 12.7
A group plays stickball in the streets of Manhattan on the one year anniversary of the 9/11 attack on the World Trade Towers.

Know the sports you shoot. I spend a lot of time staying familiar with the athletes and the trends in the sports I cover. I do this by searching for information online, by reading magazines and newspapers, and by watching television news. The more you know going into an assignment or event, the better your chances to take full advantage of every opportunity.

One of the first stories I covered for *Sports Illustrated* was a piece on Archie Manning. I went to his home to photograph him with his family. Peyton was 14 and Eli was 9. I have since followed both of these future Hall of Fame quarterbacks through their entire careers (**Figure 12.8**).

Challenge yourself. I spend a lot of time learning new things about the world of photography. Especially now, with the advent of digital cameras and editing software, everything changes quickly. Every day a new camera hits the market or a new technique is discovered, and it is important to stay abreast of the current technology.

Since 1983, I've been making images for *Sports Illustrated* and learning about my profession. The success I've known is not an accident; I work at it. I spend an hour a day studying because I've made it a point to build it into my schedule.

But perhaps the most important thing I've learned in my career is that you never know it all. There is always something new to learn and someone who knows how to do it. I have continually been amazed and humbled by the number of people who not only know more than me, but are willing to share their knowledge.

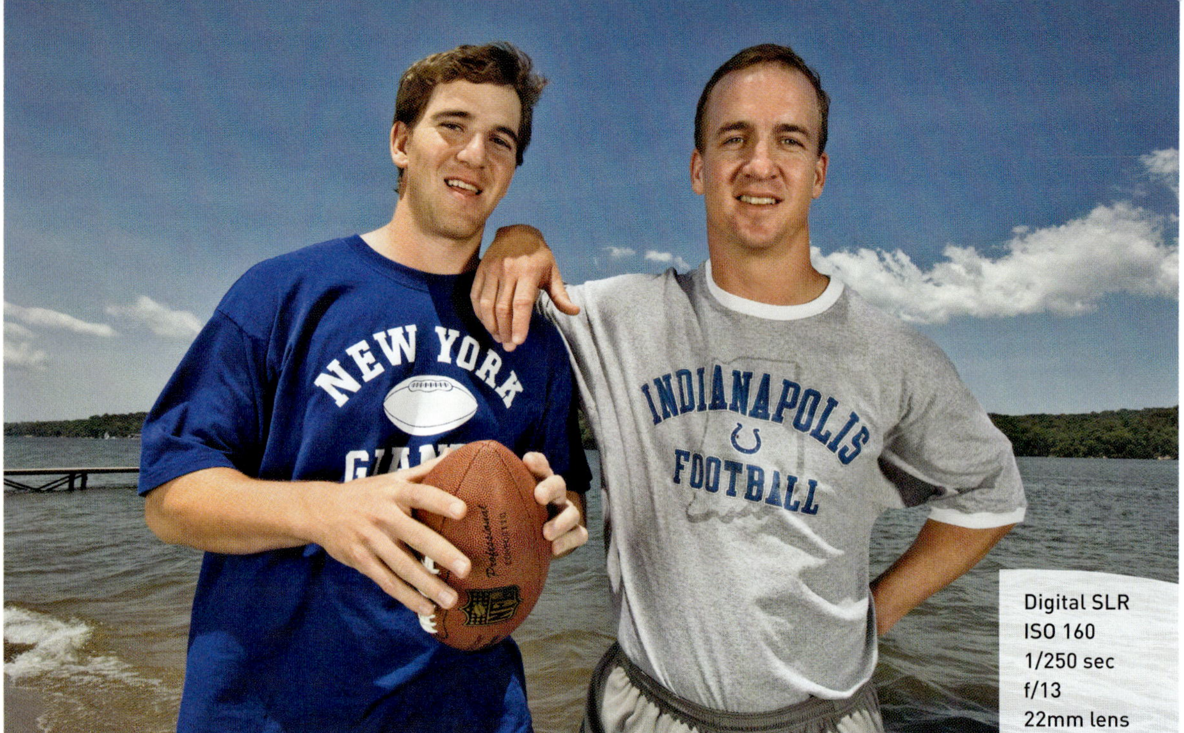

FIGURE 12.8
I still enjoy photographing Peyton and Eli Manning when they play because I feel like I know them and how they play so well.

WHAT'S NEXT?

The final question is what's next? For me the answer is more of the same—photographing games big and little wherever they may happen.

Video is also a major part of my work now. It has become an important component of game coverage, not only for traditional broadcast outlets but also as part of the storytelling done by traditional still photographers. It's simply too rich to ignore, and I suspect that my involvement with moving images will continue to grow.

The same rules apply to new and old media alike—good stories, nice moments, dedication to craft, and a desire to share.

Industry-wide I believe the same things that are in my future will be there for everyone else as well. Digital cameras have made it easier to make good quality images, and the Internet will continue to speed the distribution and increase the viewing possibilities.

Remember that at the end of the day, it's the images that matter. The camera is simply a tool that allows you to take what you have in your heart, your mind, and your soul, and translate it into a viewing mechanism on a computer screen, a mobile device, a gallery wall, or in a printed publication so that you can share it with your viewers.

Chapter 12 Assignments

Spending time working on the following assignments will help you grow your business and become a better sports photographer.

Create a Portfolio: Putting Your Best Foot Forward

The most difficult thing to do is to edit your own work effectively. Start by choosing 20 images that you like and that you think represent what you do well. Show them to others and analyze their feedback. When you are ready, reach out to an editor and ask for a critique. This is a process you will need to do for the entire time you are shooting pictures if you want to continue to grow creatively.

Study Sports Photography on the Web: Keeping Up with the Joneses

Choose your five favorite sports photography websites. Visit them once a week. Look at what the photographers who are regularly published there are doing. Study not just the content, but also try to figure out how the pictures were taken. This will help you stay current and will give you needed information to get ahead.

Stay Abreast of New Cameras and Lenses: Technology Is Your Friend

More than any other genre of photography, sports photography is affected by advances in technology. Constantly paying attention to what the new gear can do will help you in the field by opening your eyes to new image-making opportunities.

Share your results with the book's Flickr group!
Join the group here: flickr.com/groups/sportsphotographyfromsnapshotstogreatshots.

Conclusion

"You cannot possibly photograph a sport unless you understand it completely, and understand and know the men who play it. The same intensity they have to play the game you must have to record it. Not stop it, but suspend it forever in time."
—Robert Riger, Sports Artist (www.robertriger.com)

Hard work, dedication to craft, education, and the ability to fall in love every day are what it takes to be a good photographer. Add reflexes and knowledge of the games, and you have the recipe for being a good sports photographer.

To understand the future, it is important to study and value the past.

The best sports photographers have some attributes in common:

- They work very hard, taking little for granted.
- They are dedicated to their craft and art.
- They have incredible reflexes.
- They have a desire to communicate.
- They pay attention; history repeats itself in sports, often very quickly.

FRIENDS, MENTORS, AND HEROES

I am genuinely inspired by many aspects of life—art, food, music, literature, humor, and nature—and I take my cues from all of them.

Specific to sports journalism, the following list contains the folks I admire to provide inspiration and community. It is by no means an exhaustive list, and more often than not I spend my time looking at the works of photographic artists from all disciplines reading my favorite novelists, and enjoying great coffee while listening to one of the thousands of albums I have collected through my years on the road.

These are the people I consider my friends, mentors, and heroes:

- **Heinz Kluetmeier (www.heinzkluetmeier.com).** Perhaps the hardest working photographer ever, Heinz is the master of technology but not a slave to it. He never takes no for an answer and makes photographs where none should exist. Heinz has been a close friend and mentor for more than half my life and was the person who hired me at *Sports Illustrated*.

- **Walter Iooss Jr. (www.walteriooss.com).** Master of composition and light, Walter has incredible style.
- **John Zimmerman.** The original, John did it all and did it best.
- **Joe McNally (www.joemcnally.com).** A consummate photojournalist, Joe has perfected the use of the small strobe. He is also an author and a teacher.
- **Brian Lanker (www.brianlanker.com).** Pulitzer Prize winning genius and storytelling wizard, Brian is very generous with his knowledge and friendship. He was nice to me when I was a student at Arizona State, and I've always remembered the way Brian treated me when I am approached by students and aficionados.
- **Rich Clarkson (www.richclarkson.com).** Teacher, editor, photographer, publisher, and businessman, Rich has been a tremendous influence in the photographic community for nearly 60 years. He was my first boss at the Topeka Capital Journal when I was an intern there.
- **Howard Schatz (www.howardschatz.com).** A man with unquenchable curiosity, boundless energy, and technical virtuosity, Howard has a great love of the medium.
- **John Beiver.** Widely regarded as one the best action photographers of all time, I've been honored to work beside John for nearly three decades. For more information about John, see http://sportsillustrated.cnn.com/multimedia/photo_gallery/0711/gallery.canon.biever/content.1.html.
- **Adam Pretty (http://adampretty.com).** A young photographer already at the top of his game, Adam still has his career ahead of him.
- **David Burnett (www.davidburnett.com).** One of the greatest photojournalists ever, David has covered wars, sports, and daily life, and is a strong creative force.
- **Laci Perenyi (www.sportphoto-perenyi.de).** Former Olympian and a very funny man, Laci is an intense, off-the-wall artist.
- **Michael Zagaris (http://zagaris.photoshelter.com).** From the Rolling Stones to the San Francisco 49ers, Michael has been behind the scenes watching the magic happen. Michael rocks!
- **John McDonough.** A wonderful photographer, John and I have been close friends since I was 17 and colleagues for nearly 40 years. For more information about John, see http://sportsillustrated.cnn.com/multimedia/photo_gallery/2005/07/20/gallery.mcdonough/content.2.html.
- **Jimmy Colton (http://jimcolton.com).** A fantastic editor, Jimmy is my coach.
- **Scott Kelby (www.scottkelby.com).** King of Photoshop, Scott is an educator and an author.

- **Laura Heald, Film Editor (www.strawhatvisuals.com).** Cinematographer, writer, and easily the hardest working and most versatile talent I know, Laura is a great friend with a long and distinguished career ahead of her.

I draw inspiration for my career as a sports photographer from all directions. Although I enjoy looking at photographs of others, I also enjoy reading the writers who describe them. Sportswriters Tim Layden, William Nack, Edwin Pope, and Christine Brennan are all important resources for me:

- **Tim Layden, *Sports Illustrated* Senior Writer.** A great friend, Tim's dedication to craft and expansive knowledge is inspiring.
- ***Blood Sweat & Chalk*** (Sports Illustrated, 2011)
- **William Nack, journalist and author.** William's writing made me fall in love with horse racing. I began reading his prose long before I became a journalist, and I can honestly say that his words helped shape my career.
- ***Secretariat: Making of a Champion*** (Hyperion, 2010)
- ***Ruffian: A Racetrack Romance*** (ESPN, 2007)
- ***My Turf: Boxers, Blood Money and the Sporting Life*** (Da Capo Press, 2004)
- **Edwin Pope, Sports Editor the *Miami Herald*.** I didn't realize how good Edwin's writing was until I started traveling 300 days a year and reading the other columnists around the country. Only then did I know how blessed I had been to read a master every morning over breakfast.
- ***The Edwin Pope Collection*** (Taylor Pub, 1988)
- **Christine Brennan, Columnist *USA Today*.** Christine's evocative columns always make me think.
- ***Inside Edge*** (Anchor, 1997)

I've been lucky to be surrounded by people who continually inspire and invigorate me. Knowing that good work is being done every day in new and different ways makes me excited to start each morning.

Good luck.

Bill Frakes
@BillFrakes
(www.billfrakes.com)

Index

Numbers

M

N

O

P

Q

R

S

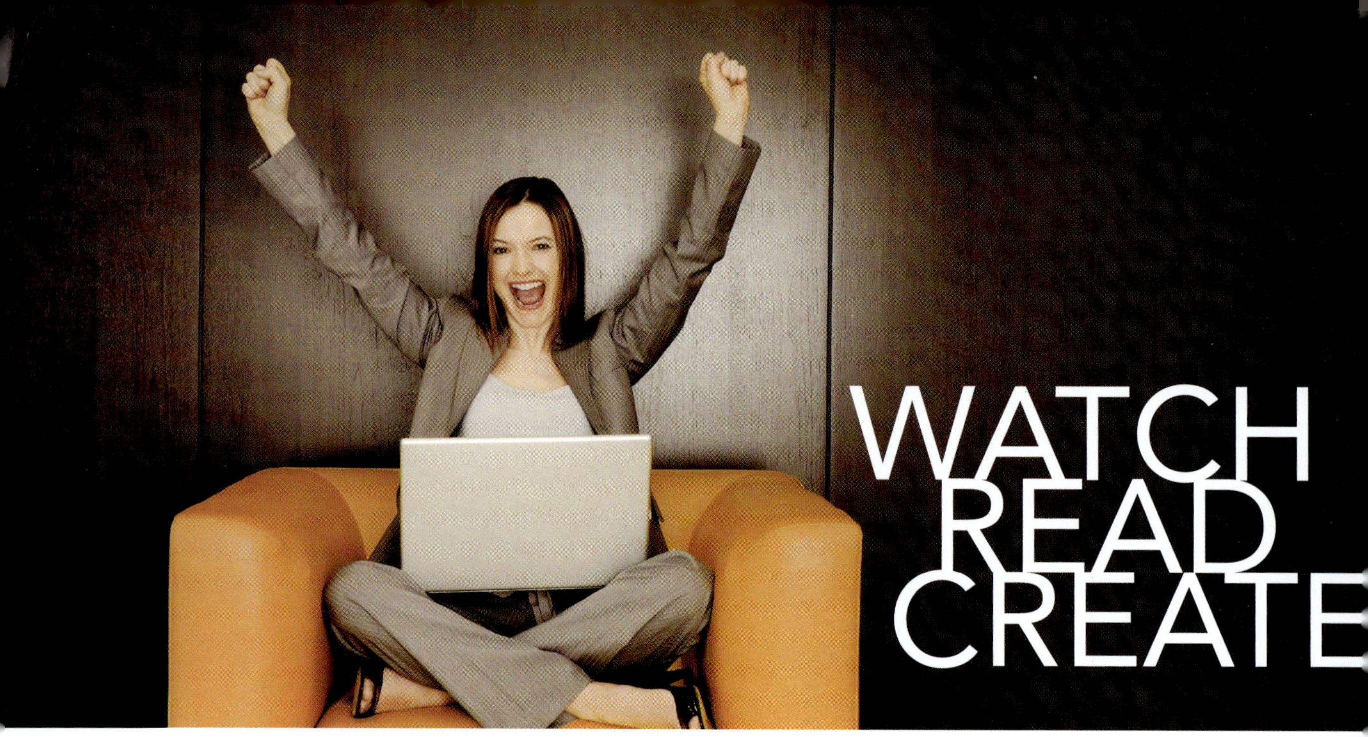